VAX
FORTRAN

VAX
FORTRAN

Charlotte Middlebrooks

Manager of Academic Computing Support
D. W. Mattson Computer Center
Tennessee Technological University
Cookeville, Tennessee

Illustrations by Mike Marshall

A RESTON COMPUTER GROUP BOOK
Reston Publishing Company, Inc. ■ Reston, Virginia
A Prentice-Hall Company

To Joe and Tracey

> EDT and DCL are proprietary software of the Digital Equipment Corporation. DEC, VAX, VMS, and VT are trademarks of the Digital Equipment Corporation.

Library of Congress Cataloging in Publication Data

Middlebrooks, C. H. (Charlotte H.)
  VAX FORTRAN.

  "A Reston Computer Group book."
    1. VAX–11 (Computer)—Programming. 2. FORTRAN
(Computer program language) I. Title.
  QA76.8.V37M53 1984   001.64′24   83–26895
  ISBN 0-8359-8245-9
  ISBN 0-8359-8243-2 (pbk.)

Editorial/production supervision and interior design
by Barbara J. Gardetto

© 1984 by
Reston Publishing Company, Inc.
A Prentice-Hall Company
Reston, Virginia 22090

10 9 8 7 6 5 4 3 2 1

Printed in the United States of America

Contents

ACKNOWLEDGMENTS x

PREFACE xi

CHAPTER 1
Beginning to Program on the VAX 2
- 1.1 Computer Programs 3
- 1.2 A FORTRAN Program 4
- 1.3 Memory Concept 5
- 1.4 Computer Terminal 5
- 1.5 Printer 7
- 1.6 Computer Memory 7
- 1.7 Computer Configuration 9
- 1.8 Program Entry and Execution 10
- 1.9 Summary 18

CHAPTER 2
Basic Elements of FORTRAN Programming 20
- 2.1 Basic Definitions 21
- 2.2 A FORTRAN Program 22
- 2.3 Entering a FORTRAN Program 23
- 2.4 Descriptive Labels for Output 27
- 2.5 Constants, Variables and Symbolic Names 28
- 2.6 Arithmetic Expressions 29
- 2.7 Integer and Real Arithmetic 31
- 2.8 Integer and Real Declarations 34
- 2.9 Intrinsic Functions 34
- 2.10 Applications 37

2.11 Summary 42
2.12 Exercises 43

CHAPTER 3
FORTRAN Files and Data Files: Input and Output 46

3.1 Steps in Creating and Running a FORTRAN Program 48
3.2 WRITE Statement—Writing Output to a Terminal 48
3.3 READ Statement—Reading Input from a Terminal 51
3.4 VAX Files 53
3.5 Writing Output to a Disk File 58
3.6 Reading Data from a Disk File 60
3.7 Summary 65
3.8 Exercises 67

CHAPTER 4
Developing a Fortran Program: Syntax, Logic, and Problem Solving 70

4.1 Syntax of the Language 71
4.2 Logic of a Problem 74
4.3 Debugging 74
4.4 Documentation for a Program 75
4.5 Techniques for Problem Solving 77
4.6 Summary 85
4.7 Exercises 85

CHAPTER 5
Introduction to Loops: DO Loops 88

5.1 Counter 90
5.2 DO Loop with a Counter 92
5.3 DO Loop with Variable Counting Increments 100
5.4 GO TO Statement 102
5.5 Applications 106
5.6 Problem Solving 111
5.7 Summary 114
5.8 Exercises 115

CHAPTER 6
Defining the Way That Input and Output
Are Presented for Numeric Data and
Character Data 118

6.1 Alphanumeric Character Strings 120
6.2 Introduction to Format Statements for Numeric Output 122

6.3 General Description of Format Statements for Output 124
6.4 General Description of Format Statements for Input 127
6.5 General Input Format Considerations 130
6.6 Applications 134
6.7 Summary 138
6.8 Exercises 139

CHAPTER 7
Conditional Statements: IF Statements 142
7.1 Simple IF Statements 143
7.2 Conditional Statement: IF statement 145
7.3 Block IF Structure 149
7.4 IF THEN ELSE Structure 151
7.5 Complex IF THEN ELSE Structures 153
7.6 Nested IF THEN ELSE Structures 154
7.7 Case Structure: Arithmetic GO TO Statement 155
7.8 Case Structure: Computed GO TO Statement 157
7.9 Applications 158
7.10 Problem Solving 165
7.11 Summary 170
7.12 Exercises 171

CHAPTER 8
Structured Loops 174
8.1 Nested DO Loops 175
8.2 DO WHILE Structure 181
8.3 Problem Solving 185
8.4 Applications 188
8.5 Summary 195
8.6 Exercises 196

CHAPTER 9
Introduction to One-Dimensional Arrays 200
9.1 When an Array Is Necessary 201
9.2 Definition of an Array 204
9.3 Accessing the Elements of an Array With a DO Loop 207
9.4 Manipulating Data That Are Stored in an Array 213
9.5 General Approach to Writing Programs with Arrays 219
9.6 Methods of Input and Output for Arrays 221
9.7 Plotting with One-Dimensional Arrays 223
9.8 Summary 225
9.9 Exercises 226

CHAPTER 10
Applications for One-Dimensional Arrays   232

10.1   Creating Subsets of Data from a One-Dimensional Array   233
10.2   Sorting   244
10.3   Business Applications and Plotting   253
10.4   Research Applications and Plotting   256
10.5   Summary   263
10.6   Exercises   264

CHAPTER 11
Introduction to Two-Dimensional Arrays   270

11.1   Description of a Two-Dimensional Array   271
11.2   Input and Output with Implied DO Loops   291
11.3   General Approach to Writing Programs with Arrays   294
11.4   Summary   298
11.5   Exercises   299

CHAPTER 12
Subprograms: An Introduction to Functions   304

12.1   Description of a Function and Accessing a Function   305
12.2   Providing Parameters for a Function and Returning
       a Function Value   308
12.3   Passing Arrays as Arguments for a Function   311
12.4   Application   314
12.5   Summary   316
12.6   Exercises   316

CHAPTER 13
Subroutines   320

13.1   Description of a Subroutine and Accessing a
       Subroutine   321
13.2   Providing Parameters for a Subroutine and Returning
       Values to the Calling Program   324
13.3   Subroutines and Structured Programming   328
13.4   COMMON Declaration   331
13.5   Application   335
13.6   Summary   337
13.7   Exercises   338

CHAPTER 14
Applications Programming   342

14.1	Sorting	343
14.2	An Interactive Data Base Application	352
14.3	Plotting	357
14.4	Data Considerations for Applications	363
14.5	Summary	365
14.6	Exercises	365

CHAPTER 15
Developing Large Programs   370

15.1	Program Design	371
15.2	Program Structure	373
15.3	Program Correctness	375
15.4	General Programs	375
15.5	Programming Style	376
15.6	Run Time Error Recovery	376
15.7	Testing	377
15.8	Application	377
15.9	Summary	389
15.10	Exercises	390

APPENDICES   393

A	An Introduction to Using the VAX System: A Tutorial	394
	An Overview for Learning to Use the System	394
	Logging In and Using the VAX System	395
	Using the EDT Line Editor	403
	Using the EDT Full-Screen Editor	416
	Displaying, Printing, and Deleting Files Directory	471
B	An Introduction to Running FORTRAN Programs on the VAX	473
C	FORTRAN Structures: Quick Reference	481
D	FORTRAN Formats: Quick Reference	489
E	Using the VAX: Quick Reference	493
F	EDT Line Editor: Quick Reference	496

INDEX   500

Acknowledgments

I appreciate the help of those who have supported me as I have written the book. Portions of the book are in use at three universities. The introduction to the VAX that Martell Gee and Karl Fugal requested that I write for Utah State University was the beginning of the book. The tutorial for using the VAX with VT-100 compatible terminals was written and printed at Clemson University, and I appreciate the review of that material by Richard Nelson. Jim Westmoreland and Frank Bush have been helpful to me at Tennessee Technological University. Greg Mullinax's review and testing has been very helpful.

I am grateful to Mike Marshall for taking my serious approach to programming and making it lighter with his sketches. His sketches aided greatly in my development of concepts.

My thanks to Reba and Odell Hardy and to Jewell and Harold Middlebrooks for everything.

My daughter, Tracey, always inspires me with her writing—newspaper articles, public relations documents, and letters to Mom. And most of all, I appreciate the support of my dear husband Joe, who taught me the discipline of writing through his work, encourages me to write, and sometimes cooks my dinner while I write.

Preface

■ About the Book

VAX FORTRAN guides you in a systematic way from your first contact with a VAX computer through writing powerful, structured FORTRAN 77 programs. The text includes over 150 complete examples that were written and tested on a VAX and includes numerous sketches to clarify concepts. An example containing input, a complete program, and output is used to demonstrate every major concept. Appendices cover details of using the VAX and provide valuable information in a reference format.

The book is appropriate for a one-quarter or one-semester introductory programming course. No prerequisite knowledge is necessary. Students can use the tutorials in Appendices A and B to learn to use the VAX system and can then study the step-by-step introduction to programming in FORTRAN on the VAX in the text. Since the book is based on developing programs, a class should be able to move quickly into writing useful programs. The numerous examples in the text provide enough material for a teacher to use for class examples and for students to study independently.

The text can be used in a course that requires programming for applications. A new VAX user can go to a terminal and follow examples from the first contact with the VAX through writing useful applications.

The book is appropriate as a reference for knowledgeable programmers. The numerous examples demonstrate the features of FORTRAN on the VAX. The quick-reference sections in the appendices provide easy access to information.

■ The Structure of the Text

This text is an introduction to programming based on teaching by example. Examples were selected to demonstrate features of the FORTRAN language as well as applications for the language. The approach to presenting material is to develop an understanding of a concept through an example or sketch and then to present the rules assuming that the rules will be meaningful after a reader has a general understanding of the concept.

The book contains everything you need to know to begin using a VAX computer and to begin entering and running FORTRAN programs on the VAX.

The place to begin using the book is at the back. Appendix A contains a tutorial for beginning to use a VAX computer interactively. The tutorial contains examples showing everything that a user should type and all the responses the computer prints. Examples show terminal input and computer responses with directions for each entry the user should make and explanations of the messages displayed by the computer. The most effective way to use the tutorial for interactive computing is to go to a terminal and enter the examples. Entering and running the examples to learn to use the keyboard, to create, modify and delete files, and to use some of the frequently employed VAX commands should take from one to three hours depending on the user's computer experience. Detailed instructions for entering and running a FORTRAN program on the VAX are provided in Appendix B.

After learning to use the VAX computer with the material in the appendices, the reader should begin in Chapter 1. The first chapter is a very basic introduction to programming with sketches to provide a way to visualize the processes that are occurring as a program is stored, compiled, linked, and run. Chapter 2 introduces the most basic concepts of FORTRAN.

Chapter 3 provides valuable information for interactive computing. An understanding of file handling must be a part of using a computer interactively and Chapter 3 introduces, in a simple way, methods for access to files from FORTRAN on the VAX.

Chapter 4 provides a detailed development of two programs. The chapter gives a new programmer a systematic way to begin to take a set of information and to completely define the problem and finally to write the program.

Chapters 5 through 15 cover features of the FORTRAN language and applications for FORTRAN. The emphasis in the examples is to provide useful programming concepts not only to present the rules.

Charlotte Middlebrooks

VAX
FORTRAN

1

Beginning to Program on the VAX

A *computer program* is a set of instructions that specifies operations for a computer. FORTRAN is a computer language in which a set of instructions can be written for a computer. FORTRAN, an abbreviation for FORmula TRANslation, was originally designed as a scientific language to be used primarily for numeric calculations; however, the language is now a widely used general-purpose language. The language standards that most people have used were developed by the American National Standards Institute (ANSI) in 1966. New standards developed in 1977 make the language more powerful and flexible than the 66 level FORTRAN. The FORTRAN 77 language, available on the VAX™ computer, is described in this book.

1.1
COMPUTER PROGRAMS

To learn to write computer programs, you need to understand a little about how a program instructs a computer to perform operations, and you need to become familiar with some computer terminology. This chapter leads you

---

VAX™ is a trademark of Digital Equipment Corporation.

FIGURE 1.1

through an introduction to a useful way of thinking about how the computer is storing and executing your program. Just as it would be difficult to understand automobile driving instructions if you had never seen a car or a road, it is difficult to understand programming if you do not have a visual concept of the way that information is moving through the computer.

1.2
A FORTRAN PROGRAM

Look at the following simple FORTRAN computer program. The program could be entered by typing in the program at a terminal and sending the codes for the characters that were typed down the line to the computer.

The program calculates and prints the pay for someone who worked at a pay rate of four dollars per hour for three hours.

```
RATE = 4.00
HOURS = 3.0
PAY = RATE * HOURS
PRINT *, PAY
END
```

To execute the computer program, the instructions in the program must be stored inside the computer during the time that the instructions are being executed. The computer is a set of electronic circuits for storing and transfer-ring information. The set of circuits where your information is stored is called *memory*. As you use a computer, you can think of memory as a set of mailboxes.

1.3
MEMORY CONCEPT

If you wrote each of the instructions in the example program on a separate piece of paper, you could put each separate instruction into a separate mailbox with an address.

FIGURE 1.2

At some later time, a person could collect the instruction from each ad-dress, and after all the program instructions were collected, the person could then calculate the pay from the information. Each memory location can be thought of as one mailbox with an address. The computer has a control unit that keeps track of the address where information is stored so that the infor-mation can be retrieved as needed.

1.4
COMPUTER TERMINAL

The primary device in most computer installations for creating computer programs and specifying commands for a computer is a terminal, which is connected to the computer by a direct line to the computer or through a modem and telephone line to the computer. (See Figure 1.3.)

A terminal is a device with a keyboard for sending information to the computer. At a terminal, if you press the key marked with the letter [R], the terminal sends a code for an R. The code for an R might be ⎍⎍ in which the high parts of the line indicate a high-voltage current flowing and the low parts of the line indicate a low-voltage current flowing. The message is sent electronically down the wire from the terminal to the computer.

When you type a character at a computer terminal, the code is not sent until you press the key marked [RETURN]. You may type many characters before you press the [RETURN] key. When you press the [RETURN] key, the code for each character that you typed is sent one after another down the line to the computer. The dollar sign on the screen means that the VAX is waiting for a command from you. If you type the four letters HELP and press the [RETURN] key, the VAX recognizes the code for four characters H and E and L and P typed in this sequence as a request for information to be displayed at a terminal. (See Figure 1.4.)

For the computer to send information to you, there must be a way to display information at your terminal. Most often, your terminal has a keyboard and a screen, and what you type on the keyboard is displayed on your terminal screen and messages coming from the computer are displayed on the screen. A terminal may be a printing terminal. At a printing terminal, the characters that you type and the messages sent from the computer are printed on paper at the terminal.

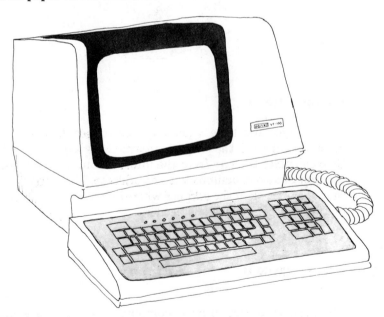

FIGURE 1.3

FIGURE 1.4

After the computer receives the code and translates the code for the characters H and E and L and P, which you typed, the computer sends a set of code down the line from the computer to the terminal. The terminal translates the code into printable characters and displays on the screen or paper a list of HELP information for the VAX.

The terminal and the computer do all the code translations, and you can simply type characters at the terminal and receive readable information from the computer at your terminal.

1.5
PRINTER

In addition to having the computer send output to your terminal, you may specify that output be directed to a printer. If you are working at a terminal with a screen, you need a printed copy, called a *hard copy,* of your program and output, so you can send output to a device that is used only for printing. Usually a high-speed printer is provided to serve all computer users or perhaps a group of users in a particular location.

1.6
COMPUTER MEMORY

There are many ways to store information for use with a computer; however, you need to consider only two ways now, *main memory* and *magnetic disk memory.* Main memory is the storage area that is actually located inside the

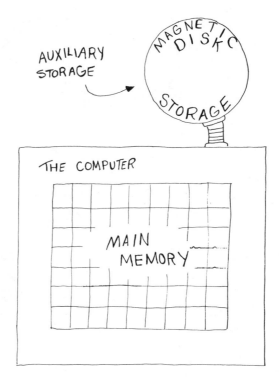

AUXILIARY STORAGE

MAGNETIC DISK STORAGE

THE COMPUTER

MAIN MEMORY

FIGURE 1.5

computer; this is where your program is at the time it is executing. Magnetic disk memory is *auxiliary storage* located outside the computer and connected to the computer by direct line. *Magnetic disk memory* is where your program is stored when you save it for ongoing storage. (See Figure 1.5.)

Although main memory is large, there is a specific and limited amount of storage space, and so space is not available to store your program and the programs of other users in main memory longer than necessary for execution. Your program must be stored in auxiliary storage when it is not in immediate use. Another reason for storing your program outside the computer is that, when the power goes off or there is an interruption in machine operation, the contents of main memory, which are controlled by electric currents, are destroyed.

Magnetic disk auxiliary storage is a form of long-term storage that provides rapid access to information by the computer. A magnetic disk pack looks somewhat like a stack of phonograph records, and information is stored in magnetic form somewhat like music is stored on a phonograph record. After information is stored on a magnetic disk, it remains there available to you through commands to the computer for recalling the information. When you specify a command to the computer to SAVE your program, the contents of the program are saved on magnetic disk.

1.7
COMPUTER CONFIGURATION

Looking at a VAX computer or any other computer, you usually see only a metal box. If you open the VAX computer, you see circuit boards and wires. It is not necessary to understand how the computer works electronically, but you need to know a little about the basic parts of the computer with which you will be interacting. Figure 1.6 shows the basic parts of a computer.

The most important thing for you to understand about computers is the way that memory works like addressable mailboxes for storing and retrieving information. You also need to know a little about how the processing occurs. Look at the diagram of a computer configuration (Figure 1.7).

The *central processing unit,* called the CPU, is the set of complex electronic circuits that comprise the heart of the computer. Control of the flow of information into, through, and out of the computer occurs in the *control unit* of the CPU, and the actual execution of the instructions in a computer program occurs in the CPU. In addition to memory and the control unit, the

FIGURE 1.6

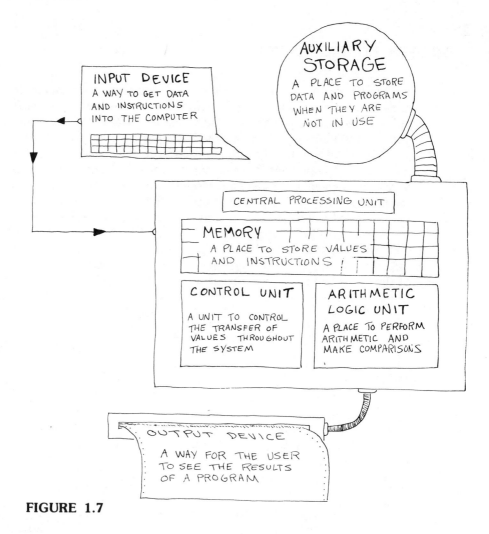

FIGURE 1.7

arithmetic logic unit, which performs calculations and comparisons, is located in the CPU.

1.8
PROGRAM ENTRY AND EXECUTION

This section provides you with a way to think about what is happening when a FORTRAN program is entered and executed. Details about commands for entering, saving, and executing a program are in the appendices.

This section covers concepts of entering and executing a program from a terminal. The concepts of translating a program into machine code, linking

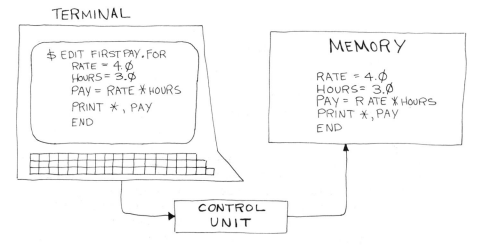

FIGURE 1.8

the translated code, and executing the code are the same whether the program is entered from cards or the terminal.

As you enter a program at the terminal, the control unit is controlling the flow of information in the form of electronic signals, and the information is stored in main memory in the form of electronic codes. Usually, you enter a new program using the EDIT command and provide a filename to give the program a name so that it can be retrieved at some later time. The filename should be nine characters or fewer, followed by a period, followed by the characters FOR, which indicate that this is a FORTRAN program. (See Figure 1.8.)

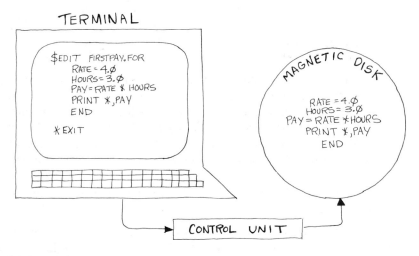

FIGURE 1.9

After you enter your program at a terminal, you can enter a command to save your program on magnetic disk. Then the program will be there until you delete it from magnetic disk. (See Figure 1.9.)

After you enter your program from a terminal into main memory and then save the program on magnetic disk, you need to give the computer commands to begin the process of executing your instructions to calculate and print the pay for the example program. The statements that you entered in this example are FORTRAN statements called *source code.* Source code is code written in a high-level language using names and expressions that are understandable to a programmer. To execute a program, the FORTRAN source code must be translated into *object code,* and the object code must be *linked* to generate a set of code that is *executable.*

The command to compile, that is, to translate, a FORTRAN program into object code is the word FORTRAN followed by the name of the FORTRAN program, as shown in Figure 1.10. Object code is also called machine code.

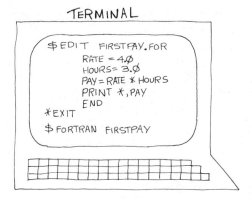

FIGURE 1.10

A *compiler* translates the source code that you have entered into object code, that is, code for specifying exact instructions for the computer. When you type the command, FORTRAN, each of your statements is translated into machine code. For example, your instruction PAY=RATE*HOURS in FORTRAN source code might be translated into three separate object code instructions, which specify exactly what operations should be performed by the computer.

PAY=RATE*HOURS instruction might translate to the following object code:

MOV 008234,ACC   The address for each of the values in your program is established. Location 8234, in this case, would be the address for the value that you called RATE. This object code statement specifies that the value in location 8234 should be MOVed into the ACCumulator, where arithmetic can be performed.

MUL 006654,ACC   Location 6654 contains the value that you called HOURS. Multiply that value times the value already stored in the ACCumulator and store the results in the ACCumulator.

MOV ACC,008442   Move the contents of the ACCumulator, which now stores the result of the multiplication RATE times HOURS, into the memory location with address 8442. Memory location 8442 would be the location that you called PAY.

After the source code is compiled, a set of object code is created and stored. The first part of the filename for the object code is the same as the name for the FORTRAN program, that is, FIRSTPAY for this example. The three letters for the extension of the filename are OBJ, so the file FIRSTPAY.OBJ is stored. The meaning of the object code is similar to that described with the specific memory locations and the ACCumulator; however, the file is coded in such a way that you cannot list the file to observe what is in the file.

After the source code is compiled and an object code file is created, the object code must be linked to produce *executable code*. The command for LINKing the code into executable form is the word LINK followed by the filename for the FORTRAN program. This creates one more file, with the name FIRSTPAY.EXE. The extension of EXE is always used for EXEcutable code. (See Figure 1.11.)

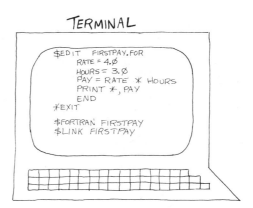

FIGURE 1.11

The LINK procedure inserts pointers into the code that point to memory locations where execution should begin or should transfer. After the LINK step is completed, all the information about executing the program is available to the computer. Finally, you can enter the command to RUN the program. (See Figure 1.12.)

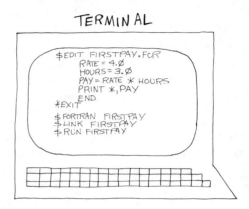

TERMINAL

```
$EDIT FIRSTPAY.FOR
   RATE = 4.0
   HOURS= 3.0
   PAY= RATE * HOURS
   PRINT *, PAY
      END
*EXIT

$ FORTRAN FIRSTPAY
$ LINK FIRSTPAY
$ RUN FIRSTPAY
```

FIGURE 1.12

Look at the following figures, which indicate conceptually the way that execution occurs. When the program executes, the EXEcutable code instructions are actually being processed. However, to understand programming, you can think about execution as if the source code instructions were being executed directly without the translation.

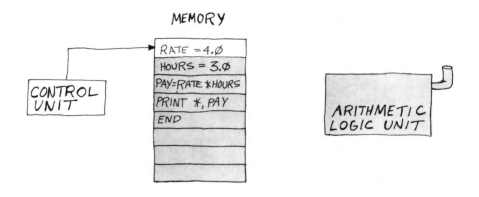

MEMORY

CONTROL UNIT

RATE = 4.0
HOURS = 3.0
PAY=RATE *HOURS
PRINT *, PAY
END

ARITHMETIC LOGIC UNIT

FIGURE 1.13

1. The computer executes the instructions one after another in the order of occurrence.

2. The control unit specifies that the first instruction should be executed. (See Figure 1.13.)

3. When the first instruction is executed, the value 4.0 is stored into the memory location named RATE. (See Figure 1.14.)

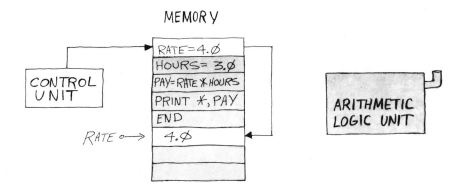

FIGURE 1.14

4. The control unit specifies that the second instruction be executed. When the second instruction executes, the value 3.0 is stored into the memory location named HOURS. (See Figure 1.15.)

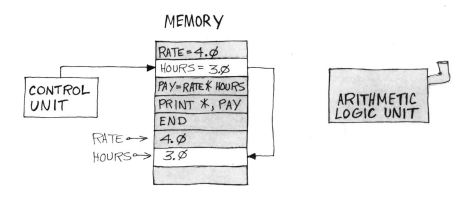

FIGURE 1.15

5. The control unit specifies that the third instruction be executed. The computer goes to the memory location named RATE, gets the value that is there, and moves that value into the arithmetic logic unit. (See Figure 1.16.)

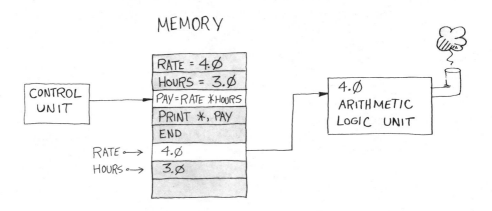

FIGURE 1.16

6. Still executing the third instruction, the computer goes to the memory location named HOURS, gets the value that is there, and multiplies the value in that memory location times the value RATE, which is already in the arithmetic logic unit. (See Figure 1.17.)

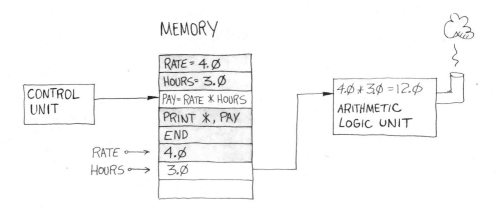

FIGURE 1.17

7. Still executing the third instruction, the computer stores the result of the multiplication into the memory location named PAY. (See Figure 1.18.)

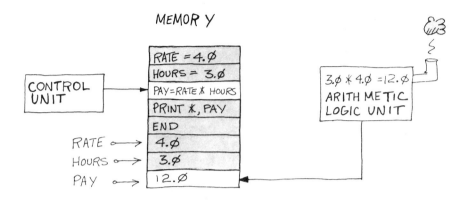

FIGURE 1.18

8. The control unit specifies that the fourth instruction be executed. The computer gets the value stored in the memory location named PAY and transfers that value to an external line to a terminal where the value can be displayed. (See Figure 1.19.)

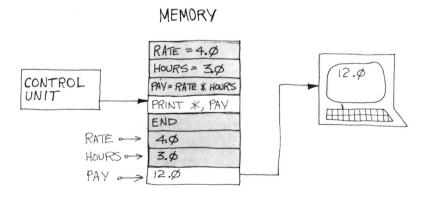

FIGURE 1.19

9. The control unit specifies that the fifth instruction be executed. The END statement indicates the end of the program. The one value printed

for the output of this program is the value 12, printed at the terminal, as shown in Figure 1.20.

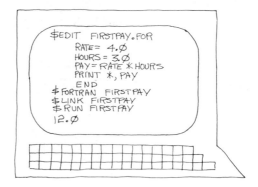

FIGURE 1.20

1.9
SUMMARY

A FORTRAN program is a set of instructions for the computer. The instructions in a program are stored in the computer in a set of addressable locations from which each instruction can be retrieved and executed one after another.

A program is usually entered with an editor from a terminal. The terminal sends codes for the characters you type to the computer. The computer sends codes down the line for each character to be displayed on the terminal screen. After your program is entered and saved, it is stored on a magnetic disk attached to the computer.

Before the instructions in a program can be executed, the instructions must be translated into machine code with the FORTRAN command and then linked with the LINK command in order to produce a code that is executable.

The RUN command initiates the process of actually executing each instruction one after another in the order of occurrence. When the program runs, each instruction containing an equal sign stores one value in a memory location and a PRINT statement displays output.

All processing in the computer occurs in the *central processing unit*, which consists of *memory*, the *control unit*, and the *arithmetic logic unit*. Instructions and values are stored in *memory*. The flow of values throughout the program is controlled by the *control unit*. Arithmetic is performed in the *arithmetic logic unit*.

When an instruction with an equal sign is executed, one value is stored in the memory location named on the left of the equal sign. When memory locations are named on the right of the equal sign, those values are retrieved from memory and used in evaluating the expression on the right of the equal sign. A PRINT statement causes a value or values to be retrieved from memory and displayed at the terminal.

2

Basic Elements of FORTRAN Programming

Symbol	Language	Program	FORTRAN
Assignment statement		Print statement	
Constant	Variable	Symbolic name	
Arithmetic operator		Arithmetic expression	
Arithmetic precedence		Integer	Real
Program entry fields		Declaration	
Intrinsic function			

2.1
BASIC DEFINITIONS

Codes for the *symbols* that can be typed at a terminal can be recognized by a computer. The computer can recognize the codes for all the letters and numbers.

ABCDEFGHIJKLMNOPQRSTUVWXYZ   0123456789

In addition, the computer can recognize special symbols such as the following.

. , + – * / ( ) < >

Some symbols have predefined meanings for the computer. A plus sign, +, specifies that addition be performed in most cases. Some groups of characters can be arranged into words that have a predefined meaning for the computer. The characters P and R and I and N and T, when joined together, specify that something should be displayed either on paper or on a terminal screen. The programmer can define *symbolic names* for the values that are to be stored in a program. PAY, COST, and TAX could be symbolic names for memory locations.

Symbols	Predefined words	Symbolic names	FORTRAN statement
+ =	PRINT END	PAY COST TAX	PAY = COST + TAX

DEFINITION: A *computer language* is a set of rules for organizing a set of symbols, predefined words, and symbolic names in a way to specify instructions for a computer.

DEFINITION: A *computer program* is a set of instructions for a computer written in the words and symbols that make up a particular language. A computer program specifies computations or manipulations to be performed, usually on a set of data.

DEFINITION: FORTRAN is a computer language that can be used to provide the instructions for a computer program. FORTRAN is a programming language that was originally designed as a scientific programming language to be used primarily for numeric calculations; however, the language has expanded to become a widely used general-purpose programming language.

2.2
A FORTRAN PROGRAM

The following is a FORTRAN program. A *program* consists of a set of *statements.* The names COSTSHIP1, COSTSHIP2, and TOTALCOST are symbolic names that represent memory locations inside the computer. The symbols +, =, and * are symbols recognized by the FORTRAN language. In general, symbolic names are separated by an operator, such as a plus sign or an equal sign, that specifies the relationship between the symbolic names. The spacing between the symbolic names and the operators is irrelevant in most cases.

For instance the statement: COSTSHIP1 = 780.00

could be written as: COSTSHIP1 = 780.00

This program might be used to store the cost of two shipments to a warehouse and to calculate and print the total cost of the shipments.

```
COSTSHIP1 = 780.00
COSTSHIP2 = 220.00
TOTALCOST = COSTSHIP1 + COSTSHIP2
PRINT *, TOTALCOST
STOP
END
```

Each line of this program is a *statement*. Each statement in a program is executed one after another in the order it occurs in a simple program such as the preceding.

The statements COSTSHIP1=780.00, COSTSHIP2 = 220.00, and TOTALCOST = COSTSHIP1 + COSTSHIP2 are called assignment statements.

DEFINITION: An *assignment statement* stores a value in computer memory in an addressable location so that the value can be retrieved. An assignment statement contains an equal sign. The meaning of an assignment statement is that the value of the expression on the right side of the equal sign is to be stored in the location named on the left side of the equal sign.

DEFINITION: A PRINT statement causes some output to be displayed. A PRINT statement causes the computer to go to the memory location that is specified by the symbolic name, get the value that is there, and print the value on an output device. If more than one symbolic name is specified in a PRINT statement, the values in each memory location specified are printed one after another on an output line.

The asterisk in the print statement specifies that the output be directed to the default device corresponding to your input. If you are using a terminal, the output will be printed at your terminal.

DEFINITION: The STOP statement in a FORTRAN program is an executable statement which specifies that execution should stop.

DEFINITION: The END statement in a FORTRAN program indicates that this is the end of a program.

2.3
ENTERING A FORTRAN PROGRAM

You can type in the program yourself at a terminal using one of the editors available on the VAX.

The instructions for entering and executing a FORTRAN program on the VAX are in Appendices A and B. Look at the section in the appendix corresponding to the way that you will be using the VAX.

One line of a FORTRAN program is 80 characters long, corresponding to an 80-column punched card. The line is an 80 character record, even if you are entering the program from a terminal. The record is divided into *fields*. FORTRAN statements must begin in column 7 or beyond and cannot go beyond column 72. Columns 7 to 72 comprise the statement field for the program. Each statement may have a *statement number,* and if there is a statement number, it is entered in columns 1 to 5.

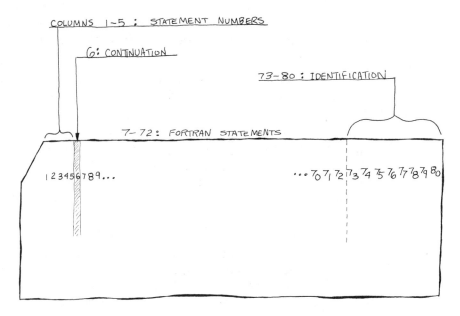

FIGURE 2.1

If you are entering a FORTRAN statement which is too long to be completed before column 72, you can continue the statement on the following line. If a statement is too long to fit on one line, just keep typing until a logical breaking point in a record before column 72 and then start a new statement on the following line. In the second line of the statement, put a character in column 6 to indicate that this is the continuation of a previous line. Column 6 is used only to indicate the *continuation of a statement.*

Columns 73 to 80 may be used for identification of statements, if you choose. Columns 73 to 80 are not used by FORTRAN in any way and can be used for your own information about records. (See Figure 2.1.)

You can enter the example program one statement per record. After the program is entered, you enter the VAX command $ FORTRAN to compile your program, the VAX command $ LINK to link your code into executable code, and then the VAX command $ RUN to cause the statements in your program to begin execution. Refer to Chapter 1 and to Appendix B for details on executing your first FORTRAN program. It is instructive to actually enter and run the examples in the text.

The examples in this book use '$ EDIT filename' to indicate that you should enter the program using an editor that is available on the VAX. Before continuing, you should look at Appendix A to learn to create and modify files and Appendix B to learn to execute a simple example. Those procedures then can be used with all the examples and all the programs that you write. You need to spend a couple of hours going through appendices A and B learning to use the VAX computer so that you can enter and execute the examples if you are to benefit most from the examples.

■ Example 2.1: Executing a Simple FORTRAN Program

You can enter the program using the EDT editor described in Appendix A or using cards as described in Appendix B. This example, like all others in this book, uses $ EDIT as an indication that you should enter the program using any procedure for entering the program.

```
$ EDIT FIRSTPROG.FOR                                    Example 2.1
      COSTSHIP1 = 780.00
      COSTSHIP2 = 220.00
      TOTALCOST = COSTSHIP1 + COSTSHIP2
      PRINT *, TOTALCOST
      STOP
      END
$ FORTRAN FIRSTPROG
$ LINK FIRSTPROG
$ RUN FIRSTPROG                                          Example 2.1
1000.0000                                                Output
```

Observe what is happening conceptually as each statement in the example program is executed. The first statement causes the value 780.00 to be stored in the memory location named COSTSHIP1. (See Figure 2.2.)

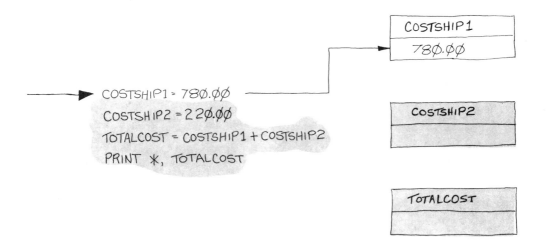

FIGURE 2.2

When the second statement executes, the value 220.00 is stored in the memory location named COSTSHIP2. (See Figure 2.3.)

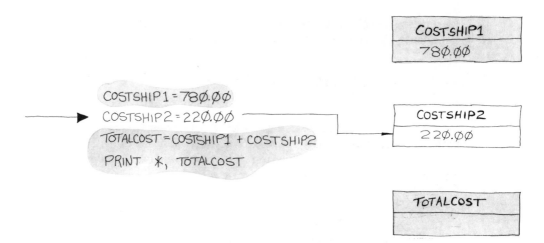

FIGURE 2.3

When the third statement is executed, the following procedures are performed. First the computer goes to the memory location named COST-SHIP1 and gets the value, 780.00, that is there. Then the computer goes to the memory location named COSTSHIP2 and gets the value, 220.00, that is there. The computer adds the two values together and stores the result in the memory location named TOTALCOST. (See Figure 2.4.)

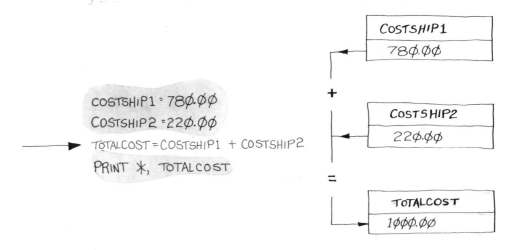

FIGURE 2.4

When the PRINT statement is executed, the computer goes to the memory location named TOTALCOST and gets the value that is there and prints the value at the terminal. (See Figure 2.5.)

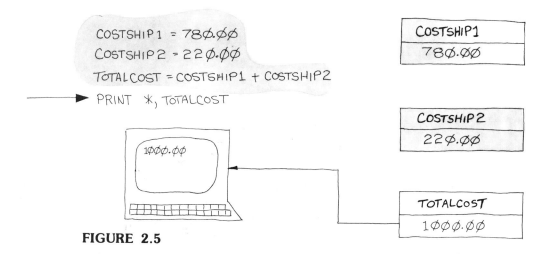

FIGURE 2.5

2.4
DESCRIPTIVE LABELS FOR OUTPUT

A PRINT statement can be used as in Example 2.1 to print the value that is stored in a memory location. In addition, strings of characters enclosed between single quotation marks can be printed. If there are no quotation marks around a string of characters in a print statement, the computer assumes that the characters are a symbolic name and goes to the memory location specified by the symbolic name, gets the value that is there, and prints the value. If there are single quotation marks around a string of characters, the computer prints the exact characters that are entered between the quotation marks.

■ Example 2.2: Labeling Output

The program stores the costs for two shipments, calculates the total cost, and prints the words THE TOTAL COST = , along with the calculated total cost.

```
$ EDIT PROGRAM2.FOR                                    Example 2.2
      COSTSHIP1 = 780.00
      COSTSHIP2 = 220.00
      TOTALCOST = COSTSHIP1 + COSTSHIP2
      PRINT *, 'THE TOTAL COST = ', TOTALCOST
      STOP
      END
$ FORTRAN PROGRAM2
$ LINK PROGRAM2
$ RUN PROGRAM2                                         Example 2.2
THE TOTAL COST =           1000.000                    Output
```

2.5
CONSTANTS, VARIABLES, AND SYMBOLIC NAMES

DEFINITION: A *constant* is a numeric value that is defined in a program. In the statement COSTSHIP1=780.00, the value 780.00 is a constant.

DEFINITION: A *variable* is a value stored in a memory location that may change during the execution of a program. A variable is a value that is referenced by a symbolic name.

DEFINITION: A *symbolic name* is a string of characters used in a computer program to identify a memory location. A symbolic name must be 31 characters or fewer. A symbolic name can contain letters, numbers, and the underline character. Symbolic names are used to identify other FORTRAN entities, such as arrays of values and functions.

As a rule you should use symbolic names that have some meaning in the program you are writing. The symbolic names X, Y, and Z could be used in the warehouse shipment example; however, notice that it is impossible to guess what the purpose of the program might be.

```
X = 780.00
Y = 220.00
Z = X + Y
PRINT *, Z
```

It is important to use symbolic names that have some meaning in your program.

The following program indicates other valid symbolic names.

```
SHIPMENT_ONE = 780.00
SHIP2 = 220.00
COST_FOR_SHIP1_AND_SHIP2 = SHIPMENT_ONE + SHIP2
PRINT *,COST_FOR_SHIP1_AND_SHIP2
```

The following are invalid symbolic names.

```
SOME  NAME
ADDRESS,CITY
AMOUNT.IN.DOLLARS
TRY?
```

No blanks can be included.
A comma cannot be included.
No periods can be included.
No special characters can be included, except for the underline character.

2.6
ARITHMETIC EXPRESSIONS

DEFINITION: An *arithmetic operator* is a symbol that specifies a numeric operation to be performed. Arithmetic operations are defined by the following symbols.

+ Addition   * Multiplication   / Division
− Subtraction   ** Exponentiation

DEFINITION: An *arithmetic expression* is a constant, a variable, or a group of constants and variables joined together by arithmetic operators and parentheses. An arithmetic expression is evaluated by a set of rules in the FORTRAN language to produce a numeric value.

DEFINITION: The order in which arithmetic expressions are evaluated is determined by the *precedence* of the operators associated with values. Exponentiation is performed before any other operations. Multiplication and division are performed before addition and subtraction. If operators of equal precedence occur side by side in an expression, the components of the expression with equivalent precedence are evaluated left to right. The following is the precedence of the operators.

First   **   Exponentiation
Second   * and /   Multiplication and division
Third   + and −   Addition and subtraction

Look at the arithmetic expression $4 + 12 − 10 / 2$
The division would be performed first giving $4 + 12 − \quad 5$
Then the leftmost addition or subtraction occurs $16 \quad − \quad 5$
And then the final result is produced 11

Look at another expression $2 * 12 / 4 * 10 ** 2 − 12$
Exponentiation is performed first $2 * 12 / 4 * \quad 100 − 12$
Perform left multiplication or division $24 / 4 * \quad 100 − 12$
Perform left multiplication or division $6 \quad * \quad 100 − 12$
Perform multiplication $600 \quad − 12$
Produce result 588

■ Example 2.3: Arithmetic Precedence

The following program includes the preceding arithmetic expressions.

```
$ EDIT EVALUATE.FOR
      A = 2
      B = 4
      C = 1Ø
      D = 12
```

Example 2.3

```
X = B + D - C / A
PRINT *, X
X = A * D / B * C ** A - D
PRINT *, X
STOP
END
$ FORTRAN EVALUATE
$ LINK EVALUATE
$ RUN EVALUATE
11.00000
588.0001
```

Example 2.3
Output

Notice that some precision was lost in the calculation of the value X. The number could not be represented exactly. A way to extend accuracy is covered in Chapter 14.

DEFINITION: Parentheses provide a level of precedence in the order of evaluation of arithmetic expressions higher than any other arithmetic operator. You can specify a particular order for the evaluation of the elements of an arithmetic expression by enclosing parts of the expression in parentheses.

First	( )	Parentheses
Second	**	Exponentiation
Third	* and /	Multiplication and division
Fourth	+ and −	Addition and subtraction

The order of the evaluation of the examples previously demonstrated is changed by inserting parentheses in the following example.

Look at the arithmetic expression	4 + (12 − 10) / 2
The subtraction would be performed first	4 + 2 / 2
Then the division would be performed	4 + 1
And then the final result is produced	5

Look at this expression with parentheses	(2*12/4*10)**2 − 12
First evaluate arithmetic inside parentheses	
Leftmost multiplication is performed first	(24 /4*10)**2 − 12
Division is performed	(6 *10)**2 − 12
Multiplication is performed	60 **2 − 12
Perform exponentiation	3600 − 12
Produce result	3588

Parentheses can be nested inside parentheses to any level.

Look at the nested parentheses	((2*12)/(4*10))**2 − 12
Evaluate expression in inside left ( )	(24 /(4*10))**2 − 12
Evaluate expression in other inner ( )	(24 / 40)**2 − 12
Evaluate expression inside remaining ( )	0.60 **2 − 12
Perform exponentiation	0.36 − 12
Produce result	−11.64

■ Example 2.4: Defining the Order of Arithmetic Precedence

The following program includes the preceding arithmetic expressions with parentheses added to specify the order of execution.

Example 2.4

```
$ EDIT PAREN.FOR
     A = 2
     B = 4
     C = 1Ø
     D = 12
     X = B + ( D - C ) / A
     PRINT *, X
     X = ( A * D / B * C ) ** A - D
     PRINT *, X
     X = ( ( A * D ) / ( B * C ) ) ** A - D
     PRINT *, X
     STOP
     END
$ FORTRAN PAREN
$ LINK PAREN
$ RUN PAREN
     5.ØØØØØØ
     3588.ØØØ
    -11.64ØØØ
```

Example 2.4
Output

2.7
INTEGER AND REAL ARITHMETIC

Various types of arithmetic can be defined and performed in a computer. The two most common types are integer arithmetic and real arithmetic.

DEFINITION: Integer arithmetic operates on integer values, that is, values with no fractional part. If you are counting apples, you would count 1, 2, 3, 4, etc. Integer arithmetic has no facility for evaluating or storing fractional parts of a number. The way that you specify to the computer the type of value to store is by the symbolic name that you assign to a memory location. If you use a symbolic name beginning with one of the letters I, J, K, L, M, or N, you indicate that an *integer* value will be stored in that memory location.

Integer arithmetic is used for applications such as counting the number of times some condition or process occurs and for addressing a particular element in a list of elements.

■ Example 2.5: Integer Arithmetic

Notice that in this example of integer arithmetic the division of 20 by 3 produces 6, because there is no provision for fractions.

```
$ EDIT WHOLENUM.FOR                                    Example 2.5
      NUMBER = 20
      M = 3
      L = NUMBER * M
      PRINT *, L
      J = NUMBER / M
      PRINT *, J
      STOP
      END
$ FORTRAN WHOLENUM
$ LINK WHOLENUM
$ RUN WHOLENUM
      60                                               Example 2.5
       6                                               Output
```

DEFINITION: Real arithmetic operates on values that are stored in memory locations in floating-point notation. The significant digits of a number are stored, and the position of the decimal point is stored for values in memory locations defined to be *real* memory locations. When real arithmetic is performed, the computer stores the maximum number of significant digits possible and records the position of the decimal point. This allows large numbers and very small numbers to be stored.

Symbolic names beginning with the letters A to H and O to Z are used to store real values, that is, values that may contain a fractional part.

Using a memory location that is specified to store a real value, a number such as 32568.1 can be stored with the location of the decimal point marked to follow the 8. A number such as 0.42563 can be stored as 42563 with the decimal point marked to be to the left of the 4. Fractions are stored as decimals in the computer. The value ½ is stored as 0.5. The value 1/3 is stored as 0.333333 and some precision is lost because the value cannot be represented exactly in the computer.

■ Example 2.6: Real Arithmetic

```
$ EDIT REALNUM.FOR                                     Example 2.6
      BIGNUMBER = 8765.99
      SMALLNUMBER = 0.039
      CALCULATION = BIGNUMBER * SMALLNUMBER
      DIVISION = BIGNUMBER / SMALLNUMBER
      PRINT *, 'THE CALCULATION IS ',CALCULATION
      PRINT *, 'THE DIVISION IS ',DIVISION
      STOP
      END
$ FORTRAN REALNUM
$ LINK REALNUM
$ RUN REALNUM
THE CALCULATION IS      341.8736
THE DIVISION IS      224769.0                          Example 2.6
                                                       Output
```

You should specify the appropriate way to store a value, either integer or real, by choosing the correct symbolic name. In addition to storing a number originally as integer or real, you must be careful of the types of storage that you define for storing the results of calculations.

Be aware that, if two integer values are used in performing an arithmetic calculation, the arithmetic is always performed as integer arithmetic. Arithmetic between real and integer values is called *mixed mode* arithmetic. If an arithmetic calculation is performed between one real number and one integer number, the arithmetic is performed as real arithmetic. Look at the output generated by the following program.

■ Example 2.7: Integer, Real, and Mixed Mode Arithmetic

```
$ EDIT MIXUP.FOR
    X = 33.9
    Y = 3.0
    N = X / Y
    PRINT *, N


    NUMERATOR = 5
    NDIVIDE = 9
    DEGREEFAHR = 212.0
    TEMPERATURE = NUMERATOR/NDIVIDE * ( DEGREEFAHR - 32.0)
    PRINT *, TEMPERATURE




    NUMERATOR = 5
    DIVIDE = 9
    DEGREEFAHR = 212.0
    TEMPERATURE = NUMERATOR/DIVIDE * ( DEGREEFAHR - 32.0)
    PRINT *, TEMPERATURE



    STOP
    END
$ FORTRAN MIXUP
$ LINK MIXUP
$ RUN MIXUP
        11
0.0000000E+00
  100.0000
```

Example 2.7

Real arithmetic is performed; however, when the result is stored in the location N, the decimal part of the number is lost.

The result produced by this calculation is zero because the division 5/9 is performed in integer arithmetic, and zero times anything is zero.

If one number in an arithmetic operation is real, then real arithmetic is performed; in this case, the anticipated temperature is calculated.

Example 2.7
Output

The output printed free format with an asterisk prints a zero in scientific notation as it is stored.

$$0.0000000E+00 \quad \text{means} \quad 0.0000000 * 10^0 = 0.0000 * 1 = 0$$

Since any number to the power of zero equals 1, the value is zero times one and that is equal to zero.

2.8

INTEGER AND REAL DECLARATIONS

Assignment statements and PRINT statements specify some instruction for the computer to execute. In addition to statements in the FORTRAN language, there are *declarations*. A declaration does not give an instruction but instead defines the way that values will be stored in memory before the execution of the program begins. If a symbolic name that would be particularly descriptive for a value that is an integer value happens to begin with a letter A to H or O to Z, you can declare the symbolic name to be INTEGER. You can declare a symbolic name that begins with I, J, K, L, M, or N to be the name of a memory location that stores a real value.

DEFINITION: A *declaration* in a FORTRAN program provides a method for specifying a way that a value should be stored. Declarations are always put before the first executable statement, because the program must know ahead of time any special way that values should be treated.

■ Example 2.8: Integer and Real Declarations

In this example, the memory location specified by the symbolic name N stores a value as a real value. A real value is stored as the maximum number of significant digits with the location of the decimal point recorded. The value stored in the memory location named Z is stored as an INTEGER value.

```
$ EDIT DECLAR.FOR                              Example 2.8
        REAL N
        INTEGER Z
        X = 33.9
        Y = 3.0
        N= X / Y
        Z = X / Y
        PRINT *,'N =',N,'Z =',Z
        STOP
        END
$ FORTRAN DECLAR
$ LINK DECLAR
$ RUN DECLAR                                   Example 2.8
N =     11.30000        Z =     11           Output
```

2.9

INTRINSIC FUNCTIONS

An *intrinsic library function* is a set of instructions stored as a part of the FORTRAN language. Library functions include operations that programmers frequently use and that might be difficult to program. Programmers often need to take the square root of a number. This set of instructions is stored as part of the FORTRAN language and given the function name SQRT. When a program includes the name of the function SQRT, the set of instructions that calculates the square root is accessed at the time the statement is executed.

Example:

$$X = SQRT (25.0)$$

The example means that the set of instructions in the function named SQRT should be executed. The value 25.0 is called a *parameter* or *argument* of the function. The argument value of 25.0 is used as a data value for the instructions in the function. The square root of the argument is calculated and the value 5.0 is then stored in the memory location named X.

An argument can be specified by a symbolic name. Some library functions require more than one argument.

The following are a few of the intrinsic library functions that are available on the VAX.

SQRT	Square root	Argument must be a real number > 0 or = 0.
LOG	Natural log	Argument must be a real number > 0.
LOG10	Common log	Argument must be a real number > 0.
EXP	Exponential	Argument must be a real number.
ABS	Absolute value	Argument must be real.
INT	Truncation	Argument must be real.
NINT	Nearest integer	Argument must be real.
REAL	Convert to REAL	Argument is integer.
MOD	Provides the remainder when the first integer argument is divided by the second integer argument	

Arguments for a trigonometric function must be a real number and must be in radians.

SIN   ASIN   COS   ACOS   TAN   ATAN

The MAXimum and MINimum functions require at least two arguments.

MAX	Finds the largest value in a list of arguments.
MIN	Finds the smallest value in a list of arguments.

■ **Example 2.9**

```
$ EDIT SQUAREROT.FOR
        X = 22.2
        Y = 44.4
        A = SQRT(X)
        PRINT *, A
        B = SQRT( X+Y)
        PRINT *, B
```

```
        N = 67
        C = SQRT(REAL(N))
        PRINT *,C
        STOP
        END
$ FORTRAN SQUAREROT
$ LINK SQUAREROT
$ RUN SQUAREROT
 4.711688
 8.160883
 8.185352
```

■ Example 2.10

```
$ EDIT INTNINT.FOR
        Z = 88.8
        M = INT(Z)
        PRINT *, M
        M = NINT(Z)
        PRINT *, M
        STOP
        END
$ FORTRAN INTNINT
$ LINK INTNINT
$ RUN INTNINT
        88
        89
```

■ Example 2.11

```
$ EDIT LOGS.FOR
        XVALUE = 100.
        A = LOG(XVALUE)
        PRINT *, A
        B = LOG10(XVALUE)
        PRINT *,B
        STOP
        END
$ FORTRAN LOGS
$ LINK LOGS
$ RUN LOGS
 4.605170
 2.000000
```

■ Example 2.12

```
$ EDIT MAXMIN.FOR
        X = 22.2
        Y = 33.3
        Z = 44.4
        XMAX = MAX(X,Y,Z)
        PRINT *,'XMAX=',XMAX
        I = 10
```

```
        J = 20
        IJMIN = MIN(I,J)
        PRINT *,'MIN=',IJMIN
        STOP
        END
$ FORTRAN MAXMIN
$ LINK MAXMIN
$ RUN MAXMIN
XMAX=        44.40000
MIN =             10
```

2.10
APPLICATIONS

The concepts in this chapter are the most basic concepts of FORTRAN programming. Realistic applications require the capability of transferring data into a program, executing statements repeatedly in a program, and making decisions based on conditions during the execution of a program. These concepts are covered in succeeding chapters.

Although the examples demonstrate some particular applications, the FORTRAN programming concepts in all the examples are useful to all programmers. It is worthwhile to look carefully at each example, because the examples can quickly demonstrate a concept that you almost certainly need to know.

■ Example 2.13: Society Award Application

In an effort to show the Home Economic Society's appreciation for the work of Dr. Joan R. MacGooden, a vote was take to determine if a special service award should be given to Dr. MacGooden. Of the 1723 members, 92% voted to present the award. Calculate the number of members voting for and against the award and print a report on the voting.

```
$ EDIT SOCIETY.FOR                                  Example 2.13
        MEMBERS = 1723
        MEMBERSFOR = 0.92 * MEMBERS
        MEMBERSAGAINST = MEMBERS - MEMBERSFOR
        PRINT *, ' HOME ECONOMICS SOCIETY'
        PRINT *, ' Joan R. MacGooden Special Award'
        PRINT *, 'For:     ',MEMBERSFOR
        PRINT *, 'Against: ',MEMBERSAGAINST
        STOP
        END
$ FORTRAN SOCIETY
$ LINK SOCIETY
```

```
$ RUN SOCIETY                                          Example 2.13
HOME ECONOMICS SOCIETY                                 Output
Joan R. MacGooden Special Award
For:            1585
Against:         138
```

Notice the use of the integer memory locations for MEMBERS, MEMBERSFOR, and MEMBERSAGAINST and the way that the values for MEMBERSFOR and MEMBERSAGAINST were calculated. The programmer has made an assumption in this program that the number of members voting for the proposal should be rounded down to the nearest even value. That may be a valid assumption, but as a programmer you must take every detail into consideration in order to produce correct results.

Look at two other approaches to programming this example. There are problems with each of the following approaches.

```
FOR = 0.92
AGAINST = 1.0 - FOR
MEMBERSFOR = FOR * 1723
MEMBERSAGAINST= AGAINST*1723
PRINT *, MEMBERSFOR
PRINT *, MEMBERSAGAINST
STOP
END
```

The output for this program would be the following.

Output

```
    1585
     137
```

Notice that in this approach the total of the members does not add up to 1723.

```
FOR = 0.92
AGAINST = 1.0 - FOR
FORMEMBERS = FOR * 1723
AGAINSTMEMBERS=AGAINST*1723
PRINT *, FORMEMBERS
PRINT *, AGAINSTMEMBERS
STOP
END
```

The output for this program would be the following.

Output

```
1585.1600
 137.8400
```

In this approach, partial members are voting.

■ Example 2.14: Bank Deposit Application – Method One

The interest rate for savings accounts is 8 percent. For each of three customers, the amount deposited in a savings account is recorded. Customer one's deposit is $420.60. Customer two's deposit is $52.16, and customer three's deposit is $100.00. Calculate and print the new balance including interest for each customer. In addition, print descriptive headings and label customer number one as 1, customer number two as 2, and customer number three as 3.

```
$ EDIT BANK.FOR                                    Example 2.14
      PRINT *, '   CUSTOMER      DEPOSIT       BALANCE'
      SAVINGSINTEREST = 0.08
      CUST1DEP = 420.60
      BALANCE1 = CUST1DEP + SAVINGSINTEREST * CUST1DEP
      PRINT *,1,CUST1DEP,BALANCE1
      CUST2DEP = 52.16
      BALANCE2 = CUST2DEP + SAVINGSINTEREST * CUST2DEP
      PRINT *,2,CUST2DEP,BALANCE2
      CUST3DEP = 100.00
      BALANCE3 = CUST3DEP + SAVINGSINTEREST * CUST3DEP
      PRINT *,3,CUST3DEP,BALANCE3
      STOP
      END
$ FORTRAN BANK
$ LINK BANK
$ RUN BANK                                         Example 2.14
   CUSTOMER     DEPOSIT       BALANCE              Output
          1    420.6000       454.2480
          2    52.16000       56.33280
          3    100.0000       108.0000
```

The column headings, CUSTOMER, DEPOSIT, and BALANCE, were created by entering spaces between the words enclosed between single quotation marks in the first PRINT statement in the program. It usually takes more than one try to get the output to line up just as you want. The output for this program is not printed with a dollar sign or with two digits following the decimal point. Chapter 6 provides information about generating formatted output.

Notice that in the arithmetic statements the multiplication is performed before the addition, calculating the interest, and then adding the interest earned to the principal.

Look at Example 2.15, which produces exactly the same output as this program, but uses the same memory locations repeatedly.

■ Example 2.15: Bank Deposit Application — Method Two

This problem is exactly the same problem as that for Example 2.14. Notice the difference in the two programs. This example stores a value in the memory location named CUSTDEP. Then the program performs a calculation, stores the result in the memory location named BALANCE, and then prints the values that are stored in the memory locations named CUSTDEP and BALANCE. Now this program stores the next customer deposit in the memory location named CUSTDEP. The first value that was stored in the memory location named CUSTDEP is destroyed, but that is all right because the value has been printed already and there is no more need for that value. Likewise, the second value stored in the memory location named BALANCE replaces the first value, but, again, the first value has been printed and is no longer needed. The third values stored in memory locations CUSTDEP and BALANCE replace the second values that were stored in those locations. Using memory locations repeatedly is an important concept in programming.

```
$ EDIT BANK.FOR                                     Example 2.15
      PRINT *, '   CUSTOMER     DEPOSIT      BALANCE'
      SAVINGSINTEREST = 0.08
      CUSTDEP = 420.60
      BALANCE = CUSTDEP + SAVINGSINTEREST * CUSTDEP
      PRINT *,1,CUSTDEP,BALANCE
      CUSTDEP = 52.16
      BALANCE = CUSTDEP + SAVINGSINTEREST * CUSTDEP
      PRINT *,2,CUSTDEP,BALANCE
      CUSTDEP = 100.00
      BALANCE = CUSTDEP + SAVINGSINTEREST * CUSTDEP
      PRINT *,3,CUSTDEP,BALANCE
      STOP
      END
$ FORTRAN BANK
$ LINK BANK
$ RUN BANK                                          Example 2.15
     CUSTOMER     DEPOSIT      BALANCE              Output
            1    420.6000     454.2480
            2    52.16000     56.33280
            3    100.0000     108.0000
```

◼ Example 2.16: Dividing the Costs Application

The microcomputer club is having a picnic and, since nobody wanted to cook, they are having it catered. The cost of the picnic is $130.00. There are 32 members in the club. It was decided that each member should pay an even dollar amount and that the remainder would be paid from the club dues. Calculate and print the amount paid by each member and the amount to be paid from the club dues.

```
$ EDIT DUES.FOR                                     Example 2.16
      INTEGER CLUBPAY
      NCOST = 130
      MEMBERS = 32
      MEMBERPAY = NCOST / MEMBERS
      CLUBPAY = MOD(NCOST,MEMBERS)
      PRINT *, 'EACH MEMBER PAYS',MEMBERPAY
      PRINT *, 'CLUBPAY',CLUBPAY
```

```
      STOP
      END
$ FORTRAN DUES
$ LINK DUES
$ RUN DUES
EACH MEMBER PAYS          4
CLUBPAY          2
```

Example 2.16
Output

The amount for each member in the example turns out to be an even amount because integer arithmetic is performed. An integer declaration makes CLUBPAY an integer value. The intrinsic function, MOD, produces the remainder of an integer division and that is exactly what is needed for this problem. The members in the club each pay an even amount, and the club pays the remainder.

■ Example 2.17: Trigonometry Application

The length of the hypotenuse of a right triangle equals the square root of the sum of the squares of its legs. For a triangle with leg lengths of 3 and 4, calculate and print the length of the hypotenuse. The following is the formula for calculating the hypotenuse r, with legs x and y.

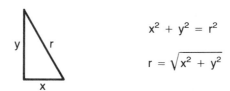

$$x^2 + y^2 = r^2$$

$$r = \sqrt{x^2 + y^2}$$

Write a FORTRAN program to calculate the length of the hypotenuse for legs x equals 3 and y equals 4.

```
$ EDIT XYR.FOR                                    Example 2.17
      X = 3.
      Y = 4.
      HYPOTENUSE = ( X*X + Y*Y ) ** 0.5
      PRINT *, HYPOTENUSE
      STOP
      END
$ FORTRAN XYR
$ LINK XYR
$ RUN XYR                                         Example 2.17
5.000000                                          Output
```

```
X = 3.
Y = 4.
HYPOTENUSE = SQRT( X*X + Y*Y )
PRINT *, HYPOTENUSE
STOP
END
```

The intrinsic function SQRT could be used instead of using the exponentiation to the ½ power, as shown in the preceding example.

■ Example 2.18: Sine and Cosine Applications

Using intrinsic functions, calculate and print the COS of 60 degrees and the SIN of 30 degrees. The degrees must be in radians for the SIN and COS functions.

$$180° = \pi \text{ radians} = 3.141593 \text{ radians}$$

```
$ EDIT PI.FOR                                        Example 2.18
      PI = 3.141593
      DEGREE60 = 60. * PI / 180.
      COS60 = COS(DEGREE60)
      PRINT *, 'COS(60) =', COS60
      DEGREE30 = 30. * PI / 180.
      SIN30 = SIN(DEGREE30)
      PRINT *, 'SIN(30) =',SIN30
      STOP
      END
$ FORTRAN PI
$ LINK PI
$ RUN PI
COS(60) =        0.5000000                           Example 2.18
SIN(30) =        0.5000000                           Output
```

2.11
SUMMARY

■ Entering a FORTRAN Program

Characters entered at a terminal and recognized by the computer may be letters, numbers, or special symbols such as =, ( ), *, +, etc.

- Special symbols usually have predefined meanings to the computer. The plus sign usually indicates that addition be performed.

- Predefined words are a group of characters joined together that have a certain meaning to the computer. The characters, PRINT, are recognized by the computer and some action occurs.

- Symbolic names are created by a programmer to represent memory locations.

A *statement* is a group of symbols, predefined words, and symbolic names joined together to specify some action to the computer.

A *program* is a group of statements that perform some task.

■ Elements of a FORTRAN Program

An *editor* is used to enter the statements in the program. Statements in a FORTRAN program are entered beginning in column 7 and going up to, or through, column 72. Statement numbers are entered in columns 1–5. A character in column 6 indicates that the current line is a continuation of the statement from the previous line.

- The FORTRAN command is used to compile the program.
- The LINK command is used to generate code for execution.
- The RUN command begins the execution of the program.

■ Executing Statements in a FORTRAN Program

An *assignment statement* is a statement containing an equal sign, and it stores one value in a memory location. When the computer processes an assignment statement, the expression on the right side of the equal sign is evaluated and that value is stored in the memory location named on the left of the equal sign.

One symbolic name, specifying the location where one value is to be stored, is to the left of the equal sign in an assignment statement.

An arithmetic expression is to the right of the equal sign in an assignment statement. An arithmetic expression can be: a *constant,* a *symbolic name,* or a group of *constants, symbolic names, arithmetic operators,* and parentheses.

When a PRINT statement executes, a value is copied from the memory location specified to a terminal screen.

■ Types of Arithmetic

Integer arithmetic is performed with no fractional parts of numbers. INTEGER values are stored in memory locations with symbolic names beginning with the letters I,J,K,L,M, or N or in locations specified to be integer locations with the *integer* declaration.

Real arithmetic is performed with both the integer and the fractional parts of numbers. REAL values are stored in memory locations with symbolic names beginning with the letters A–H and O–Z or in locations specified to be REAL locations with the REAL declaration.

2.12
EXERCISES

2.1. Fill in the blanks of the following definitions:

    a. A computer program is a set of _____ that specify some operations for a computer.

    b. A value, stored in a memory location, that may change during the execution of a program is called _____.

c. A _____ is the name given to a memory location by a programmer in order to be able to reference the location in a program.

d. The meaning of an assignment statement is that the _____ ____ on the right side of the equal sign is evaluated and that value is stored in _____ .

e. There can be _____ memory location named on the left of the equal sign in an assignment statement because that memory location is the place where one value is to be stored.

f. An _____ value has no fractional part.

g. A _____ value is stored as a series of significant digits along with the position of the decimal point.

2.2. Mark beside each of the following an I if the name is a symbolic name for an integer number, an R if the name is a symbolic name for a real number, or an X if the name is an invalid symbolic name.

NUM _____   TIMES __   AMOUNT ____   TOTAL _____
XI _____   XYZ ____   KOUNT _____   LAST AMOUNT _____
ONE.NAME __   J _____ A_VERY_LONG_SYMBOLIC_NAME __

2.3. What is the output for each of the following FORTRAN programs? If you are ever in doubt about what the computer will do, you can type in a program with PRINT statements to observe the output.

```
a.  N = 20              b.  X = 44.8           c.  A = 66.9
    M = 10                  Y = 2.0                N = 3
    L = N * M / 2          Z = X / Y + 11.2       B = A / N + N
    PRINT *, L             PRINT *, Z             PRINT *, B
    STOP                   STOP                   STOP
    END                    END                    END

d.  N = 20              e.  I = 18
    M = 10                  J = 3
    X = N / M + 0.67       N = 6
    PRINT *, X            K = 25
    STOP                   NUM = ((I/J*100)/N)/10*K
    END                    PRINT *, NUM
                           STOP
                           END

f.  A = 3.25            g.  TUITION = 306.75
    B = 1.75               FEES = 76.87
    C = 5.0                NUM = 12700
    D = 0.5               REVENUE = NUM * (TUITION+FEES)
    R = ((A+B)*C)**0.5     PRINT *,REVENUE
    PRINT *, R            STOP
    STOP                   END
    END
```

2.4. Twelve people are going on a picnic. A member of the group wrote the following program to print the cost for each person. What is wrong with the program?

```
COST_FOR_PICNIC = 9.87
MONEY_FOR_EACH = COST_FOR_PICNIC / 12
PRINT *, MONEY_FOR_EACH
STOP
END
```

2.5. Write FORTRAN programs using intrinsic functions to calculate and print values for the following:

   a. The integer part of the number 63.972

   b. The square root of the number 27

   c. The maximum of the three numbers 6, 19, and 8

   d. The minimum of the four numbers 2, 3, 1, and 5

   e. The remainder of the number 20 divided by 3

   f. The sine of an angle of 45 degrees

2.6. Write a FORTRAN program for each of the following problems:

   a. A library has 87,000 books. The library is going to give away 12,700 unused books and purchase 1000 new books. The program should store each of the book values and calculate the new book count.

   b. The program should store three grades for a student and calculate and print the average of the three grades.

   c. Apples are selling for 18 cents each, pears are selling for 23 cents each, and peaches are selling for 27 cents each. The program should store the cost for each fruit and calculate and print the total cost of purchasing 5 apples, 4 pears, and 10 peaches.

   d. The formula for calculating the amount of an investment after simple interest is paid on the investment is the following:

   Investment = investment * (1 + interest rate)

   Write a program to store an investment value of $345 and an interest rate of 6 percent. The program should calculate and print the value of the investment after the interest is paid.

   e. There are three rooms in a house. The rooms are 10 x 12 feet, 14 x 18 feet, and 9 x 11 feet. The cost of carpet for the house is $18 per square yard. The program should store all the known values and calculate and print the total cost of the carpet for the three rooms.

3

FORTRAN Files and Data Files: Input and Output

The procedures demonstrated in this chapter for defining input and output using files with the VAX should be followed throughout the text. The input and output for all example programs in the text are given; however, the details about how to provide input and how to direct output are provided only in this chapter. To learn the most from these examples, you should enter and run the examples.

For most computer applications, you must provide data in a form that can be accessed quickly as a program executes. You will often have reason to enter data from a terminal; however, large amounts of data are most often stored on magnetic disk. *Input* is the process of transferring values into the computer as a program is executing. For some applications, you may need to print the results of a computer program at the terminal; however, it is often preferable to direct the results to be stored on magnetic disk so that the results can be accessed at a later time. *Output* is the process of transferring values from a storage area internal to a program's working area to an external area, either another storge area inside the computer or a terminal or some other device.

To understand how files are being created and how to access files, you must type in some examples and observe the results. The examples in this chapter are designed to demonstrate how to store and retrieve data from files. You should enter the programs using an editor. Detailed information about using an editor is available in Appendix A. After your program is entered and saved, you should use the FORTRAN command to compile your program, that is, to translate your program into machine code. You should next enter the LINK command to link your program into a form that is executable. As the final step, you should RUN the program and produce output.

3.1
STEPS IN CREATING AND RUNNING A FORTRAN PROGRAM

$ EDIT filename.FOR

> Enter your program using the EDT editor. (Details about using an editor to enter a file and run a program can be found in Appendices A and B.)

* EXIT — End and save the program.
$ FORTRAN filename — Translate the program into machine code.
$ LINK filename — Link the program into executable code.
$ RUN filename — Execute the instructions in the program.

3.2
WRITE STATEMENT—WRITING OUTPUT TO A TERMINAL

The PRINT statement in a FORTRAN program is used to display information on the terminal screen where you are working. The PRINT statement is the simplest way to specify that output be printed; however, a WRITE statement provides more flexibility in defining where and how output should be directed.

■ Example 3.1: Writing Output to a Terminal

The following program on the left uses a WRITE statement to print output at your terminal, as does the program on the right.

```
$EDIT WRITEOUT.FOR              $EDIT PRINTOUT.FOR        Example 3.1
    COST1 = 780.00                  COST1 = 780.00
    COST2 = 220.00                  COST2 = 220.00
    TOTALCOST = COST1 + COST2       TOTALCOST = COST1 + COST2
    WRITE (6,*) TOTALCOST           PRINT *, TOTALCOST
    STOP                            STOP
    END                             END
$ FORTRAN WRITEOUT              $ FORTRAN WRITEOUT
$ LINK WRITEOUT                 $ LINK WRITEOUT
$ RUN WRITEOUT                  $ RUN PRINTOUT
1000.000           Output      1000.000              Output
```

In the statement WRITE (6,*) TOTALCOST, the 6 is a device number used to specify by default that the output from the WRITE statement be directed to the terminal where you are working. It is possible in FORTRAN to use format statements to specify how many decimal points to print for numbers and exactly how output should look. The asterisk in this WRITE statement specifies that the output should be printed in free format; that is, neither the number of decimal points nor the position for printing on an output line is specified. The following is the meaning of the WRITE statement in the program.

WRITE (6,*) TOTALCOST
WRITE (to the terminal, unformatted) the value stored in memory
                                    location named TOTALCOST

■ Example 3.2: Writing More Than One Value on a Line of Output

More than one value can be printed on one line of output. The following example prints three values on one output line.

```
$ EDIT WRITE3NUM.FOR                              Example 3.2
    COST1 = 780.00
    COST2 = 220.00
    TOTALCOST = COST1 + COST2
    WRITE (6,*) COST1, COST2, TOTALCOST
    STOP
    END
$ FORTRAN WRITE3NUM
$ LINK WRITE3NUM
$ RUN WRITE3NUM                                   Example 3.2
780.0000    220.0000    1000.000                  Output
```

■ Example 3.3: Writing More Than One Line of Output

Each WRITE statement in the following program produces one line of output. Each WRITE statement in a program produces one line of output unless there are many values to print or unless output is directed by a format to print on more than one line.

```
$ EDIT WRIT3LINE.FOR                                    Example 3.3
      COST1 = 780.00
      COST2 = 220.00
      TOTALCOST = COST1 + COST2
      WRITE (6,*) COST1
      WRITE (6,*) COST2
      WRITE (6,*) TOTALCOST
      STOP
      END
$ FORTRAN WRIT3LINE
$ LINK WRIT3LINE                                        Example 3.3
$ RUN WRIT3LINE                                         Output
780.0000
220.0000
1000.000
```

DEFINITION: A WRITE statement produces a copy of a value from a location in memory and transfers that copy to an external logical unit or into a specified internal file. Output for more than one value can be produced in one WRITE statement.

WRITE (unitnumber,*) sn1,sn2,sn3, . . .

The predefined FORTRAN word WRITE specifies that output from a program should be produced. The output to be produced should be the values stored in the locations represented by symbolic name 1, symbolic name 2, symbolic name 3, etc. Because a logical unit number of 6 is assigned by default to the terminal for output from the VAX, a 6 is usually the appropriate unit number for a WRITE statement. Examples of other unit numbers are given in Example 3.10.

The asterisk in the WRITE statement specifies that the output should be list directed; that is, the output for each element in the list should be produced one value after another according to the kind of value, real or integer, that is stored. The asterisk also means that the program is not specifying a format for the number of decimal points to be printed for a value or the location on the output line where the value should be printed.

DEFINITION: Output is data that are being transferred out of a program as it executes. Output is the value or set of values that is copied from memory locations internal to a program's designated storage area to an area external to the program.

By using one of the following statements you may allow output to be printed by default at your terminal.

PRINT *,sn1,sn2,sn3, ...
WRITE(6,*)sn1,sn2,sn3, ...

3.3
READ STATEMENT — READING INPUT
FROM A TERMINAL

The cost for all shipments to a warehouse do not have values of 780.00 and 220.00. A program should have the capability of transferring values into the computer. A READ statement allows values to be transferred into the computer at the time when a program executes. You may provide values for a computer program from a terminal at execution time with READ statements.

■ **Example 3.4: READing Input**
from a Terminal

As the following program executes, the program stops at each READ statement and waits for a value to be entered from the terminal. When the first READ statement is executed, the computer pauses and waits for a value to be entered. After the value is entered, that value is stored in the memory location named COST1. When the second READ statement is executed, the computer pauses and waits for a value to be entered. After the second value is entered, that value is stored in the memory location named COST2.

```
$ EDIT READDAT.FOR                           Example 3.4
      READ (5,*) COST1
      READ (5,*) COST2
      TOTALCOST = COST1 + COST2
      WRITE (6,*) COST1
      WRITE (6,*) COST2
      WRITE (6,*) TOTALCOST
      STOP
      END
$ FORTRAN READDAT
$ LINK READDAT
$ RUN READDAT                                Example 3.4
780                                  You type this value at the
220                                  terminal.


780.00000                            The following values are
220.00000                            printed by the program at
1000.0000                            the terminal.
```

In the statement READ (5,*) COST1, the unit number of 5 specifies that by default the input is coming from the terminal, and the asterisk specifies that the input is unformatted.

The executable code for the Example 3.4 program is still stored in a file named READDAT.EXE. You can run the program again using another set of data.

```
$ RUN READDAT
110.12
3.10


110.1200
3.100000
113.2200
```

Example 3.4

You type a value at the terminal.

You type another value at the terminal.

The following values are printed by the program at the terminal.

RUN the program again, providing other values for input, and observe the output.

DEFINITION: INPUT is data that are being transferred into a program. INPUT is a value or a set of values that is copied from an external area into memory locations that are in a designated storage area for a program.

DEFINITION: A READ statement transfers a value or a set of values into memory locations that are in a designated storage area for a program.

READ (unitnumber,*) sn1, sn2, sn3, ...

The predefined FORTRAN word READ specifies that input from a location external to the program should be accepted. The first data value that is input should be stored in the memory location with symbolic name 1; the second data value that is input should be stored in the memory location with symbolic name 2; and so on. Because a logical unit number of 5 is assigned to the terminal for input to the VAX, a 5 is usually the appropriate unit number for a READ statement. Examples of other unit numbers are given in Example 3.10.

The asterisk in the READ statement specifies that the input should be list directed; that is, the input for each element in the list should be accepted one value after another according to the kind of value, real or integer, that is stored and defined by a symbolic name. The asterisk also means that the program is accepting unformatted input without regard for exact positions on an input line.

DEFINITION: Providing data for an unformated read statement is accomplished by entering one data value for each symbolic name in the READ statement, matching the value to be entered with an appropriate symbolic name to store a real value or an integer value. If there are five symbolic names in a READ statement, you should provide five data values when the READ statement executes as the program runs.

READ (5,*) PRICE1, PRICE2, KOST1, KOST2, TAX

You would type at the terminal five values, separated by commas or spaces.

22.56, 36.98, 2, 55, 0.04

The first two values, 22.56 and 36.98, contain decimal points and fractional parts of a number and will be stored in real memory locations specified by symbolic names PRICE1 and PRICE2. The second two values, 2 and 55, contain no fractional part and will be stored in integer memory locations specified by the symbolic names KOST1 and KOST2. The fifth value, 0.04, contains a decimal point and a fractional part of a number and will be stored in a real memory location specified by the symbolic name TAX.

3.4
VAX FILES

You may often choose to have output displayed at the terminal; however, the output is displayed only once as the program executes and you cannot observe the output after it has gone off the screen. If you want to observe your output at some time other than the time when the program executes, or if you want to modify the output in some way, or if you want to use the output from your program as input to another program, then you can specify that the output from your program be stored in an internal file on magnetic disk.

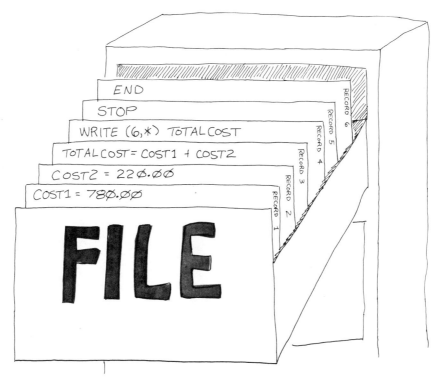

FIGURE 3.1

Being able to store and access information at various locations inside the computer is critically important for using a computer effectively in practical applications. A WRITE statement can be used to direct output to a file stored inside the computer so that the output can be accessed at a later time.

First you need to consider in general what a file is, and then you should learn how to direct output from a program to be stored in a computer file.

DEFINITION: A *file* is a set of information stored in a computer. The set of information is stored in a group of logically related records that are arranged in a specific order. The set of records in a file must be assigned a name and treated as a unit. A *record* is a set of data items entered as a unit inside the file.

One record usually, but not always, refers to one line of information (think of one line of type). In the warehouse example, each statement is a record in the file. (See Figure 3.1.)

When you enter the source code for a FORTRAN program from a terminal using an editor and save the program, you create a file in internal computer storage. The file is saved on magnetic disk where it can be accessed immediately and transferred into main memory. The file is stored in magnetic code; however, you can think about the file as if it were stored in a file cabinet. You could write a set of instructions and store them in a file folder containing a name for identification and store that file folder in a file cabinet. (See Figure 3.2.)

If you edit the FORTRAN program again, the computer locates the file

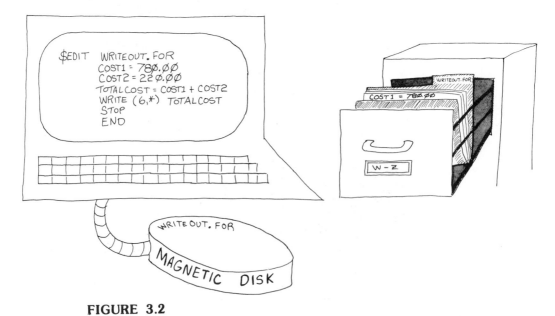

FIGURE 3.2

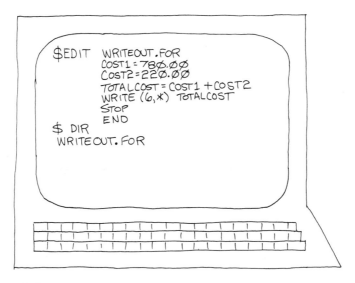

FIGURE 3.3

by the filename, and you can make additions or changes to the file and save the modified file. (See Figure 3.3.)

When you compile the program by entering the FORTRAN command, a file containing object code is stored on magnetic disk with the filename that you specified and the extension OBJ. The DIRECTORY command displays the name of the files that are present in your directory. (See Figure 3.4.)

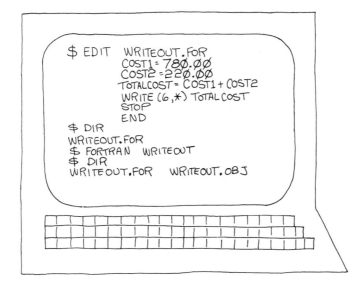

FIGURE 3.4

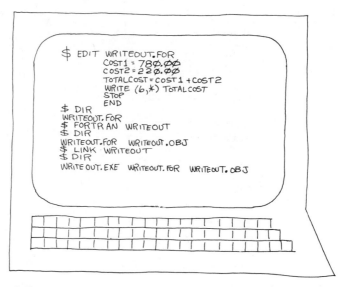

FIGURE 3.5

When you link the program by entering the LINK command, a file containing executable code is stored on magnetic disk with the filename that you specified and the extension EXE. The DIRECTORY command displays the name of the files that are present in your directory. (See Figure 3.5.)

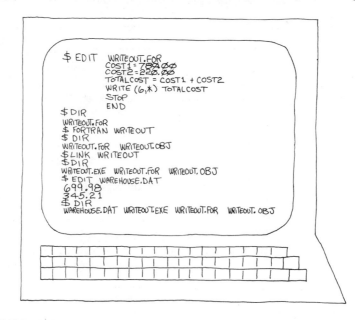

FIGURE 3.6

In addition to files that contain source code, object code, or executable code for FORTRAN programs, you can create *data files* that are stored in the computer for ongoing use. A data file can be created with an editor, and the data can be entered at the terminal and stored with a specified filename so that the file can be accessed at a later time. Details of creating and modifying files are available in Appendix A. You could create a file containing the values for the warehouse costs, the cost of shipment 1, and the cost of shipment 2 using an editor and then use the appropriate commands to save the file. After you save the file, you can enter the DIRECTORY command to see that you have a file named WAREHOUSE.DAT stored. (See Figures 3.6 and 3.7.)

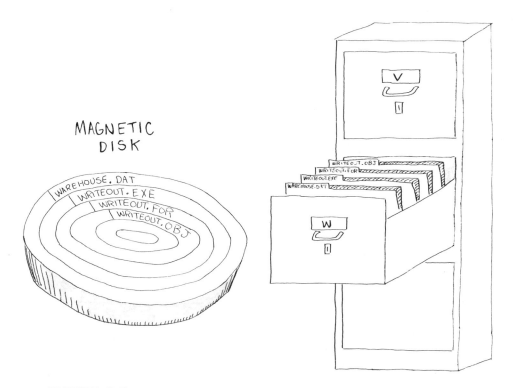

FIGURE 3.7

The WAREHOUSE.DAT file was created just as an example of creating a data file with the editor. The file is not used anymore in these examples. In fact, all the files that have been created so far can be deleted. Appendix A contains details on deleting files.

```
$ DEL WAREHOUSE.*;*
$ DEL WRITEOUT.*;*
```

3.5
WRITING OUTPUT TO A DISK FILE

The input for a FORTRAN program can come from a data file, and the output from a FORTRAN program can be directed to a data file. The OPEN statement allows you to specify a file for a logical unit number, which you can reference in a READ or a WRITE statement. Files on the VAX that have been opened are normally closed when a program completes execution; however, it is good practice to use the CLOSE statement to CLOSE the files that are OPENed in a program.

■ **Example 3.5: Writing Output**
to a Disk File

The following example WRITEs output to a file named OUTDATA.DAT.

```
$ EDIT OPENFOR.FOR                                    Example 3.5
        OPEN(6,FILE='OUTDATA.DAT',STATUS='NEW')
        COST1 = 780.00
        COST2 = 220.00
        TOTALCOST = COST1 + COST2
        WRITE (6,*) TOTALCOST
        CLOSE(6)
        STOP
        END
$ FORTRAN OPENFOR
$ LINK OPENFOR
$ RUN OPENFOR                                         Example 3.5
                                                      The output for the program
                                                      is stored in a data file
                                                      named OUTDATA.DAT.
                                                      You can use the TYPE
                                                      command to print the file
                                                      at your terminal.

$ TYPE OUTDATA.DAT                                    Example 3.5
1000.0000                                             Output
```

The OPEN statement in this example creates a NEW file because the STATUS of the file is specified to be NEW. The name of the new file is OUTDATA.DAT, as specified in the OPEN statement. The 6 in the OPEN statement is used to associate the new file named OUTDATA.DAT to output produced by the WRITE statement that references logical unit 6. When the WRITE statement in the program executes, the value stored in the memory location named TOTALCOST is not printed at the terminal. Instead the value is stored in the file named OUTDATA.DAT.

```
OPEN (6,FILE = 'OUTDATA.DAT',STATUS = 'NEW')

WRITE (6,*) TOTALCOST
```

Now that the output is stored in the data file named OUTDATA.DAT, you can enter the TYPE command to print the file at the terminal as often as you want to observe the contents of the file. You can PRINT the file on the printer whenever you need. You can EDIT the file or use the data in the file as input to another program.

`$ TYPE OUTDATA.DAT`	Print file at the terminal.
`$ PRINT OUTDATA.DAT`	Print output on printer.
`$ EDIT OUTDATA.DAT`	Bring file into main memory. You can use the editor to observe the file or modify the file.

Enter the DIRECTORY command to display the names of all the files that have been created.

```
$ DIR
OPENFOR.EXE    OPENFOR.FOR    OPENFOR.OBJ    OUTDATA.DAT
```

The following methods have been used in creating files.

- Files have been created by entering records with an EDITor.
- Files have been created by compiling programs with the FORTRAN command.

FIGURE 3.8

- Files have been created by linking programs with the LINK command.
- A file has been created by the output from a FORTRAN program using a WRITE statement associated with an OPEN statement.

Data stored in files can be printed on a printer. (See Figure 3.8.)

3.6
READING DATA FROM A DISK FILE

If you have 100 data records to input for a computer program, it is not practical to enter the records from the terminal as the program runs, because it is unlikely that you could enter that many records without making typing mistakes and generating invalid results. You can enter the data using an editor, and then you can print the file and verify that the data are correct. Using the editor, you can make changes if you discover errors in your data; then, after you are certain that the data are correct, you can use that data file as input to a program.

If data are stored in a disk file, you can use an OPEN statement to associate the logical unit in a READ statement with the unit number in the OPEN statement in order to access the data file.

■ Example 3.6: READing Input from a Disk File

Now you can write another program to read the data from the file named OUTDATA.DAT, which was created in Example 3.5. This time the READ statement accesses the file. The file in the OPEN statement has a STATUS of OLD because the file already exists. First TYPE the disk data file at the terminal.

```
$ TYPE OUTDATA.DAT                                    Example 3.6
1000.000                                              Input

$ EDIT READFILE.FOR                                   Example 3.6
      OPEN (5,FILE='OUTDATA.DAT',STATUS='OLD')
      READ (5,*) TOTALCOST
      WRITE (6,*) TOTALCOST
      CLOSE(5)
      STOP
      END
$ FORTRAN READFILE                                    Example 3.6
$ LINK READFILE                                       Output is printed at the
$ RUN READFILE                                        terminal.
1000.0000
```

When the OPEN statement in the program executes, the file named OUTDATA.DAT is opened. When the READ statement executes, the computer associates the logical unit 5 in the READ statement with the unit number 5 in the OPEN statement, and the input for the memory location named TOTALCOST is copied from the file named OUTDATA.DAT. When the WRITE statement executes, the output is printed at the terminal, because unit 6 is the terminal by default, and no OPEN statement is associated with unit 6 in this program.

■ **Example 3.7: READing Input**
from a Disk File and WRITing Output
to a Disk File

Look at one more example of READing data from a data file and WRITing data to another data file. First create and save the input data file with one of the editors available on the VAX.

```
$ EDIT DATAFILE.DAT                         Example 3.7
25.27, 16.03, 31.45                         Input
34.61, 52.14, 4.63
54.13, 41.25, 72.52
9.1, 8.2, 7.3
```

You could print the file on a printer and check carefully that you have typed the numbers correctly.

```
$ PRINT DATAFILE.DAT
```

Now you can use the editor to enter a FORTRAN program to read the three numbers per record and write the average of the three numbers to an output file named NEWDAT.DAT.

In the following program, if you did not include the two OPEN statements in the program, the program would pause and wait for you to enter the values from the terminal and would display the output at the terminal.

```
$ EDIT FILEOUT.FOR                          Example 3.7
       OPEN(5,FILE='DATAFILE.DAT',STATUS='OLD')
       OPEN(6,FILE='NEWDAT.DAT',STATUS='NEW')
       READ(5,*)VALUE1,VALUE2,VALUE3
       WRITE(6,*) (VALUE1+VALUE2+VALUE3)/3.0
       READ(5,*)VALUE1,VALUE2,VALUE3
       WRITE(6,*) (VALUE1+VALUE2+VALUE3)/3.0
       READ(5,*)VALUE1,VALUE2,VALUE3
       WRITE(6,*) (VALUE1+VALUE2+VALUE3)/3.0
       READ(5,*)VALUE1,VALUE2,VALUE3
       WRITE(6,*) (VALUE1+VALUE2+VALUE3)/3.0
       CLOSE (5)
```

```
        CLOSE (6)
        STOP
        END
$ FORTRAN FILEINOUT
$ LINK FILEINOUT
$ RUN FILEINOUT
```
Example 3.7

After the program executes, the output data are stored in the file named NEWDAT.DAT. You can TYPE the file at your terminal and print the file on printer.

```
$ TYPE NEWDAT.DAT
24.25000
30.46000
55.96667
8.200001
```
Example 3.7
Output

```
$ PRINT NEWDAT.DAT
```

Since both the files named FILEDAT.DAT and NEWDAT.DAT are still stored on disk, you can look at the files at any time and you can use the data as input to programs at any time. If you type the data in as a program runs, you must retype the data each time you run the program. It is advisable to create a data file containing your input data and to include an OPEN statement to reference the data file in your program. The OPEN statement has no effect on the rest of your program.

■ Example 3.8: Destructive READ

When a READ statement is executed, values are transferred into the memory locations specified by the symbolic names in the READ statement. The next time that a READ statement stores values in the same memory locations, the previous values are destroyed. This example is given to point out that you cannot read all four records using the same memory location names and then print out all the records. Using these symbolic names, you must read a record, perform the calculation, and print the result before going on to the next record. Look at Example 3.7 and notice the difference.

```
$ TYPE DATAFILE.DAT
25.27, 16.03, 31.45
34.61, 52.14, 4.63
54.13, 41.25, 72.52
9.1, 8.2, 7.3
```
Example 3.8
Input

```
$ EDIT WRONG.FOR
        OPEN(5,FILE='DATAFILE.DAT',STATUS='OLD')
        READ(5,*)VALUE1,VALUE2,VALUE3
        READ(5,*)VALUE1,VALUE2,VALUE3
```
Example 3.8

```
        READ(5,*)VALUE1,VALUE2,VALUE3
        READ(5,*)VALUE1,VALUE2,VALUE3
        WRITE(6,*) (VALUE1+VALUE2+VALUE3)/3.0
        WRITE(6,*) (VALUE1+VALUE2+VALUE3)/3.0
        WRITE(6,*) (VALUE1+VALUE2+VALUE3)/3.0
        WRITE(6,*) (VALUE1+VALUE2+VALUE3)/3.0
        CLOSE (5)
        STOP
        END
$ FORTRAN WRONG
$ LINK WRONG
$ RUN WRONG
8.200001
8.200001
8.200001
8.200001
```

Example 3.8
Output

The calculation and value printed are based on the values that were read from the last record in the file. A READ statement destroys whatever value was in the memory location specified by the symbolic name prior to the input.

■ Example 3.9: Solving the Destructive READ Problem

There are usually many ways to write a program to produce the same results. This program produces the same output as Example 3.7. The output is printed at the terminal instead of output to disk. This program solves the problem created in Example 3.8 by using different variable names for the input values.

```
$ TYPE DATAFILE.DAT
25.27,  16.03,  31.45
34.61,  52.14,  4.63
54.13,  41.25,  72.52
9.1,  8.2,  7.3
```

Example 3.9
Input

```
$ EDIT MANYNAMES.FOR
        OPEN(5,FILE='DATAFILE.DAT',STATUS='OLD')
        READ(5,*)A1,A2,A3
        READ(5,*)B1,B2,B3
        READ(5,*)C1,C2,C3
        READ(5,*)D1,D2,D3
        WRITE(6,*) (A1+A2+A3) / 3.0
        WRITE(6,*) (B1+B2+B3) / 3.0
        WRITE(6,*) (C1+C2+C3) / 3.0
        WRITE(6,*) (D1+D2+D3) / 3.0
        CLOSE (5)
        STOP
        END
$ FORTRAN MANYNAMES
$ LINK MANYNAMES
```

Example 3.9

```
$ RUN MANYNAMES
24.25000
30.46000
55.96667
8.200001
```

Example 3.9
Output

■ Example 3.10: Merging Files with a Program

If you have two records stored in a file named PART1.DAT and three records stored in a file named PART2.DAT, and you want to put the records together into one file named BOTHPARTS.DAT, you can include an OPEN statement for each file in the program. Unit numbers other than 5 and 6 can be used. The unit number for each of the READ statements should correspond to the appropriate OPEN statement that references file PART1.DAT or file PART2.DAT. The unit number for the WRITE statement should correspond to the OPEN statement that references the file named BOTH-PARTS.DAT.

```
$ EDIT PART1.DAT
31 56 89 77 65
22 98 62 19 28
```

Example 3.10
Input

```
$ EDIT PART2.DAT
67 58 49 20 21
23 33 44 12 29
90 89 76 65 33
```

Example 3.10
Input

```
$ EDIT MERGE.FOR
      OPEN(11,FILE='PART1.DAT',STATUS='OLD')
      OPEN(20,FILE='PART2.DAT',STATUS='OLD')
      OPEN(99,FILE='BOTHPARTS.DAT',STATUS='NEW')
      READ(11,*)NUM1,NUM2,NUM3,NUM4,NUM5
      WRITE(99,*)NUM1,NUM2,NUM3,NUM4,NUM5
      READ(11,*)NUM1,NUM2,NUM3,NUM4,NUM5
      WRITE(99,*)NUM1,NUM2,NUM3,NUM4,NUM5
      READ(20,*)NUM1,NUM2,NUM3,NUM4,NUM5
      WRITE(99,*)NUM1,NUM2,NUM3,NUM4,NUM5
      READ(20,*)NUM1,NUM2,NUM3,NUM4,NUM5
      WRITE(99,*)NUM1,NUM2,NUM3,NUM4,NUM5
      READ(20,*)NUM1,NUM2,NUM3,NUM4,NUM5
      WRITE(99,*)NUM1,NUM2,NUM3,NUM4,NUM5
      CLOSE(11)
      CLOSE(20)
      CLOSE(99)
      STOP
      END
$ FORTRAN MERGE
$ LINK MERGE
$ RUN MERGE
```

Example 3.10

```
$ TYPE BOTHPARTS.DAT                          Example 3.10
31 56 89 77 65                                Output
22 98 62 19 28
67 58 49 20 21
23 33 44 12 29
90 89 76 65 33
```

3.7
SUMMARY

A READ statement transfers data into a program as a program executes. The unit number of 5 specifies by default that input should come from the terminal where you are working.

```
READ (5,*) sn1, sn2, sn3, . . .
```

You can associate unit number 5 with a disk file by including an OPEN statement in your program before the READ statement.

```
OPEN (5,FILE = 'filename.ext',STATUS = 'OLD')
READ (5,*) sn1, sn2, sn3, . . .
```

A WRITE statement transfers data from a program to an area external to the program as the program executes. The unit number of 6 specifies by default that output should be displayed at the terminal where you are working.

```
WRITE (6,*) sn1, sn2, sn3, . . .
```

You can associate unit number 6 with a disk file by including an OPEN statement in your program before the WRITE statement.

```
OPEN (6,FILE = 'filename.ext',STATUS = 'NEW')
WRITE (6,*) sn1, sn2, sn3, . . .
```

The CLOSE statement is used to close a file that was opened with an OPEN statement. Files are closed by default when a program terminates; however, it is good practice to include a CLOSE statement for each file that is opened.

Unit numbers other than 5 for input and 6 for output may be used.

```
OPEN (unitnumber,FILE = 'filename.ext',STATUS = 'OLD')
READ (unitnumber,*) sn1, sn2, sn3, . . .
```

OPEN (unitnumber,FILE = 'filename.ext',STATUS = 'NEW')
WRITE (unitnumber,*) sn1, sn2, sn3, . . .

The READ(5,*) statement in the following program pauses and waits for the user to enter two values from the terminal as the program is executing. The WRITE(6,*) statement causes the output to be printed at the terminal. (See Figure 3.9.)

FIGURE 3.9

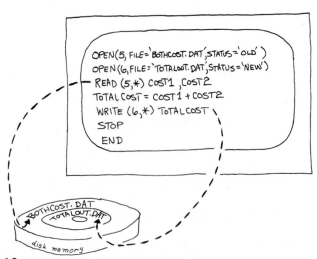

FIGURE 3.10

OPEN statements in the program in Figure 3.10 specify that the input for the READ(5,*) statement should come from a disk file named BOTHCOST.DAT and that the output for the WRITE(6,*) statement should go to a disk file named TOTALOUT.DAT.

3.8
EXERCISES

3.1. Fill in the blanks of the following statements. Possible answers are FORTRAN, READ, asterisk, WRITE, file, LINK, RUN, input, output, OPEN, assignment, function.

a. A computer _____ is a set of related records stored as a unit.

b. _____ is the data transferred into a computer program.

c. Values transferred out of a computer program are called _____ _____ .

d. A FORTRAN _____ statement causes a value or values to be transferred into a program during the execution of the program.

e. A FORTRAN _____ statement causes a value or values to be transferred out of a program during the execution of the program.

f. An _____ statement in a FORTRAN program is used to associate a logical unit with a READ statement or a WRITE statement in order to specify from where the input should come or to where the output should go.

g. If you create a FORTRAN program named SOMEONE.FOR using an editor, what are the commands to compile, link, and run the program?

```
$ EDIT SOMEONE.FOR
$ _____          Compile the program
$ _____          Link the program
$ _____          Run the program
```

3.2. In each of the following programs, specify from where the input will come and to where the output will go when the program executes.

a. READ(5,*)HOURS
READ(5,*)RATE
PAY = RATE*HOURS
WRITE(6,*)PAY
STOP
END

Input from _____
Output to _____

b. OPEN(5,FILE = 'RH.DAT',STATUS = 'OLD')
READ(5,*)HOURS,RATE
PAY = RATE*HOURS
WRITE(6,*)PAY
STOP
END

Input from_____
Output to _____

c. OPEN(5,FILE = 'RATEHOURS.DAT',STATUS = 'OLD')
OPEN(6,FILE = 'PAYOUT.DAT',STATUS = 'NEW')
READ(5,*)HOURS
READ(5,*)RATE
PAY = HOURS * RATE
WRITE (6,*) PAY
STOP
END

Input from _____
Output to _____

3.3. In the OPEN statement associated with a READ statement, the STATUS of the file must always be STATUS='_____', because the program could not READ from a file that does not already exist.

3.4. Enter and run the following FORTRAN program. Refer to Appendix A for details about creating and saving files with the EDT editor and to Appendix B for details about entering and running a FORTRAN program.

```
$ EDIT THISFILE.FOR
        BREAD = .89
        NUMBER = 10
        COST = NUMBER * BREAD
        WRITE (6,*) COST
        STOP
        END
```

```
$ FORTRAN THISFILE
$ LINK THISFILE
$ RUN THISFILE
```

a. What is the output for the program?

b. Where does the output go?

c. If you enter the DIRECTORY command, what files are stored?

3.5. Change the program in Exercise 3.4 and run the program for each of the following specifications.

a. The program should put the output into a data file named PROBFIVE.DAT.

b. The program should allow you to enter the data values for BREAD and NUMBER from the terminal. Enter the values one value per line of input.

c. The program should allow you to enter the data values for BREAD and NUMBER from the terminal. Enter both values on the same line of input.

d. Create a data file named BREADNUM.DAT that contains the values for BREAD and NUMBER, with each value in a separate record in the file. Modify the program so that the input for the program will come from the file BREADNUM.DAT.

3.6. a. The homework assignments for a class have a possible total cumulative score of 50. The five grades recorded for a student are 7, 9, 10, 10, and 6. Write and run a FORTRAN program that will allow you to enter each score on a separate line for the student. Then the program should calculate and print the total cumulative score for the student and calculate and print the percentage of the possible total score for the student. All data values should be input from the terminal, and the output should be printed at the terminal.

b. Run the program for another student who has scores of 5, 9, 10, 7, and 6. Enter the data from the terminal and print the output at the terminal.

c. Create a data file that contains the scores 8, 9, 9, 10, and 8 for a student. Rewrite the program to read the scores from the data file. Print the output at the terminal.

d. Use the input data file from part c and this time write the output to a data file.

4

Developing a FORTRAN Program: Syntax, Logic and Problem Solving

There are two primary considerations in developing a computer program. You must use correct *syntax* when writing a program; that is, you must use correct symbols and symbolic names that are formed correctly, and the symbols and symbolic names must be provided in programming structures according to the rules of FORTRAN. And you must use correct logic; that is, you must specify the correct instructions in the correct order to make the program perform the procedures necessary to solve a problem.

4.1
SYNTAX OF THE LANGUAGE

DEFINITION: The *syntax* of a computer language, like the syntax of any language, is the way in which the symbols and words of the language are put together to form expressions, statements, and structures.

The following statement contains a *syntax error* because the FORTRAN language does not allow a multiplication symbol to follow a plus sign. In this case, the computer could not decide whether to add or multiply, and so it prints a message that there is a syntax error when it tries to compile this statement.

TOTALCOST= SHIP1 + * SHIP2   Syntax Error

■ Example 4.1: Program with an Error

The following statement has a syntax error because there can be only one memory location specified on the left of the equal sign. The computer would not be able to determine in which memory location to store a value. Remember that the meaning of an assignment statement is that the expression on the right of the equal sign should be evaluated and the result stored in the one memory location named on the left of the equal sign.

SHIP1 + SHIP2 = TOTALCOST   Syntax Error

If there are syntax errors in your program, they are detected when you use the $FORTRAN command to compile your program. Messages are printed specifying all the errors in symbols, symbolic names, and the way that structures are formed. Look at the following program, which contains a syntax error, and the message that is printed when the $FORTRAN command is entered to translate the program into machine code.

```
$ EDIT LOOKERROR.FOR
       SHIP1 = 780.00                          Example 4.1
       SHIP2 = 220.00
       SHIP1 + SHIP2 = TOTALCOST               Invalid Statement
       WRITE (6,*) TOTALCOST
       STOP
       END
$ FORTRAN LOOKERROR
```

The following error message
is printed.

```
% FORT-F-INVLEFSID,Left side of assignment must be a variable or
                   an array element.
       [IP1 + SHIP2 =] in module LOOKERROR$MAIN at line 3.
% FORT-F-ENDNOOBJ, complete with 1 diagnostic - object deleted.
```

You can create a listing of the FORTRAN compilation by using the LIST parameter following the word FORTRAN. The error messages still come on the screen, but, in addition, a file with your program name and the extension LIS is created, so you can TYPE the file or PRINT the file to study your errors. Another advantage to this procedure is that the error messages are listed where they occur in your program.

```
$ FORTRAN/LIST LOOKERROR

$ TYPE LOOKERROR.LIS
                        VAX
        SHIP1 = 780.00
        SHIP2 = 220.00
        SHIP1 + SHIP2 = TOTALCOST
% FORT-F-INVLEFSID,Left side of assignment must be a variable or
                an array element.
        [IP1 + SHIP2 =] in module LOOKERROR$MAIN at line 3.
        WRITE (6,*) TOTALCOST
        STOP
        END
% FORT-F-ENDNOOBJ, complete with 1 diagnostic - object deleted.

COMMAND QUALIFIERS
   .    .
   .    .
Run Time        0.25 seconds
Elapsed Time:   5.07 seconds

$ PRINT LOOKERROR.LIS
```

■ Example 4.2: Correcting the Program in Example 4.1

You need to use the editor to correct the third statement in the program, and then try to compile the program again. Searching for and correcting an error in a computer program is called *debugging*.

```
$ EDIT LOOKERROR.FOR                          Example 4.2
        SHIP1 = 780.00
        SHIP2 = 220.00
        TOTALCOST = SHIP1 + SHIP2
        WRITE (6,*) TOTALCOST
        STOP
        END
$ FORTRAN LOOKERROR
$ LINK LOOKERROR
$ RUN LOOKERROR                               Example 4.2
1000.0000                                     Output
```

You learn the syntax of the language as you go through the rules of FORTRAN. Following the examples in this book, it is relatively simple to develop correct statements and correct FORTRAN structures. If there are syntax errors in your program, the computer provides descriptive error messages and you know what to correct. Logic is the more difficult part of programming.

4.2
LOGIC OF A PROGRAM

DEFINITION: The *logic* of a computer program is the sequence of execution of the statements in the program. It is necessary to arrange the statements in a program in a logical order.

■ **Example 4.3: Program with Logic Problems**

Look at the rearranged version of Example 4.2. The program would execute; there are no syntax errors. But the output would be meaningless, because the statements are not arranged in a logical order.

```
$ EDIT LOGICERR.FOR

      WRITE(6,*) TOTALCOST

      TOTALCOST = SHIP1 + SHIP2


      SHIP2 = 220.00
      SHIP1 = 780.00



      STOP
      END
$ FORTRAN LOGICERR
$ LINK LOGICERR
$ RUN LOGICERR
0.000000E+00
```

Example 4.3

The value in TOTALCOST has not been defined. The values in SHIP1 and SHIP2 are undefined, so the addition is meaningless. The values for the shipments are stored in the memory locations SHIP1 and SHIP2, but the values are not used to calculate the total, because the total has already been calculated.

Example 4.3
Output

The output for the program would be zero, because at the time that the WRITE statement was executed, the value stored in TOTALCOST was undefined; however, the computer assumes the value to be zero. The unformatted output for the value zero on the VAX is printed in scientific notation.

4.3
DEBUGGING

An error in a computer program is usually called a *bug*. An error can be a syntax error, as in Example 4.1, where the FORTRAN compiler provides messages to indicate syntax errors. An error can be a logic error, as in Example 4.3, and then your program will execute but you will get invalid results.

Finding and correcting the errors in either case may be called *debugging*.

DEFINITION: Debugging is the process of identifying and correcting both syntax and logic errors.

Debugging a program for a logic error may be difficult. In the simple program in Example 4.3, it is easy to see that the order of the statements is wrong, but in a larger program it is not always so obvious. When there is a problem, you can look at the output and try to determine what might cause that output to occur. If that is not enough of a clue, you should step through the program yourself as if you were the computer. Draw boxes for the memory locations and, as each statement executes, write the value that would be stored in a memory location or the value that would be input or output. You can usually find the error in this way.

4.4
DOCUMENTATION FOR A PROGRAM

DEFINITION: Documentation for a program is the information provided for a program about the development of the program, how to use the program, what data should be provided for the program, how the program executes, and what results are produced by the program.

Documentation is extremely important for a program that will be used more than once. Comments included in a program are one form of documentation for a program. Perhaps, in addition, a written document is necessary to explain the purpose and use of a program.

Comments should be used in a program to provide information about the development of a program, including the date of development, the author, the installation, and the like. Comments should be used to inform the user of a program what data must be provided for the program. Comments should be used to explain the meaning of the code so that, when you or someone else needs to use or modify the program at some later date, you will not have to start from scratch in figuring out the code.

DEFINITION: A *comment statement* in a FORTRAN program is a statement that begins with a C in column 1. A comment statement is recognized by the FORTRAN compiler as a statement that should not be executed. Comment statements are used for documenting a program. Comment statements can be entered in upper or lower case letters.

■ Example 4.4: Comment Statements

The computer prints the comment statements when the program is edited or displayed on the screen or printed on a printer; however, when the program executes, these statements are ignored.

The output for this example is the same as the output for Example 4.2, which contains no comment statements.

```
$ EDIT EXPLAINIT.FOR                                          Example 4.4
C*****************************************
C    PROGRAM EXPLAINIT.FOR
C    Written by Dr. Larry Stands
C    October 10, 1983
C    Tennessee Tech University  VAX 11/780
C*****************************************
C
C      The program calculates the cost of two shipments
C      received at the Tech warehouse in October.
C      There is no input to the program.

C      Variables
       REAL SHIP1
C                           Stores the value of shipment one.
       REAL SHIP2
C                           Stores the value of shipment two.
       REAL TOTALCOST
C                           Stores the calculated total cost.

       SHIP1 = 780.00
       SHIP2 = 220.00

C      Total cost is the sum of the two shipments.
       TOTALCOST = SHIP1 + SHIP2

C      Print the output.
       WRITE (6,*) TOTALCOST

       STOP
       END


$ FORTRAN EXPLAINIT
$ LINK EXPLAINIT
$ RUN EXPLAINIT                                               Example 4.4
1000.000                                                     Output
```

If a C is typed in column 1, the statement is recognized as a comment and neither spacing nor the information on the line is relevant to the computer. Blank lines can be inserted in a program to emphasize a statement or groups of statements. The asterisk character, *, and the exclamation mark, !, can also be used in column 1 to indicate that a line of code is a comment.

Documentation is an important part of programming. A style of writing and documenting programs should be developed to enhance the readability of programs.

4.5
TECHNIQUES FOR PROBLEM SOLVING

Writing FORTRAN code to specify instructions for a computer is usually straightforward, after the steps for solving the problem are completely defined. When you have a problem to solve with the computer, you must go through several steps in organizing the problem in such a way that it can be solved by a computer. It is impossible to introduce the complexities of solving large problems before you have had a chance to do some programming, so a few general concepts are introduced in this chapter.

To organize a problem in such a way that the problem can be solved using the computer, you must go through a systematic set of steps.

First: Analyze the problem. Define the information that you have available. Define the results that you need to produce.

Second: Generate a list of the logical steps that are necessary to produce the results which should be produced from the information that you have available. The list of logical steps arranged in a correct order to solve a program is called an *algorithm*.

Third: Write the FORTRAN code to implement the logical steps for producing the necessary results from the available information.

The following example provides a systematic approach to solving a problem. Problem solving is an individual process. No two people would solve a substantial problem in exactly the same way. Because it is generally not possible to write code directly from the information stated in a problem, it is necessary to use a systematic approach for generating a set of steps for developing a computer program to solve a problem. The procedures in this chapter present a method for problem solving that works for many people.

■ Example 4.5: Solving a Problem

The Problem.   A microcomputer dealer has various devices for sale. The dealer usually sells a computer, a television for a monitor, and a printer each time a sale is made. The dealer has a discount on printers this week, with the cost for the printer being reduced by 10 percent of the price of the computer. The prices for a microcomputer, for a television to use for a monitor, and for a printer are available. Sales tax in the state is 4 percent. For a customer purchasing all three items, write a FORTRAN program to input the price for each item and to calculate and print the total cost to the customer for purchasing a microcomputer, a television monitor, and a printer. Run the program with the costs being $800 for the microcomputer, $250 for the television, and $450 for the printer.

The Analysis. The best way to begin the analysis for a problem is to write down everything that you know about a problem and all the results that you need to produce. It may be helpful to actually number the list in order to be sure that you are thinking in terms of one fact or procedure at a time. You could begin by writing down each detail in the problem in the order in which the information is provided.

1. Printer cost is reduced by 10 percent of computer cost.
2. Computer cost is available.
3. Television cost is available.
4. Printer cost is available.
5. Tax is 4 percent.
6. Input the price for each item.
7. Calculate the total cost for purchasing the computer, television, and printer.
8. Print the total cost for purchasing the computer, television, and printer.

You now have a list of what you know and the result that the program should produce. The items on the list are not defined completely, and the list is not in the correct order to perform the steps that need to be performed; however, the list describes the problem better than the rambling paragraph did.

You need to rearrange the list into a logical order and define the steps. Since the program should perform some computations based on the cost of the computer, television, and printer, and since you know that the cost data are available for input to the program, rearrange the list with the input statement at the beginning.

1. Printer cost is reduced by 10 percent of computer cost.
2. Computer cost is available.
3. Television cost is available.
4. Printer cost is available.
5. Tax is 4 percent.
6. Input the price for each item.
7. Calculate the total cost for purchasing the computer, television, and printer.
8. Print the total cost for purchasing the computer, the television, and the printer.

Step 1 is defined now.

1. Input computer cost, television cost, printer cost.
2. Printer cost is reduced by 10 percent of computer cost.

3. Tax is 4 percent.

4. Calculate the total cost for purchasing the computer, television, and printer.

5. Print the total cost for purchasing the computer, television, and printer.

The procedure for calculating the reduced cost of the printer should be defined in step 2. The procedure for calculating the tax must be defined in step 3. To calculate the tax, you must first calculate the total sale. The total sale will be the cost of the computer plus the cost of the television plus the reduced cost of the printer. Then the tax is 4 percent of the total sale. Rewrite the steps.

1. Input computer cost, television cost, printer cost.

2. Printer cost will be the input printer cost minus 10 percent of the computer cost.

3. Total sale will be the cost of the computer plus the cost of the television plus the reduced cost of the printer.

4. Tax will be 4 percent of the total sale.

5. Calculate the total cost for purchasing the computer, television, and printer.

6. Print the total cost for purchasing the computer, television, and printer.

DEFINITION: An *algorithm* is a set of steps that are necessary to solve a problem.

You need to define the calculation for the total cost in the final two steps in the list in order to complete the algorithm for solving the problem.

The Algorithm.   When the information in the problem is carefully specified and organized, it is easy to see how to write a FORTRAN program from this information. The carefully specified and organized list of steps that follows is an algorithm for solving the problem.

1. Input computer cost, television cost, printer cost.

2. Printer cost will be the input printer cost minus 10 percent of the computer cost.

3. Total sale will be the cost of the computer plus the cost of the television plus the reduced cost of the printer.

4. Tax will be 4 percent of the total sale.

5. Total cost will be the total sale plus the tax.

6. Write the total cost.

The Flow Chart.   A *flow chart* is a tool that is available for providing a pictorial display of the algorithm.

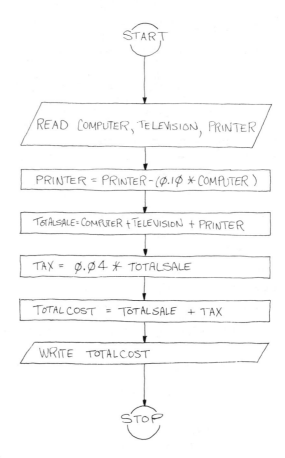

FIGURE 4.1

DEFINITION: A flow chart is a graphical representation of the steps that are necessary to solve a problem. Specific symbols are used for the various processes that occur in a computer program. The parallelogram shape is used to represent input and output. A rectangle is used to represent a process. A diamond-shaped symbol is used to indicate decision steps, which are covered in Chapter 7. (See Figure 4.1.)

Finally, after these steps are followed, writing the FORTRAN code is simple.

The Code.   You can enter the code and run the FORTRAN program.

The FORTRAN Code to Solve the Problem.   The input for the program would be that specified by the problem. The input could be stored in a data file or typed at the terminal as the program executes.

```
800,250,450                                          Example 4.5
                                                     Input
$ EDIT SOLVEIT.FOR
      READ(5,*)COMPUTER,TELEVISION,PRINTER           Example 4.5
      PRINTER = PRINTER - 0.10*COMPUTER
      TOTALSALE = COMPUTER + TELEVISION + PRINTER
      TAX = 0.04 * TOTALSALE
      TOTALCOST = TOTALSALE + TAX
      WRITE (6,*) TOTALCOST
      STOP
      END
$ FORTRAN SOLVEIT
$ LINK SOLVEIT
$ RUN SOLVEIT                                         Example 4.5
  1476.8000                                           Output
```

■ Example 4.6: Code That Is Difficult to Read

Almost always there are many ways to write a computer program. Programs can be written with complex statements; however, it is best to write programs in a straightforward way. If long and complicated statements are written, it is easy to introduce errors into a program, and it is difficult for other people to read your program. This program produces exactly the same result as the code in Example 4.5.

```
                                                     Example 4.6
800,250,450                                          Input

$ EDIT BADCODE.FOR                                   Example 4.6
      READ(5,*)COMPUTER, TELEVISION, PRINTER
      WRITE(6,*)COMPUTER+TELEVISION+(PRINTER - 0.10*COMPUTER) +
    - 0.04*( COMPUTER + TELEVISION+ PRINTER - 0.10*COMPUTER)
      STOP
      END
$ FORTRAN BADCODE
$ LINK BADCODE
$ RUN BADCODE                                         Example 4.6
  1476.8000                                           Output
```

It is important to write a program in a form that is as readable as possible. It is easier to write correct code if the statements have some meaning to you, and it is certainly easier to pick up a program six months from now and understand it if the statements have some meaning. Using symbolic names that are descriptive and writing statements in a readable way simplify the process of finding logical errors in a program.

Observe that the following code uses the same instructions as that in Example 4.6; however, the symbolic names have been changed from meaningful names to X, Y, and Z. This code is even more difficult to understand than the code in Example 4.6.

```
READ(5,*)X, Y, Z
WRITE(6,*)X +  Y  + ( Z −0.10*X)  +
−0.04*(X  +  Y  +  Z −0.10*X)
STOP
END
```

■ Example 4.7: Another Problem to Solve

A small company employs two workers. Write a FORTRAN program to input from the first record the hourly pay rate for each employee and then to input from the second record the number of hours worked by each employee. Both employees always work a minimum of 40 hours per week. For all hours worked over 40, the pay is twice the normal hourly rate. Write a program that will calculate and print each employee's pay and calculate and print the total pay for the company. The following might be the data for the problem:

4.65,5.60   Pay rates
44,47   Hours worked

The Analysis.   First, write down everything that you know about the problem and all the results that you need to produce.

1. A small company employs two workers.

2. Input from the first record the hourly pay rate for each employee.

3. Input from the second record the number of hours worked by each employee.

4. Both employees always work a minimum of 40 hours per week.

5. For all hours worked over 40, the pay is twice the normal hourly rate.

6. Calculate and print each employee's pay.

7. Calculate and print the total pay for the company.

Look at step 4. Since employees always work a minimum of 40 hours per week, the overtime hours can be calculated by subtracting 40 from the number of hours worked. That is what you really need to figure out from step 4.

1. A small company employs two workers.

2. Input from the first record the hourly pay rate for each employee.

3. Input from the second record the number of hours worked by each employee.

4. Overtime hours will be the hours worked minus 40.

5. For all hours worked over 40, the pay is twice the normal hourly rate.

6. Calculate and print each employee's pay.

7. Calculate and print the total pay for the company.

Step 1 indicates that there are two workers. You could check each step in the analysis and make sure that operations are provided for two employees in all the procedures and remove step 1 from the list. You could carefully define each step to be performed. It might take several revisions of the list before you develop the algorithm that completely defines all the steps necessary to solve the problem. If you continue to clarify the steps in your list and check to see if the order of the instructions is correct, you can eventually develop an algorithm for the problem.

The Algorithm

1. Input from the first record the hourly pay rate for each of the two employees.

2. Input from the second record the number of hours worked by each of the two employees.

3. Overtime hours for employee 1 will be the number of hours for employee 1 minus 40.

4. Overtime hours for employee 2 will be the hours worked for employee 2 minus 40.

5. Overtime pay for employee 1 will be 2 times the hourly pay rate times overtime hours for employee 1.

6. Overtime pay for employee 2 will be 2 times the hourly pay rate times overtime hours for employee 2.

7. Pay for employee 1 will be the hourly pay rate times 40 plus the overtime pay for employee 1.

8. Pay for employee 2 will be the hourly pay rate times 40 plus the overtime pay for employee 2.

9. Total pay for the company will be the pay for employee 1 plus the pay for employee 2.

10. Write pay for employee 1.

11. Write pay for employee 2.

12. Write pay for company.

The Code for the Problem.   The code for the problem is listed here as a program to execute. The following example would be the input for the program.

```
4.65,5.60                                          Example 4.7
44,47                                              Input

$ EDIT PAYOVER.FOR                                 Example 4.7
        READ (5,*) RATE1, RATE2
        READ (5,*) HOURS1, HOURS2
        OVERHOURS1 = HOURS1 - 40
        OVERHOURS2 = HOURS2 - 40
        OVERPAY1 = OVERHOURS1 * RATE1 * 2
        OVERPAY2 = OVERHOURS2 * RATE2 * 2
        PAY1 = 40 * RATE1 + OVERPAY1
        PAY2 = 40 * RATE2 + OVERPAY2
        COMPANYPAY = PAY1 + PAY2
        WRITE (6,*) PAY1
        WRITE (6,*) PAY2
        WRITE (6,*) COMPANYPAY
        STOP
        END
$ FORTRAN PAYOVER
$ LINK PAYOVER
$ RUN PAYOVER                                      Example 4.7
223.2000                                           Output
302.4000
525.6000
```

■ Example 4.8: Another Program for the Problem of Example 4.7

You might have developed the algorithm for the problem in a different way and written this program for Example 4.7. The following would be the input for the program.

```
4.65,5.60                                          Example 4.8
44,47                                              Input

$ EDIT PAYOVER2.FOR                                Example 4.8
        READ (5,*) RATE1, RATE2
        READ (5,*) HOURS1, HOURS2
        PAY1 = 40 * RATE1 + ( RATE1 *2 * (HOURS1-40) )
        PAY2 = 40 * RATE2 + ( RATE2 *2 * (HOURS2-40) )
        COMPANYPAY = PAY1 + PAY2
        WRITE (6,*) PAY1
        WRITE (6,*) PAY2
        WRITE (6,*) COMPANYPAY
        STOP
        END
$ FORTRAN PAYOVER2
$ LINK PAYOVER2
```

```
$ RUN PAYOVER2
223.2000
302.4000
525.6000
```

Example 4.8
Output

4.6
SUMMARY

You must use correct syntax when writing a program; that is, you must use correct symbols and symbolic names that are formed correctly, and the symbols and symbolic names must be provided in programming structures according to the rules of FORTRAN.

You must use correct logic; that is, you must specify the correct instructions in the correct order to make the program perform the procedures necessary to solve a problem. It is usually necessary to use a systematic approach for developing an algorithm, which specifies the list of logical steps arranged in the correct order to solve a problem. The following is one approach to problem solving.

First: Write down everything that you know about a problem and all the results that you need to produce. Make a detailed list.

Next: Clarify each item of information. Join together items that are related. Rearrange the information into the order necessary to solve the problem. Continue to clarify and rearrange the list of steps until you feel that this is a specific algorithm for solving the problem.

After you have created a detailed list of the steps that need to be followed to produce the needed results, you can write the FORTRAN code. Practice is necessary to become proficient at developing algorithms. Developing algorithms for problems, writing the code, running the programs on the computer, and debugging them is the best way to improve logic skills.

Documentation is extremely important for computer programs. Documentation can be included in FORTRAN programs by typing a C in column 1; then that line will be used only for comments in the source code and will be ignored when the program is executed.

4.7
EXERCISES

4.1. A hospital linen supply room is ordering 500 bed sheets, 500 pillow cases, and 50 surgical gowns. Sheets cost $6.50 each, pillow cases cost

$2.30 each, and surgical gowns cost $11.25 each. There is no discount on the first $1000.00, but there is a discount of 10 percent on all the purchases over $1000.00. Develop an algorithm using a systematic approach, and write the FORTRAN code to calculate and print the total cost for the purchase.

4.2. A librarian needs a computer program that will allow him to evaluate the use of the library books each year. The program should allow the user to input the number of books that belong to the library for the categories of art, history, and science. The program should then allow the user to enter the number of books that have been checked out during the year in each category. For each category, the program should calculate and print the percentage of available books that have been checked out during the year. In addition, the program should calculate and print the overall percentage of books that have been checked out during the year. First develop the algorithm and then write the code for solving the problem.

4.3. The length of a track at an athletic field is $^1/_8$ mile. Otis daily runs 20 laps. Develop an algorithm and write a FORTRAN program to calculate the daily distance Otis runs in miles, feet, and meters.

$$1\text{ mile} = 5280\text{ feet}$$

$$1\text{ meter} = 3.28\text{ feet}$$

4.4. Dean Beckman is running for state representative. He must win the majority vote in his district, which includes three counties. Of the 90,000 voters in Hillsboro County, the polls indicate that he can expect to receive 73,000 votes. Of the 65,000 voters in Prairie County, the polls indicate that he can expect to receive 51,000 votes. There has been no poll conducted in Green County, the final county in his district. If the polls are correct in Hillsboro and Prairie counties, how many votes must Mr. Beckman get in Green County in order to win a majority vote in the district? Develop an algorithm and write a FORTRAN program to input the known values, to calculate the number of votes needed in Green County, and to print a report of the known and generated information.

4.5. Three brands of orange juice are being evaluated by the home economics department in order to determine the cost for each brand for obtaining 100 percent of the daily vitamin C requirement. To get 100 percent of the daily requirement of vitamin C, you need to drink 5 ounces of brand A, 7 ounces of brand B, or 4 ounces of brand C. A 16-ounce can of brand A costs $1.34. A 12-ounce can of brand B costs $1.03. A 12-ounce can of brand C costs $1.19. Develop an algorithm and write a FORTRAN program that calculates the appropriate values and prints out a chart somewhat like the following.

NUTRITIONAL STUDY
VITAMIN C

	COST PER OUNCE	COST FOR 100% OF DAILY VITAMIN C REQUIREMENT
BRAND A		
BRAND B		
BRAND C		

5

Introduction to Loops: DO Loops

A set of instructions can be entered in a program and each instruction can be executed one time. The method of providing one statement for every operation that should be performed is demonstrated in Chapters 1 to 4. The real power of a computer program, however, is in its ability to execute a set of instructions repeatedly.

The following set of instructions could be executed to input the rate of pay and the hours worked and then to calculate and print the pay for one employee.

```
READ (5,*) RATE,HOURS
PAY = RATE * HOURS
WRITE (6,*) 'THE  PAY  IS ',PAY
```

These three instructions could be executed 50 times if there were 50 employees.

```
┌──► DO these instructions 50 times
│        READ (5,*)RATE,HOURS
│        PAY = RATE * HOURS
│        WRITE (6,*) 'THE PAY IS ',PAY
└───── END DO
```

A *DO loop* is a structure in FORTRAN for executing a set of instructions repeatedly. One form of a DO loop counts the number of times a set of instructions is executed. The following is a DO loop in the FORTRAN language that allows the pay rate and hours worked to be input and calculates and prints the pay for 50 employees. The statements between the DO statement and the END DO statement are executed 50 times.

```
DO NUMBER_EMPLOYEE = 1, 50
   READ (5,*) RATE,HOURS
   PAY = RATE * HOURS
   WRITE (6,*) 'THE PAY IS ',PAY
END DO
```

5.1
COUNTER

A *counter* is a programming term for a memory location that is being used to record the number of times some process or condition occurs. Counters are used often in computer programs.

Study the following example to understand how a counter works before reading the remainder of the chapter, which shows some applications for counters.

■ Example 5.1: A Simple Counter

Usually a counter works something like a person counting the number of occurrences of some condition. This program might represent a teacher counting each student as the students come through the door on the first day of class. As each of the three students in the class is counted, the count is printed. Often, but not always, counters are integer values. Statement numbers are included in columns 1 through 5 to identify the statements in this program.

```
$ EDIT COUNT.FOR                                        Example 5.1
100     KOUNTSTUDENT=0
200     KOUNTSTUDENT = KOUNTSTUDENT + 1
300     WRITE(6,*) 'STUDENT NUMBER ', KOUNTSTUDENT
400     KOUNTSTUDENT = KOUNTSTUDENT + 1
```

```
500     WRITE(6,*) 'STUDENT NUMBER ', KOUNTSTUDENT
600     KOUNTSTUDENT = KOUNTSTUDENT + 1
700     WRITE(6,*) 'STUDENT NUMBER ', KOUNTSTUDENT
800     STOP
900     END
$ FORTRAN COUNT
$ LINK COUNT
$ RUN COUNT
STUDENT NUMBER       1
STUDENT NUMBER       2
STUDENT NUMBER       3
```

Example 5.1
Output

Description of Example 5.1. Now consider the meaning of the statements in the program. Before the first student enters the room, the count for the number of students is set to zero. Store the value, 0, in the memory location named KOUNTSTUDENT in order to initialize the count.

Memory location
KOUNTSTUDENT

100   KOUNTSTUDENT = 0

| 0 | |

When the first student enters the room, the value 1 is added to the count for the number of students. To add 1 to the count when statement number 200 is executed, the value 0, which is in location KOUNTSTUDENT, is retrieved and the value 1 is added to the 0; finally, the new sum of 1 is stored in location KOUNTSTUDENT.

KOUNTSTUDENT

200   KOUNTSTUDENT = KOUNTSTUDENT + 1

| 0̸ 1 | |

Now the value stored in location KOUNTSTUDENT is 1. WRITE the characters STUDENT NUMBER and the value that is stored in location KOUNTSTUDENT.

300   WRITE (6,*) ' STUDENT NUMBER ',KOUNTSTUDENT

Count the next student by adding 1 to the value stored in location KOUNTSTUDENT. This is done by first taking the value from location KOUNTSTUDENT, adding 1 to that value, and storing the incremented value in location KOUNTSTUDENT.

KOUNTSTUDENT

400   KOUNTSTUDENT = KOUNTSTUDENT + 1

| 0̸ 1̸ 2 | |

The value stored in location KOUNTSTUDENT is now 2. WRITE the characters STUDENT NUMBER and the value stored in location KOUNTSTUDENT.

500   WRITE (6,*) ' STUDENT NUMBER ',KOUNTSTUDENT

Add 1 to the student count for the third student and print the count.

                                                               KOUNTSTUDENT

600   KOUNTSTUDENT = KOUNTSTUDENT + 1 | Ø̶ 1̶ 2̶ 3 |

700   WRITE (6,*) ' STUDENT NUMBER ',KOUNTSTUDENT

Terminate the program.

800   STOP
900   END

This program serves only to demonstrate the way that counters work. If you were to expand Example 5.1 to count 100 students, you would have 100 pairs of statements

KOUNTSTUDENT = KOUNTSTUDENT + 1

and

WRITE (6,*) ' STUDENT COUNT ',KOUNTSTUDENT

5.2
DO LOOP WITH A COUNTER

DEFINITION: A DO loop is a structure that causes a set of statements to be executed repeatedly. One form of a DO loop provides a counter for automatically controlling the number of times the statements are executed. A form of a DO loop with a counter is the following.

DO count_name = initial_value, final_value
    statement(s) to be executed repeatedly
END DO

When a DO loop executes, all the statements between the DO statement and the END DO statement are executed the number of times specified in the DO statement. After the statements following the DO statement are executed, the execution loops from the END DO statement back to the DO

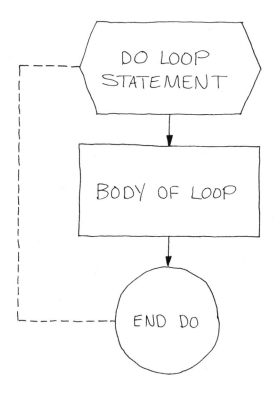

FIGURE 5.1

statement. The variable count_name is a location used to store the count for the loop. The first value for count_name is the initial_value specified on the right of the equal sign. Each time through the loop, an increment of 1 is added to the value in count_name until the counter for the loop reaches the final_value.

The flow chart in Figure 5.1 indicates the structure for a DO loop.

Another form of the DO LOOP with a counter is the following.

DO   num   count_name = initial_valu, final_valu

statement(s) to be executed repeatedly

num   CONTINUE

In this form of the DO LOOP, the loop is defined by the DO statement and the CONTINUE statements. The statements between the DO and the

CONTINUE statements are executed the number of times specified between the initial_valu and the final_valu. NUM is a statement number.

The DO LOOP with a statement number is the standard form for a DO LOOP. The DO LOOP terminated with an END DO statement is a VAX extension of FORTRAN 77.

The symbolic name for the counter for a DO loop must reflect the type of number stored in the location; that is, symbolic names beginning with I, J, K, L, M, or N should be used if whole numbers are being counted. In general, integer variables are used for counters in DO loops, because inaccurate values can be produced with the repeated increments to a value. Real values can be used if decimal numbers are used in the DO statement.

■ Example 5.2: A DO LOOP

This example uses a DO loop to perform the same counting and printing as in Example 5.1. This example produces exactly the same output as Example 5.1.

```
$ EDIT DOWAY.FOR                                    Example 5.2
      DO   KOUNTSTUDENT = 1,3
           WRITE(6,*) ' STUDENT NUMBER ',KOUNTSTUDENT
      END DO
      STOP
      END
$ FORTRAN DOWAY
$ LINK DOWAY
$ RUN DOWAY                                         Example 5.2
STUDENT NUMBER        1                             Output
STUDENT NUMBER        2
STUDENT NUMBER        3
```

Description of Example 5.2.   A DO structure executes everything between the DO statement and the END DO statement the number of times specified for the counter. In Example 5.2, the location named KOUNTSTUDENT is used to store the count value for the DO loop. The 1,3 specifies that the initial value stored in KOUNTSTUDENT is 1 and that each time through the loop an increment of 1 is added to the value in the location named KOUNTSTUDENT until the value in KOUNTSTUDENT exceeds 3. After the DO loop has been executed the number of times specified in the counter, the program execution transfers to the first statement following the END DO statement.

The program executes as if the statements were written repeatedly as in Example 5.1.

KOUNTSTUDENT

DO for KOUNTSTUDENT equal to 1

1

    WRITE(6,*) ' STUDENT NUMBER ',KOUNTSTUDENT
END DO

KOUNTSTUDENT

DO for KOUNTSTUDENT equal to 2

X̶ 2

    WRITE(6,*) ' STUDENT NUMBER ',KOUNTSTUDENT
END DO

KOUNTSTUDENT

DO for KOUNTSTUDENT equal to 3

X̶ Z̶ 3

    WRITE(6,*) ' STUDENT NUMBER ',KOUNTSTUDENT
END DO

STOP
END

The WRITE statement is executed three times, once each time through the loop. The first time through the loop the value stored by the DO statement in location KOUNTSTUDENT is 1. When the WRITE statement executes, the characters STUDENT NUMBER, which are between quotation marks, are printed, and then the value stored in the location named KOUNTSTUDENT is printed. When the END DO statement is executed, a transfer is made back to the DO statement, adding 1 to the value in the location named KOUNTSTUDENT. The WRITE statement is executed a second time, printing the characters STUDENT NUMBER and the value 2, which is stored in the location named KOUNTSTUDENT. The END DO statement again transfers execution back to the DO statement, which increments the value in location KOUNTSTUDENT, making the value 3. The WRITE statement is executed one more time, printing STUDENT NUMBER 3.

When the END DO statement is executed a third time, a transfer is made again to the DO statement. Each time the value KOUNTSTUDENT is incremented at the top of the loop, a comparison is made to see if the value is greater than the final value specified, in this case 3. After three times through the DO loop, a 1 is added to the value in KOUNTSTUDENT, making the value 4. Since the value 4 is greater than 3, which is defined to be the final value for the DO loop, execution of the program is transferred to the first statement following the END DO statement, in this case the STOP statement, and the program terminates.

■ Example 5.3: Another Program That Needs a Loop

Study this example in order to understand how the statements are being executed. The program generates a total cost for five items received at a warehouse. After you understand how this program works, look at Example 5.4 to see how a program with a DO loop generates the same results as this program.

The values 25, 30, 10, 40, and 15 could be the cost of five items received at a warehouse. The following computer program could be used to transfer each of the warehouse costs into computer memory using a READ statement, to calculate the total cost of the shipment, and to print the total cost.

```
25
3Ø
1Ø
4Ø
15
```

Example 5.3
Input

```
$ EDIT TOTALCOST.FOR
        TOTAL = Ø
        READ (5,*) COST
        TOTAL = TOTAL + COST
        READ (5,*) COST
        TOTAL = TOTAL + COST
        READ (5,*) COST
        TOTAL = TOTAL + COST
        READ (5,*) COST
        TOTAL = TOTAL + COST
        READ (5,*) COST
        TOTAL = TOTAL + COST
        WRITE (6,*) 'CALCULATED TOTAL',TOTAL
        STOP
        END
$ FORTRAN TOTALCOST
$ LINK TOTALCOST
$ RUN TOTALCOST
CALCULATED TOTAL      12Ø.ØØØØ
```

Example 5.3

Example 5.3
Output

Description of Example 5.3.   When the program runs, the value 0 is stored in the location named TOTAL.

TOTAL = 0

TOTAL
0

Then the program encounters the READ statement, so the first data value is stored in the location named COST.

READ (5,*) COST

COST	TOTAL
25	0

Next the third statement is executed. The computer goes to the location named TOTAL and gets the value that is there. The value in TOTAL would be 0. The value 25, which is currently in the location named COST, is added to the value in the location named TOTAL, and the result is stored in the location named TOTAL.

TOTAL = TOTAL + COST

COST	TOTAL
25	Ø 25

The program would continue by first transferring a value into location COST each time a READ statement is encountered and then adding the value stored in COST to the TOTAL value.

READ (5,*) COST
TOTAL = TOTAL + COST

COST	TOTAL
2̶5̶ 30	Ø 2̶5̶ 55

After three more pairs of READ(5,*)COST and TOTAL = TOTAL + COST statements are executed, the WRITE statement causes the final value that is stored in the location named TOTAL to be printed.

COST	TOTAL
2̶5̶ 3̶0̶ 1̶0̶ 4̶0̶ 15	Ø 2̶5̶ 5̶5̶ 6̶5̶ 1̶0̶5̶ 120

WRITE (5,*) 'CALCULATED TOTAL',TOTAL

If there were 50 items in the warehouse shipment for the program in Example 5.3, it would be necessary to have 50 pairs of statements for READing each of the values and for adding each value to the total value. If there were 1000 items in the shipment, it would be necessary to have 1000 pairs of statements to READ each value and calculate the TOTAL. Now see Example 5.4, which puts the READ and TOTAL statements in a DO loop to be executed repeatedly.

■ Example 5.4: Processing in a DO Loop

This problem is the same as for Example 5.3. The program written to process the data in this example contains a DO loop for executing statements repeatedly, whereas the previous example contains no loop.

The data to be processed might be the costs for five shipments to a warehouse. The cost values might be 25, 30, 10, 40, and 15. The program allows five cost values to be READ as the program runs and calculates and prints the total cost of the shipment. Since there are five items in the shipment, the DO loop is executed five times. The number of times the DO loop is executed is controlled by the counter for the DO loop.

```
        25                                              Example 5.4
        30                                              Input
        10
        40
        15

        $EDIT DOREAD.FOR                                Example 5.4
              TOTAL = 0
              DO ITEMNUMBER = 1,5
                 READ (5,*) COST
                 TOTAL = TOTAL + COST
              END DO
              WRITE (6,*) 'CALCULATED TOTAL',TOTAL
              STOP
              END
        $ FORTRAN DOREAD
        $ LINK DOREAD
        $ RUN DOREAD                                    Example 5.4
        CALCULATED TOTAL      120.0000                  Output
```

The output for the program is the same as the output for Example 5.3. If you do not understand this program after reading the program description, study Example 5.3 again.

Description of Example 5.4. The program would execute as if the statements were written in the following way.

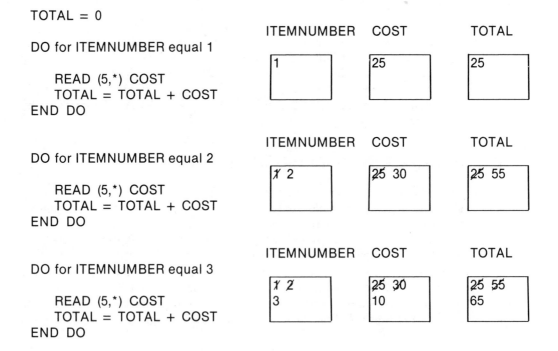

```
TOTAL = 0

DO for ITEMNUMBER equal 1

    READ (5,*) COST
    TOTAL = TOTAL + COST
END DO


DO for ITEMNUMBER equal 2

    READ (5,*) COST
    TOTAL = TOTAL + COST
END DO


DO for ITEMNUMBER equal 3

    READ (5,*) COST
    TOTAL = TOTAL + COST
END DO
```

```
                           ITEMNUMBER   COST         TOTAL
DO for ITEMNUMBER equal 4
                           1  2         25  30       25  55
   READ (5,*) COST         3  4         10  40       65  105
   TOTAL = TOTAL + COST
END DO
```

```
                           ITEMNUMBER   COST         TOTAL
DO for ITEMNUMBER equal 5
                           1  2         25  30       25  55
   READ (5,*) CCOST        3  4         10  40       65  105
   TOTAL = TOTAL + COST     5           15           120
END DO
```

```
WRITE (6,*) 'CALCULATED TOTAL',TOTAL
STOP
END
```

The first statement causes the TOTAL value to be initialized by storing the value 0 in the location named TOTAL. When the DO loop begins to execute, the value 1 is stored in the location named ITEMNUMBER. Location ITEMNUMBER is the counter for the DO loop. When the READ statement is executed, the first data value is stored in the location named COST. The next statement is executed, causing the value stored in COST to be added to the value stored in TOTAL and the sum to be stored in location TOTAL, replacing the previous value for TOTAL. The END DO statement is reached and execution transfers to the DO statement, incrementing the counter, ITEMNUMBER, for the loop. The READ statement and the calculating statement are executed again. The READ (5,*) COST and TOTAL = TOTAL + COST statements are executed five times, just as if the statements were written as they appear in Example 5.3. After the statements in the loop have executed five times, processing moves to the WRITE statement and the output is printed at the terminal.

Loops in programs provide great power. Using a DO loop, you can easily change the Example 5.4 program to calculate the total costs for 50 items or for 1000 items, as the following program segments indicate.

```
DO ITEMNUMBER = 1,50
   READ (5,*)COST
   TOTAL = TOTAL + COST
END DO

DO ITEMNUMBER = 1,1000
   READ (5,*)COST
   TOTAL = TOTAL + COST
END DO
```

■ **Example 5.5: Using DO Loop**
   Counters for Calculations

Often the counter values in a DO loop are used for calculations. You might print a table of degrees Fahrenheit and degrees Celsius using the counter in a DO loop. The DO loop counter in this example could represent Fahrenheit temperatures from 0 to 212 degrees.

```
$ EDIT DEGREES.FOR                                    Example 5.5
      FIVENINTHS = 5.0 / 9.0
      DO 10 DEGREEF = 0.0 , 212.0
         DEGREEC = FIVENINTHS * ( DEGREEF - 32.0 )
         WRITE (6,*) INT(DEGREEF), NINT(DEGREEC)
10       CONTINUE
         STOP
         END
$ FORTRAN DEGREES
$ LINK DEGREES
$ RUN DEGREES                                         Example 5.5
      0           -18                                 Output
      1           -17
      2           -17
      :            :
     32            0
      :            :
    212           100
```

The values for calculation in Example 5.5 are generated by the DO loop. The program generates 213 lines of output. The INT function causes the DEGREEF values to be printed as integers, and the NINT function in the WRITE statement rounds the output for the DEGREEC values to the nearest integer. Only a part of the output is listed.

5.3
DO LOOP WITH VARIABLE COUNTING INCREMENTS

A DO loop is a structure that provides control for executing a statement or a group of statements repeatedly. One application for DO loops is the use of the DO loop as a counter to cause the statements in the loop to be executed some number of times. Using a DO loop simply as a counter incremented by 1 each time through the loop, as in Examples 5.2, 5.4, and 5.5, is a common use of DO loops.

DEFINITION: The general form of a DO loop used as a counter provides the capability of executing the statements in a DO loop repeatedly, with the loop control variable assuming values beginning with the beginning value specified in the DO statement, changing each time through the loop with the increment value specified, and ending with the ending value specified.

DO loop_control_value = begin_value, end_value, increment

    statements to be executed repeatedly

END DO

The standard FORTRAN 77 DO loop includes a statement number and a CONTINUE statement instead of the END DO statement.

DO num   loop_value = begin_value, end_value, increment

    statements to be executed repeatedly

num   CONTINUE

The beginning value, ending value, and increment values in a DO loop can be symbolic names and can be provided in an assignment statement preceding the DO loop, can be generated by some process in the program, or can be READ into the program. The beginning value, ending value, and increment values can be FORTRAN expressions that produce an integer or a real value.

The symbolic names for the beginning value, ending value, and increment values must reflect the type of number, integer or real, being used in the DO loop processing, just as the symbolic name for the control value must be appropriate for integer or real. Symbolic names beginning with I, J, K, L, M, and N should be used if whole numbers are being used for loop control, and symbolic names beginning with other letters should be used if decimal numbers are being used in the DO statement. Integer or real declarations can be used to specify a data type.

All FORTRAN statements must begin in column 7 or beyond. It is not necessary to indent statements within a DO loop beyond column 7, however, it is good programming practice to indent statements in a DO loop to make the structure easily identifiable in a program.

DO loops can be nested one inside another. Nested DO loops are covered in Chapter 8. DO WHILE loops allow a set of statements to be executed repeatedly while a specified condition exists. DO WHILE loops are also covered in Chapter 8.

■ **Example 5.6: DO Loops**
   with Variable Counters

This example demonstrates several DO loops in one program and the use of real and integer loop control values and a negative step value.

```
$ EDIT DOMANY.FOR                              Example 5.6
        MIN = 14
        MAX = 26
        INC = 4
        DO I = MIN, MAX, INC
           WRITE (6,*) I
        END DO
        DO 10 I = MIN * 2, MAX + 6, INC/2
           WRITE (6,*) I
10      CONTINUE
        XMIN = 0.5
        XMAX = 1.5
        XSTEP = 0.5
        DO 20 XVALUE = XMIN, XMAX, XSTEP
           WRITE (6,*) XVALUE
20      CONTINUE
        DO XVALUE = XMAX * 2, XMIN + 1.0, -0.5
           WRITE (6,*) XVALUE
        END DO
        STOP
        END
$ FORTRAN DOMANY
$ LINK DOMANY
$ RUN DOMANY
        14                                     Example 5.6
        18                                     Output
        22
        26
        28
        30
        32
0.5000000
1.0000000
1.5000000
3.0000000
2.5000000
2.0000000
1.5000000
```

5.4
GO TO STATEMENT

The GO TO statement in the FORTRAN language causes an unconditional transfer of control to a specified statement number in the program. Structures of the FORTRAN language can provide a managed transfer of control in a program, and the use of GO TO statements is discouraged.

GO TO statement number

■ Example 5.7: Unconditional Transfer of Control

In following program, the first three statements in the program are executed one after another. When the fourth statement, the GO TO statement, executes, execution transfers to statement 60 and execution continues from there. Notice that the values for N and M are not set to zero, and the second WRITE statement is not executed.

A warning message will be printed when this program is compiled, indicating that there are statements that could never be executed because there is no path to the statements. The purpose of the example is to indeed indicate that there is no path to these statements.

Example 5.7

```
$ EDIT GOTO.FOR
        N = 5
        M = 2
        WRITE (6,*) 'FIRST WRITE STATEMENT',N,M
        GO TO 60
        N = 0
        M = 0
        WRITE (6,*) 'SECOND WRITE STATEMENT',N,M
60      WRITE (6,*) 'THIRD WRITE STATEMENT',N,M
        STOP
        END
$ FORTRAN GOTO
  Warning
  %FORT-W-NOPATH, No path to statement in module GOTO$MAIN line 5
$ LINK GOTO
$ RUN GOTO                                          Example 5.7
FIRST WRITE STATEMENT        5        2             Output
THIRD WRITE STATEMENT        5        2
```

When the program in Example 5.7 is compiled with the FORTRAN command, a warning message is provided to indicate that there are statements which could never be executed because there is no path to the statements, but the warning message does not keep the program from compiling and the program will execute.

■ Example 5.8: A Loop with a GO TO Statement

A GO TO statement can be used to create a loop in a program; however, unlike the DO loop, which provides a control for exiting the loop, the GO TO statement alone has no control mechanism.

When the program reaches the GO TO statement in this program, execution transfers to statement 10. The set of statements to input a number and print the number is executed three times. There is no way out of the loop, however.

Example 5.9 provides a good solution to the problem in this example.

NOTE: An explanation for entering data follows the example.

```
5                                                          Example 5.8
11                                                         Input
23
$ EDIT NOEND.FOR                                           Example 5.8
10    READ (5,*) NUMBER
      WRITE (6,*) NUMBER
      GO TO 10
      STOP
      END
$ FORTRAN NOEND
$ LINK NOEND
$ RUN NOEND                                                Example 5.8
      5                                                    Output
     11
     23
Error occurred  - end of file
```

Description of Example 5.8.   Consider the way that the program would execute if you were entering data from a terminal. Each time that a READ statement is executed, the program would stop and wait for you to enter a value. The value would immediately be echoed at the terminal, and execution would transfer to statement 10 and again wait for you to enter a value. If you planned to enter only 3 values, the program would wait for you all day. There is no systematic way to terminate the loop. You would have to terminate the processing of the program with a CONTROL/Y or create an End of File with a CONTROL/Z which in turn would create an error in the program and terminate execution.

■ Example 5.9: Reading a Variable Number of Records

This particular use of the GO TO statement provides a useful function for the GO TO statement; however, there are ways to perform the same function using structured programming techniques. If you have a set of data stored on disk and you do not know how many records there are, you can read the data record after record until you reach the End of File (EOF). In Example 5.8, the program terminated when the READ statement tried to execute and there was not another data record available. By including an END= clause in the READ statement, you can instruct the program to transfer execution to some statement when the End of File is encountered.

For most programming applications, the data is stored in a data file, and the data file is shown here to reemphasize that data is usually stored in a file when the technique of reading to the End of File is employed.

```
$ EDIT THREEREC.DAT
5                                                   Example 5.9
11                                                  Input
23
$ EDIT ENDOFFILE.FOR                                Example 5.9
    OPEN(5,FILE='THREEREC.DAT',STATUS='OLD')
    KOUNT = 0
    TOTAL = 0
10  READ (5,*,END=20) VALUE
    KOUNT = KOUNT + 1
    WRITE (6,*) KOUNT, VALUE
    TOTAL = TOTAL + VALUE
    GO TO 10
20  AVERAGE = TOTAL/KOUNT
    WRITE (6,*) 'THE NUMBER OF RECORDS IN THE FILE IS',KOUNT
    WRITE (6,*) 'THE AVERAGE IS ',AVERAGE
    STOP
    END
$ FORTRAN ENDOFFILE
$ LINK ENDOFFILE
$ RUN ENDOFFILE                                     Example 5.9
          1         5.000000                        Output
          2        11.00000
          3        23.00000
THE NUMBER OF RECORDS IN THE FILE IS         3
THE AVERAGE IS        13.000000
```

Description of Example 5.9. The program reads the first value, a 5. The program adds 1 to the location KOUNT, which is being used to count the number of data records. The program adds the value 5 to the TOTAL value and writes the KOUNT of 1 and the value 5 that was READ. The GO TO statement causes execution to transfer to statement 10, and the READ statement executes a second time, causing the value 11 to be input for the program. The KOUNT is incremented by 1, and the value 11 is added to the TOTAL value, and the KOUNT and the VALUE are WRITten out. Again the GO TO statement causes execution to transfer to statement 10, READing the value 23, incrementing the KOUNT, adding the value 23 to the TOTAL, and WRITing out the KOUNT and the VALUE.

After the value 23 has been READ in and processed and WRITten out, the GO TO statement again causes execution to transfer to statement 10. This time there are no more records to read; the END OF FILE has been reached. Since the END= clause is in the READ statement, the program transfers to the statement specified in the END= clause, this time to statement 20. Processing begins at statement 20 now. The average of the values is calculated and printed, and the program terminates.

5.5
APPLICATIONS

The following applications for DO loops in business, science, and the social sciences are intended only as an indication of applications in general. Because different concepts are covered in each example, you can gain information by reviewing each. For the business application, two programs are printed to emphasize that there is more than one correct way to write a computer program. Rarely do two programmers write exactly the same program.

■ Example 5.10: A Science Application

The precipitation increased every month during the months from February through May. There were 3 inches of rain in February, $4\frac{1}{2}$ inches of rain in March, 6 inches of rain in April, and $7\frac{1}{2}$ inches of rain in May. Write a program that prints the month number, and calculates and prints the number of inches of rain for each month, along with calculating and printing the average rainfall for the four months.

```
$ EDIT RAIN.FOR                                          Example 5.10
      TOTALRAIN = 0
      DO 30 MONTH = 2,5
         RAIN = 1.5 * MONTH
         TOTALRAIN = TOTALRAIN + RAIN
         WRITE(6,*)'MONTH',MONTH,'    RAINFALL',RAIN
30    CONTINUE
      WRITE(6,*)'AVERAGE RAINFALL',TOTALRAIN/4
      STOP
      END
$ FORTRAN RAIN
$ LINK RAIN
$ RUN RAIN                                               Example 5.10
MONTH       2    RAINFALL      3.000000                  Output
MONTH       3    RAINFALL      4.500000
MONTH       4    RAINFALL      6.000000
MONTH       5    RAINFALL      7.500000
AVERAGE RAINFALL      5.250000
```

■ Example 5.11: An Economics Application

A DO loop provides an easy way to calculate and print the effects of inflation. This example requires, as input to the program, the cost for some item, the rate of inflation, and the beginning and ending years for calculating the inflated cost of the item. Try running the program with an item such as a toaster costing $25 and a television set costing $500. The following is a formula for calculating the increasing cost of the item, including the inflation cost.

$$\text{Cost} = \text{cost} * (1 + \text{rate of inflation})$$

```
20,0.11,1984,1986

$ EDIT INFLATION.FOR
      INTEGER YEARBEGIN,YEAREND
C     THE PROGRAM CALCULATES AND PRINTS THE COST FOR THE ITEM
C     OVER THE YEARS INPUT
      READ (5,*) COST, RATE, YEARBEGIN, YEAREND
      WRITE (6,*)'COST', COST, 'INFLATION RATE', RATE*100,'%'
      DO N = YEARBEGIN, YEAREND
         COST = COST * (1+RATE)
         WRITE (6,*) N, COST
      END DO
      STOP
      END
$ FORTRAN INFLATION
$ LINK INFLATION
$ RUN INFLATION
COST      20.00000         INFLATION RATE     11.00000  %
          1984       22.20000
          1985       24.64200
          1986       27.35262
```

Example 5.11 Input
Example 5.11

Example 5.11 Output

You could run the program again with a different set of data.

```
 500,0.07,1985,1990

 $ RUN INFLATION

COST      500.0000         INFLATION RATE     7.00000   %
          1985     535.0000
          1986     572.4500
          1987     612.5215
          1988     655.3981
          1989     701.2760
          1990     750.3654
```

Example 5.11 Input
Example 5.11 Output

■ Example 5.12: A Math Application

The factorial of a number is used in many mathematical computations; however, the purpose of this example is to demonstrate a kind of iteration that might be used in any type of application. The following is the formula for calculating the factorial of a number. The exclamation point indicates a factorial. Zero factorial is defined to be 1.

$$n! = n(n - 1)(n - 2)(n - 3) \ldots (1)$$

For example,

$$3! = 3(2)(1) = 6 \quad \text{and} \quad 5! = 5(4)(3)(2)(1) = 120$$

The memory location used for storing the factorial in the program is a real location, because locations defined to be real locations can store larger numbers than locations defined to be integer locations, and the factorial number gets to be large very quickly.

```
6
$ EDIT ITERATE.FOR
      READ (5,*) NUMBER
      FACTORIAL = 1
      DO MULTIPLY = 1, NUMBER
        FACTORIAL = FACTORIAL * MULTIPLY
      END DO
      WRITE (6,*) NUMBER, FACTORIAL
      STOP
      END
$ FORTRAN ITERATE
$ LINK ITERATE
$ RUN ITERATE
      6     720.0000
```

Example 5.12
Input
Example 5.12

Example 5.12
Output

■ Example 5.13: A Business Application

Two example programs are written for this simple problem.

Certificates for savings deposits can be obtained for 3-, 6-, 9-, and 12-month periods. Simple interest is paid based on the number of months the deposit is held. The simple interest is 1% per month. Therefore, for a 3-month period, the interest is 3%, for a 6-month period the interest is 6%, for 9 months the interest is 9%, and for 12 months the interest is 12%.

Calculate and print the value of a $1000 deposit that is held for 3, 6, 9, and 12 months.

```
$ EDIT ONEWAY.FOR                                         Example 5.13a
      DEPOSIT = 1000.00
      DO 10 MONTHS = 3,12,3
        VALUE = DEPOSIT + (DEPOSIT * MONTHS * 0.01)
        WRITE(6,*) 'MONTHS DEPOSITED',MONTHS,' TOTAL VALUE',VALUE
10    CONTINUE
      STOP
      END
```

```
$ FORTRAN ONEWAY
$ LINK ONEWAY
$ RUN ONEWAY                                              Example 5.13a
MONTHS DEPOSITED     3 TOTAL VALUE    1030.0000           Output
MONTHS DEPOSITED     6 TOTAL VALUE    1060.0000
MONTHS DEPOSITED     9 TOTAL VALUE    1090.0000
MONTHS DEPOSITED    12 TOTAL VALUE    1120.0000
```

Notice in Example 5.13a that the value for MONTHS was used as the counter for the DO loop and the interest rate was developed based on the counter for MONTHS. In Example 5.13b, the counter for the DO loop is the interest rate, and the value for months is generated based on the interest rate.

```
$ EDIT ANOTHER.FOR                                        Example 5.13b
      DEPOSIT = 1000.00
      DO 10 RATEINTEREST = 0.03, 0.12, 0.03
       VALUE = DEPOSIT + (DEPOSIT * RATEINTEREST)
       MONTHS = RATEINTEREST * 100
       WRITE(6,*) 'MONTHS DEPOSITED',MONTHS,' TOTAL VALUE',VALUE
10     CONTINUE
       STOP
       END
$ FORTRAN ANOTHER
$ LINK ANOTHER
$ RUN ANOTHER                                             Example 5.13b
MONTHS DEPOSITED     3 TOTAL VALUE    1030.0000           Output
MONTHS DEPOSITED     6 TOTAL VALUE    1060.0000
MONTHS DEPOSITED     9 TOTAL VALUE    1090.0000
MONTHS DEPOSITED    12 TOTAL VALUE    1120.0000
```

■ Example 5.14: A Social Science Problem

Youngsters in grades 6, 8, and 10 were tested to determine the class participation and comprehension for a particular subject. The result was the following. Forty percent of the students in the sixth grade completely understood the material, 60 percent of the students in the eighth grade understood the material, and 80 percent of the students in the tenth grade understood the material. The trend in class participation was the opposite. Students in the lower grades participate more than students in the upper grades. Fifty percent of the students in the sixth grade participate, 30 percent of the students in the eighth grade participate, and 10 percent of the students in the tenth grade participate. Write a program that uses a DO loop to print out the grade number along with the comprehension and participation for each grade. To gain experience with logic, generate the percentages based on the counter for the DO loop and values that are calculated in the DO loop.

Practical application problems are rarely stated systematically. Whenever you start to write a computer program, it is useful to write down a summary of everything that you know. For this problem, when you have organized what you know, you are well on the way to solving the problem. After carefully reading the problem description and writing down what you read, you might make the following notes.

NOTES	GRADE	COMPREHENSION	PARTICIPATION
	6	40%	50%
	8	60%	30%
	10	80%	10%

What you need to do for this program is to write out a table that looks something like the notes that were made from the problem description. The difficulty in this problem lies in determining the relationship between the grade number and the percentages of comprehension and participation. This is a logic problem.

Before you begin to write code, you should determine the relationship between the grade and the comprehension and participation. In many cases, it takes a considerable amount of thought before you can develop a relationship that can be used in a program. For this problem, a relationship between grades and comprehension is (grade − 2)*10.

$$(6 - 2) * 10 = 40 \qquad (8 - 2) * 10 = 60 \qquad (10 - 2) * 10 = 80$$

The percentages, 50, 30, and 10 percent, for grades 6, 8, and 10 are simple values decreasing by 20 percentage points for each grade. There appears to be no relationship between the grades and the percentages, so the DO loop can be used as a means for decrementing these values, if the original value is set to 70.

It is often necessary to develop a logical relationship among values in programming.

```
$ EDIT ASSOCIATE.FOR                                    Example 5.14
      WRITE(6,*)' GRADE',' % COMPREHENSION',' % PARTICIPATION'
      NPARTICIPATION = 70
      DO NGRADE = 6, 10, 2
         NCOMPREHENSION = (NGRADE - 2) * 10
         NPARTICIPATION = NPARTICIPATION - 20
         WRITE(6,*)NGRADE,NCOMPREHENSION,NPARTICIPATION
      END DO
      STOP
      END
$ FORTRAN ASSOCIATE
$ LINK ASSOCIATE
$ RUN ASSOCIATE                                         Example 5.14
                                                        Output

   GRADE        % COMPREHENSION        % PARTICIPATION
      6              40                 50
      8              60                 30
     10              80                 10
```

5.6
PROBLEM SOLVING

The best place to start in problem solving is to write down everything that you know about a problem and all the results that you need to generate. After you make a list of the general information in a problem, you can begin to organize the facts into a logical order for solving the problem. You may draw arrows to indicate a loop. This initial development of order for the problem is usually the most difficult part of problem solving.

After you arrange the list of facts in a logical order and draw arrows to indicate loops for sets of processes that need to be performed more than once, you may actually draw a flow chart. The formal flow chart serves primarily to precisely define what you have already developed in your organized list, with arrows indicating flow of processing. The formal flow chart may be necessary for programs written for other people, but the most important part of your own problem solving is making a list of facts and organizing the list into a logical sequence with arrows or some other notation to indicate the order for processing. Writing the FORTRAN code is usually relatively simple after the problem has been solved by organizing the facts.

■ **Example 5.15: Solving a Problem**
That Requires a Loop

A new county planner has been hired. The planner is studying each of the developments in the area and wants some tabulated information about the High Valley Flats development. All the land parcels in High Valley Flats are rectangular. For each parcel the length and width of the parcel are recorded in feet. The new planner requests that you write a FORTRAN program to generate a listing including some information about each parcel of land and county total information.

The planner would like to have printed a total area in square miles for the county. In addition, the length, width, and area in square feet should be printed for each parcel, along with the plot number. The data are arranged in order of plot numbers. The first pair of length and width is for plot 1, the second pair is plot 2, and so on. The following are the lengths and widths for each of the parcels for High Valley Flats:

2160, 4585	2570, 3220
3230, 9027	3718, 1063
2130, 1108	

Solving the Problem.   First, write down the general information that you know. Sometimes you must read carefully to find all the relevant facts.

1.   There are five parcels of land.

2. Area for each parcel recorded by length and width in square feet.

3. Print total area in square miles.

4. For each parcel, print the length, width, and total area in square feet along with the parcel number.

At this point you have listed the general information about the problem. The flow of a computer program is still not apparent. You need to break down the problem into more precise facts and rearrange the order of the process. From what you know about programming, you know that you need to add the size of each parcel to the total size in order to generate a total, so the total should be printed as a last step in a program, and not before the parcels have been accessed separately.

1. DO the calculations for each of the five parcels.

2. Input length and width for each parcel in feet.

3. Calculate area for each parcel in square feet.

4. Print parcel number, length, width, and area.

5. Add parcel area to total area.

6. Calculate area in square miles for area in square feet.

7. Print area in square miles.

Now that you have broken down the problem into precise steps and you have the steps arranged in a logical order, you need only to draw an arrow to indicate the loop for processing the steps for the five parcels.

```
┌─►DO the calculations for each of the five parcels
│      Input length and width for each parcel in feet
│      Calculate area for each parcel in square feet
│      Print parcel number, length, width, and area
│      Add parcel area to total area
└── CONTINUE calculations for parcels
    Square miles = 5280 feet times 5280 feet
    Calculate area in square miles from the area in square feet
    Print area in square miles
```

Now the flow of the program is completely defined and coding is straightforward. The flow chart in Figure 5.2 describes the flow of the program to solve the problem.

```
2160, 4585
3230, 9027
2130, 1108
2570, 3220
3718, 1063
$ EDIT HIGHVALEY.FOR
```

Example 5.15
Input

Example 5.15

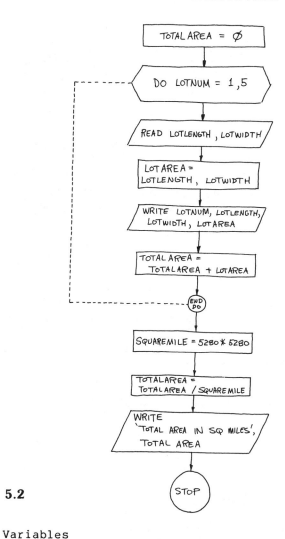

FIGURE 5.2

```
C        Variables
         REAL LOTNUM,LOTLENGTH,LOTWIDTH,LOTAREA,
    -        TOTALAREA, SQUAREMILE
         TOTALAREA = Ø
         DO 1Ø LOTNUM = 1, 5
            READ(5,*) LOTLENGTH, LOTWIDTH
            LOTAREA =  LOTLENGTH * LOTWIDTH
            WRITE(6,*) LOTNUM, LOTLENGTH, LOTWIDTH, LOTAREA
            TOTALAREA = TOTALAREA + LOTAREA
1Ø       CONTINUE
         SQUAREMILE=528Ø * 528Ø
         TOTALAREA = TOTALAREA / SQUAREMILE
         WRITE(6,*) 'TOTAL AREA IN SQUARE MILES ',TOTALAREA
         STOP
         END
$ FORTRAN HIGHVALEY
$ LINK HIGHVALEY
```

```
$ RUN HIGHVALEY                                        Example 5.15
                                                          Output
        1          2160.0000        4585.0000      9903600.
        2          3230.0000        9027.0000      2.9157210E+07
        3          2130.0000        1108.0000      2360040.
        4          2570.0000        3220.0000      8275400.
        5          3718.0000        1063.0000      3952234.
TOTAL AREA IN SQUARE MILES        1.924375
```

Note that the area for lot 2 is printed in scientific notation. The number is large. When numbers are greater than about seven significant digits, some accuracy may be lost. In this case the accuracy is probably acceptable, but there is the capability of using double precision for storing values and performing calculations if greater accuracy is needed.

5.7
SUMMARY

A *counter* is a memory location that is used to keep track of the number of times a process occurs.

A DO LOOP structure in the FORTRAN language contains a counter as a part of the structure.

■ A Standard FORTRAN 77 DO LOOP

DO num loop-control = begin__value, end__value, increment

    statements to be executed repeatedly

num   CONTINUE

■ VAX Extension for DO LOOPS that Require No Statement Number

DO loop-control = begin__value, end__value, increment

    statements to be executed repeatedly

END DO

Calculating a *cumulative total* for a set of values is accomplished by retrieving a value from a memory location, adding a value to that value, and storing the new total back into the memory location.

$$
\begin{array}{ccccc}
\downarrow & & \uparrow & & \uparrow \\
\text{store} & & \text{retrieve} & & \text{add} \\
\downarrow & & \uparrow & & \uparrow \\
\text{total} & = & \text{total} & + & \text{value}
\end{array}
$$

A good approach to solving problems in general is to write down everything you know about a problem and everything you need to generate in list form and then refine and rearrange the list until each step to the solution is defined.

5.8
EXERCISES

5.1. Write a FORTRAN program to print your name exactly 10 times.

5.2. What is the output for each of the following FORTRAN programs? The easiest way to determine the output is to draw a box that represents each of the memory locations for the variables in the program. Then write in the boxes the value of each variable as the program would execute. At the point where a PRINT statement is executed, the value that is in the memory location specified is printed; so if you write what is in each memory location at each step as the program executes, you know what is in the memory location at that time.

```
a.    LOOPTOTAL = 0
      DO 10 LOOP = 1,3
         LOOPTOTAL = LOOPTOTAL + LOOP
         PRINT *, LOOP, LOOPTOTAL
10    CONTINUE
      STOP
      END


b.    DO I = 3,8
         IVALUE = I - 3
         PRINT *, I, IVALUE
      END DO
      STOP
      END


c.    DO 2 KOUNT = 100,2000,100
         KOUNTYEAR=((KOUNT-100)/100)+1
         PRINT *,'CENTURY',KOUNTYEAR
2     CONTINUE
      STOP
      END
```

(Continued)

```
d.    L=3
      M=6
      N=24
      INDEXADD=10
      ITOT=0
      DO INDEX = M,N,L
        ITOT=INDEX+INDEXADD
        PRINT INDEX,ITOT
        IALL=IALL + ITOT
      END DO
      PRINT *,IALL
      STOP
      END
```

5.3. For the integers 1 to 15, write a FORTRAN program to print a table of the numbers and the squares and cubes of the numbers.

$$
\begin{array}{ccc}
1 & 1 & 1 \\
2 & 4 & 8 \\
3 & 9 & 27 \ \text{etc.}
\end{array}
$$

5.4. Write a program to print all the odd numbers (1, 3, 5 . . . 99) less than 100.

5.5. Create a conversion table for miles and kilometers with a FORTRAN program. Begin with 10 miles and use increments of 10 miles up to 100 miles. One kilometer = 1.61 mile.

5.6. Write a FORTRAN program with a DO loop to READ in the cost for six items and calculate the average cost for the six items. Run your program twice with two different sets of data.

a. Costs for data set 1 are: .89   .63   1.25   3.24   .52   .12

b. Costs for data set 2 are: .94   .57   1.64   4.38   .67   .17

5.7. An antique item was purchased in 1940 for $30. The value of the item has doubled every five years since the purchase. Write a FORTRAN program to calculate and print the value of the item in 1985.

5.8. BUSINESS PROBLEM

A wealthy person has agreed to donate money to a deserving cause over the next year. The person is considering two options for donating. Write a FORTRAN program to print the value of the donation for each of the following donation plans.

Plan 1: Donate one penny on the first day of the year and double the donation on each of the succeeding 364 days of the year. Each day's donation is added to the previous amount donated (i.e., the first day the donation is one cent; the next day the donation is 2 cents, so the total donation by the second day is 3 cents; on the third day, the donation is 4 cents and the total donation is 7 cents).

Plan 2: Donate $100 in January and double the value of each donation each month for twelve months.

	Plan 1		Plan 2
Donation	Total value	Donation	Total value
.01	.01	100.00	100.00
.02	.03	200.00	300.00
.04	.07	400.00	700.00
.08	.15	800.00	1500.00
Continue through 365 days		Continue through twelve months	

5.9. SCIENCE PROBLEM

Under test conditions in a small body of water, the temperature increases by 0.01% for every 100 kilograms of pollutants added to the water. The temperature at the beginning of the test period was 68 degrees Celsius. Calculate and print the water temperature after 100 kilograms have been added, after 200 kilograms have been added, after 300 kilograms, after 400, and so on, and finally after 2000 kilograms of pollutants have been added. Write a FORTRAN program with a DO loop to perform the calculations and print the temperature as each 100 kilograms of pollutant is added.

5.10. SOCIAL SCIENCE PROBLEM

A school library currently has 10,000 books. Old books should be removed. The librarian is planning to remove 100 old books per year while increasing the number of new books by 5 percent per year over the next five years. The old books will be removed before the calculation for the number of new books to purchase is made. How many books will be in the library at the end of five years? Write a FORTRAN program with a DO loop to solve this problem.

5.11. LOGIC PROBLEMS

It is often necessary to determine a relationship between numbers in order to write a computer program. Write a FORTRAN program with a DO loop to calculate the sum of each of the following expressions. Include a READ statement in your programs to input the value for n in the examples that require a value for n.

a. $1 + 2 + 3 + \cdots + n$

b. $2 + 5 + 8 + 11 + 14 + \cdots + 44$

c. $(0.22) + (0.22)^2 + (0.22)^3 + \cdots + (0.22)^n$

d. $1 + 3 + 5 + 7 + \cdots + (2n - 1)$

e. $1 + \frac{1}{2} + \frac{1}{3} + \frac{1}{4} + \cdots + \frac{1}{n}$

f. $1 - \frac{1}{2} + \frac{1}{3} - \frac{1}{4} + \cdots - \frac{1}{100}$

g. $1 + \frac{1}{4} + \frac{1}{9} + \frac{1}{16} + \cdots + \frac{1}{n^2}$

h. $1 + \frac{1}{2} + \frac{1}{4} + \frac{1}{8} + \cdots + \frac{1}{2^n}$

6

Defining the Way
That Input and Output
Are Presented for Numeric
Data and Character Data

Character data contain letters, numbers, and special characters such as #, &, and $. The names and addresses in the following data are called *alpha-numeric character* data. The numbers at the right of each record are *numeric* data.

Dixon, Jewel   Apt#28, 23 Cheery Lane, Jacksonville, Fla.   9234.56
Talen, Bob   R&R Village, Lake Tahoe, California   1867.38

Character data are specified with a CHARACTER declaration at the beginning of a FORTRAN program.

It is often necessary or useful to enter data in columns in a specific way for READing into a program and it is often useful to be able to print output in orderly tables with descriptive headings. FORMAT statements allow you to control input and output by specifying the way that values should be input and the way that output should occur.

For unformatted input, numeric data can be typed one value after another in a record with the values separated by commas or blanks. For unformatted output, the values are printed one after another according to the default printing characteristics of FORTRAN on the VAX. Exact descriptions for the way that the data are to be input or output can be provided in a FORMAT statement, and the way that output should be positioned on a page can be described in a FORMAT statement. A FORMAT statement is used with input and output statements to indicate for each field the type of data stored. The type could be alphanumeric character data, integer numeric data, real numeric data, or other types of data. This chapter describes input and output for character, integer, and real data.

6.1
ALPHANUMERIC CHARACTER STRINGS

Unless you specify otherwise in a program, values that are stored in memory locations with symbolic names beginning with the letters A to H and O to Z are real numeric values by default, and values stored in memory locations with symbolic names beginning with the letters I to N are integer values by default. If you want to store and be able to print the words HAPPY BIRTHDAY, you must declare in the program that data should be stored as CHARACTER data. (See Figure 6.1.)

FIGURE 6.1

DEFINITION: The CHARACTER data type is used to store strings of letters, numbers, and special characters including blanks. If a program contains character data, a CHARACTER declaration must be at the beginning of a program before any executable statements.

The maximum number of characters that can be stored in a character field must be specified in the CHARACTER declaration following an asterisk. Alphanumeric data can be stored in an assignment statement by enclosing the characters between single quotation marks.

CHARACTER BOYSNAME*14, GIRLSNAME*12,SPACENAME*4

BOYSNAME = 'EDWARD CHARLES'
GIRLSNAME = 'LINDA TRACEY'
SPACENAME = 'E.T.'

A FORMAT statement is used with a WRITE statement to specify that alphanumeric characters should be printed.

```
        WRITE(6,100)BOYSNAME,GIRLSNAME,SPACENAME
100     FORMAT(' ',A,5X,A,5X,A)
```

In the WRITE statement, the 6 indicates that the output should be printed at the terminal, unless you have specified some other destination. In the WRITE statement, the 100 indicates that the description for the way the output should be printed is in FORMAT statement 100. In FORMAT statement 100, the blank enclosed between single quotation marks indicates that the output should be printed on the next available line, that is, single spaced. The A is a field description which indicates that the value to be printed in this field is alphanumeric character data. Each value to be printed, BOYSNAME, GIRLSNAME, and SPACENAME, is to be printed as alphanumeric characters. The 5X indicates that 5 blank spaces should be left on the output line between the printed strings.

■ **Example 6.1: Storing and Printing Characters**

There is no input to the program. The alphanumeric values are stored in assignment statements in the program.

```
$ EDIT ALPHACHAR.FOR                              Example 6.1
        CHARACTER BOYSNAME*14, GIRLSNAME*12,SPACENAME*4
        BOYSNAME = 'EDWARD CHARLES'
        GIRLSNAME = 'LINDA TRACEY'
        SPACENAME = 'E.T.'
        WRITE(6,100)BOYSNAME,GIRLSNAME,SPACENAME
100     FORMAT(' ',A,5X,A,5X,A)
```

```
          STOP
          END
$ FORTRAN ALPHACHAR
$ LINK ALPHACHAR
$ RUN ALPHACHAR                                        Example 6.1
EDWARD CHARLES     LINDA  TRACEY      E.T.             Output
```

6.2
INTRODUCTION TO FORMAT
STATEMENTS FOR NUMERIC OUTPUT

A FORMAT statement can be used to specify the way that a value or values are printed or stored as output from a program, including the number of decimal points for each value and the location of the value in the output record.

The following two programs are the same except for the output being unformatted in Example 6.2 and the output being formatted in Example 6.3. Observe the differences.

■ Example 6.2: Unformatted Output

Look at Example 6.3 to see formatted output for the same problem.

```
$ EDIT SIMPLEOUT.FOR                                  Example 6.2
C    THE PROGRAM PRODUCES TWO OUTPUT RECORDS USING
C    NO FORMAT WITH THE  WRITE STATEMENTS
     COST = 112.96
     MONTHS = 6
     RATEOFINTEREST = 0.07
     WRITE (6,*) 'COST               MONTHS   RATE OF INTEREST'
     WRITE (6,*) COST,MONTHS,RATEOFINTEREST
     STOP
     END
$ FORTRAN SIMPLEOUT
$ LINK SIMPLEOUT
$ RUN SIMPLEOUT
COST            MONTHS   RATE OF INTEREST      Example 6.2
   112.9600         6   7.0000000-02           Output
```

The first WRITE statement prints the string of characters between the quotation marks. The second WRITE statement prints the values. It is difficult to line up the headings without formats, and the numbers are definitely not printed in a desirable way without formats.

■ Example 6.3: Formatted Output

This program is the same as that in Example 6.2 except that the output for the previous example is unformatted.

Example 6.3

```
$ EDIT FORMATOUT.FOR
C     THE PROGRAM PRODUCES TWO OUTPUT RECORDS USING
C     FORMAT STATEMENTS WITH THE  WRITE STATEMENTS
      COST = 112.96
      MONTHS = 6
      RATEOFINTEREST = 0.07
      WRITE (6,100)
100   FORMAT(' ','COST   MONTHS   RATE OF INTEREST')
      WRITE (6,200) COST, MONTHS, RATEOFINTEREST
200   FORMAT(' ',F6.2,4X,I2,4X,F4.2)
      STOP
      END
$ FORTRAN SIMPLEOUT
$ LINK SIMPLEOUT
$ RUN SIMPLEOUT
COST   MONTHS   RATE OF INTEREST
112.96     6     0.07
```

Example 6.3
Output

The WRITE(6,100) statement specifies that FORMAT statement number 100 is used to determine how to print information to unit 6, which is defined to be the terminal by default. FORMAT 100 contains a carriage control for single spacing and then a string of characters to be printed on an output line.

Look at the WRITE statement for the numeric values and the 200 FORMAT statement. The WRITE statement specifies the names of the three memory locations that contain values to be printed. The FORMAT statement specifies the way that the three values should be printed.

WRITE (6,200) COST, MONTHS, RATEOFINTEREST
> The 200 in the WRITE statement specifies that the description for the way that each of the values should be printed is defined in FORMAT statement 200.

200 FORMAT(' ',F6.2,I2,4X,F4.2)
> The 200 is the statement label that identifies the FORMAT statement. Whenever a 200 is used in a WRITE statement in the program, this format statement is used for specifying the way that the output should be produced.

Following are descriptions of the elements of this FORMAT statement.

200   FORMAT(' ',F6.2,4X,I2,4X,F4.2)
> The blank enclosed by single quotes is a CARRIAGE CONTROL. The blank space used as a carriage control indicates that the output from the WRITE statement should begin on the next available line as in single spacing with a typewriter.

WRITE (6,200) COST, MONTHS, RATEOFINTEREST
> F6.2 is the description for the way that the value stored in memory location COST should be printed.

200   FORMAT(' ',F6.2,4X,I2,4X,F4.2)

The F in F6.2 means that a floating-point value should be printed. A floating-point value is a value stored in a memory location that has been given a name beginning with the letters A to H and O to Z or that has been declared to be real. The 6 means that the entire number should be six character positions wide and that includes the decimal point. The 2 means that there should be two digits printed after the decimal point.

An X in a FORMAT statement indicates that print positions on the output line should be skipped over, and so the two occurrences of 4X in this FORMAT statement indicate that four print positions should be skipped after printing the COST and after printing the MONTHS.

WRITE (6,200) COST, MONTHS, RATEOFINTEREST
> The I2 is the description for the way that the value stored in memory location MONTHS should be printed.

200   FORMAT(' ',F6.2,4X,I2,4X,F4.2)

The I means that an integer value should be printed. An integer value is a value that has been given a name beginning with the letters I, J, K, L, M, or N or has been declared to be integer with an INTEGER declaration. The integer described in this example is two digits wide.

WRITE (6,200) COST, MONTHS, RATEOFINTEREST
> The F4.2 is the description for the way the value stored in location RATEOFINTEREST should be printed.

200   FORMAT(' ',F6.2,4X,I2,4X,F4.2)

The value stored in location RATEOFINTEREST is a real floating-point value, which should be printed with 4 print positions including a decimal point, and 2 digits should be printed following the decimal point.

6.3
GENERAL DESCRIPTION OF FORMAT STATEMENTS FOR OUTPUT

A FORMAT statement specifies the way that an input line or an output line should look. There are common descriptions used in defining the format for input and output, but the application of formats in input and output are different and so the examples in this section cover only output formats.

DEFINITION: A FORMAT *statement* used with a WRITE statement defines how the values to be output from the program will be produced, including the number of characters or digits to produce, and for numeric values whether or not a decimal should be output and possibly the number of digits following the decimal point. For printed output, a carriage control character must be included to specify line spacing.

The following is a general form for an output format statement.

statement-number   FORMAT   (carriage control, field descriptions)

The statement-number is used by a WRITE statement to reference a FORMAT statement.

WRITE(unit,statement-number)v1,v2,v3, . . . vn
where v1, v2, v3, etc., represent the values to be printed in each field

The carriage control character defines the line spacing for output to a printer. A carriage control character can be one of the following:

' '   blank   Print on the next line (single spacing)
'0'   zero   Skip one line (double spacing)
'1'   one   Start on a new page
'+'   plus   Print on the same line as previous print (may be used if you want to strike over)

The field descriptions describe the way that each output value should be produced. For each value to be output in a WRITE statement, there should be a field description in the FORMAT statement.

DEFINITION: A *field* is a set of character positions on an output line.

An output line might contain three fields.

field1   field2   field3

If a WRITE statement contains three values to print, there must be at least three field descriptions in a format statement. Extra field descriptions can be included to specify fields that should be left blank and fields that contain quoted character strings.

An I format is used for integer numbers. An F format is used for real numbers.

In   Defines a field to contain an integer value with n digits.
Fw.d   Defines a field to contain a real value with a *width* of w characters, includes the decimal point, with d digits after the decimal point.

Each numeric value is right justified in its respective field; that is, each value is printed at the right of the specified field, and if there are more print positions specified than are necessary to print the number, the blank spaces occur to the left of the number.

A number in front of the I format or the F format specifies the number of times for using that format. Look at the following format statements with equivalent meanings.

```
100     FORMAT(' ',3I2,4F8.1)
200     FORMAT(' ',I2,I2,I2,F8.1,F8.1,F8.1,F8.1)
```

Each format statement indicates that 3 integer values 2 digits wide should be printed on the output line followed by 4 real values 8 positions wide with 1 digit after the decimal point.

The X format and the T format are used to control spacing across the output line. The X format specifies the number of spaces that should be skipped. The T format is a tab format and specifies a particular column at which to begin the next field.

nX   Defines a field to be a blank field *n* character positions wide.
Tn   Defines a column *n* at which the next printed field should begin.

The A format is used to output alphanumeric characters. It is used for printing strings of characters that include letters, numbers, and special characters.

Characters between quotation marks in a FORMAT statement are printed on an output line just as the characters appear.

/// Slashes are used in an output format to specify that a line or lines should be skipped before resuming printing. One slash causes output to move to the following line. Multiple slashes cause one fewer blank lines to occur than the number of slashes. A carriage control must be included in an output format following new line specifications caused by slashes. Examples of slashes in output formats are given in Section 6.6.

■ Example 6.4: Integer and Real Output

```
$ EDIT NUMOUT.FOR                              Example 6.4
        I = 2
        J = 23
        N = 356
        X = 27.87
        Y = 179.003
        Z = 0.00567
        WRITE (6,100) I, J, N, X, Y, Z
100     FORMAT(' ',I1,I2,I3,F5.2,F7.3,F7.5)
        WRITE (6,200) I, J, N, X, Y, Z
200     FORMAT(' ',I5,I5,I5,F10.5,F10.5,F10.5)
        WRITE (6,300) I, J, N, X, Y, Z
300     FORMAT(' ',3I5,F8.2,2F10.5)
```

```
      WRITE (6,400) I, J, N, X, Y, Z
400   FORMAT(' ',I5,T10,I5,T20,I5,T30,F5.2,T40,F7.3,T50,F7.5)
      STOP
      END
$ FORTRAN NUMOUT
$ LINK NUMOUT
$ RUN NUMOUT
22335627.87179.0030.00567
    2    23   356   27.87000 179.00301    0.00567
    2    23   356   27.87 179.00301    0.00567
    2    23         356       27.87     179.003   0.00567
```

Example 6.4
Output

6.4
GENERAL DESCRIPTION OF FORMAT STATEMENTS FOR INPUT

Often data are stored in 80-character records, because a punched card contains 80 punch positions. If you have many data values to input for each record, there may not be room to include commas or blanks between values. A FORMAT description could be used to indicate where values begin and end for each variable and where the decimal point should be positioned in the variable.

These input data could be read without a format specification because numbers are separated by commas and the decimal position is marked.

These input data can be read only with a format specification because the beginning and ending for each number are not defined and the decimal positions for numbers are not marked.

25,33.56,0.047,10978.3
22,28.09,0.234,89765.1

2533560047109783
2228090234897651

DEFINITION: A *FORMAT statement* used with a READ statement describes each field of data that is to be transferred into the program, as well as fields in the input record that are to be skipped over.

The following is a general form for an input format statement.

statement-number   FORMAT (field descriptions)

The statement-number is used in a READ statement to reference the FORMAT statement.

READ (unit,statement-number)v1,v2,v3, . . . vn
where v1, v2, v3, etc., represent the values to be transferred into memory according to the field descriptions in the FORMAT statement.

For an input record, a FORMAT statement must describe each field that contains input data and must specify all fields that should be skipped.

An I format is used to describe a field that contains an integer number. An F format is used to describe a field that contains a real number.

In   Defines a field that contains an integer value *n* digits wide.

Fw.d   Defines a field that contains a real number with a total width of *w*. If no decimal point is entered, the program records the position of the decimal point to be located *d* positions from the right of the number when the value is stored by the program. If a decimal point is actually entered, the location of the actual decimal point is stored.

The X format and the T format are used to skip over fields that contain blanks or information that should be ignored.

nX   Defines *n* character positions to skip over.

Tn   Defines a specific column n for positioning.

The A format is used to input alphanumeric characters, that is, strings of characters that include letters, numbers, and special characters. The number of characters to be input for a variable is specified in the CHARACTER declaration in the program.

■ **Example 6.5: A Simple Example of Formatted Input and Output**

Four records containing numeric data are stored. For each of four persons, a record contains the account number and balance owed. The account number is stored in columns 1 to 4 as an integer. The balance is stored in columns 6 to 12.

```
2376    1203.67
3302      21.98
4459     100.00
5986     987.98
```

The format for the first field would be an I format because the account number is an integer. The format for the second field would be an F format because the number is a real number. The way that a decimal is stored internally allows the decimal to *float* conceptually in order to store the maximum number of significant digits, and so the F stands for the floating-point numbers, which are more often called real numbers. The machine needs to be able to store values like 389432.1 and 0.000345, and so the capability of storing the significant digits along with the location of the decimal point is called *floating point*.

The integer value for the data in this example contains 4 digits. Then there is a blank space in the record, and then the real value contains 7 character positions including the decimal point. The width of the field includes the number of positions. There are two positions after the decimal point. The input format could be the following:

FORMAT(I4,1X,F7.2)

Often the blank space or spaces before a value are included as part of the format for a field. Blank positions to the left of a field have no effect on the value stored in a field. The following format includes the blank space in front of the balance value in the format for the balance.

FORMAT(I4,F8.2)

Column numbers are printed vertically above the data. Column numbers 1 to 40 are shown.

```
          1         2         3         4          Column
1234567890123456789012345678901234567890          Numbers
----------------------------------------------------------
2376 1203.67                                      Example 6.5
3302   21.98                                      Input
4459  100.00
5986  987.98

----------------------------------------------------------
$ EDIT FORMATIN.FOR                               Example 6.5
C     THE PROGRAM READS TWO VALUES FROM EACH OF FOUR RECORDS.
C     AFTER EACH RECORD IS READ, THE TWO INPUT VALUES ARE
C     PRINTED.
100   FORMAT(I4,F8.2)
200   FORMAT(' ',I4,F8.2)
      DO I = 1,4
         READ(5,100)NUMACCOUNT,BALANCE
         WRITE(6,200)NUMACCOUNT,BALANCE
      END DO
      STOP
      END
$ FORTRAN FORMATIN
$ LINK FORMATIN
$ RUN FORMATIN                                    Example 6.5
2376 1203.67                                      Output
3302   21.98
4459  100.00
5986  987.98
```

Description of Example 6.5.   The DO loop causes the statements between the DO statement and the END DO statement to execute the number of times specified in the DO statement. In this case the only statements in the DO loop are a READ statement for transferring data into the program and a WRITE statement that transfers data out of the program. The READ statement and the WRITE statement are executed four times, once for each record in the data file.

Each time the READ statement executes, the program transfers into memory two values, which are stored according to the field descriptions in FORMAT statement 100. Each time the WRITE statement executes, two values are output from the program according to the field descriptions in FORMAT statement 200. It is not necessary to use exactly the same format for output as the format that was used for input.

6.5
GENERAL INPUT
FORMAT CONSIDERATIONS

The way that you store data in a set of records for input to a computer program is important. Data can be stored in one way and accessed in several ways depending on the READ statement and the FORMAT statement. Any one of the FORMAT statements following the example data might be appropriate. Only you or the person who stored the data can specify a correct format. Of course, some formats that are written slightly differently can actually input identical data.

The numbers above the data are column numbers. The column numbers are printed vertically here. Columns 1 to 40 are shown.

Column	1	2	3	4
Numbers		1234567890123456789012345678901234567890		

Data	23 502 333 4 25.5 26.789 23 .11

```
        FORMAT(I3,2X,I5,I3,F7.1,3X,F6.3,I4,F4.2)
or      FORMAT(I2,I3,2I5,I6,2F7.2,I3,F4.2)
```

There are many other possibilities for the way that the data could be READ. Only the person who knows how the data are stored can write a correct format. The following examples indicate the meaning of input formats. Before going on to the examples, look at the following row of data. Certainly, only a person who has information about the data could determine the format.

Column	1	2	3	4
Numbers		1234567890123456789012345678901234567890		

Data	8767654323460765432345678765

Now study the following examples of FORMAT statements for input.

■ Example 6.6: Input Data Formats

Data might be stored in a record in the following fields. A real number is stored in columns 1 to 5, a real number is stored in columns 10 to 14, an integer number is stored in columns 20 to 25, and real numbers are stored in columns 30 to 35 and 37 to 42. There are blank spaces in columns 6 to 9, 15 to 19, 26 to 29, and 36.

```
         1         2         3         4         5    Column
1234567890123456789012345678901234567890  Numbers
```

5.892	23.87	205331	2309.1	3488.5	Example 6.6
1.345	55.66	133502	9034.3	6754.1	Input
9.987	34.22	200300	6721.8	5591.2	

```
$ EDIT INOUT.FOR                                        Example 6.6
C      THE PROGRAM READS INPUT FROM THREE RECORDS ACCORDING TO
C      FORMAT 100 AND WRITES THE OUTPUT RECORDS FREE FORMAT.
C
100    FORMAT(F5.3,4X,F5.2,5X,I6,4X,F6.1,1X,F6.1)
       DO I = 1, 3
          READ(5,100)A,B,N,C,D
          WRITE(6,*)A,B,N,C,D
       END DO
       STOP
       END
$ FORTRAN INOUT
$ LINK INOUT                                            Example 6.6
$ RUN INOUT                                             Output
   5.892000     23.87000        205331     2309.100     3488.500
   1.345000     55.66000        133502     9034.300     6754.100
   9.987000     34.22000        200300     6721.800     5591.200
```

■ Example 6.7: Describing Input Data with a Format

For this example, the same data are stored in each record as in Example 6.6, but the data are accessed in a different way.

Perhaps you discover after data are collected that the first data value for each record is accurate only to one decimal point, but that accuracy is adequate and so you continue to use the data. Perhaps the second data value is not relevant to the current programming project and you want to skip over that value. You can use the input format statement to skip over the rightmost decimal parts of the first number and completely skip over the second number.

The digits in columns 20 to 25 might represent two integer fields. A two-digit integer field might be in columns 20 to 21 and a four-digit integer field in columns 22 to 25.

The multiple field description is used to describe the final two fields in each record with one field description.

```
          1         2         3         4         5      Column
123456789012345678901234567890123456789012345678990      Numbers
---------------------------------------------------------------------
5.892    23.87     205331    2309.1 3488.5           Example 6.7
1.345    55.66     133502    9034.3 6754.1           Input
9.987    34.22     200300    6721.8 5591.2
---------------------------------------------------------------------
```

```
$ EDIT INOUT2.FOR
```
                                                     Example 6.7

```
C     THE PROGRAM READS INPUT FROM THREE RECORDS ACCORDING TO
C     FORMAT 100 AND WRITES THE OUTPUT RECORDS FREE FORMAT.
C
100     FORMAT(F3.1,T20,I2,I4,3X,2F7.1)
        DO I = 1, 3
           READ(5,100)A,N,M,C,D
           WRITE(6,*)A,N,M,C,D
        END DO
        STOP
        END
$ FORTRAN INOUT2
$ LINK INOUT2
$ RUN INOUT2
```
                                                     Example 6.7
                                                     Output
```
5.800000          20          5331      2309.100       3488.500
1.300000          13          3502      9034.300       6754.100
9.900000          20           300      6721.800       5591.200
```

■ Example 6.8: Input Formats for Data with No Spaces

The data from Example 6.7 could be stored with no spaces between values and no decimal points entered. By using the correct format, the data could be entered into the program correctly. For this example, a real number is stored in columns 1 to 4, a real number is stored in columns 5 to 8, an integer number is stored in columns 9 to 14, and real numbers are stored in columns 15 to 19 and 20 to 24.

```
          1         2         3         4         Column
123456789012345678901234567890123456789990        Numbers
-----------------------------------------------------------
58922387205331230913485                    Example 6.8
13455661335029034367541                    Input
99873422200300672185512
```

```
$ EDIT INOUT3.FOR                                    Example 6.8

C       THE PROGRAM READS INPUT FROM THREE RECORDS ACCORDING TO
C       FORMAT 100 AND WRITES THE OUTPUT RECORDS FREE FORMAT.
C
100       FORMAT(F4.3,F4.2,I6,2F5.1)
          DO I = 1, 3
             READ(5,100)A,B,N,C,D
             WRITE(6,*)A,B,N,C,D
          END DO
          STOP
          END
$ FORTRAN INOUT3
$ LINK INOUT3                                         Example 6.8
$ RUN INOUT3                                          Output
5.892000       23.87000        205331    2309.100      3488.500
1.345000       55.66000        133502    9034.300      6754.100
9.987000       34.22000        200300    6721.800      5591.200
```

■ Example 6.9: VAX Formatted Input

For an input number stored with no decimal and accessed according to an I format, the value in the input record is the value that will be stored. Blanks and zeros to the left of an integer number are ignored.

For an input number that is accessed according to an F format, there are two ways for determining the value that is to be stored. In the w width field specified by the format Fw.d, if a decimal point is included in the number, the value will be stored exactly as typed in the input record. In the w width field specified by the format Fw.d, if a decimal point is not typed in the input record, the value to be stored is the number typed with a decimal point inserted d digit positions from the right of the field.

The data for this example are accessed with the following format.

```
100     FORMAT(3I5,I2,I5,I3,3X,F6.3,3X,F7.2)
```

Observe the way the data look according to this format. The top two rows of numbers are column numbers 1 through 50.

```
     |       1|11111|11|11222|222|222|233333|333|3344444|444445
12345|67890|12345|67|89012|345|678|901234|567|8901234|567890
     |     |     |  |     |   |   |      |   |       |
 2300|45600|23900|70|89000|200|   |23.45 |   |345.786|
5    |5    |3    |6 | 7    |235|   |1.988 |   |4567.89|
    1|   70| 33  |  |      |   |6  |0.78  |   |.0031  |


     1         2          3          4          5      Column
12345678901234567890123456789012345678901234567890   Numbers

2300456002390070890000200   23.45    345.786
5    5    3    6  7    235   1.988    4567.89          Example 6.9
    1   70 33            6   0.78     .0031            Input
```

```
$ EDIT SEEVALUES.FOR                                    Example 6.9
      DO IRECORD = 1, 3
          READ(5,100)I,J,K,L,M,N,X,Y
          WRITE(6,200)I,J,K,L,M,N,X,Y
      END DO
100   FORMAT(3I5,I2,I5,I3,3X,F6.3,3X,F7.2)
200   FORMAT(' ',6(I5,2X),F8.3,5X,F8.3)
      STOP
      END
$ FORTRAN SEEVALUES
$ LINK SEEVALUES                                        Example 6.9
$ RUN SEEVALUES                                         Output
  2300   45600   23900      70   89000     200    23.450     345.786
 50000   50000   30000      60    7000     235     1.988    4567.890
     1      70    3300       0       0       6     0.780       0.003
```

6.6

APPLICATIONS

■ Example 6.10: Generating a Formatted Table

An accountant in the credit department of a store might write the following program. The program reads some information about each charge customer. For the example, there are only four customers. For each customer, there is a record. The first 25 columns in the record contain the customer name followed by three fields that are 8 positions wide containing dollar values. The first numeric value is the old balance for the customer. The second numeric field is the amount of payment for the month for the customer, and the third numeric field is the amount purchased for the month.

For each customer, read in the name, the old balance, the payment, and the purchase amount for the month. Calculate the new balance for each customer, and print the customer number, the name, the old balance, the amount paid, the amount purchased, and the new balance. The first customer is customer 1, the second customer is customer 2, and so on. In addition, calculate and print the totals for the old balance and the new balance. Produce output in a report format.

A slash in the middle of a format statement causes the output to move to a new line to begin printing. More than one slash in the middle of a format statement or slashes at the beginning or end of a format statement cause a blank line or blank lines to appear in the output.

```
Corvette, Henry A.      1258.67 1000.00 1582.79      Example 6.10
Goodman, Kevin            31.16    8.20    4.15       Input
Jezak, Shane             411.37  311.37 1900.08
Kane, Kim                906.55  500.00  112.15
```

Example 6.10

```
$ EDIT EASYCHARG.FOR
      CHARACTER NAME*25
C
100   FORMAT('1',T22,'EASY CHARGE CREDIT REPORT',//,
     - ' ',T28,' APRIL 1983',///)
200   FORMAT(' ',T33,'OLD',T61,'NEW',/,' ',' NAME',T31,
     - 'BALANCE',T40,'PAYMENT',T49,'PURCHASE',T59,'BALANCE',/)
300   FORMAT(A,3F8.2)
400   FORMAT(/,' ',I1,1X,A,4(1X,F8.2))
500   FORMAT('0','TOTALS',T30,F8.2,T57,F8.2)
      WRITE(6,100)
      WRITE(6,200)
      DO NUMBERCUST = 1,4
         READ(5,300)NAME,OLDBAL,PAY,PURCHASE
         TOTALOLD = TOTALOLD + OLDBAL
         BALNEW = OLDBAL - PAY + PURCHASE
         TOTALNEW = TOTALNEW + BALNEW
         WRITE (6,400)NUMBERCUST,NAME,OLDBAL,PAY,PURCHASE,BALNEW
      END DO
      WRITE (6,500) TOTALOLD,TOTALNEW
      STOP
      END
$ FORTRAN EASYCHARG
$ LINK EASYCHARG
$ RUN EASYCHARG
```

Example 6.10
Output

EASY CHARGE CREDIT REPORT

APRIL 1983

NAME	OLD BALANCE	PAYMENT	PURCHASE	NEW BALANCE
1 Corvette, Henry A.	1258.67	1000.00	1582.79	1841.46
2 Goodman, Kevin	31.16	8.20	4.15	27.11
3 Jezak, Shane	411.37	311.37	1900.08	2000.08
4 Kane, Kim	906.55	500.00	112.15	518.70
TOTALS	2607.75			4387.35

■ Example 6.11: Generating Mailing Labels

If you have a set of data including names and addresses, you can create mailing labels. Probably the input data are stored in a disk file. Information about creating files is given in Chapter 3 and Appendix A. If your computer center has mailing label forms, you can request that the special forms paper be mounted and print the mailing labels on the appropriate forms.

Example 6.11
Input

```
         1         2         3         4         5        Column
12345678901234567890123456789012345678901234567890123456789012345678 Number

Bret Borman         205 Ocean Rd.     Arcata      CA94755
John Deer           8096 Western Hwy  Kansas CityKA34555
Fletcher Strong     110 Orange St.    Clemson     SC29631
```

Example 6.11

```
$ EDIT  MAILLABEL.FOR
        CHARACTER STUDENT*19,STREET*19,CITY*11,STATE*2,ZIP*5
100     FORMAT(5A)
200     FORMAT(' ',A,/,' ',A,/,' ',A,', ',A,5X,A,//)
        DO I = 1,3
           READ (5,100)STUDENT,STREET,CITY,STATE,ZIP
           WRITE(6,200)STUDENT,STREET,CITY,STATE,ZIP
        END DO
        STOP
        END
$ FORTRAN MAILLABEL
$ LINK MAILLABEL
$ RUN MAILLABEL
```

Example 6.11
Output

```
Bret Borman
205 Ocean Rd.
Arcata      , CA     94755


John Deer
8096 Western Hwy.
Kansas City, KA     34555


Fletcher Strong
110 Orange St.
Clemson     , SC     29631
```

■ Example 6.12: Reading an Unknown Number of Records

Some plants were used in an experiment. Each plant was treated with a different fertilizer. For each plant, the growth in inches after one month is recorded and the growth after two months is recorded. If the data are stored in a data file, you often do not know how many records are stored, so this program reads data until it reaches the End of File.

The program calculates the average growth over the two months for each plant. The program counts the number of plants for which there are data and calculates the overall average growth.

Example 6.12
Input

```
$ EDIT PLANTS.DAT
 1.7    2.3
 0.4    0.7
 2.1    1.4
 0.9    1.6
```

Example 6.12

```
$ EDIT GROWTH.FOR
100     FORMAT(' ',T15,'RESEARCH REPORT',//,
      - ' ',T20,'GROWTH',//,' ',T10,40('-'),//,
      - ' ',T12,'FIRST MONTH',T25,'SECOND MONTH',T40,'AVERAGE',//)
200     FORMAT('0','PLANT',I3,T15,F4.1,T28,F4.1,T41,F5.2)
300     FORMAT('0','PROJECT AVERAGE',T41,F5.2)
400     FORMAT(F4.1,3X,F4.1)
        OPEN(5,FILE='PLANTS.DAT',STATUS='OLD')
        WRITE (6,100)
        KOUNT = 0
        TOTAL = 0
10      READ(5,400,END=20)GROW1,GROW2
            KOUNT = KOUNT + 1
            PLANTTOTAL = GROW1 + GROW2
            TOTAL = TOTAL + PLANTTOTAL
            PLANTAVERAGE = PLANTTOTAL /2
            WRITE (6,200)KOUNT,GROW1,GROW2,PLANTAVERAGE
        GO TO 10
20      PROJECTAVERAGE = TOTAL / (KOUNT*2)
        WRITE (6,300)PROJECTAVERAGE
        CLOSE(5)
        STOP
        END
$ FORTRAN GROWTH
$ LINK GROWTH
```

```
$ RUN GROWTH                                          Example 6.12
                                                      Output
                    RESEARCH REPORT
                        GROWTH
         -------------------------------------------
                  FIRST MONTH   SECOND MONTH    AVERAGE

   PLANT   1         1.7           2.3          2.00

   PLANT   2         0.4           0.7          0.55

   PLANT   3         2.1           1.4          1.75

   PLANT   4         0.9           1.6          1.25

   PROJECT AVERAGE                              1.39
```

6.7
SUMMARY

When using alphanumeric character data in a computer program, the locations assigned to store the values must be defined to be CHARACTER locations. A CHARACTER declaration, which must appear before any executable statement in your program, specifies the symbolic name for the character string and the maximum number of characters that can occur in the string of characters.

FORMAT statements are used to specify the descriptions of data fields for input and output as well as carriage controls for output.

	READ(unit,statement-number)v1,v2,v3, . . . vn
statement-number	FORMAT(f1,f2,f3, . . . fn)

where f1, f2, etc., are the field descriptions for the values in v1, v2, etc., to be transferred into memory

	WRITE(unit,statement-number)v1,v2,v3, . . . vn
statement-number	FORMAT(carriage-control,f1,f2,f3, . . . fn)

Carriage Control
' ' blank	Print on the next line (single spacing)
'0' zero	Skip one line (double spacing)
'1' one	Start on a new page
'+' plus	Print on the same line as previous print
/	Skip to next line (requires a carriage control character to follow)

Field Descriptions

In	Integer value n digits wide
Fw.d	Real number w digits wide with d positions after the decimal point
nA	n occurrences of an alphanumeric field(s)
nX	n character positions to skip over
Tn	Positions next input or output at the specified column n

6.8
EXERCISES

6.1. For each of the following input records, write a READ statement and associated FORMAT statement to input the data and a WRITE statement with associated FORMAT statement to print the data with descriptive headings.

```
Column            1         2         3
Numbers    12345678901234567890123 4567890

           _____
Record 1     23.57    0.562     11      22
Record 2     2 4    67  876    38.97   2233   1
```

6.2. Write a FORTRAN program that will read in the following three records and print the records with descriptive headings.

```
Column            1         2         3         4
Numbers    1234567890123456789012345678901234567890

           _____
           Burt Reynolds      1983     9.7
           John Wayne         1970     6.2
           Clark Gable        1950    10.0
```

6.3. Write a FORTRAN program to input the following letter to Mom and print the letter. *Note:* You can declare the length for the CHARACTER string to be 80, the usual maximum length of a record, and read one record after another without regard for the actual number of characters in the line.

April 20, 1983

Dear Mom,

This is my first computer letter. I have stored all these records on a device called magnetic disk. Sometimes I put the records on cards. Anyway I can read the records with a FORTRAN program and print the records.

This is great!

Love,
Francis

6.4. The following data are stored in records as shown.

This is the
entire line.
And this is
another line.

Write a FORTRAN program to READ the data and print the following output.

This is the entire line.
And this is another line.

6.5. Write a FORTRAN program that will read in information for each of several salespeople. For each salesperson, read in a sales area, a sales amount, and a commission. For each salesperson, print the salesperson's number, the area, the sales, and the commission. In addition, calculate and print the average commission for the salespersons. Format all input and output. Include a report title for the year 1984. The district names are the first records in each set of data. Run the program with the following two sets of data.

Set 1			Set 2		
WEST DISTRICT			EAST DISTRICT		
624	5986.79	0.067	546	6722.15	0.059
578	9795.68	0.087	617	8922.11	0.099
343	9854.62	0.046	965	3427.78	0.035
578	6895.26	0.077	234	7634.25	0.042
777	6589.97	0.082			

6.6. Write a FORTRAN program for the following problem and print the results in a report format. Three candidates are running for office in the election in the Clemmons city election. The program should perform the necessary calculations and print a report including the name of each candidate, the number of votes received, and the percentage for each candidate of the total votes received. (*Note:* With the information covered to this point in the text, you need to write this program without a loop.) The following is the name and the number of votes for each candidate.

Steve Amos   423
Susan Dods   579
Jane Stone   62

7

Conditional Statements: IF Statements

A conditional statement in a computer program provides a programming structure for executing different sets of instructions based on the condition of some value or values stored in memory at the time that the instruction is executed.

7.1
SIMPLE IF STATEMENTS

The form of a simple IF statement is the following.

```
IF (condition) consequent statement
```

The condition is a comparison between two or more values. Examples 7.1 and 7.2 provide an introduction to IF statements.

■ Example 7.1: Simple IF Statements

```
$ EDIT IFPROGRAM.FOR                                    Example 7.1
      POINTS = 21.0
      IF (POINTS.GE.21.0) WRITE(6,*) 'GAME ENDED'
      IF (POINTS.LT.21.0) WRITE(6,*) 'PLAY MORE'
      STOP
      END
$ FORTRAN IFPROGRAM
$ LINK IFPROGRAM
$ RUN IFPROGRAM
GAME ENDED                                              Example 7.1
                                                        Output
```

The value 21 is stored in the memory location named POINTS in the first statement.

The characters between the parentheses in each IF statement provide a CONDITION for the statement.

IF (POINTS .EQ. 21.0) WRITE (6,*) 'GAME ENDED'

The CONDITION in the first IF statement is the following: (Is the value stored in the memory location named POINTS greater than or equal to the value 21.0). In this case, the value stored in location POINTS in the previous statement is indeed 21, and so the CONDITION is *true*. Since the CONDITION is true, the WRITE statement is executed and the characters GAME ENDED are printed.

IF (POINTS .LT. 21.0) WRITE (6,*) 'PLAY MORE'

The CONDITION in the second IF statement is the following: (Is the value stored in the memory location named POINTS less than 21). In this case, the value stored in the memory location named POINTS in the first

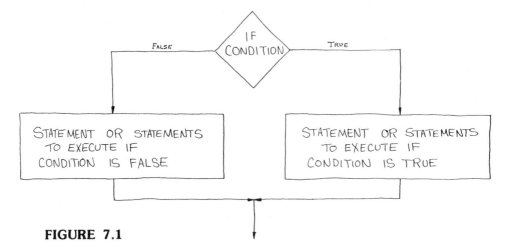

FIGURE 7.1

statement is 21 and that value has not changed. Since the value stored in location POINTS is not less than 21, the condition is *false,* and so the WRITE statement is not executed. The characters PLAY MORE are not printed.

The symbol for an IF statement in a flow chart is a diamond. If a condition is true, the flow of the program branches one way. If a condition is false, the flow of the program branches another way. The block IF structure covered later in this chapter allows an entire group of statements to be executed based on a condition at execution time. (See Figure 7.1.)

■ Example 7.2: Another Simple IF Statement

The following program inputs one value and stores the value in the memory location named POINTS. If the value that is stored in the memory location named POINTS is equal to 21, then the words GAME ENDED are printed. If the value stored in the memory location named POINTS is less than 21, then the words PLAY MORE are printed.

```
17                                                      Example 7.2
$ EDIT READIF.FOR                                       Input
        READ (5,*)  POINTS                              Example 7.2
        IF (POINTS.EQ.21.0) WRITE(6,*) 'GAME ENDED'
        IF (POINTS.LT.21.0) WRITE(6,*) 'PLAY MORE'
        STOP
        END
$ FORTRAN READIF
$ LINK READIF
$ RUN READIF                                            Example 7.2
PLAY MORE                                               Output
```

When the READ statement is executed in this example, the value 17 is provided as input. The value 17 is stored in the memory location named POINTS. Then the first IF statement is executed. Since the value stored in the location named POINTS is not equal to 21, the characters GAME ENDED are not printed. Then the second IF statement is executed. Since the value stored in the location named POINTS is indeed less than 21, the characters PLAY MORE are printed.

7.2
CONDITIONAL STATEMENT:
IF STATEMENT

DEFINITION: A FORTRAN IF *statement,* called a *conditional statement,* allows or prohibits the execution of some instruction or instructions based on whether the condition specified is *true* or *false.*

IF (condition) consequent statement

The condition specifies a comparison to be made between two or more values. The result of the comparison is either true or false. If the result is *true,* the consequent statement is executed. If the result is false, the consequent statement is not executed.

The primary *relational operators* are the following.

LT	Less than	GT	Greater than
EQ	Equal	NE	Not equal
LE	Less than or equal	GE	Greater than or equal

A condition can contain an *expression* or another *condition.* A condition may include compound conditions. The following are compound conditional operators.

AND   Adjoining conditions must be true.

OR   One condition of adjoining conditions must be true.
           Both conditions of adjoining conditions may be true.

XOR   The eXclusive OR allows one and only one of adjoining conditions to be true.

NOT   The opposite of the stated condition must be true.

Real values should be compared only with real values, and integer values should be compared only with integer values. Because of the way that data are stored in the computer, comparisons between real and integer values may produce erroneous results. (See Figure 7.2.)

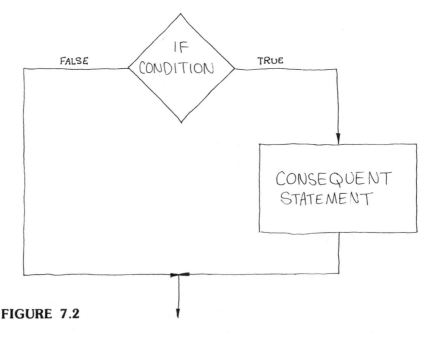

FIGURE 7.2

■ Example 7.3: Relational Operators

This program provides examples of relational operators. WRITE statements in the program are executed or are not executed based on whether or not the condition in the IF statement is true.

Example 7.3

```
$ EDIT OPERATE.FOR
       REAL INCOME
       INCOME =  350.00
       EXPENSE = 310.00
       FUNMONEY = INCOME - EXPENSE
       WISHMONEY = 100.00
       IF (INCOME.GT.EXPENSE) WRITE(6,*) 'MONEY LEFT OVER'
       IF (INCOME.LT.EXPENSE) WRITE(6,*) 'TROUBLE'
       IF (WISHMONEY.LE.FUNMONEY) WRITE(6,*) 'GREAT !!'
       IF (WISHMONEY.GE.FUNMONEY) WRITE(6,*) 'WISH FOR MORE'
       IF ((INCOME-EXPENSE).LT.(0.2 * INCOME))
     -     WRITE(6,*) 'SHOULD CUT EXPENSES'
       STOP
       END
$ FORTRAN OPERATE
$ LINK OPERATE
$ RUN OPERATE
MONEY LEFT OVER
WISH FOR MORE
SHOULD CUT EXPENSES
```

Example 7.3
Output

■ Example 7.4: Compound Conditions
in IF Statements

This program demonstrates the use of compound conditions in IF statements.

Example 7.4

```
$ EDIT COMPOUND.FOR
       NUMBER = 16
       IF (NUMBER.GT.10.AND.NUMBER.LT.15) WRITE(6,100)
100    FORMAT(' ',' .AND.   CONDITION IS TRUE')
       IF (NUMBER.LT.100.OR.NUMBER.GT.1000) WRITE(6,200)
200    FORMAT(' ',' .OR.    CONDITION IS TRUE')
       X = 7.8
       IF (.NOT.X.EQ.5.0) WRITE(6,300)
300    FORMAT(' ',' .NOT.   CONDITION IS TRUE')
       STOP
       END
$ FORTRAN COMPOUND
$ LINK COMPOUND
$ RUN COMPOUND
 .OR.    CONDITION IS TRUE
 .NOT.   CONDITION IS TRUE
```

Example 7.4
Output

■ Example 7.5: Character Comparisons

There is a collating sequence for characters, and so a program may sort names into alphabetical order. For purposes of comparisons, an A is less than B, B is less than C, and so on.

Particular characters in a character string can be specified by including the beginning and ending character positions in parentheses following the symbolic name for the character string. A colon is used to separate the beginning and ending character positions. The second through the fifth characters in an alphanumeric character string named SOMENAME could be accessed with the following: SOMENAME(2:5).

```
$ EDIT ALPHA.FOR                                            Example 7.5
        CHARACTER COMPARENAME*10,NAME1*10,NAME2*10
        COMPARENAME = 'JONES'
        NAME1 = 'SMITH'
        NAME2 = 'JONES'
        IF (NAME1.EQ.COMPARENAME) WRITE(6,100) NAME1
100     FORMAT('  ',A,' IS THE SAME AS COMPARENAME')
        IF (NAME2.EQ.COMPARENAME) WRITE(6,100) NAME2
        IF (NAME2(1:2).EQ.'JO') WRITE (6,200) NAME2(1:2)
200     FORMAT(' THE FIRST 2 CHARACTERS ARE ',A)
        IF ('A'.GT.'B')WRITE (6,300)
300     FORMAT( ' A IS GREATER THAN B IN THE COLLATING SEQUENCE')
        IF ('B'.GT.'A')WRITE (6,400)
400     FORMAT( ' B IS GREATER THAN A IN THE COLLATING SEQUENCE')
        IF ('ALEXANDER'.LT.'ZETWICK')WRITE(6,500)
500     FORMAT(' ','ALEXANDER',/,' ','ZETWICK')
        STOP
        END
$ FORTRAN ALPHA
$ LINK ALPHA
$ RUN ALPHA                                                 Example 7.5
JONES      IS THE SAME AS COMPARENAME                       Output
THE FIRST 2 CHARACTERS ARE JO
B IS GREATER THAN A IN THE COLLATING SEQUENCE
ALEXANDER
ZETWICK
```

■ Example 7.6: Selection

There are often some criteria that data must meet in order to be considered valid. If you are calculating the payroll for the local school district and you discover a pay rate of $300 an hour, you know that something is wrong. Before you write a program to perform data analysis, you might write a little program just to go through the data and print out any data values that seem to be out of a logical range for your project. You could print out the record number so that you would know where to look for the problem data.

Six months of monthly rainfall data have been collected. For each of the six months, a record contains the amount of rainfall in inches at the upstate

South Carolina weather station, the month name, and the year. Only the rainfall data values are used in this program, but it is always helpful to record data with all the relevant information, such as month and date in this case, so that you can figure out how to use the data again. If data are not well documented, it is almost impossible to use at a later time.

Amounts of rainfall less than 0.5 inches or greater than 8.0 inches should be checked for validity with the original data recorded at the weather station. The following program reads the six data records and prints out the data values that should be examined.

```
4.7        JAN    1982                                    Example 7.6
8.2        FEB    1982                                    Input
6.1        MAR    1982
5.7        APR    1982
Ø.1        MAY    1982
4.9        JUN    1982
$ EDIT CHECKDATA.FOR                                      Example 7.6
100        FORMAT(' DATA WHICH SHOULD BE CHECKED FOR ACCURACY')
200        FORMAT(' ',I3,2X,F4.1)
           WRITE(6,100)
           DO MONTH = 1,6
              READ (5,*)RAIN
              IF (RAIN.LT.Ø.5.OR.RAIN.GT.8.Ø)WRITE(6,200)MONTH,RAIN
           END DO
           STOP
           END
$ FORTRAN CHECKDATA
$ LINK CHECKDATA
$ RUN CHECKDATA                                           Example 7.6
DATA WHICH SHOULD BE CHECKED FOR ACCURACY                 Output
   2    8.2
   5    Ø.1
```

7.3
BLOCK IF STRUCTURE

There may be several operations that need to be performed if some condition is true. A block of statements can be executed based on the result of some condition.

```
IF (condition) THEN
    block of statements to execute if condition is true
END IF
```

The IF (condition) THEN must be in one statement alone. There must be at least one statement between the IF and the END IF statements. The END IF statement must be a statement alone. It is not necessary to indent the block of statements, but indentation improves readability. If the block of

FIGURE 7.3

statements is indented, you can immediately identify what will happen if the condition is true and these statements are executed. (See Figure 7.3.)

■ Example 7.7: Block Structured IF

The following program stores the value 87.0 in the memory locaton named GRADE. The condition in the IF statement compares the value in the memory location named GRADE to the value 70.00. Since the value in the memory location named GRADE is greater than 70.00, the condition is true. Since the condition is true, the statements between the IF statement and the END IF statement are executed.

```
$ EDIT IFBLOCK.FOR                          Example 7.7
      GRADE = 87.0
      IF (GRADE.GT.70.0) THEN
            WRITE (6,*)'PASSING'
            WRITE (6,*)'GOOD STUDENT'
      END IF
      STOP
      END
$ FORTRAN IFBLOCK
$ LINK IFBLOCK
$ RUN IFBLOCK                               Example 7.7
PASSING                                     Output
GOOD STUDENT
```

■ **Example 7.8: Boat Fee**

Needing additional revenue as usual, the legislature has imposed a luxury fee on all boats over 22 feet long. The fee is 2 percent of the value of the boat. The assessor needs a program to go through the records of boat owners and calculate the fee, and to print the names of owners of boats that exceed 22 feet and the fee to be paid by each.

Each data record contains the length of the boat, the value of the boat, and the name of the owner.

```
24    13678.68   Joe Edwards
15     7345.19   Shirley Grimes
16     5781.22   Don Livermore
23    12632.13   Tracey Logan
$ EDIT BOATFEE.FOR
        CHARACTER NAME*20
100     FORMAT(I2,2X,F9.2,A)
200     FORMAT(' ',A,F6.2)
        DO NOWNER = 1,4
           READ(5,100)LENGTH,VALUE,NAME
           IF (LENGTH.GT.22) THEN
              FEE = 0.02 * VALUE
              WRITE (6,200) NAME,FEE
           END IF
        END DO
        STOP
        END
$ FORTRAN BOATFEE
$ LINK BOATFEE
$ RUN BOATFEE
Joe Edwards          273.57
Tracey Logan         252.64
```

Example 7.8
Input

Example 7.8

Example 7.8
Output

7.4
IF THEN ELSE STRUCTURE

In many cases when a condition exists in a program, one block of statements should be executed if the condition is true and another block of statements should be executed if the condition is false. The IF THEN ELSE structure provides this capability.

IF (condition) THEN

    block of statements to execute if condition is true

ELSE

    block of statements to execute if condition is false

END IF

The IF(condition)THEN must be a statement alone. The END IF must be a statement alone. The ELSE must be a statement alone unless it is followed by another IF statement. Indentation of blocks of statements to be executed is not required, but it is best to indent the blocks. If you prefer to line up the THEN and the ELSE to emphasize the opposite conditions, you can use a line continuation marker in column 6 in the line following the IF statement and continue with the THEN printed on the following line.

```
IF (condition)
—   THEN
        block of statements to execute if condition is true
     ELSE
        block of statements to execute if condition is false
  END IF
```

■ Example 7.9: IF THEN ELSE structure

The following program simply stores the value 63.0 in the memory location named GRADE. The condition in the IF statement compares the value in the memory location named GRADE to the value 70.0. Since the value in the memory location named GRADE is not greater than 70.0, the condition is not true. Since the condition is false, the statement in the ELSE part of the structure is executed, printing the words NOT PASSING.

```
$ EDIT IFELSE.FOR                                    Example 7.9
      GRADE = 63.0
      IF (GRADE.GT.70.0) THEN
          WRITE (6,*)'PASSING'
        ELSE
          WRITE (6,*)'NOT PASSING'
      END IF
      STOP
      END
$ FORTRAN IFELSE
$ LINK IFELSE
$ RUN IFELSE                                         Example 7.9
NOT PASSING                                          Output
```

■ Example 7.10: Boat Tax

Taxes on boats might be based on the length of the boat. For boats that are less than or equal to 20 feet, the boat tax might be 1 percent of the value of the boat. For boats that are longer than 20 feet, the tax might be 1.5 percent. The following FORTRAN program reads boat data and determines if the boat is less than or equal to 20 feet. If the boat is less than 20 feet, the program calculates the tax of 1 percent and prints the owner's name and the tax;

otherwise, the program calculates the tax of 1.5 percent and prints the owner's name and the tax.

Each data record contains the length of the boat, the value of the boat, and the name of the owner.

```
24    13678.68   Joe Edwards                            Example 7.10
15     7345.19   Shirley Grimes                         Input
16     5781.22   Don Livermore
23    12632.13   Tracey Logan
$ EDIT BOATTAX.FOR                                      Example 7.10
        CHARACTER OWNER*20
100     FORMAT(I2,2X,F9.2,A)
200     FORMAT(' ',A,F6.2,'    BOAT IS LESS THAN OR EQUAL 20 FT.')
300     FORMAT(' ',A,F6.2,'    BOAT IS LONGER THAN 20 FT.')
        DO NOWNER = 1,4
            READ(5,100)LENGTH,VALUE,OWNER
            IF (LENGTH.LE.20) THEN
                    TAX = 0.01 * VALUE
                    WRITE (6,200)OWNER,TAX
                ELSE
                    TAX = 0.015 * VALUE
                    WRITE (6,300)OWNER,TAX
            END IF
        END DO
        STOP
        END
$ FORTRAN BOATTAX
$ LINK BOATTAX
$ RUN BOATTAX                                           Example 7.10
                                                        Output
Joe Edwards          205.18   BOAT IS LONGER THAN 20 FT.
Shirley Grimes        73.45   BOAT IS LESS THAN OR EQUAL 20 FT.
Don Livermore         57.81   BOAT IS LESS THAN OR EQUAL 20 FT..
Tracey Logan         189.48   BOAT IS LONGER THAN 20 FT.
```

7.5
COMPLEX IF THEN ELSE STRUCTURES

A block of statements to be executed in an IF THEN ELSE structure could contain another IF THEN ELSE structure.

```
IF (condition) THEN
        IF (condition) THEN
            block of statements
        ELSE
            block of statements
        END IF
    ELSE
        IF (condition) THEN
            block of statements
        ELSE
            block of statements
        END IF
END IF
```

This structure provides a powerful decision-making tool. Care must be taken to structure the IF's, ELSE's, and END IF's correctly. Example 7.21 contains an example of a complex IF THEN ELSE structure.

7.6
NESTED IF THEN ELSE STRUCTURES

Another form of the IF THEN ELSE statement allows the use of multiple ELSE statements to be associated with one primary IF statement and one END IF statement. The independence of an IF statement is determined by the necessity of an END IF statement to close the block.

```
IF (condition) THEN
     block of statements
   ELSE IF (condition) THEN
     block of statements
   ELSE IF (condition) THEN
     block of statements
END IF
```

In this structure, as soon as a condition is met, the block of statements immediately following is executed, and then the END IF is executed and the complete IF structure is exited.

■ Example 7.11: Nested IF Statements

For a group of children in grade levels 1 through 12, the following program assigns the student to elementary school, middle school, or high school.

```
 3  Carol Lowell                             Example 7.11
11  Gary Williamson                          Input
12  Loren Brown
 8  John Martinez
$ EDIT PICKSCHOL.FOR                         Example 7.11
       CHARACTER STUDENT*20,SCHOOL*17
100    FORMAT(I2,2X,A)
200    FORMAT(' ',2A)
       DO I = 1,4
          READ (5,100)LEVEL,STUDENT
          IF (LEVEL.LT.7) THEN
             SCHOOL = 'ELEMENTARY SCHOOL'
          ELSE IF (LEVEL.LT.10) THEN
             SCHOOL = 'MIDDLE SCHOOL'
          ELSE
             SCHOOL = 'HIGH SCHOOL'
          END IF
```

```
        WRITE (6,200)STUDENT,SCHOOL
        END DO
        STOP
        END
$ FORTRAN PICKSCHOL
$ LINK PICKSCHOL
$ RUN PICKSCHOL
Carol Lowell          ELEMENTARY SCHOOL
Gary Williamson       HIGH SCHOOL
Loren Brown           HIGH SCHOOL
John Martinez         MIDDLE SCHOOL
```

Example 7.11
Output

7.7
CASE STRUCTURE: ARITHMETIC
GO TO STATEMENT

The ARITHMETIC GO TO statement in the FORTRAN language provides a structure for transferring execution directly to a specified statement number (sn) based on whether the expression evaluates to a negative value, a zero value, or a positive value.

IF (expression) sn1, sn2, sn3

where execution transfers to
    sn1 if the value of the expression is negative
    sn2 if the value of the expression is zero
    sn3 if the value of the expression is positive

The statement is not a part of a structure that contains an exit and therefore in most cases requires GO TO statements to go around the statements that should not be executed; therefore, the ARITHMETIC GO TO statement is not used in structured programs.

■ Example 7.12: Arithmetic
GO TO Statement

The example program reads five values. For each value that is input, the arithmetic GO TO statement causes execution to transfer to statement 10 if the value is negative, statement 20 if the value is zero, or statement 30 if the value is positive. Observe the GO TO statements that are necessary to go around the inappropriate statements.

```
0
-4.5
6.3
-0.9
2.4
```

Example 7.12
Input

```
$ EDIT MATHGO.FOR                                    Example 7.12
      DO I = 1,5
         READ (5,*) VALUE
         IF (VALUE)10,20,30
10       WRITE (6,*) 'VALUE IS NEGATIVE', VALUE
         GO TO 40
20       WRITE (6,*) 'VALUE IS ZERO',VALUE
         GO TO 40
30       WRITE (6,*) 'VALUE IS POSITIVE',VALUE
40    END DO
      STOP
      END
$ FORTRAN MATHGO
$ LINK MATHGO
$ RUN MATHGO                                         Example 7.12
VALUE IS ZERO    0.0000000E+00                       Output
VALUE IS NEGATIVE    -4.500000
VALUE IS POSITIVE     6.300000
VALUE IS NEGATIVE    -0.9000000
VALUE IS POSITIVE     2.400000
```

A nested IF statement could be used instead of the arithmetic GO TO statement. The following example produces the same result as this example with a nested IF statement.

■ Example 7.13: An IF THEN ELSE Implementation of an Arithmetic GO TO Structure

Since an exit is not a part of the arithmetic GO TO structure, the arithmetic GO TO is not appropriate for use in most structured programs. This example provides the same capabilities for selecting a specific case as in Example 7.12; however, the IF THEN ELSE implementation in this example provides a systematic exit from the structure.

```
0                                                    Example 7.13
-4.5                                                 Input
6.3
-0.9
2.4
$ EDIT MATHGO.FOR                                    Example 7.13
      DO I = 1,5
         READ(5,*) VALUE
         IF (VALUE.LT.0.0)THEN
            WRITE (6,*) 'VALUE IS NEGATIVE', VALUE
         ELSE IF (VALUE.EQ.0.0) THEN
            WRITE (6,*) 'VALUE IS ZERO',VALUE
         ELSE
            WRITE (6,*) 'VALUE IS POSITIVE',VALUE
         END IF
      END DO
```

```
        STOP
        END
$ FORTRAN MATHGO
$ LINK MATHGO
$ RUN MATHGO
VALUE IS ZERO     0.0000000E+00
VALUE IS NEGATIVE   -4.500000
VALUE IS POSITIVE    6.300000
VALUE IS NEGATIVE   -0.9000000
VALUE IS POSITIVE    2.400000
```

Example 7.13
Output

7.8
CASE STRUCTURE: COMPUTED GO TO STATEMENT

Another form of a conditional GO TO statement is the *computed* GO TO statement. The computed GO TO statement causes execution to transfer to a specified statement number (sn) based on the value of an integer variable.

GO TO (sn1, sn2, sn3, ... snn), integervariable

Where execution transfers to
sn1 if the value of the integervariable is 1
sn2 if the value of the integervariable is 2
sn3 if the value of the integervariable is 3
.
.
.
snn if the value of the integervariable is n

■ Example 7.14: Computed GO TO

The example program calculates and prints the pay for a group of employees. The program reads the number of employees from the first record. The program then reads the three rates of pay. For this example pay rate 1 is 3.50. Pay rate 2 is 4.75. Pay rate 3 is 5.30.

The program goes through a DO loop for each employee. For each employee, the program reads the name, the code for the pay rate for the employee, and the number of hours worked. The code for the pay rate is a 1, 2, or 3, which corresponds to the three rates of pay that are entered with the second read statement in the program. The GO TO (10,20,30), KODEPAY causes execution to transfer to statement 10 if the value stored in the location named KODEPAY is equal to 1. If the value stored in the location named KODEPAY is equal to 2, execution transfers to statement 20. If the value stored in the location named KODEPAY is equal to 3, execution transfers to statement 30 and the appropriate description of the value is printed.

```
        3                                                   Example 7.14
        3.50, 4.75, 5.30                                    Input
        Keri Shayne          3     42.5
        Cindy Lowry          1     39.0
        Jim Johnson          2     41.2
        $ EDIT COMPUTEGO.FOR                                Example 7.14
                CHARACTER NAME*20
                WRITE (6,100)
                READ (5,*) NUMBER_OF_EMPLOYEES
                READ (5,*) RATE1,RATE2,RATE3
                DO I = 1, NUMBER_OF_EMPLOYEES
                    READ (5,50)NAME, KODEPAY,HOURS
                    GO TO (10,20,30), KODEPAY
        10          PAY = HOURS * RATE1
                    WRITE (6,200)NAME,RATE1,PAY
                    GO TO 40
        20          PAY = HOURS * RATE2
                    WRITE (6,200)NAME,RATE2,PAY
                    GO TO 40
        30          PAY = HOURS * RATE3
                    WRITE (6,200)NAME,RATE3,PAY
        40      END DO
        50      FORMAT(A,I1,F8.2)
        100     FORMAT(' ','NAME',T25,'RATE',T35,'PAY')
        200     FORMAT(' ',A,T23,F7.2,T33,F7.2)
                STOP
                END
        $ FORTRAN COMPUTEGO
        $ LINK COMPUTEGO
        $ RUN COMPUTEGO                                     Example 7.14
        NAME                     RATE        PAY            Output
        Keri Shayne              5.30        225.25
        Cindy Lowry              3.50        136.50
        Jim Johnson              4.75        195.70
```

7.9
APPLICATIONS

■ Example 7.15: Selecting Records with an IF Statement

A set of data for the nine entrants in the Walhalla road race is available. A research team is using the data to select all the runners who are over 25 years of age and who are nonsmokers for a research project. The researchers want a list of all the over-25 nonsmokers and a research project number for each. The first over-25 nonsmoking runner is runner 1, the second over-25 non-smoking runner is runner 2, and so on.

For input data, a Y or an N is stored in column 1 to indicate if the runner is a smoker or a nonsmoker, the age is stored in columns 3 and 4, and the name is stored in columns 6 to 25.

```
Y 24 Cindy Ballard                                    Example 7.15
N 25 Jim Blaton                                       Input
N 26 Aaron Cullins
N 28 Barbara Child
Y 26 John Cracken
N 31 Dan Frazier
Y 27 Mike Goddard
N 29 Lisa Melbourne
N 27 Amie Gosh
$ EDIT GETRUNERS.FOR                                  Example 7.15
      CHARACTER NAME*20,SMOKE*1
100   FORMAT(A,1X,I2,1X,A)
200   FORMAT(' ',I2,1X,A,I5)
      NUM_RUNNER = 0
      DO I = 1, 9
         READ (5,100)SMOKE,NAGE,NAME
         IF (NAGE.GT.25.AND.SMOKE.EQ.'N') THEN
            NUM_RUNNER = NUM_RUNNER + 1
            WRITE (6,200) NUM_RUNNER,NAME,NAGE
         END IF
      END DO
      STOP
      END
$ FORTRAN GETRUNERS
$ LINK GETRUNERS
$ RUN GETRUNERS                                       Example 7.15
 1 Aaron Cullins         26                           Output
 2 Barbara Child         28
 3 Dan Frazier           31
 4 Lisa Melbourne        29
 5 Amie Gosh             27
```

■ Example 7.16: IF THEN ELSE

A small company has a record for each of its three employees. For each employee, the record contains the employee name, the number of hours worked, and the rate of pay.

If the employee works 40 hours or fewer, the pay is calculated simply as the rate times the hours. If the employee works more than 40 hours, the pay for the hours over 40 are compensated at 1.5 times the base pay rate. The following FORTRAN program calculates and prints the base pay for each employee and the overtime pay for the employees working over 40 hours.

```
Carol Robards             46.5 11.20          Example 7.16
Edwin Martin              38.0  4.75          Input
John Williams             41.4  7.50
$ EDIT PAYIF.FOR                              Example 7.16
      CHARACTER NAME*25
100   FORMAT(A,2F6.2)
200   FORMAT(' ','NAME',T30,'BASE PAY',T40,'OVERTIME PAY'
300   FORMAT(' ',A,T30,F8.2,T40,F8.2)
      WRITE(6,200)
```

```
        DO I = 1,3
           READ(5,100)NAME,HOURS,RATE
           IF (HOURS.LE.40.0) THEN
              PAY = RATE * HOURS
              WRITE (6,300) NAME,PAY
           ELSE
              BASEPAY = RATE * 40
              OVERPAY = (HOURS-40.) * (RATE*1.5)
              WRITE (6,300) NAME, BASEPAY, OVERPAY
           END IF
        END DO
        STOP
        END
$ FORTRAN PAYIF
$ LINK PAYIF
$ RUN PAYIF
```

Example 7.16
Output

NAME	BASE PAY	OVERTIME PAY
Carol Robards	448.00	109.20
Edwin Martin	180.50	
John Williams	300.00	15.75

■ Example 7.17: Finding the Maximum Value in a Set of Data

It is often necessary to find the maximum value in a set of data values. For this example, four data values are stored one value per record. The procedure for finding the largest value is to first assume that the first value is the largest and then compare the next value with the largest value to that point. Anytime a compared value is larger than the recorded largest value, the largest value is replaced by the new largest value. At the end, the final recorded largest value is indeed the largest value.

The following is the algorithm for finding the largest value in a set of data values read one value per record.

Read the first value.

Set the maximum value to be the first value, because at this point the first value is the maximum value.

┌─► If there are more data values
│   Read next value
│   If this value is greater than the recorded largest value, then record the
└── largest value to be this value

Write the largest value

This procedure assumes that there is a unique largest value or that the first occurrence of multiple occurrences of the value that is the largest is found.

In most cases, a READ statement or an assignment statement should be outside the loop for establishing the first value for the initial comparison. If you set the largest value to be zero and all the values are negative numbers, then the largest value would be recorded as zero and that would be an incorrect result.

The flow chart in Figure 7.4 indicates the procedure for finding a maximum value.

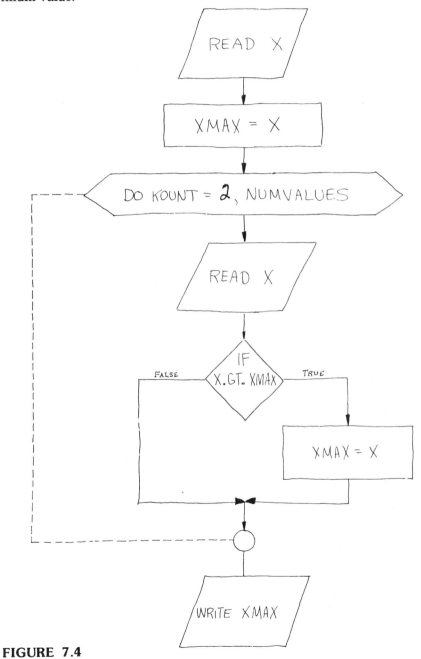

FIGURE 7.4

```
23.5                                                Example 7.17
39.8                                                Input
45.5
15.6
$ EDIT FINDMAX.FOR                                  Example 7.17
        READ (5,*) X
        XMAX = X
        DO NUMX = 2, 4
            READ (5,*) X
            IF (X.GT.XMAX) XMAX = X
        END DO
        WRITE (6,*) 'THE MAXIMUM VALUE IS ', XMAX
        STOP
        END
$ FORTRAN FINDMAX
$ LINK FINDMAX
$ RUN FINDMAX                                       Example 7.17
THE MAXIMUM VALUE IS          45.50000              Output
```

■ Example 7.18: Finding a Maximum Value and the Location of the Value in a Set of Values

In addition to finding the maximum value in a set of values, you may need to know which of the values was the maximum value. Perhaps there are six students in a class. A grade for each student is recorded. The following program finds the maximum grade for the class and the ID number for the student who has the maximum grade. In addition, the program writes out the count for the student who has the maximum grade.

Notice that the student ID number, a social security number, is stored as character data. Nine-digit integer numbers are too large to be stored as numeric values in single precision. Double precision is explained later in the text.

This program assumes that there is a unique maximum value. If there is more than one occurrence of the value that is the largest, the first occurrence of the largest value is recorded.

```
478234321 59                                        Example 7.18
348987621 73                                        Input
582123774 63
564392212 82
378987635 79
278653234 75
$ EDIT WHOMAX.FOR                                   Example 7.18
        CHARACTER ID*9,ID_FOR_MAX*9
        INTEGER GRADE
100     FORMAT(A,I3)
200     FORMAT(' ','STUDENT NUMBER ',I1,' ID ',A,' MAX GRADE ',I3)
        READ(5,100)ID,GRADE
        ID_FOR_MAX = ID
        MAX = GRADE
```

```
            NUMBER_STUDENT = 1
            DO NUMSTUD = 2, 6
               READ (5,100)ID,GRADE
               IF (GRADE.GT.MAX) THEN
                  MAX = GRADE
                  NUMBER_FOR_STUDENT = NUMSTUD
                  ID_FOR_MAX = ID
               END IF
            END DO
            WRITE (6,200) NUMBER_FOR_STUDENT, ID_FOR_MAX, MAX
            STOP
            END
      $ FORTRAN WHOMAX
      $ LINK WHOMAX
      $ RUN WHOMAX
      STUDENT NUMBER 4 ID 564392212 MAX GRADE  82
```

Example 7.18
Output

■ **Example 7.19: Finding the Minimum**
Value of the Values in a Record

In the previous two examples, a maximum value was found for values that were entered one after another on succeeding records. In the data for this example, there are three values for each record. The program selects the minimum value for each record.

For each of four students, there is a record containing the student's name and three scores. For each student, the program writes out the student's name and the minimum score that is determined.

```
Kallman, Chris       87 93 99
Morton, Terri        69 73 77
Revel, Keith         95 86 97
Zimmerman, Jane      89 80 82
```

Example 7.19
Input

```
      $ EDIT MINREC.FOR
            CHARACTER NAME*20
      100   FORMAT(A,3I3)
      200   FORMAT(' ',A,3I3,'   MINIMUM = ',I3 )
            DO NUMSTUD = 1,4
               READ(5,100)NAME,NSCORE1,NSCORE2,NSCORE3
               MIN = NSCORE1
               IF (NSCORE2.LT.MIN) MIN = NSCORE2
               IF (NSCORE3.LT.MIN) MIN = NSCORE3
               WRITE (6,200) NAME, NSCORE1,NSCORE2,NSCORE3,MIN
            END DO
            STOP
            END
      $ RUN MINREC
      Kallman, Chris       87 93 99  MINIMUM = 87
      Morton, Terri        69 73 77  MINIMUM = 69
      Revel, Keith         95 86 97  MINIMUM = 86
      Zimmerman, Jane      89 80 82  MINIMUM = 80
```

Example 7.19

Example 7.19
Output

The minimum values for each student could be found in the following way instead of as shown in the program. The value MIN is initialized to NSCOR1 in case there is not a unique minimum value.

```
      DO NUMSTUD = 1,4
          READ(5,100)NAME,NSCOR1,NSCOR2,NSCOR3
  —       MIN = NSCORE1
          IF (NSCOR1.LT.NSCOR2.AND.NSCOR1.LT.NSCOR3)
  —       MIN = NSCOR1
          IF (NSCOR2.LT.NSCOR1.AND.NSCOR2.LT.NSCOR3)
  —       MIN = NSCOR2
          IF (NSCOR3.LT.NSCOR1.AND.NSCOR3.LT.NSCOR2)
  —       MIN = NSCOR3
          WRITE (6,200) NAME, MIN
      END DO
```

Look at this another way. You can assume that NSCOR1 is less than NSCOR2 and NSCOR3. If this assumption is not correct, one of the conditions in the IF statements will be satisfied and the assumption will prove invalid; again correct output will be produced.

```
      DO NUMSTUD = 1,4
          READ(5,100)NAME,MIN,NSCOR2,NSCOR3
          IF (NSCOR2.LT.NSCOR1.AND.NSCOR2.LT.NSCOR3)
  —       MIN = NSCOR2
          IF (NSCOR3.LT.NSCOR1.AND.NSCOR3.LT.NSCOR2)
  —       MIN = NSCOR3
          WRITE (6,200) NAME, MIN
      END DO
```

■ **Example 7.20: Finding the Minimum Value for Each Record and the Minimum Value for a Set of Records**

If you knew that no grade could be less than zero, then you could set the minimum value to be zero and not have to use the initializing set of statements outside the DO loop. In this case you could probably do that, but it is always important to consider what might happen if someone made zero and had ten points taken off for some dreadful deed.

Taking care of the few odd possible occurrences takes a great deal of time in programming. When an error occurs in a program that has been working for a while, maybe an error in a bill from a utility company, it may be that one of the odd possible occurrences that the programmer didn't think about happened.

```
        Kallman, Chris      87 93 99                        Example 7.20
        Morton, Terri       69 73 77                        Input
        Revel, Keith        95 86 97
        Zimmerman, Jane     89 80 82
      $ EDIT MINCLASS.FOR                                   Example 7.20
              CHARACTER NAME*20
        100   FORMAT(A,3I3)
        200   FORMAT(' ',A,3I3,'  MINIMUM = ',I3)
        300   FORMAT(' ','CLASS MINIMUM',I3)
              READ(5,100)NAME,NSCORE1,NSCORE2,NSCORE3
              MIN = NSCORE1
              IF (NSCORE2.LT.MIN) MIN = NSCORE2
              IF (NSCORE3.LT.MIN) MIN = NSCORE3
              WRITE (6,200) NAME,NSCORE1,NSCORE2,NSCORE3, MIN
              MINCLASS = MIN
              DO NUMSTUD = 2,4
                 READ(5,100)NAME,NSCORE1,NSCORE2,NSCORE3
                 MIN = NSCORE1
                 IF (NSCORE2.LT.MIN) MIN = NSCORE2
                 IF (NSCORE3.LT.MIN) MIN = NSCORE3
                 WRITE (6,200) NAME,NSCORE1,NSCORE2,NSCORE3, MIN
                 IF (MIN.LT.MINCLASS) MINCLASS = MIN
              END DO
              WRITE (6,300) MINCLASS
              STOP
              END
      $ FORTRAN MINCLASS
      $ LINK MINCLASS
      $ RUN MINCLASS                                        Example 7.20
        Kallman, Chris      87 93 99  MINIMUM = 87          Output
        Morton, Terri       69 73 77  MINIMUM = 69
        Revel, Keith        95 86 97  MINIMUM = 86
        Zimmerman, Jane     89 80 82  MINIMUM = 80
        CLASS MINIMUM IS   69
```

7.10
PROBLEM SOLVING

Most problems require considerable analysis before it is possible to begin writing code for a computer program for the problem. A computer program for a realistic problem usually contains several interrelated structures or nested structures. Observe the approach to solving the problem in this example.

Programming concepts used in examples in the text can always be extended to your own field whatever it might be. The following example involves assigning seats in a plane for the smoking and nonsmoking sections of the plane; however, the concepts could apply equally to a medical research team who was assigning treatments to rats and putting rats on particular waiting lists for treatments, depending on the characteristics of each rat. The same kinds of assignments could be made in any field of application.

■ Example 7.21: Program Containing a Complex IF THEN ELSE Structure

A list of seat assignments for passengers on a small airplane is being made. There is a record for each passenger. The record includes a three-character field indicating whether the passenger wants a SMoKing seat or a NONsmoking seat. In addition, the record indicates whether the passenger will accept a SUBstitute seat in the section other than the preferred section or whether a SUBstitute is NOt acceptable. And the record includes the name of the passenger.

```
SMK SUBNO THOMPSON
NON SUB   JACKSON
```

There are five seats in the smoking section and five seats in the nonsmoking section of the plane. The program first checks to see if a seat is available in the section preferred by the passenger; if it is, the next available seat is assigned to the passenger. If there are no more seats in the preferred section, the program checks to see if the passenger would be willing to sit in the other section and if there is a seat available in the other section. If the passenger is willing to substitute and there is a seat available in the other section, the passenger is assigned the next available seat in the other section. If the passenger is unwilling to change sections or there are no more seats in the other section, the passenger is put on the waiting list for the preferred section.

You need to determine all the possibilities for assigning seats. It usually takes several trials before a problem is completely defined.

The following sets of questions could be asked of a passenger at the ticket counter; however, for this program the answers are prerecorded in the data records. One of the following sets of questions and answers is applicable for every passenger.

■ Possibility 1:

Do you want a nonsmoking seat?
yes
   Is a nonsmoking seat available?
   yes
      Add 1 to the count for nonsmoking seats and print the nonsmoking seat number and passenger name.

■ Possibility 2:

Do you want a nonsmoking seat?
yes
   Is a nonsmoking seat available?
   no
      Will you accept a substitute seat in the smoking section and is a seat available in the smoking section?   yes

Add 1 to the count for smoking seats and print the smoking seat number and passenger name.

■ **Possibility 3:**

Do you want a nonsmoking seat?

yes

Is a nonsmoking seat available?

no

Will you accept a substitute seat in the smoking section and is a seat available in the smoking section?

no

Add 1 to the count for the waiting list for nonsmoking seats and print the nonsmoking waiting list number and passenger name.

■ **Possibility 4:**

Do you want a nonsmoking seat?

no

Is a smoking seat available?

yes

Add 1 to the count for smoking seats and print the smoking seat number and passenger name.

■ **Possibility 5:**

Do you want a nonsmoking seat?

no

Is a smoking seat available?

no

Will you accept a substitute seat in the nonsmoking section and is a seat available in the nonsmoking section?

yes

Add 1 to the count for nonsmoking seats and print the nonsmoking seat number and passenger name.

■ **Possibility 6:**

Do you want a nonsmoking seat?

no

Is a smoking seat available?

no

Will you accept a substitute seat in the nonsmoking section and is a seat available in the nonsmoking section?

no

Add 1 to the count for the waiting list for smoking seats and print the smoking waiting list number and passenger name.

To put all these possibilities into a computer program, a relationship between the possibilities must be established in a way that can be represented in a program. The IF THEN ELSE structure provides the exact capability that is needed. The flow chart in Figure 7.5 indicates the possibilities for the program.

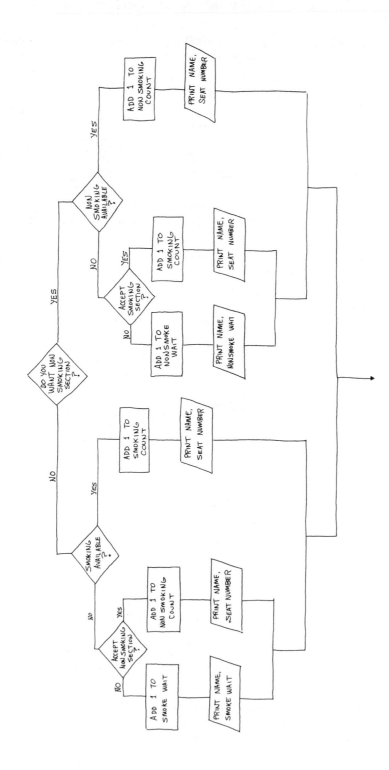

FIGURE 7.5

```
SMK SUBNO THOMPSON                                    Example 7.21
SMK SUB   JOHNSON                                     Input
NON SUBNO BROOKS
SMK SUB   PERIN
NON SUBNO HARDY
NON SUB   GARDNER
NON SUBNO ROLLINS
SMK SUBNO CARLIN
SMK SUB   JACKSON
SMK SUB   SANDERS
SMK SUBNO GREEN
NON SUBNO LATEN
$ EDIT PLANESEAT.FOR                                  Example 7.21
        CHARACTER NAME*10,SMOK_OR_NONSMOK*3,SUBSTUT*5
50      FORMAT(//,' ','WAITING',T50,'WAITING',/,' NON SMOKERS',
      - T18,'NON SMOKERS',T32,'SMOKERS',T50,'SMOKERS',/,' ',
      - T15,30('-') )
100     FORMAT(A,1X,A,1X,A)
200     FORMAT(' ',T15,'| ',I1,2X,A,T45,'|')
300     FORMAT(' ',I1,2X,A,T15,'|',T45,'|')
400     FORMAT(' ',T15,'|',T32,I1,2X,A,T45,'|')
500     FORMAT(' ',T15,'|',T45,'|',T49,I1,2X,A)
600     FORMAT(' ',T15,30('-') )
        WRITE (6,50)
        NUM_SMOK_SEATS = 5
        NUM_NONSMOK_SEATS = 5
        KNTSMOK = 0
        KNTSMOK_WAIT = 0
        KNTNON = 0
        KNTNON_WAIT = 0

        DO IPASSENGER = 1,12
           READ (5,100) SMOK_OR_NONSMOK, SUBSTUT, NAME
           IF (SMOK_OR_NONSMOK .EQ. 'NON' ) THEN
              IF (KNTNON .LT. NUM_NONSMOK_SEATS) THEN
                 KNTNON = KNTNON + 1
                 WRITE (6,200) KNTNON, NAME
              ELSE
              IF(SUBSTUT.EQ.'SUB'.AND.KNTSMK.LT.NUM_SMOK_SEATS)THEN
                 KNTSMOK = KNTSMOK + 1
                 WRITE (6,400) KNTSMOK, NAME
              ELSE
                 KNTNON_WAIT = KNTNON_WAIT + 1
                 WRITE (6,300) KNTNON_WAIT, NAME
              END IF
              END IF
           ELSE
              IF (KNTSMOK .LT. NUM_SMOK_SEATS) THEN
                 KNTSMOK = KNTSMOK + 1
                 WRITE (6,400) KNTSMOK, NAME
              ELSE
                 IF (SUBSTUT.EQ.'SUB'.AND.KNTNON.LT.NUM_NONSMOK_SEATS)THEN
                    KNTNON = KNTNON + 1
                    WRITE (6,200) KNTNON, NAME
                 ELSE
                    KNTSMOK_WAIT = KNTSMOK_WAIT + 1
                    WRITE (6,500) KNTSMOK_WAIT, NAME
                    END IF
                  END IF
              END IF
           END DO
           WRITE (6,600)
           STOP
```

```
        END
$ FORTRAN PLANESEAT
$ LINK PLANESEAT
$ RUN PLANESEAT
```

Example 7.21
Output

```
WAITING                                           WAITING
NON SMOKERS      NON SMOKERS    SMOKERS            SMOKERS

                              1 THOMPSON
                              2 JOHNSON
              1 BROOKS
                              3 PERIN
              2 HARDY
              3 GARDNER
              4 ROLLINS
                              4 CARLIN
                              5 JACKSON
              5 SANDERS
  1 LATEN                                        1 GREEN
```

7.11

SUMMARY

Conditional statements provide the capability in a program to execute different sets of instructions based on existing conditions as a program executes.

IF (condition) consequent-statement

IF the comparison between values in the *condition* is *true*, then the *consequent statement* is executed. IF the comparison between values in the *condition* is *false*, then the *consequent statement* is not executed.

The *relational operators* between individual values are the following:

LT   Less Than   GT   Greater Than
EQ   Equal   NE   Not Equal
LE   Less than or Equal   GE   Greater than or Equal

The following are *compound conditional operators:*

AND   Adjoining conditions must be true.
OR   One condition of adjoining conditions must be true.
       Both conditions of adjoining conditions may be true.
XOR   The eXclusive OR allows one and only one of adjoining conditions
       to be true.
NOT   The opposite of the stated condition must be true.

The IF THEN structure allows a block of statements to be executed if the condition in an IF statement is true.

```
    IF (condition) THEN
        block of statements to execute if the condition is true
    END IF
```

The IF THEN ELSE structure allows one block of statements to be executed if the condition in an IF statement is true or another block of statements to be executed if the condition is false.

```
IF (condition) THEN
    block of statements to execute if condition is true
ELSE
    block of statements to execute if condition is false
END IF
```

A block of statements inside an IF THEN or IF THEN ELSE structure could contain other IF structures or DO structures.

7.12
EXERCISES

7.1. What are the meanings of the following relational operators?

EQ _____   LE _____   GE _____
NE _____   LT _____   GT _____

7.2. Fill in each blank with the proper compound conditional operator that corresponds to the description of the operator.

AND   OR   XOR   NOT

_____ The opposite of the stated condition must be true.
_____ One condition of adjoining conditions must be true.
_____ One and only one of adjoining conditions must be true.
_____ Adjoining conditions must be true.

7.3. For each of the following conditions, write an IF statement.

a. If N equals zero, set X equal to 10.

b. If $A > B$, print A.

c. If $X > Y$ and $A < B$, set C equal to Z.

d. If $X > 0$, set Y equal to the square root of X.

7.4. What is the printed output for each of the following programs?

```
a.  X = 25.2
    Y = 16.3
    IF (X.EQ.Y)WRITE(6,*)'SAME'
    IF (X.GT.Y)WRITE(6,*)'X IS BIG'
    IF (X.LT.Y)WRITE(6,*)'Y IS BIG'
    IF ((Y + 10.2).GT.X)WRITE(6,*)'ADDS BIG'
    STOP
    END
```

b. N = 12
M = 10
IF ((N.GT.M) .AND. ((M + 5) .LT. 20)) WRITE(6,*)'AND TRUE'
IF ((M.GT.N) .OR. (N.GT.11)) WRITE (6,*)'OR TRUE'
STOP
END

c. DO I = 1,10
        IF (I GT.7) WRITE (6,*)I
END DO
STOP
END

d. DO I = 1,6
        READ (5,*)NUMBER
        IF (NUMBER.GT.10) KNT = KNT + 1
        END DO
        WRITE (6,*) KNT
        STOP
        END

This is the input data for problem d: 9, 14, 23, 6, 7, 19

7.5. A set of data records is available for books in the library. The first character field contains the type of book, fiction or nonfiction. The next field contains the year of publication. The third field contains the title. The following are some of the data records.

```
FICTION   1972 SUMMER MEMORIES
NONFICT   1980 CAMP FUN
NONFICT   1981 NUCLEAR ENERGY
NONFICT   1979 FISHING SPOTS
FICTION   1982 FISHING STORIES
FICTION   1981 THE BAND
```

Write a FORTRAN program that will generate a list of the books under the following headings.

FICTION		NONFICTION	
BEFORE 1980	1980–PRESENT	BEFORE 1980	1980–PRESENT

7.6. Write a program to generate a student registration listing for a small school. There are exactly 800 students in the school. Write a FORTRAN program to do the following. For each student, read a social security number, number of credit hours, and a code to indicate if tuition is paid late (code 1 = late, code 0 = on time). If the number of credit hours is less than 10, the fee per credit hour is $25 per hour. If the number of credit hours is greater than or equal to 10, the tuition is always $250. A late fee of 10 percent of the calculated tuition is added if the late code is 1. Write out the student's social security number and total tuition.

7.7. A manufacturing company makes three models of computer terminals. Model 1 costs $620. Model 2 costs $954. Model 3 costs $1282. There are currently in stock 220 model 1 terminals, 123 model 2 terminals, and 84 model 3 terminals.

Orders are placed for terminals. Each order record contains a model number, that is, a 1, 2, or 3. In addition, each record contains the quantity of terminals being ordered for that model and the name of the firm placing the order. The following are sample records.

```
3  15   Software House
3   6   Floeming Restaurant Supply
1   8   Clemson Marina
2  10   Mountain Power
```

Write a FORTRAN program that calculates the cost for each order and prints a report of the orders. In addition, the program should print an inventory record of the initial quantities and values of inventory and an updated inventory record following the processing of the orders.

7.8. For the following data entered one value per record, write the FORTRAN programs specified.

```
  13
   0
  -5
  23
  -2
 879
```

a. Find the maximum value in the set of data.

b. Find the minimum value in the set of data.

c. Find both the largest value and the second largest value.

d. Find the smallest value that is greater than zero.

7.9. For the following data entered three values per record, write the FORTRAN programs specified.

```
 16   -23   125
  0    210   111
-82     9   925
```

a. Find the maximum value for each record.

b. Find the minimum value for the entire set of data.

c. Find the minimum value greater than zero for the entire set of data.

d. Find the largest negative number for the entire set of data.

8

Structured Loops

A DO structure in the FORTRAN language provides a method for executing a block of statements repeatedly. There are two primary forms for the DO structure. One form causes a block of statements to be executed a specified number of times, and the other form causes a block of statements to be executed WHILE some condition is true. A DO loop structure that contains another DO loop is called a *nested* DO *loop.* There are many applications for nested DO loops. The DO WHILE structure is a combination of the looping capability of the DO loop along with the conditional capability of an IF statement.

8.1
NESTED DO LOOPS

The following DO structure, which is described in Chapter 5, provides a method for executing a block of statements a specified number of times.

```
DO ikount = ibegin, iend, istep

    block of statements to be executed

END DO
```

A block of statements inside a DO loop can contain another DO loop. A DO loop that contains one or more DO loops is called a nested DO loop.

```
DO ikount = ibegin, iend, istep
    DO jkount = jbegin, jend, jstep

        block of statements to be executed

    END DO
END DO
```

The inside loop is executed completely before execution returns to the outside loop. The counter for the outside loop is held constant while utilizing each of the values for the inside loop.

The following is the standard FORTRAN form for the nested DO structure. In this structure, inum is a statement number that delimits the outside loop, and jnum is a statement number that delimits the inside loop.

```
DO inum ikount = ibegin, iend, istep
    DO jnum jkount = jbegin, jend, jstep

        block of statements to be executed

jnum    CONTINUE
inum  CONTINUE
```

Because the nested DO structure is used in many applications, several examples are provided in this chapter.

■ Example 8.1: Nested Do Loop

This example demonstrates the order of processing for a nested DO loop. Observe that the inside loop is executed three times each time the outside loop is executed.

```
$ EDIT NESTDO.FOR                                    Example 8.1
      DO IOUTSIDE = 1,2
          WRITE (6,*) 'OUTSIDE LOOP    TOP'
          DO INSIDE = 1,3
              WRITE (6,*) 'INSIDE LOOP'
          END DO
```

```
                WRITE (6,*) 'OUTSIDE LOOP     BOTTOM'
            END DO
            STOP
            END
$ FORTRAN NESTDO
$ LINK NESTDO
$ RUN NESTDO
OUTSIDE LOOP     TOP
INSIDE LOOP
INSIDE LOOP
INSIDE LOOP
OUTSIDE LOOP     BOTTOM
OUTSIDE LOOP     TOP
INSIDE LOOP
INSIDE LOOP
INSIDE LOOP
OUTSIDE LOOP     BOTTOM
```

Example 8.1
Output

■ Example 8.2: Rows and Columns

It is often necessary to be able to represent index values for rows and columns. A nested DO loop provides an easy way to do this. For an example, a classroom might contain three rows with four seats per row. The seats are lined in columns.

ROW1	SEAT1	SEAT2	SEAT3	SEAT4
ROW2	SEAT1	SEAT2	SEAT3	SEAT4
ROW3	SEAT1	SEAT2	SEAT3	SEAT4

You can print a listing of the seats in the class by row with this program.

```
$ EDIT ROWSEAT.FOR                              Example 8.2
        DO IROW = 1,3
            WRITE (6,*) 'ROW',IROW
            DO ISEAT = 1,4
                WRITE (6,*)'SEAT    ',ISEAT
            END DO
        END DO
        STOP
        END
$ FORTRAN ROWSEAT
$ LINK ROWSEAT
$ RUN ROWSEAT                                    Example 8.2
ROW          1                                  Output
SEAT              1
SEAT              2
SEAT              3
SEAT              4
ROW          2
SEAT              1
SEAT              2
SEAT              3
```

(Continued)

(Continued)

```
SEAT                4
ROW             3
SEAT                1
SEAT                2
SEAT                3
SEAT                4
```

The general approach to accessing and printing rows across the page with implied DO loops is covered in Chapters 9 and 11.

■ Example 8.3: Row and Column Indexes

Instead of specifying a row and seat number, you often have need simply to specify a row and column number. For the situation in Example 8.2, with three rows each with four seats, the following index values represent the rows and columns.

```
1, 1    1, 2    1, 3    1, 4
2, 1    2, 2    2, 3    2, 4
3, 1    3, 3    3, 4    3, 5
```

You can print a vertical listing of the indexes for the seats in the class by row and column with this program.

```
$ EDIT ROWCOLUMN.FOR                          Example 8.3
100     FORMAT(' ',I1,',',I1)
        DO IROW = 1,3
            DO ISEAT = 1,4
                WRITE (6,100)IROW,ISEAT
            END DO
        END DO
        STOP
        END
$ FORTRAN ROWCOLUMN
$ LINK ROWCOLUMN
$ RUN ROWCOLUMN                               Example 8.3
1,1                                           Output
1,2
1,3
1,4
2,1
2,2
2,3
2,4
3,1
3,2
3,3
3,4
```

■ Example 8.4: Variable Nested DO Loops

Many applications require that the counter for an inside loop be controlled by a value outside the loop. The maximum count for the inside loop in this example is always the value of the counter for the outside loop.

```
$ EDIT VARYDO.FOR                                    Example 8.4
100     FORMAT(' ',I1,',',I1)
        DO KOUNTOUT = 2,4
            DO INSIDE = 1,KOUNTOUT
                WRITE (6,100)KOUNTOUT,INSIDE
            END DO
        END DO
        STOP
        END
$ FORTRAN VARYDO
$ LINK VARYDO
$ RUN VARYDO                                         Example 8.4
2,1                                                  Output
2,2
3,1
3,2
3,3
4,1
4,2
4,3
4,4
```

■ Example 8.5: Controlling the Number of Times a Process Occurs

This program READs the names and three scores for each of four students and calculates and prints the average for each student. For each student, there is a name stored in one record, and each of the three scores for the student is stored on succeeding records.

```
BOX, BARBARA                                         Example 8.5
88                                                   Input
67
92
CARR, KAREN
76
72
79
HARDING, REBA
92
87
91
```

```
        TERRELL, TOM
        85
        81
        87
        $ EDIT DOSCORE.FOR                                    Example 8.5
                CHARACTER NAME*20
        100     FORMAT(A)
        200     FORMAT(F3.0)
        300     FORMAT(' ',A,F5.1)
                DO ISTUDENT = 1,4
                    READ (5,100) NAME
                    TOTAL = 0
                        DO ISCORE = 1,3
                            READ (5,200) SCORE
                            TOTAL = TOTAL + SCORE
                        END DO
                    AVERAGE = TOTAL / 3.0
                    WRITE (6,300) NAME, AVERAGE
                END DO
                STOP
                END
        $ FORTRAN DOSCORE
        $ LINK DOSCORE
        $ RUN DOSCORE                                        Example 8.5
        BOX, BARBARA        82.3                             Output
        CARR, KAREN         75.7
        HARDING, REBA       90.0
        TERRELL, TOM        84.3
```

The outside loop contains the READ statement for the name, the statement to initialize the TOTAL for this student, the statement to calculate the average, and the WRITE statement, because each of those functions should occur only once for each student. The inside DO loop is executed three times, once for each of the three scores for the student.

Notice that the total must be set to zero for each student. Otherwise, the score would be accumulating for all the students. Try taking out the statement TOTAL=0 and observe the problem that occurs.

■ Example 8.6: Iterative Processing

DO loops provide an excellent structure for performing calculations repetitively based on the previous calculation. For this example, a teacher is trying to predict the final scores for students. In the past, a teacher has discovered that with succeeding exams the score for each student increases 5 percent. Based on the first exam score, the teacher has written this program to predict the final score.

Example 8.6
Input

```
69 Sandy Adams
75 Howard Caskill
63 Robert Jackson
```

```
   82 Pete Tucker
   79 Shirley Wilson
$ EDIT PREDICT.FOR                                    Example 8.6
        CHARACTER NAME*20
100     FORMAT(F3.0,1X,A)
200     FORMAT(' ',A,2I4)
        DO ISTUDENT = 1,5
           READ (5,100) SCORE, NAME
           PREDICT = SCORE
           DO JSCORE = 2,4
              PREDICT = PREDICT * 1.05
           END DO
           WRITE (6,200)NAME,INT(SCORE),INT(PREDICT)
        END DO
        STOP
        END
$ FORTRAN PREDICT
$ LINK PREDICT
$ RUN PREDICT                                         Example 8.6
Sandy Adams          69   79                          Output
Howard Caskill       75   86
Robert Jackson       63   72
Pete Tucker          82   94
Shirley Wilson       79   91
```

The output is printed as integers by using the INTeger intrinsic function.

8.2
DO WHILE STRUCTURE

The DO WHILE structure causes a block of statements to be executed repeatedly while a specified condition is true. The DO WHILE statement can be used with an associated statement number or without a statement number as shown.

```
        DO num WHILE(condition)      DO WHILE (condition)
           block of statements          block of statements
num     END DO                       END DO
```

The condition in a DO WHILE statement can be any condition as described in Chapter 7.

■ Example 8.7: DO WHILE

This example indicates the processing for a DO WHILE structure. In this example, the value KOUNT is being incremented in the DO loop. The DO loop continues to execute WHILE the value of KOUNT is less than 5. When the processing begins at the top of the loop for the fifth time and the condition is evaluated and determined to be false, the processing moves to the first statement following the END DO statement for the loop.

```
$ EDIT DOWHILE.FOR                                          Example 8.7
      KOUNT = 1
      DO WHILE (KOUNT .LT. 5)
         WRITE (6,*) 'KOUNT',KOUNT
         KOUNT = KOUNT + 1
      END DO
      STOP
      END
$ FORTRAN DOWHILE
$ LINK DOWHILE
$ RUN DOWHILE                                               Example 8.7
KOUNT        1                                              Output
KOUNT        2
KOUNT        3
KOUNT        4
```

■ Example 8.8: Iterative Processing with a DO WHILE Loop

The DO WHILE structure provides an excellent way to control processing while some condition exists. For this example, a person has a loan of $500. The monthly repayment plan is the following. The person should always pay 50 percent of the unpaid balance until the balance is less than $30. When the balance becomes less than $30, the person should pay the final payment of the entire unpaid balance. The program calculates and prints the payments that should be made.

```
$ EDIT LOAN.FOR                                             Example 8.8
100      FORMAT(' PAYMENT = ',F7.2)
         BALANCE = 500.00
         DO WHILE ( BALANCE .GT. 30.00)
            PAYMENT = 0.50 * BALANCE
            WRITE (6,100) PAYMENT
            BALANCE = BALANCE - PAYMENT
         END DO
         WRITE (6,100) BALANCE
         STOP
         END
$ FORTRAN LOAN
$ LINK LOAN
$ RUN LOAN                                                  Example 8.8
  PAYMENT =   250.00                                        Output
  PAYMENT =   125.00
  PAYMENT =    62.50
  PAYMENT =    31.25
  PAYMENT =    15.63
  PAYMENT =    15.63
```

Notice that the total repayment adds to $500.01. A penny was gained in the process. You should be aware that the computer cannot represent most floating-point numbers in exact form. Iterative processing, rounding, and truncating always provide some opportunity for error.

■ Example 8.9: A Flag for End of File

Often you do not know how many records are in a file. You may simply want to perform some processing until there are no more records in the file. For the final record in a file, you can insert a record that can be used as a FLAG to indicate that this is the final record, and then your program can check each time to determine if the current record is the final record.

For this example, the data values are all known to be positive. The data values are entered one value per record. To indicate to a program when the final data record is reached, you can insert a record that *flags* the program. In this example, the value −999 is inserted as the final record. The program continues to process records while the value in memory location named NUMBER is not equal to −999.

```
23                                                      Example 8.9
3478                                                    Input
999
1289
-999
$ EDIT FLAGNUM.FOR                                      Example 8.9
        READ (5,*) NUMBER
        DO WHILE (NUMBER .NE. -999)
            WRITE (6,*) NUMBER
            READ (5,*) NUMBER
        END DO
        STOP
        END
$ FORTRAN FLAGNUM
$ LINK FLAGNUM
$ RUN FLAGNUM                                           Example 8.9
        23                                              Output
        3478
        999
        1289
```

Notice the order of the READ and WRITE statements. The first READ statement is outside the DO WHILE loop. If there were only the flag record in the file, no numbers would be echoed. If the first record is a valid number, then the DO WHILE loop begins to execute and the record is echoed. Since the READ statement is the final statement in the loop, the processing immediately transfers to the top of the loop following the data input to determine if execution should continue in the loop or if the loop should be exited based on the input number.

■ Example 8.10: Input/Output Status

If an option such as the END clause covered in Example 5.9 or the IOSTAT clause in this example is not included in a READ statement, the program would terminate with an error if the program tries to read from a record after the end of the file has been reached. The IOSTAT clause can be included in a READ statement to return a code to a memory location indicating that a record was read successfully, that there was an input/output error, or that the end of file was reached. Including the IOSTAT clause allows processing to continue following an I/O error or an end of file.

IOSTAT is a key word in a READ statement. IOSTAT returns the status of the input operation each time the READ statement is executed and stores the status code in the integer variable with the symbolic name specified following the equal sign. The value of IOSTAT is zero if no error or no end of file is encountered. The value of IOSTAT is positive if an error occurs or negative if the end of file is encountered.

For this example, three names are entered, one name per record. The program contains a DO WHILE loop to READ and echo each record WHILE the status of the input returned by IOSTAT does not indicate that an error or an end of file occurred. The data would probably be stored in a data file. For this example, a file named THREENAME.DAT is created.

Example 8.10
Input

```
$ EDIT THREENAME.DAT
FOX
GEE
HAM
```

```
$ EDIT IOSTATUS.FOR                            Example 8.10
        OPEN(5,FILE='THREENAME.DAT',STATUS='OLD')
        READ (5,100,IOSTAT=IEND) NAME
        DO WHILE (IEND .EQ. 0)
           WRITE (6,200) NAME
           READ (5,100,IOSTAT=IEND) NAME
        END DO
100     FORMAT(A)
200     FORMAT(' ',A)
        STOP
        END
$ FORTRAN IOSTATUS
$ LINK IOSTATUS
$ RUN IOSTATUS                                 Example 8.10
FOX                                            Output
GEE
HAM
```

The first READ statement precedes the DO WHILE loop, setting an initial value for IEND for the condition in the DO WHILE loop. The value of the condition (IEND. EQ. 0) is evaluated at the beginning of the DO WHILE loop. If the value of IEND is indeed equal to zero, then the statements between the DO and the END DO are executed.

The statements in the DO WHILE loop continue to execute until the value in IEND is not equal to zero, and the value of IEND is set to a nonzero value when the end of file is encountered by a READ statement.

8.3
PROBLEM SOLVING

The following is an example of compound interest. For the example, assume that you make an investment of $100 at $2\frac{1}{2}$% interest compounded monthly. The following procedure is used to calculate the compound interest.

The original investment is 100.00.

Calculate the interest for the first month.
$100.00 * 0.025 = 2.50$

Add the interest for the first month to the 100.00 that you already had.
$100.00 + 2.5 = 102.50$

You now have 102.50. The next month you get more interest. This time the interest is calculated based on the amount you have after the first month.
$102.50 * 0.025 = 2.5625$

Add the interest for the second month to the 102.50 that you have.
$102.50 + 2.56 = 105.0625$

You now have 105.06. Calculate the interest for the third month.
$105.0625 * 0.025 = 2.62656$

Add the interest for the third month to the current balance.
$105.0625 + 2.62656 = 107.68906$

At the end of the third month, you have $107.69.

■ Example 8.11: Compound Interest

This example program performs the compound interest calculations described in Section 8.3. For an initial investment of $100.00, the program calculates the interest and the value of the investment for an interest rate of 2.5% compounded monthly for three months.

```
$ EDIT COMPOUND.FOR                                    Example 8.11
100     FORMAT(' ','MONTH',I3,'  INTEREST',F7.2,'
        CURRENTVALUE = 100.00
        DO MONTH = 1,3
           AMOUNTINTEREST = CURRENTVALUE * 0.025
           CURRENTVALUE = CURRENTVALUE + AMOUNTINTEREST
           WRITE (6,100)MONTH,AMOUNTINTEREST,CURRENTVALUE
        END DO
```

```
        STOP
        END
$ FORTRAN COMPOUND
$ LINK COMPOUND
$ RUN COMPOUND                                              Example 8.11
MONTH  1  INTEREST    2.50  CURRENT VALUE 102.50           Output
MONTH  2  INTEREST    2.56  CURRENT VALUE 105.06
MONTH  3  INTEREST    2.63  CURRENT VALUE 107.69
```

■ Example 8.12: Another Way to Calculate Compound Interest

This example program calculates the value of an investment as interest is compounded and added to the previous value of the investment. For an initial investment of $100.00, the program calculates the value of the investment for an interest rate of 2.5% compounded monthly for three months.

The difference between this program and the program in Example 8.11 is that the previous program calculates the interest earned each month as a separate value, which can be printed, and this program simply calculates the current value of the investment.

```
$ EDIT COMPOUND1.FOR                                       Example 8.12
100     FORMAT(' ','MONTH',I3,'  CURRENT VALUE',F7.2)
        CURRENTVALUE = 100.00
        DO MONTH = 1,3
            CURRENTVALUE = CURRENTVALUE * 1.025
            WRITE (6,100) MONTH,CURRENTVALUE
        END DO
        STOP
        END
$ FORTRAN COMPOUND1
$ LINK COMPOUND1
$ RUN COMPOUND1                                            Example 8.12
MONTH  1  CURRENT VALUE 102.50                             Output
MONTH  2  CURRENT VALUE 105.06
MONTH  3  CURRENT VALUE 107.69
```

■ Example 8.13: Prime Numbers

This program determines and prints all the prime numbers between 1 and 300. A number is prime if it has no factors except 1 and itself. For example, the number 13 is prime because no number other than the number 13 itself and the number 1 can be an even divisor of 13.

$$1 \overline{\smash{)}13} \quad \frac{13}{} \qquad 13 \overline{\smash{)}13} \quad \frac{1}{}$$

One way to determine if a number has factors other than 1 and itself is to divide by successive numbers from 2 through the square root of the number.

If there is a remainder on each division, it means that no division comes out even and, hence, there are no factors. If there is an instance of a zero remainder, the number is not prime.

$$2\,\overline{\smash{\big)}\,13} \qquad 3\,\overline{\smash{\big)}\,13} \qquad 4\,\overline{\smash{\big)}\,13}$$

Obviously, no even number other than 2 is prime. Even numbers could be eliminated from consideration in the outside DO loop by using the increment feature of the DO loop. Furthermore, it is unnecessary to test division by even numbers, because all multiples of even numbers are in turn even numbers, and even numbers other than 2 are not prime. This is controlled in the inside loop.

The MOD library function returns the remainder of an integer division.

M = MOD(27, 4)   The remainder of 27 divided by 4 is stored in the memory location named M. In this case the value 3 is stored in M.

L1 = 21
L2 = 7
L3 = MOD(L1, L2)   In this example, when the division is performed in the MOD function, there is a 0 remainder, so the value zero is stored in memory location L3. Since there is at least one number that divides evenly into 21, the number 21 is *not* a prime number.

The number 1 is a unique number and the numbers 2 and 3 can be assumed to be prime and printed without a mathematical test.

Example 8.13

```
$ EDIT PRIME.FOR
100     FORMAT(' ','PRIME NUMBERS BETWEEN 1 AND 300',//)
200     FORMAT(10X,I3)
        WRITE (6,100)
        WRITE (6,200)1
        WRITE (6,200)2
        WRITE (6,200)3
        DO NUM = 5,300,2
            IDIVIDE = 1
            IMOD = 1
            MAX = SQRT(FLOAT(NUM)) + 1
            DO WHILE (IDIVIDE.LT.MAX)
                IDIVIDE = IDIVIDE + 2
                IMOD = MOD(NUM,IDIVIDE)
                IF (IMOD.EQ.0) IDIVIDE = MAX
            END DO
            IF (IMOD.NE.0) WRITE (6,200) NUM
        END DO
        STOP
        END
$ FORTRAN PRIME
$ LINK PRIME
```

```
$ RUN PRIME                                          Example 8.13
                                                     Output
PRIME NUMBERS BETWEEN 1 AND 300
```

```
                1
                2
                3
                5
                7
               11
               13
               17
               19
               23
                :
                :
              269
              271
              277
              281
              283
              293
```

It is simple to write an integer remainder formula, since this formula is all carried out in integer arithmetic.

Example:
$N = 37$
$M = 6$
Leftover $= N - (N/M*M)$

$37 - (37/6)*6$
$37 - 6*6$
$37 - 36$
Leftover $= 1$ indicates that 6 is not a factor of 37

8.4
APPLICATIONS

■ Example 8.14: Interest Table

An investment counselor needs to produce an investment table to show to clients. The counselor would like to show returns for investments held for six months with the interest compounded monthly. The value of investments from $1000 to $10,000 at intervals of $1000 should be shown for monthly interest rates of 1%, 2%, and 3%.

Example 8.14

```
$ EDIT INTEREST.FOR
100     FORMAT(' ',T20,'HOMETOWN INVESTMENT COMPANY')
200     FORMAT(/,' ',T22,'COMPOUND INTEREST TABLE',//,' ',
       - T13,'INTEREST COMPOUNDED MONTHLY FOR SIX MONTHS',/)
```

```
300       FORMAT(' ',T16,'RETURN AT',T36,'RETURN AT',T56,'RETURN AT',
   -    /,' ','INVESTMENT',T19,'1%',T39,'2%',T59,'3%',/,' ',T15,
   -    'INTEREST RATE',T35,'INTEREST RATE',T55,'INTEREST RATE',/)
400       FORMAT(' ',2X,'$',I5,T18,I5,T38,I5,T58,I5)
          WRITE (6,100)
          WRITE (6,200)
          WRITE (6,300)
          DO INVEST = 1000, 10000, 1000
              RETURN1 = INVEST
              RETURN2 = INVEST
              RETURN3 = INVEST
              DO MONTH = 1, 6
                  RETURN1 = RETURN1 * 1.01
                  RETURN2 = RETURN2 * 1.02
                  RETURN3 = RETURN3 * 1.03
              END DO
              WRITE (6,400)INVEST,INT(RETURN1),INT(RETURN2),INT(RETURN3)
          END DO
          STOP
          END
$ FORTRAN INTEREST
$ LINK INTEREST
$ RUN INTEREST
```

Example 8.14
Output

HOMETOWN INVESTMENT COMPANY

COMPOUND INTEREST TABLE

INTEREST COMPOUNDED MONTHLY FOR SIX MONTHS

INVESTMENT	RETURN AT 1% INTEREST RATE	RETURN AT 2% INTEREST RATE	RETURN AT 3% INTEREST RATE
$ 1000	1061	1126	1194
$ 2000	2123	2252	2388
$ 3000	3184	3378	3582
$ 4000	4246	4504	4776
$ 5000	5307	5630	5970
$ 6000	6369	6756	7164
$ 7000	7430	7883	8358
$ 8000	8492	9009	9552
$ 9000	9553	10135	10746
$10000	10615	11261	11940

■ Example 8.15: Using the IOSTAT Clause in a READ Statement and a DO WHILE Loop to Input Data and Process to the End of File

Taxes on boats might be based on the length of the boat. The tax rate for boats that are less than 20 feet long is 1 percent. The tax rate for boats that are 20 feet or longer is 1.5 percent. This example accepts records of boat owners as input and calculates and prints a tax table for output.

The data file named BOATDATA.DAT contains information about boat owners. For each owner, a record contains the length of the boat, the value of the boat, and the owner's name.

```
$ TYPE BOATDATA.DAT                                        Example 8.15
24   13678.68 Joe Edwards                                  Input
15    7345.19 Ami Indiana
16    5781.22 Chris Kallman
23   12632.13 Tracey Logan
$ EDIT BOATTAX.FOR                                         Example 8.15
        CHARACTER OWNER*20
        OPEN(5,FILE='BOATDATA.DAT',STATUS='OLD')
        WRITE (6,100)
        READ(5,200,IOSTAT=IEND)LENGTH,VALUE,OWNER
        DO WHILE (IEND.EQ.0)
           IF (LENGTH.LE.20) THEN
              TAX = 0.01 * VALUE
              WRITE(6,300)OWNER,VALUE,TAX
           ELSE
              TAX = 0.015 * VALUE
              WRITE (6,400)OWNER,VALUE,TAX
           END IF
           READ(5,200,IOSTAT=IEND)LENGTH,VALUE,OWNER
        END DO

100     FORMAT(' ',T46,'UNDER',T56,'20 FEET',/,
      - ' ','OWNER',18X,'VALUE',6X,'TAX',T45,'20 FEET',T55,'OR LONGER')
200     FORMAT(I2,2X,F9.2,A)
300     FORMAT(' ',A,2F9.2,T48,'X')
400     FORMAT(' ',A,2F9.2,T60,'X')

        STOP
        END
$ FORTRAN BOATTAX
$ LINK BOATTAX
$ RUN BOATTAX                                              Example 8.15
                                                           Output
```

OWNER	VALUE	TAX	UNDER 20 FEET	20 FEET OR LONGER
Joe Edwards	13678.68	205.18		X
Ami Indiana	7345.19	73.45	X	
Chris Kallman	5781.22	57.81	X	
Tracey Logan	12632.13	189.48		X

Description of Example 8.15. The program reads the first record. The IOSTAT clause in the READ statement is used to determine when there are no more data records to be input.

READ(5,200,IOSTAT = IEND)LENGTH,VALUE,OWNER

IOSTAT is a key word in a READ statement. IOSTAT returns the status of the input operation each time the READ statement is executed and stores the status code in the variable with the symbolic name IEND. The value of IOSTAT is zero if no error or no end of file is encountered. The value of IOSTAT is negative if the end of file is reached.

DO WHILE(IEND.EQ.0)

Then the program executes the DO WHILE loop to calculate the tax, print an output tax record, and READ another record WHILE the status of the input returned by IOSTAT does not indicate that an end of file occurred.

Observe that the IF THEN ELSE structure is inside the DO WHILE structure. The READ statement is the last statement in the DO WHILE structure. When the end of file is reached and the value of IOSTAT stored in variable IEND is not zero, no more statements in the DO WHILE loop will be executed.

■ Example 8.16: Contributions — A Good Problem in Logic

A community group is keeping records for a project to raise money to build a community park. It is necessary that the group keep contribution records for each individual contributor for tax purposes. Each contribution is entered in one data record along with the name of the contributor. One person may make several contributions, and all the contributions for one person are in succeeding data records.

The logic for this problem is difficult to develop without careful consideration. It is necessary to save a contributor's name. If the next contributor has the same name as the one just read in, add the contribution for this contributor to the total for this person. If the name of the new contributor is different from the name of the last one, the total for the last contributor should be written out, and the information about the new contributor should be used to initialize memory locations. It is necessary to consider the end of the data. After there are no more contributors, the last contributor's total should be printed and the grand total printed.

```
NEWHOUSE   56.                                         Example 8.16
NEWHOUSE   5.                                           Input
NEWHOUSE   2.
FILLMORE   16.
FILLMORE   9.
JENNINGS   4.
JENNINGS   27.5
JENNINGS   19.75
DYSART     6.5
CARDIN     15.2
CARDIN     6.8
NOMORE
$ EDIT  PARKFUND.FOR                                    Example 8.16
        CHARACTER THISDONOR*1Ø, DONOR*1Ø
100     FORMAT(A,F1Ø.2)
```

```
200     FORMAT(1X,A,F10.2)
300     FORMAT(' GRAND TOTAL ',F10.2)
400     FORMAT(' ID   CONTRIBUTION')
        WRITE (6,400)
        GRANDTOTAL = 0
        READ(5,100) THISDONOR, THISCONTRIBUTION
        DONOR = THISDONOR
        CONTRIBUTION = 0
        DO WHILE (THISDONOR .NE. 'NOMORE')
            IF (THISDONOR .EQ. DONOR) THEN
                CONTRIBUTION = CONTRIBUTION + THISCONTRIBUTION
            ELSE
                GRANDTOTAL = GRANDTOTAL + CONTRIBUTION
                WRITE (6,200) DONOR, CONTRIBUTION
                DONOR = THISDONOR
                CONTRIBUTION = THISCONTRIBUTION
            END IF
            READ (5,100) THISDONOR, THISCONTRIBUTION
        END DO
        WRITE (6,200) DONOR, CONTRIBUTION
        GRANDTOTAL = GRANTOTAL + CONTRIBUTION
        WRITE (6,300) GRANDTOTAL
        STOP
        END
$ FORTRAN PARKFUND
$ LINK PARKFUND
$ RUN PARKFUND
ID   CONTRIBUTION
NEWHOUSE       63.00
FILLMORE       25.00
JENNINGS       51.25
DYSART          6.50
CARDIN         22.00
GRAND TOTAL    167.75
```

Example 8.16
Output

■ Example 8.17: A Natural Resources Problem

The Lupine Forest was declared a wilderness area 4 years ago. A forestry researcher is studying the accuracy of the district's population predictions for the four years following the wilderness declaration.

In 1980, at the time when the forest was declared a wilderness area, a count of the number of animals for several species was conducted. At that time, the yearly percentage of population increase was estimated for each species. At the end of 1984, an actual population count was conducted.

The researcher has written the following program to produce a report on the animals in the wilderness area. The program first READs a data record that contains the number of animals in the project. Then, for each of the species, the program inputs a name, the 1980 population, the predicted yearly percentage of increase, and the 1984 population. For each species, the program calculates the predicted population for 1984 and prints the 1980 population, the percentage of increase predicted, the predicted population, the 1984 population, and the difference between the predicted population and the actual 1984 population. The ABSsolute value of the difference is printed using the ABSolute intrinsic function. If the actual population is greater than the predicted population, the program prints the word OVER. If the actual population is less than the predicted population, the program prints the word UNDER. In addition, the total number of animals in 1980, the total of the predicted number of animals for 1984, and the actual number of animals for 1984 are calculated and printed.

```
   8                                                      Example 8.17
BEARS      224 .02 268                                    Input
CAYOTE     610 .05 820
DEER       420 .04 600
EAGLES      30 .01  32
ELK         97 .01  92
FOXES       68 .02  60
RABBIT    3050 .105020
WOLVES      79 .01  93
```

```
$ EDIT ANIMALS.FOR                                        Example 8.17
        CHARACTER ANIMAL*8,OVERUNDER*5
        INTEGER POPULATION80,POPULATION84
100     FORMAT('0',T31,'LUPINE DISTRICT',//,' ',1X,T21,
      - 'ANALYSIS OF POPULATION PREDICTION',//,1X,T32,
      - '1980 - 1984',//)
200     FORMAT(' ',
      -         T13,'P                   P F        P             A',
      - /, ' ',T13,'O     P   I     P O O        O        D   P N',
      - /, ' ',T13,'P 1   R Y N     R P R      A P 1    I B R D',
      - /, ' ',T13,'U 9   E E C     E U        C U 9    F E E',
      - /, ' ',T13,'L 8   D A R     D L 1      T L 8    E T D A',
      - /, ' ',T13,'A 0   I R E     I A 9      U A 4    R W I C',
      - T57,'O   U')
201     FORMAT(
      -         ' ',T13,'T     C L A     C T 8      A T      E E C T',
      - T57,'V O U',
      - /, ' ',T13,'I     T Y S     T I 4      L I      N E T U',
      - T57,'E R D',
      - /, ' ',T13,'O     E E     E O        O        C N E A',
      - T57,'R   E',
      - /, ' ',T13,'N     D         D N          N      E   D L',T61,'R',
      - /, ' ',T13,'----  -----   ------     ------   -------',
      - T57,'------',/)
300     FORMAT(I3)
400     FORMAT(A,I4,F4.2,I4)
500     FORMAT(' ',A,T12,I4,T22,I2,'%',T30,I4,T39,I4,T47,I4,T57,A)
600     FORMAT('0',T11,I5,T29,I5,T38,I5)
        WRITE (6,100)
        WRITE (6,200)
        WRITE (6,201)
        TOTAL80 = 0
        TOTAL84 = 0
        TOTALPREDICT = 0
        READ (5,300) NUMBERANIMALS
```

```
      DO 10 I = 1, NUMBERANIMALS
         READ (5,400)ANIMAL,POPULATION80,PERCENTPREDICT,POPULATION84
         TOTAL80 = TOTAL80 + POPULATION80
         TOTAL84 = TOTAL84 + POPULATION84
         PREDICT = POPULATION80
         DO 20 IYEAR = 81,84
            PREDICT = PREDICT + PREDICT * PERCENTPREDICT
20       CONTINUE
      TOTALPREDICT = TOTALPREDICT + PREDICT
      PERCENT = PERCENTPREDICT * 100
      DIFERENCE = POPULATION84 - PREDICT
      IF (DIFERENCE .GT.0) THEN
         OVERUNDER = 'OVER'
      ELSE IF (DIFERENCE .LT. 0) THEN
         OVERUNDER = 'UNDER'
      END IF
      IF (ABS(DIFERENCE) .LT. 1) OVERUNDER = '       '
      WRITE (6,500)ANIMAL,POPULATION80,INT(PERCENT),INT(PREDICT),
    -             POPULATION84,INT(ABS(DIFERENCE)),OVERUNDER
10    CONTINUE
      WRITE (6,600)INT(TOTAL80),INT(TOTALPREDICT),INT(TOTAL84)
      STOP
      END
$ FORTRAN ANIMALS
$ LINK ANIMALS
$ RUN ANIMALS
```

Example 8.17
Output

                    LUPINE DISTRICT

              ANALYSIS OF POPULATION PREDICTION

                       1980 - 1984

P				P F	P		A	
O	P	I	P O O	O	D	P N	
P 1	R Y N	P R	A P 1	I B R D	
U 9	E E C	R P U	C U 9	F E E	
L 8	D A R	E U	T L 8	E T D A	
A 0	I R E	D L 1	U A 7	R W I C	O U
T	C L A	I A 9	A T	E E C T	V O N
I	T Y S	C T 8	L I	N E T U	E R D
O	E E	T I 4	O	C N E A	R E
N	D	E O	N	E D L	R
BEARS	224	2%	242	268	25	OVER
CAYOTE	610	5%	741	820	78	OVER
DEER	420	4%	491	600	108	OVER
EAGLES	30	1%	31	32	0	
ELK	97	1%	100	92	8	UNDER
FOXES	68	2%	73	60	13	UNDER
RABBIT	3050	10%	4465	5020	554	OVER
WOLVES	79	1%	82	93	10	OVER

                     4578   6228   6985

8.5
SUMMARY

A NESTED DO LOOP allows the statements in the inside DO LOOP to execute repeatedly for each time through the outside DO LOOP.

The standard FORTRAN 77 nested DO loop can be used.

```
          DO inum ikount = ibegin, iend, istep
               DO jnum jkount = jbegin, jend, jstep
                    block of statements to be executed
jnum          CONTINUE
inum     CONTINUE
```

The VAX extension for the nested DO loop without statement numbers can be used.

```
          DO ikount = ibegin, iend, istep
               DO jkount = jbegin, jend, jstep
                    block of statements to be executed
               END DO
          END DO
```

The DO WHILE structure provides a loop structure that executes while some condition is true.

The DO WHILE structure is a common extension to FORTRAN 77.

```
          DO num WHILE (condition)
               block of statements
num     CONTINUE
```

```
          DO WHILE (condition)
               block of statements
          END DO
```

The IOSTAT option in a READ statement allows data to be input from a file until there is no more data to input. The READ statement is usually used in association with a DO WHILE loop to read to the end of file.

```
          READ(unitnum,formatnum,IOSTAT = integername)variable-list
```

```
          DO num WHILE(integername.eq.0)
               READ(unitnum,formatnum,IOSTAT = integername)variable-list
num     CONTINUE
```

The IOSTAT option in a READ statement returns the status of the input operation each time the READ statement is executed and stores the status code in the location represented by the symbolic integername following the equal sign. The value of IOSTAT is zero if no error or no end of file is encountered. The value of IOSTAT is positive if an error occurs or negative if the end of file is encountered.

The statements in the DO WHILE loop will continue to execute until the value in the symbolic integername is not equal to zero, and that value will be set to a negative value when the end of file is encountered in a READ statement.

It is important to note that rounding errors occurred in printing the integer values for the predicted number of animals; however, a decimal value would be inappropriate for the number of animals. Such problems must often be considered in developing a program. Rounding errors should be explained in a report or presentation of computer output.

8.6
EXERCISES

8.1. Write a FORTRAN program to print the number of cents in a nickel and to print the number of cents for five nickels. An example of the expected output is the following.

```
1     cent
2     cent
3     cent
4     cent
5     cent
1     nickel
1     cent
2     cent
⋮     ⋮
```

8.2. What is the output for each of the following FORTRAN programs? The best way to keep track of the value in each memory location as the program executes is to draw a box for each memory location represented by a symbolic name in the program and then to record what value would be stored in that location as you step through the program as the computer would.

```
a.      DO 10 IOUTSIDE = 1, 2        b.  DO I = 1, 4
            DO 20 INSIDE = 1, 3             DO J = 1, 2
                WRITE (6,*) 'DO LOOP'            WRITE (6,*)I,J
    20      CONTINUE                        END DO
    10  CONTINUE                        END DO
        STOP                            STOP
        END                             END
```

c. DO ITIMES = 1,5
    DO I = ITIMES,ITIMES + 3
      WRITE (6,*)ITIMES,I
    END DO
  END DO
  STOP
  END

d. DO KOUNT = 2, 4
    KTOT = KOUNT
    DO L = KOUNT, 5
      KTOT = KTOT + L
    END DO
    WRITE (6,*)KTOT
  END DO
  STOP
  END

8.3. A company has seven districts. Each district has five stores. Write a FORTRAN program to input sales and to calculate and print the average sales for each district. The data records are created with the total sales for one store in one record, and all five store records for one district are together. The following is part of the data for the districts.

40,000 ⎫
50,000 ⎪
30,000 ⎬   five stores in district 1
20,000 ⎪
10,000 ⎭
60,000 ⎫
40,000 ⎬
30,000 ⎭   five stores in district 2
 ⋮

The output for the program should be somewhat like the following.

DISTRICT 1 AVERAGE 30000
DISTRICT 2 AVERAGE   ⋮
   ⋮   ⋮   ⋮   ⋮

8.4. It is not known how many districts a company has and it is not known how many stores are in each district, but the total sales for each store in each district are recorded in a record that contains the sales data and the name of the district. Write a FORTRAN program to calculate and write the total sales for each district along with the district name. In addition, calculate and write the total sales for the company. The following are the data for the program. All the sales for one district are together record after record.

25,000 EASTERN   21,800 MOUNTAIN
13,005 EASTERN   48,762 PACIFIC
26,000 EASTERN   69,876 PACIFIC
32,500 CAROLINAS
18,670 CAROLINAS

8.5. There are five nominees to an agricultural extension and research position. The two primary categories for considering the nominees are extension work and research. Extension work contains two subcategories, teaching and fieldwork. Research includes three subcategories, theoretical research, applied research, and papers published. Each applicant is scored in each subcategory by the selection committee. The applicant who gets the job is the one who has the highest average between the research and extension categories. The extension category average is determined by adding the two scores and dividing by 2. The research category average is determined by adding the three scores and dividing by 3. Write a FORTRAN program to analyze the data and select the successful candidate. Use nested DO loops for data input and analysis. The data are stored one record after another as shown. The following would be the data for the first two candidates.

ALFREDO

8	Teaching
7	Fieldwork
3	Theoretical research
5	Applied research
4	Papers published

BARRON

5	Teaching
4	Fieldwork
4	Theoretical research
6	Applied research
4	Papers published

Calculations for Alfredo

$$8 + 7 = 15$$

$$3 + 5 + 4 = 12$$

$$\frac{7.5}{2\,|\,15} \qquad \frac{4}{3\,|\,12}$$

$$\frac{5.75}{2\,|\,7.5 + 4}$$

8.6. A mathematical series that is produced by summing the two preceding terms is the Fibonacci series. The first two elements of the series are 1 by definition. The following are the first eight terms of the series.

1	1	2	3	5	8	13	21	34	55
		$1+1$	$1+2$	$2+3$	$3+5$	$5+8$	$8+13$	$13+21$	$21+34$

a. Write a FORTRAN program to calculate and print the first 50 integers in the Fibonacci series.

b. Write a FORTRAN program to calculate and print the first 50 elements of the real numbers that are the inverse of the Fibonacci series. These numbers should be calculated and printed as the decimal equivalent of the values.

$$\frac{1}{1} = 1 \qquad \frac{1}{1} = 1 \qquad \frac{1}{2} = 0.5 \qquad \frac{1}{3} = 0.33 \qquad \frac{1}{5} = 0.2 \qquad \frac{1}{8} = \ldots$$

c. The quotient of successive terms in the Fibonacci series converges to the value 0.618. Write a FORTRAN program to demonstrate through 50 elements of the series the convergence of the series.

$\frac{1}{1}$	$\frac{1}{2}$	$\frac{2}{3}$	$\frac{3}{5}$	$\frac{5}{8}$	$\frac{8}{13}$	$\frac{13}{21}$	$\frac{21}{34}$	$\frac{34}{55}$
	0.50	0.666	0.600	0.625	0.615	0.619	0.618	0.618

8.7. A car dealer finances the automobiles that are sold. The dealer has three different interest rates. The interest rate on new cars sold is 12% annually. The interest rate on used cars is 18% annually. The interest rate on demonstration cars is 14% annually. Write a FORTRAN program to input for each car sold the selling price and the status of the car and to calculate and print the interest costs for a period of three years. The following data might be used.

```
 3,250.78    USED
 4,938.22    DEMO
12,698.55    NEW
 9,213.45    NEW
 2,896.77    USED
```

An Introduction to One-Dimensional Arrays

For many computing purposes, it is efficient to read one record and perhaps perform calculations and print out a result before reading the next record. This method of computing is used in Chapters 1 to 8. It is often necessary, however, to be able to store all of a set of data values in memory at one time in order to perform calculations or comparisons based on a summary of the data. Data can be stored in a FORTRAN structure called an *array*. The array structure provides an efficient way for storing and accessing large amounts of data with a computer program.

9.1
WHEN AN ARRAY IS NECESSARY

After a little experience with arrays, you will find that the array structure simplifies most programming problems. Most programs are written with arrays because large programs are easy to write with arrays and because it is easy to document and to read programs with arrays.

For some problems, arrays provide the only practical approach for writing a program. Look at the program in Example 9.1, which indicates a need for an array. The programs in Examples 9.2 and 9.3 indicate the way that data are accessed in an array, and then Example 9.4 provides the first practical program with an array.

■ Example 9.1: Assigning Student Scores

A teacher's grade book usually has a row of numbers down the side. By each number, there is a name, followed by one or more scores for the student. A grade book might look like the following.

```
GRADE BOOK
1   Adams, Kenny      70
2   Cain, Carolyn     80
3   Carr, Kevin       60
4   Miller, Mindy     80
5   Zimes, Zeke       60
```

If you refer to student 1, you refer to Kenny Adams. If you refer to student 2, you refer to Carolyn Cain. If you refer to student 5, you refer to Zeke Zimes.

This program assigns the score for each student to a memory location with the symbolic name of STUDENT, followed by the number of the student, and calculates the average for the class. Then the program compares each score with the class average and writes out the student number and score for each student whose score is greater than the average class score.

The important thing to note about this program is that you must have the score for each student in memory after the average is calculated in order to perform the comparisons with the average score. Each score must have a memory location assigned to it. If there were 30 students in the class, you would need to have 30 pairs of statements to READ the score and add the score to the total and another statement for each student to make the comparison with the average score.

The purpose of this program is to demonstrate the need for an array and to clarify what is happening in Example 9.2, which performs exactly the same function as this program except that Example 9.2 contains an array.

```
$ EDIT ASSIGN.FOR                              Example 9.1
        TOTAL = 0
        STUDENT1 = 70
        TOTAL = TOTAL + STUDENT1
        STUDENT2 = 80
        TOTAL = TOTAL + STUDENT2
        STUDENT3 = 60
        TOTAL = TOTAL + STUDENT3
        STUDENT4 = 80
        TOTAL = TOTAL + STUDENT4
```

```
        STUDENT5 = 60
        TOTAL = TOTAL + STUDENT5
        AVERAGE = TOTAL / 5.0
        WRITE (6,*) ' THE AVERAGE IS ',AVERAGE
        IF (STUDENT1.GT.AVERAGE) WRITE(6,*) '1',STUDENT1,' ABOVE AVE'
        IF (STUDENT2.GT.AVERAGE) WRITE(6,*) '2',STUDENT2,' ABOVE AVE'
        IF (STUDENT3.GT.AVERAGE) WRITE(6,*) '3',STUDENT3,' ABOVE AVE'
        IF (STUDENT4.GT.AVERAGE) WRITE(6,*) '4',STUDENT4,' ABOVE AVE'
        IF (STUDENT5.GT.AVERAGE) WRITE(6,*) '5',STUDENT5,' ABOVE AVE'
        STOP
        END
$ FORTRAN ASSIGN
$ LINK ASSIGN
$ RUN ASSIGN                                        Example 9.1
 THE AVERAGE IS      70.00000                       Output
2   80.00000      ABOVE AVE
4   80.00000      ABOVE AVE
```

■ Example 9.2: Assigning Student Scores to an Array

This example uses an array to perform exactly the same function as Example 9.1.

GRADE BOOK

1	Adams, Kenny	70
2	Cain, Carolyn	80
3	Carr, Kevin	60
4	Miller, Mindy	80
5	Zimes, Zeke	60

In the teacher's grade book, the score for student 1 is 70, the score for student 2 is 80, and the score for student 5 is 60.

An array can be set up to store each score for the students. An *array* is a group of memory locations that have a common name and are accessed by specifying the number for the particular location in the array. For this example, the array is named STUDENT. The score for student 1 is stored in loca-

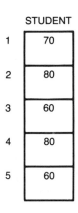

FIGURE 9.1

tion 1 in the array. The score for student 2 is stored in location 2 in the array, and so on. (See Figure 9.1.)

The array is set up in memory by a DIMENSION statement in a FORTRAN program. The way that the program accesses a particular element of an array is with a subscript specifying the particular location in the array. STUDENT(1) references the first score in the array named STUDENT, that is, the value 70. STUDENT(3) references the third score in the array named STUDENT, that is, the value 60.

Look at the example program, which assigns the score for each student to a memory location in the array named STUDENT and calculates the average for the class. Then the program compares each score stored in the array named STUDENT with the class average and writes out the student number and score for each student whose score is greater than the average class score.

```
$ EDIT ASIGNARAY.FOR                                    Example 9.2
      DIMENSION STUDENT(5)
      TOTAL = 0
      STUDENT(1) = 70
      TOTAL = TOTAL + STUDENT(1)
      STUDENT(2) = 80
      TOTAL = TOTAL + STUDENT(2)
      STUDENT(3) = 60
      TOTAL = TOTAL + STUDENT(3)
      STUDENT(4) = 80
      TOTAL = TOTAL + STUDENT(4)
      STUDENT(5) = 60
      TOTAL = TOTAL + STUDENT(5)
      AVERAGE = TOTAL / 5.0
      WRITE (6,*) ' THE AVERAGE IS ',AVERAGE
      IF (STUDENT(1).GT.AVERAGE) WRITE(6,*) '1',STUDENT(1),' ABOVE AVE'
      IF (STUDENT(2).GT.AVERAGE) WRITE(6,*) '2',STUDENT(2),' ABOVE AVE'
      IF (STUDENT(3).GT.AVERAGE) WRITE(6,*) '3',STUDENT(3),' ABOVE AVE'
      IF (STUDENT(4).GT.AVERAGE) WRITE(6,*) '4',STUDENT(4),' ABOVE AVE'
      IF (STUDENT(5).GT.AVERAGE) WRITE(6,*) '5',STUDENT(5),' ABOVE AVE'
      STOP
      END
$ FORTRAN ASIGNARAY
$ LINK ASIGNARAY
$ RUN ASIGNARAY                                          Example 9.2
 THE AVERAGE IS     70.00000                             Output
2    80.00000      ABOVE AVE
4    80.00000      ABOVE AVE
```

9.2
DEFINITION OF AN ARRAY

An *array* is a group of related storage locations that have the same symbolic name. A DIMENSION statement sets aside a group of memory locations to be used with one variable name and to be accessed with a location number called a *subscript* or *index* number. A DIMENSION statement declares the number of memory locations that should be made available to the program as it executes. You may declare that more locations than are actually used be allocated. Since you are allocating memory that subsequently cannot be used for other operations, you should estimate the size of your array with only a reasonable amount of overflow from the expected number of elements. The DIMENSION statement, like other declarations, must precede all executable FORTRAN statements in the program. (See Figure 9.2.)

```
DIMENSION ARRAYNAME (3)
```

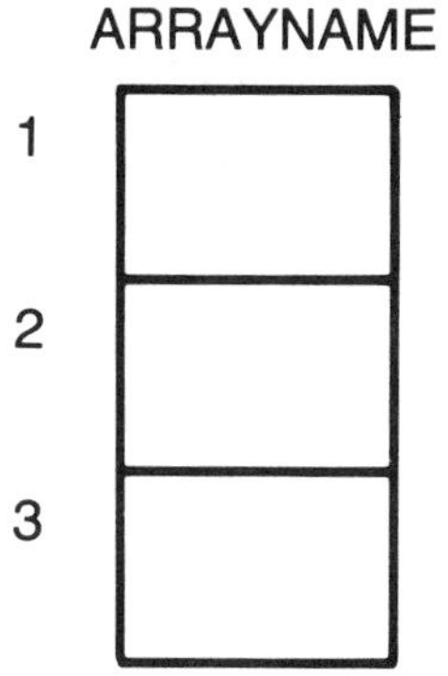

FIGURE 9.2

An element of the group is accessed by the use of the number that designates its location within the group. The numbers that represent the location in the array are called index numbers or subscripts. The variables in the array are called *subscripted variables*.

As always, a computer can reference only one memory location at one time. The subscript number is used to specify the one memory location that is being accessed.

Arrays can contain data types that are normally used in FORTRAN programs, including integer, real, and character data.

You can declare that 1000 memory locations be set aside for a particular array and you may use only 500 of the locations. You may never, however, use more locations than you have declared; the locations will not be available at execution time. If you try to access an array element beyond the bounds of the DIMENSION declaration, the program produces an error when it executes. This is one of the most common errors that occurs as a program executes. For instance, the following program segment would produce an error.

```
DIMENSION X(10)
X(11) = 44.5                        An execution error would
                                                    occur.
```

■ Example 9.3: Reading Student Scores into an Array

This example performs exactly the same function as Example 9.2 except that the data values are READ into the array named STUDENT instead of the values being assigned to the memory locations.

GRADE BOOK

1	Adams, Kenny	70
2	Cain, Carolyn	80
3	Carr, Kevin	60
4	Miller, Mindy	80
5	Zimes, Zeke	60

In the teacher's grade book, student 1 is Kenny Adams, student 2 is Carolyn Cain, etc.

In this example, the DIMENSION statement establishes an array named STUDENT, which allocates space for storing the student grades.

This program READs the score for each student into a memory location in the array named STUDENT and calculates the average for the class. Then the program compares each score stored in the array named STUDENT with the class average and writes out the student number and score for each student whose score is greater than the average class score.

For this example and Example 9.4, the student data are stored in the following way. For each student, a record includes the score for the student in columns 1 to 3, and the name follows the score. The name is not used.

```
70   Adams, Kenny                                        Example 9.3
80   Cain, Carolyn                                       Input
60   Carr, Kevin
80   Miller, Mindy
60   Zimes, Zeke
$ EDIT READARAY.FOR                                      Example 9.3
      DIMENSION STUDENT(5)
      TOTAL = 0
      READ (5,*) STUDENT(1)
      TOTAL = TOTAL + STUDENT(1)
      READ (5,*) STUDENT(2)
      TOTAL = TOTAL + STUDENT(2)
      READ (5,*) STUDENT(3)
      TOTAL = TOTAL + STUDENT(3)
      READ (5,*) STUDENT(4)
      TOTAL = TOTAL + STUDENT(4)
      READ (5,*) STUDENT(5)
      TOTAL = TOTAL + STUDENT(5)
      AVERAGE = TOTAL / 5.0
      WRITE (6,*) ' THE AVERAGE IS ',AVERAGE
      IF (STUDENT(1).GT.AVERAGE) WRITE(6,*) '1',STUDENT(1),' ABOVE AVE'
      IF (STUDENT(2).GT.AVERAGE) WRITE(6,*) '2',STUDENT(2),' ABOVE AVE'
      IF (STUDENT(3).GT.AVERAGE) WRITE(6,*) '3',STUDENT(3),' ABOVE AVE'
      IF (STUDENT(4).GT.AVERAGE) WRITE(6,*) '4',STUDENT(4),' ABOVE AVE'
      IF (STUDENT(5).GT.AVERAGE) WRITE(6,*) '5',STUDENT(5),' ABOVE AVE'
      STOP
      END
```

```
$ FORTRAN READARAY
$ LINK READARAY
$ RUN READARAY
  THE AVERAGE IS      70.00000
2   80.00000      ABOVE AVE
4   80.00000      ABOVE AVE
```

Example 9.3
Output

Description of the Execution of Example 9.3. When the first READ statement is executed, the value 70 is transferred into location 1 in the array named STUDENT. (See Figure 9.3.)

As each READ statement is executed, the input value is stored in the location in the array that is specified by the subscript value. Then each value is available throughout the execution of the program.

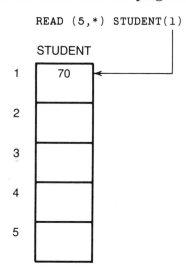

FIGURE 9.3

9.3
ACCESSING THE ELEMENTS OF AN ARRAY WITH A DO LOOP

A DO loop provides a structure for accessing the elements in an array one after another. Most often, a DO loop and an array are used together. The index value for the counter in the DO loop may be used as the subscript for an array.

DO kount = 1, number_elements_in_array

    array(kount)

■ **Example 9.4: Accessing an Array in a DO Loop**

Example 9.3 indicates the method for declaring and accessing an array. The purpose of this example is to demonstrate specifically how the subscripts are used to access the individual locations in an array. Refer to Example 9.3 to clarify the function of this example, because the two programs perform exactly the same function.

This program READs the score for each student into a memory location in the array named STUDENT and calculates the average for the class. Then the program compares each score stored in the array named STUDENT with the class average and writes out the student number and score for each student whose score is greater than the average class score.

```
70   Adams, Kenny                                              Example 9.4
80   Cain, Carolyn                                             Input
60   Carr, Kevin
80   Miller, Mindy
60   Zimes, Zeke
$ EDIT DOARRAY.FOR                                            Example 9.4
      DIMENSION STUDENT(5)
      TOTAL = 0
      DO NUM = 1,5
         READ (5,*) STUDENT(NUM)
         WRITE(6,*)'STUDENTNUMBER',NUM,' SCORE IS',STUDENT(NUM)
         TOTAL = TOTAL + STUDENT(NUM)
      END DO

      AVERAGE = TOTAL / 5.0
      WRITE (6,*) ' THE AVERAGE IS ',AVERAGE

      DO N = 1,5
         IF(STUDENT(N).GT.AVERAGE) WRITE(6,*)N,STUDENT(N),' ABOVE AVE'
      END DO

      STOP
      END
$ FORTRAN DOARRAY
$ LINK DOARRAY
$ RUN DOARRAY                                                 Example 9.4
STUDENT NUMBER        1    SCORE IS    70.00000               Output
STUDENT NUMBER        2    SCORE IS    80.00000
STUDENT NUMBER        3    SCORE IS    60.00000
STUDENT NUMBER        4    SCORE IS    80.00000
STUDENT NUMBER        5    SCORE IS    60.00000
 THE AVERAGE IS     70.00000
        2    80.00000       ABOVE AVE
        4    80.00000       ABOVE AVE
```

Description of the Execution of Example 9.4. Look at the first DO loop in the program. The statements in the loop are executed five times.

```
DO NUM = 1,5
    READ (5,*) STUDENT(NUM)
    WRITE(6,*)'STUDENTNUMBER',NUM,' SCORE IS',STUDENT(NUM)
    TOTAL = TOTAL + STUDENT(NUM)
END DO
```

The first time through the DO *loop,* the value stored in the loop counter specified by the symbolic name NUM is 1 (Figure 9.4).

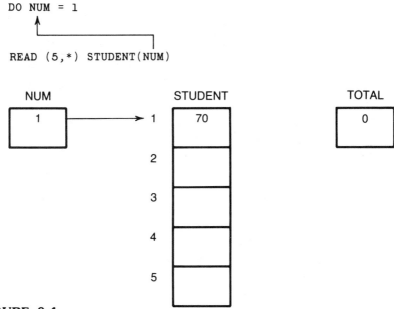

FIGURE 9.4

The READ statement specifies that a data value is input. The first data value provided for input to the program is 70. That value is stored in the array named STUDENT in the location specified by the value that is stored in the memory location named NUM.

Then WRITE out the value stored in the memory location named NUM and the value stored in the array called STUDENT in the location specified by the value in NUM (Figure 9.5).

Then add the value stored in the array called STUDENT in the location specified by the value of NUM to the value stored in the memory location named TOTAL. The value stored in the location named TOTAL was zero. (See Figure 9.6.)

The *second time through the* DO *loop* the value stored in the memory location named NUM is 2.

```
WRITE(6,*)'STUDENTNUMBER',NUM,' SCORE IS',STUDENT(NUM)
```

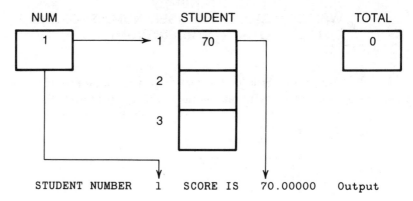

FIGURE 9.5

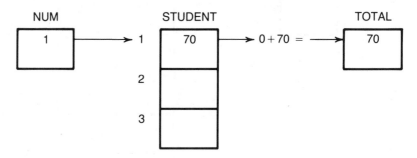

FIGURE 9.6

```
DO NUM = 1,5
```

READ the second value and store the value in the location pointed to by the value of NUM. Then WRITE out the value stored in the memory location named NUM and the value stored in the array called STUDENT in the location specified by the value in NUM. Then add the value stored in the array called STUDENT in the location specified by the value of NUM to the value stored in the memory location named TOTAL. The value stored in the location named TOTAL is 70 before this calculation. (See Figure 9.7.)
Each succeeding time through the DO *loop,* the value stored in the loop counter specified by the symbolic name NUM is incremented by 1 until the loop has completed execution for the value of NUM being equal to 5.

```
DO NUM = 1,5
```

READ the next value and store the value in the location pointed to by

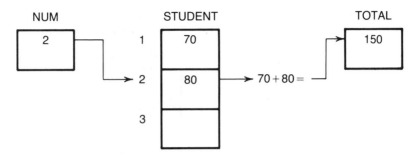

FIGURE 9.7

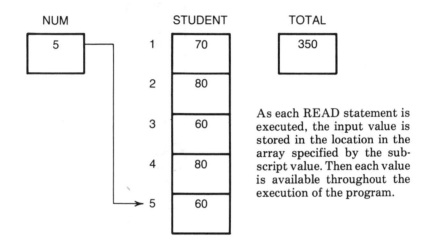

As each READ statement is executed, the input value is stored in the location in the array specified by the subscript value. Then each value is available throughout the execution of the program.

FIGURE 9.8

the value of NUM. WRITE out the value stored in the location named NUM and in the array named STUDENT in the location specified by the value of NUM. And add the value in the array called STUDENT in the location specified by the value of NUM to the value stored in the memory location specified by the symbolic name TOTAL. (See Figure 9.8.)

A value is calculated and stored in the memory location named AVERAGE and that value is printed. (See Figure 9.9.)

Comparisons are made for each student with the class average. The value of N is 1 the first time through the loop. Location 1 in the array named STUDENT contains the value 70. The value in location 1 in the array named STUDENT is compared with the value in the memory location named AVERAGE; 70 is not greater than 70, and so no output is printed. (See Figure 9.10.)

The value of N is 2 the second time through the loop. Location 2 in the array named STUDENT contains the value 80. The value in location 2 in the

```
AVERAGE = TOTAL / 5.0
WRITE (6,*) ' THE AVERAGE IS ',AVERAGE
```

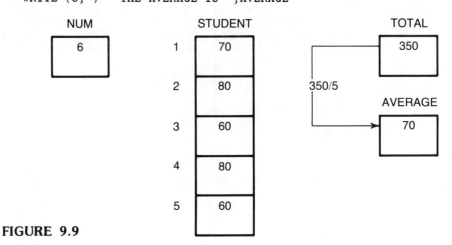

FIGURE 9.9

```
DO N = 1,5
    IF(STUDENT(N).GT.AVERAGE) WRITE(6,*)N,STUDENT(N),' ABOVE AVE
END DO
```

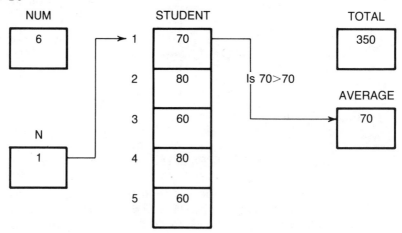

FIGURE 9.10

array named STUDENT is compared with the value in the memory location named AVERAGE; 80 is greater than 70, and so the output is printed. (See Figure 9.11.)

The value of the counter for the DO loop that is the subscript for the array continues to increment each time through the loop. Each value in the array is compared with the value in the memory location named AVERAGE, and a line of output is printed if the condition is met.

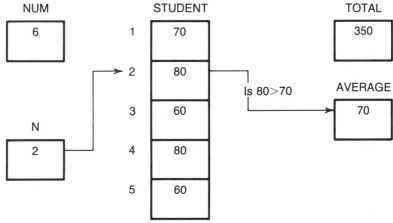

FIGURE 9.11

9.4
MANIPULATING DATA
THAT ARE STORED IN AN ARRAY

One advantage to using arrays is the capability that is provided in the structure for storing elements in an array and accessing the elements in the array according to processing needs. One way to access and store elements is sequentially in the array, as indicated in Examples 9.2 to 9.4.

You may need to access particular elements in an array in some way other than sequentially. Example 9.5 indicates a method for storing data in an array according to index values that are provided as data. Examples 9.6 and 9.7 provide additional information about storing and accessing data for various kinds of applications.

■ Example 9.5: Ordering Data Input
to an Array

The records containing student data can be provided in any order and can be arranged in the appropriate order by the program if index values are provided as a part of the data. This program uses the same student data as in Example 9.4 except that these data are arranged in another order, and an index value between 1 and 5 is provided to indicate the student number. In addition, the first record contains the count for the number of records of data, in this case five records.

Notice that the DIMENSION statement in the program indicates that there may be as many as 10 students in the class.

```
5                                                        Example 9.5
3 60 Carr, Kevin                                         Input
1 70 Adams, Kenny
5 60 Zimes, Zeke
2 80 Cain, Carolyn
4 80 Miller, Mindy
$ EDIT ORDER.FOR                                         Example 9.5
      DIMENSION STUDENT(10)
C     Initialize the total to zero.
      TOTAL = 0
C     Input the count for the number of students.
      READ (5,*) NUMBER_OF_STUDENTS

C     For each of the students, input the student number and the
C     score for the student.  WRITE the student number and the
C     student score as they are READ.  Add the student score
C     to the  total score for the class.
      DO N = 1, NUMBER_OF_STUDENTS
         READ (5,*) NUMSTUD, STUDENT(NUMSTUD)
         WRITE(6,*)'STUDENT NUM',NUMSTUD,' SCORE IS',STUDENT(NUMSTUD)
         TOTAL = TOTAL + STUDENT(NUMSTUD)
      END DO

C     WRITE each of the student records which is now stored in the
C     appropriate place in the array named STUDENT.
      WRITE(6,*)'     RECORDS ARRANGED IN ORDER IN THE ARRAY'
      DO NUM = 1, NUMBER_OF_STUDENTS
         WRITE(6,*)'STUDENT_NUM',NUM,' SCORE IS',STUDENT(NUM)
      END DO

C     Calculate and print the average score
      AVERAGE = TOTAL / NUMBER_OF_STUDENTS
      WRITE (6,*) ' THE AVERAGE IS  ',AVERAGE

C     For each of the five students, compare the student's score
C     with the average score for the class and print the scores
C     which are above average.
      DO N = 1, NUMBER_OF_STUDENTS
         IF(STUDENT(N).GT.AVERAGE)WRITE(6,*)N,STUDENT(N),' ABOVE AVE'
      END DO
      STOP
      END
$ FORTRAN ORDER
$ LINK ORDER
$ RUN ORDER                                              Example 9.5
STUDENT NUM        3 SCORE IS    60.00000                Output
STUDENT NUM        1 SCORE IS    70.00000
STUDENT NUM        5 SCORE IS    60.00000
STUDENT NUM        2 SCORE IS    80.00000
STUDENT NUM        4 SCORE IS    80.00000
    RECORDS ARRANGED IN ORDER IN THE ARRAY
STUDENT NUM        1 SCORE IS    70.00000
STUDENT NUM        2 SCORE IS    80.00000
STUDENT NUM        3 SCORE IS    60.00000
STUDENT NUM        4 SCORE IS    80.00000
STUDENT NUM        5 SCORE IS    60.00000
 THE AVERAGE IS     70.00000
        2   80.00000    ABOVE AVE
        4   80.00000    ABOVE AVE
```

Description of the Execution of Example 9.5.   In general, the limit for
the count for DO loops should be a variable as in this program. In this example, the number of students is input as a data value. The symbolic name
NUMBER__OF__STUDENTS stores the upper limit for the elements that
should be accessed in the array. If, for another class, there are eight
students, it is not necessary to change the program, but only to change the
data.

For this example, consider the way that data values are stored in the array according to the index value that is READ as input. In the first DO loop,
the counter for the DO loop is controlling the number of times the
statements in the loop are executed, but the counter is not used as an index
for the location in the array.

```
DO N = 1, NUMBER__OF__STUDENTS
    READ (5,*) NUMSTUD, STUDENT(NUMSTUD)
    WRITE(6,*)'STUDENT__NUM',NUMSTUD,' SCORE IS',STUDENT
-    (NUMSTUD)
    TOTAL = TOTAL + STUDENT(NUMSTUD)
END DO
```

The first time through the first DO loop, a record is input containing the
value of 3, which is stored in the memory location named NUMSTUD. The
value stored in NUMSTUD is then used to specify the location in the array
named STUDENT where the data value of 60 should be stored. The value 60
is then added to the value in the memory location named TOTAL. (See
Figure 9.12.)

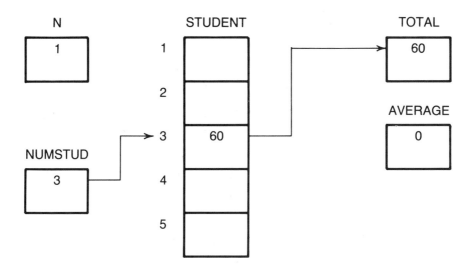

FIGURE 9.12

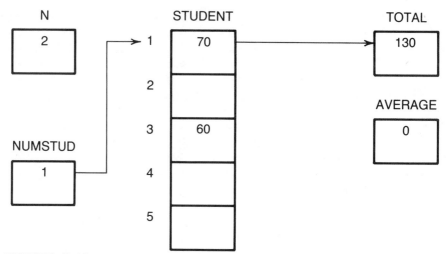

FIGURE 9.13

The second time through the first DO loop, a record is input containing the value of 1, which is stored in the memory location named NUMSTUD. The value stored in NUMSTUD is then used to specify the location in the array named STUDENT where the data value of 70 should be stored. The value 70 is then added to the value in the memory location named TOTAL. (See Figure 9.13.)

After the first DO loop has executed five times, each student score is stored in the appropriate location in the array named STUDENT.

```
DO N = 1, NUMBER_OF_STUDENTS
    IF(STUDENT(N).GT.AVERAGE)WRITE(6,*)N,STUDENT(N),' ABOVE AVE'
END DO
```

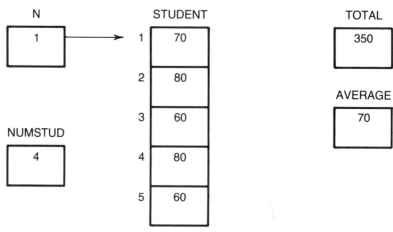

FIGURE 9.14

In the second and third DO loops, the values are already stored in the array sequentially corresponding to student numbers, so the counter for the DO loop is used as the subscript for the array. Look at the third DO loop. (See Figure 9.14.)

The comparison and printing in the final DO loop perform exactly as in Example 9.4, because the records are stored exactly as they were in that example.

■ Example 9.6: Integer, Real, and Character Arrays

An integer or a real declaration followed by the number of elements in an array can be used to declare an array instead of using a DIMENSION statement. If a number of elements for an array is included in a character declaration, then an array is created for a program that can be used to store alphanumeric data.

This program contains four arrays. There are three data records for the program. The CHARACTER NAME(3)*20 declaration sets up an array for alphanumeric data, which has 3 fields, each with 20 character positions. The arrays SCORE1 and SCORE2 are declared to be INTEGER arrays with three elements each, and the array MEAN is declared to be an array of three elements containing numbers stored in a floating-point form.

For each of the three students, the program READs two scores and the student name and calculates and stores the average score for the student. Then the program WRITEs the student name along with the average score for the student.

```
87 85 HAROLD HUGGINS                            Example 9.6
79 82 THOMAS STARK                              Input
89 86 JAN STEVENS
$ EDIT CHARACTER.FOR                            Example 9.6

      CHARACTER NAME(3)*20
      INTEGER SCORE1(3),SCORE2(3)
      REAL MEAN(3)

      DO I = 1,3
         READ(5,100)SCORE1(I),SCORE2(I),NAME(I)
         MEAN(I)=( SCORE1(I) + SCORE2(I) ) / 2.0
      END DO

      DO I = 1,3
         WRITE (6,200) NAME(I),MEAN(I)
      END DO

100   FORMAT(2I3,A)
200   FORMAT(' ',A,5X,F6.1)
      STOP
      END
```

```
$ FORTRAN CHARACTER
$ LINK CHARACTER
$ RUN CHARACTER                      86.0
  HAROLD HUGGINS                     80.5
  THOMAS STARK                       87.5
  JAN STEVENS
```
Example 9.6
Output

■ Example 9.7: Manipulating Data

A teacher might have two scores for each student.

GRADE BOOK
1 Adams, Kenny   70 80
2 Cain, Carolyn   80 90
3 Carr, Kevin   60 60
4 Miller, Mindy   80 70
5 Zimes, Zeke   60 70

When the first exam was given, perhaps a record for each student with the first exam score was typed.

70
80
60
80
60

When the second exam was given, another record for each student was typed, and the entire set of second exam scores was placed after the first set of exam scores.

80
90
60
70
70

This example program inputs the two scores and calculates the total score for each student in one array and writes out the total for each student.

```
70
80
60
80
60
80
90
60
70
70
$ EDIT TWOSCORES.FOR
       DIMENSION ISTUD(5)
```
Example 9.7
Input

Example 9.7

```
100      FORMAT(I3)
200      FORMAT(' ','TOTAL SCORE FOR EACH STUDENT')
300      FORMAT('0','STUDENT',/,' ','NUMBER',7X,'SCORE')
400      FORMAT(' ',1X,I3,10X,I3)

C        Reads the first score for each student into the
C        array named ISTUD.
         DO NUMSTUD = 1,5
             READ(5,100) ISTUD(NUMSTUD)
         END DO

C        READs the second score for each student and adds that
C        score to the value which is already stored in array ISTUD.
         DO NUMSTUD = 1,5
             READ (5,100) ISECONDSCORE
             ISTUD(NUMSTUD) = ISTUD(NUMSTUD) + ISECONDSCORE
         END DO

C        Write a heading for the output.
         WRITE (6,200)
         WRITE (6,300)

C        WRITEs the student number and the total score for each.
         DO NUMSTUD = 1,5
             WRITE (6,400)NUMSTUD,ISTUD(NUMSTUD)
         END DO
         STOP
         END
$ FORTRAN TWOSCORES
$ LINK TWOSCORES
$ RUN TWOSCORES
TOTAL SCORE FOR EACH STUDENT

STUDENT
NUMBER          SCORE
     1           150
     2           170
     3           120
     4           150
     5           130
```

Example 9.7
Output

9.5
GENERAL APPROACH TO WRITING
PROGRAMS WITH ARRAYS

There are several goals for writing a computer program. Correctness, efficiency, and readability are important goals. Another goal is to make a program *general* so that the program can be used for various sets of data without the need to modify the program. The number of students in a class of graduate students might be fewer than 10. The number of students in an introductory undergraduate class could be 30. If you were teaching both kinds of classes, you would want to have a grading program that could be used for both classes.

The IOSTAT clause in the READ statement allows a program to READ and process data until the end of the file is reached and then to store a negative value in the location specified. Then that location can be tested. The program can count the number of records and use that value as the maximum value for DO loops that access each element of an array.

Processing in a program using arrays can usually be divided into segments, each containing a definable task. It is important to write programs that can be understood by others and by yourself at a later date. Developing a program as a series of definable tasks and then documenting each task facilitates writing good programs that will continue to be useful. Look at the following example.

■ Example 9.8: Counting the Number of Elements Stored in an Array

In this example the program counts the number of records that are input before the end of file and stores that count in the memory location named NUMSTUD.

The program inputs the name and three scores for each student and determines the maximum score for each student. The maximum score for each student is stored in an array named SCOREMAX. For each student, if the maximum score is greater than 90, then the characters EXCELLENT are stored in an array named ADDON and a bonus of 5 points is given.

```
$ EDIT IN.DAT                                        Example 9.8
Jewell Dixon                   82    91    83        Input
Theodore H. Azore              79    83    87
Robert H. Brooks               84    90    83
$ EDIT GENERAL.FOR                                   Example 9.8
       CHARACTER STUDENT(30)*25,ADDON(30)*9
       DIMENSION SCOREMAX(30)
       OPEN(5,FILE='IN.DAT',STATUS='OLD')

C      Initialize the number of students and read first record.
C      The status of IOSTAT is zero and the value of the
C      variable IEND will remain zero as long as an end
C      of file or error is not encountered in a READ statement.
       NUMSTUD = 0
       READ (5,100,IOSTAT=IEND)STUDENT(1),S1,S2,S3

C      While the end of file has not been reached, add one to the
C      count for the number of students and find the maximum
C      score for this student.  Then READ another record if there
C      is more data.
       DO WHILE (IEND.EQ.0)
           NUMSTUD = NUMSTUD + 1
           SCOREMAX(NUMSTUD) = S1
           IF (S2.GT.SCOREMAX(NUMSTUD)) SCOREMAX(NUMSTUD)=S2
           IF (S3.GT.SCOREMAX(NUMSTUD)) SCOREMAX(NUMSTUD)=S3
           READ(5,100,IOSTAT=IEND)STUDENT(NUMSTUD+1),S1,S2,S3
       END DO
```

```
C          If the maximum score for the student is greater than or
C          equal to 90, then a bonus of 5 points is added to the
C          maximum score for the student and the characters EXCELLENT
C          are stored in the array named ADDON.
           DO NUM = 1, NUMSTUD
              IF (SCOREMAX(NUM).GE.90) THEN
                 SCOREMAX(NUM) = SCOREMAX(NUM) + 5.0
                 ADDON(NUM) = 'EXCELLENT'
              END IF
           END DO

C          Write out the student name, the maximum score including
C          the 5 point bonus if added and either a blank or the
C          word EXCELLENT.
           DO NUM = 1, NUMSTUD
              WRITE (6,200)STUDENT(NUM),SCOREMAX(NUM),ADDON(NUM)
           END DO
100        FORMAT(A,3F5.0)
200        FORMAT(' ',A,F5.0,5X,A)
           STOP
           END
$ FORTRAN GENERAL
$ LINK GENERAL
$ RUN GENERAL                                               Example 9.8
Jewell Dixon               96.      EXCELLENT               Output
Theodore H. Azore          83.
Robert H. Brooks           95.      EXCELLENT
```

9.6
METHODS OF INPUT
AND OUTPUT FOR ARRAYS

Data are often provided and output one value per record, and the input and output for arrays covered in Examples 9.2 through 9.8 are appropriate. However, it may be necessary to read multiple data values that are stored in one record into an array or to write out data values across an output line instead of one record after another. An *implied* DO *loop* provides the structure necessary for controlling input and output that are not input or output one record after another.

An implied DO loop is used only for input and output and cannot be used for other processing in a program. The following is a form of an implied DO loop for a one-dimensional array.

READ(unit,format) (arrayname(kount),kount = kbegin,kend)
WRITE(unit,format) (arrayname(kount),kount = kbegin,kend)

The values for the array with the symbolic name arrayname are input or output for the subscript value of kount first being equal to kbegin and incrementing by 1 until the value in the location specified by kend has been processed.

Just as all input and output statements interact with a format statement, the combination of the input or output statement along with the format statement actually determines the way that data are stored or output. The following example indicates some of the possibilities for input and output.

■ Example 9.9: Input and Output with Implied DO Loops

The example provides various ways to input and output data.

```
25                                              Example 9.9
45                                              Input
30
25
15 20 23 34
$ EDIT DOIMPLIED.FOR                            Example 9.9
      DIMENSION N(4),M(4)

100     FORMAT(I3)
200     FORMAT(' ',I3)
300     FORMAT(' ',4I3)
400     FORMAT(4I3)

      READ(5,100)(N(I),I=1,4)       ;Reads the first 4 values
                                    ;one value per record
      WRITE(6,*)' N ARRAY OUTPUT WITH DO LOOP'
      DO I = 1,4
         WRITE(6,200)N(I)
      END DO

      WRITE(6,*)' N ARRAY OUTPUT ONE VALUE PER RECORD'
      WRITE(6,*)' OUTPUT IS CONTROLLED BY FORMAT 200'
      WRITE(6,200)(N(I),I=1,4)

      WRITE(6,*)' N ARRAY OUTPUT- ALL VALUES IN ONE RECORD'
      WRITE(6,*)' OUTPUT IS CONTROLLED BY FORMAT 300'
      WRITE(6,300)(N(I),I=1,4)

      READ(5,400)(M(I),I=1,4)       ;Reads the next 4 values all
                                    ;4 values from one record
      WRITE(6,*)' M ARRAY OUTPUT WITH DO LOOP'
      DO I = 1,4
         WRITE(6,200)M(I)
      END DO

      WRITE(6,*)' M ARRAY OUTPUT ONE VALUE PER RECORD'
      WRITE(6,*)' OUTPUT IS CONTROLLED BY FORMAT 200'
      WRITE(6,200)(M(I),I=1,4)

      WRITE(6,*)' M ARRAY OUTPUT- ALL VALUES IN ONE RECORD'
      WRITE(6,*)' OUTPUT IS CONTROLLED BY FORMAT 300'
      WRITE(6,300)(M(I),I=1,4)
```

```
      STOP
      END
$ FORTRAN DOIMPLIED
$ LINK DOIMPLIED
$ RUN DOIMPLIED
N ARRAY OUTPUT WITH DO LOOP
25
45
30
25
N ARRAY OUTPUT ONE VALUE PER RECORD
OUTPUT IS CONTROLLED BY FORMAT 200
25
45
30
25
N ARRAY OUTPUT- ALL VALUES IN ONE RECORD
OUTPUT IS CONTROLLED BY FORMAT 300
25 45 30 25
M ARRAY OUTPUT WITH DO LOOP
15
20
23
34
M ARRAY OUTPUT ONE VALUE PER RECORD
OUTPUT IS CONTROLLED BY FORMAT 200
15
20
23
34
M ARRAY OUTPUT- ALL VALUES IN ONE RECORD
OUTPUT IS CONTROLLED BY FORMAT 300
15 20 23 34
```

Example 9.9
Output

9.7
PLOTTING WITH ONE-DIMENSIONAL ARRAYS

The implied DO loop provides the output capability to produce simple line printer graphics.

A single dimension array is usually thought of as a vertical array of elements; however, with the implied DO loop, the array of elements can be printed across the page. An array could be defined to contain character data and might contain an asterisk in some locations and blanks in other locations.

> You can think of an array as being vertical or horizontal. A character array could contain asterisks, which could be used for plotting symbols. (See Figure 9.15.)

The three asterisks would be the output for the program in Figure 9.15. Other symbols could be used.

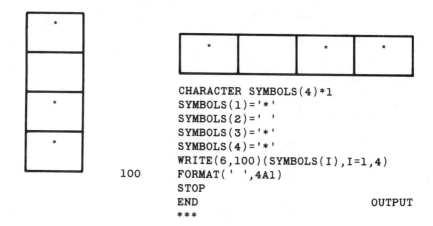

```
                            CHARACTER SYMBOLS(4)*1
                            SYMBOLS(1)='*'
                            SYMBOLS(2)=' '
                            SYMBOLS(3)='*'
                            SYMBOLS(4)='*'
                            WRITE(6,100)(SYMBOLS(I),I=1,4)
             100            FORMAT(' ',4A1)
                            STOP
                            END                      OUTPUT
                            ***
```

FIGURE 9.15

■ Example 9.10: Graphical Line Output

Six months of rainfall data are recorded. For each month, the number of days of rain and the name of the month are included in a record.

This example reads the number of days of rainfall and the month name and prints an asterisk on an output line to indicate the number of rainy days.

```
21 January                                      Example 9.10
13 February                                     Input
 9 March
26 April
19 May
 5 June
$ EDIT RAINYDAY.FOR                             Example 9.10
        CHARACTER MONTHNAME*8,DAYS(31)*1
100     FORMAT(' PLOT FOR DAYS OF RAIN IN THE FIRST SIX MONTHS OF YEAR')
200     FORMAT(I2,1X,A)
300     FORMAT(' ',A,31A1)

C       Initialize each element in  line of DAYS to a blank character
        DO NDAY = 1,31
            DAYS(NDAY)=' '
        END DO

        WRITE (6,100)

C       READ the number of days of rain and the month name.
C       Store an asterisk in the location which corresponds to the
C       number of days of rainfall.  Print the month name and the
C       line of blank characters with the asterisk placed at the
C       position which represents the number of days of rainfall.
C       Then store a blank character in the days of rainfall for
C       this month to initialize the array for the next month.
```

```
        DO MONTH = 1,6
            READ(5,200)NUMDAYS,MONTHNAME
            DAYS(NUMDAYS) = '*'
            WRITE(6,300)MONTHNAME,(DAYS(I),I=1,31)
            DAYS(NUMDAYS)=' '
        END DO
        STOP
        END
$ FORTRAN RAINYDAY
$ LINK RAINYDAY                                    Example 9.10
$ RUN RAINYDAY                                     Output
PLOT FOR DAYS OF RAIN IN THE FIRST SIX MONTHS OF YEAR
January                                *
February                     *
March               *
April                             *
May                      *
June            *
```

9.8
SUMMARY

An *array* is a group of memory locations that have a common name and each element is accessed by an index value for a particular location in the array. An *array* can be established in memory with one of the following declarations:

CHARACTER arrayname (number_elements) * number_characters
DIMENSION arrayname (number_elements)
INTEGER arrayname (number_elements)
REAL arrayname (number_elements)

A counter in a DO LOOP provides a systematic approach for accessing each of the elements in an array.

DO   kount = 1, number_elements_in_array

    array(kount)

An IMPLIED DO LOOP can be used for array input and output.

READ(unit,format) (arrayname(kount),kount = kbegin,kend)
WRITE(unit,format) (arrayname(kount),kount = kbegin,kend)

If data are stored in arrays, a program can usually be divided into definable tasks. The code can be written to perform some task with each of the elements in the array and then to perform succeeding tasks with each of the elements in the array, each task being documented in the program.

9.9
EXERCISES

9.1. A set of memory locations to be accessed as an array is allocated at the beginning of a program with a _____ statement.

9.2. A particular element of an array is accessed with a _____ enclosed in parentheses following the array name.

9.3. Describe the locations that will be allocated with the following FORTRAN statements.

    a. DIMENSION X(100)   **b.** INTEGER VALUES(25)
    c. REAL NUMBERS(50)   **d.** CHARACTER FIRSTNAMES(8)*15

9.4. What is the output for the following FORTRAN program?

```
DIMENSION X(4)
X(1) = 11.1
X(2) = 22.2
X(3) = 33.3
X(4) = 44.4
TOTAL = 0
DO I = 1, 4
    TOTAL = TOTAL + X(I)
END DO
WRITE(6,*)TOTAL
END
```

9.5. What is the output for the following FORTRAN program?

```
DIMENSION N1(3),N2(3),N3(3)
N1(1) = 55
N1(2) = 65
N1(3) = 60
N2(1) = 65
N2(2) = 75
N2(3) = 80
DO I = 1,3
    N3(I) = (N1(I) + N2(I))/2
END DO
DO I = 1,3
    WRITE(6,*)I,N1(I),N2(I),N3(I)
END DO
STOP
END
```

9.6. What is the output for the following FORTRAN program?

```
DIMENSION NUM(6)
DO I = 1,6
    NUM(I) = I*I
END DO
DO K = 1, 6
    WRITE(6,*)K,NUM(K)
END DO
END
```

9.7. What is the output for the following FORTRAN program?

```
      DIMENSION SUM(10)
      DO 10 I = 2, 6, 2
          SUM(I) = 0
          MAX = I
          DO 20 J = 1, MAX
              SUM(I) = SUM(I) + J
20        CONTINUE
          WRITE (6,100)I,SUM(I)
10    CONTINUE
100   FORMAT(' ',I2,I5)
      STOP
      END
```

9.8. What is the output for the following program with the input data shown?

Input
4 2
3 4
1 6
2 2

```
      DIMENSION ISTORE(5),NEWONE(3)
      ISTORE(5) = 0
      DO 10 I = 1,4
          READ(5,*)INDEX,ISTORE(INDEX)
10    CONTINUE
      DO 20 J = 1,3
          INDEX = J + 2
          NEWONE(J) = ISTORE(INDEX)
20    CONTINUE
      DO 30 K = 1,3
          WRITE(6,*)K,ISTORE(K),NEWONE(K)
```

```
30      CONTINUE
        DO 40 K = 4,5
            WRITE(6,*)K,ISTORE(K)
40      CONTINUE
        STOP
        END
```

9.9. **a.** There are 20 records with two integer values per record. The first value is in columns 1 to 3, and the second value is in columns 6 to 10. Write the FORTRAN statements to store, for each record, the first value in array X and the second value in array Y.

b. After the 20 values are stored in the arrays X and Y, write the values in the arrays. Then calculate and write the average of the values in the X array and the average of the values in the Y array.

9.10. **a.** There are data records with two integer values per record. Value 1 is in columns 3 to 8, and value 2 is in columns 10 to 15. Assume that you do not know how many data records there are, but there would never be more than 500 records. Devise a method to indicate when there are no more data values.

b. Write the FORTRAN statements necessary to store the first value in each record in the array X and the second value in each record in the array Y as long as there are more data.

c. After all the data values are stored, write out the count for the number of data records and all the data read into arrays X and Y. Calculate and print the average of the values in the X and Y arrays. Remember that the average can be based only on the number of valid values read.

d. Create a third array, Z, that contains the average of the corresponding values in the X and Y arrays. Write the three arrays.

$$Z(1) = (X(1) + Y(1))/2$$
$$Z(2) = (X(2) + Y(2))/2 \quad \text{etc.}$$

9.11. There is an introductory math class with a maximum of 230 students in the class. The teacher wants you to write the following FORTRAN program. Make up some data to test the program.

First input the number of students.

Then input and store in an array one score for each student.

Calculate the average score for the class.

If the exam was too difficult, the teacher is adjusting the grades upward. If the class average is less than 63, add 2 points to each student's score.

If the exam was too easy, the teacher is adjusting the grades downward. If the class average is greater than 83, subtract 2 points from each student's score.

The program should write the final score for each student.

9.12. This program segment allocates the storage for an array named NUMBER and reads 100 values into the array.

```
DIMENSION NUMBER(100)
READ(5,*)(NUMBER(I),I = 1,100)
```

Write the remaining statements necessary to do the following.

a. Find the sum of all the negative values.

b. The count for the number of negative values.

c. Write out the index value for each location that contains a zero.

9.13. A small company has exactly 30 employees. For each employee, the following information is available: employee name, hours worked, and pay rate. The input data might look like the following:

Nancy Adams	27	3.75
Bob Bough	32	4.25
Cindy Crossman	21	4.00

Write a FORTRAN program to do the following.

a. Set aside memory locations for all the arrays to be used in the program.

b. Input and store the data in three singly dimensioned arrays.

c. For each employee, calculate the pay. Write out the name and pay for each employee. PAY = RATE*HOURS

d. Calculate the average pay for all the employees.

e. Write out the names of all the employees whose pay is greater than the average pay.

9.14. A balsa wood bridge-building contest is held each year during Engineering Week. Pressure was applied to each model bridge and the strength of the bridge was measured in pounds per square inch (psi) at the breaking point. Over the 12 years that the contest has been held, the students have become better at building the bridges. Each year the psi measure has increased.

Write a FORTRAN program that reads the 12 psi values measured into an array named PSI. Then go through each year after the first and store in another array the percentage of increase over the previous year. For every year after the first, write out the psi value and the percentage of increase over the previous year. In addition, calculate and write out the percentage of increase for the final year over the first year of the contest.

Input
817
926
1011
⋮ ⋮

9.15. Write the following FORTRAN program. Set up two arrays of 100 locations each, one called XNUM, which will contain a numerator for a division problem, and one called DEN for the denominator values. The program should input one numerator and one denominator per record, storing the values in the two arrays specified until the end of file is encountered.

A division by zero is an error that causes a FORTRAN program to terminate execution. It is advisable to test each division in a program to prevent a possible division by zero and to flag any occurrences of an attempt to divide by zero.

The program should step through the arrays XNUM and DEN, dividing the numerator by the denominator and storing the result of the division in the numerator array unless the denominator is zero. If the denominator is zero, the division should not be performed; instead, the location in the array where the zero denominator occurred should be written out, and a −999.9 should be stored in the numerator in that location. In addition, a count should be kept of the number of zero denominators encountered in the array.

Finally, after all the calculations have been made, you should write out the entire numerator array, which now contains the results. And then write out the count for the number of times a zero denominator occurred.

9.16. A small local store has a number of customers who have charge accounts. There are never more than 25 customers who have charge accounts. Write a FORTRAN program to do the following:

READ in the number of customers. For each customer, read an account number, a name, a balance, the monthly payment, and the total of the purchases made this month. Store this information in five arrays as the information is input. Write out all the information for each customer immediately after the information is read in.

For each customer, calculate the new balance by subtracting the payment from the current balance and adding the purchase. This new balance should now be stored in the array that you were using for the input balance.

This is a very small store and the proprietor expects the customers to keep their balances under $100.00. For each customer whose balance is greater than or equal to $100.00, the program should add a $2.00 service charge to the balance and again store that balance in the array you have been using for the balance. Write out all the customer's names who were charged the $2.00 service charge.

Find and write out the name of the customer who has the largest updated balance.

Finally, step through the array and print each customer's index number, account number, name, and updated balance.

The program should print appropriate headings above each different kind of output.

Use the following data to test your program.

8877	Carolyn Keene	69.21	5.00	7.16
6225	Joyce Miller	73.56	10.00	17.98
7336	Keri Shay	109.16	15.00	21.79
6379	Willis Ritten	93.56	5.00	2.98
9736	Alton Jenner	85.82	12.00	57.60
5779	Odell Harper	21.79	3.00	0.00
1627	Ann Ames	87.98	8.00	76.77

10

Applications for One-Dimensional Arrays

Most FORTRAN programs written for general applications contain arrays. To use arrays effectively in programs, it is necessary to incorporate sets of instructions for selecting and arranging elements in an array and for interfacing more than one array.

As you begin to write realistic programs, you find a need to access data stored in arrays in many different ways. The examples in this chapter provide an overview of various approaches to solving problems that you will encounter. Rarely will two problems be exactly the same, but the approaches included in this chapter will give you a place to start.

10.1
CREATING SUBSETS OF DATA
FROM A ONE-DIMENSIONAL ARRAY

There is often a need to select a subset of the elements stored in an array. Example 10.1 demonstrates a method for selecting subsets of data based on the value of the elements in an array. Subsets of data are created for sunny, cloudy, and rainy days.

If you have a large set of data, you may need to choose a small set of data for testing or for some preliminary data analysis. A method for selecting a random subset of values is demonstrated in Example 10.2.

Example 10.3 demonstrates a method for storing values in an associated array using program logic to access the appropriate elements in the primary array and in the array being created.

■ Example 10.1: Selecting a Subset of Data Based on Data Values

The data for this example might be used in a study of bacterial growth in a body of water.

Example 10.1
Input

```
CLOUD 400
SUN   200
RAIN  500
RAIN  800
CLOUD 400
CLOUD 500
SUN   200
SUN   300
SUN   300
CLOUD 400
CLOUD 500
RAIN 900
RAIN  800
RAIN  700
RAIN 800
CLOUD 700
SUN   300
SUN   200
SUN   100
SUN   200
SUN   400
SUN   300
SUN   400
CLOUD 500
CLOUD 600
SUN   900
RAIN  800
RAIN  900
CLOUD 800
SUN   400
```

The input data includes a description of the weather and a bacteria count for each of the 30 days in one month. The weather description should be input and stored in an array named WEATHER, and the bacteria count should be input and stored in an array named RAW-DATA.

After the input data are stored, three subsets of data should be created based on the weather. A subset of data should be created for the bacteria counts for sunny weather, for cloudy weather, and for rainy weather.

The first data value was recorded for day 1 in the month, the second data value for day 2 in the month, third data value for day 3, and so on. Create an array for the sunny days that contains the date for each bacteria count for the sunny days. Create an array for the bacteria count for the cloudy days and an array for the dates of the cloudy days. And create an array for the bacteria count and dates for rainy days.

For the sunny days, cloudy days, and rainy days, print the date and bacteria count arrays, and calculate and print the average bacteria count for each weather type.

Example 10.1

```
$ EDIT BACTERIA.FOR
        CHARACTER WEATHER(30)*5
        INTEGER RAWDATA(30),SUNDATA(30),CLOUDDATA(30),RAINDATA(30)
        INTEGER SUNDATE(30),CLOUDDATE(30),RAINDATE(30)
        DATA KNTSUN,KNTCLOUD,KNTRAIN,TOTSUN,TOTCLOUD,TOTRAIN/6*0/

C       Input the bacteria counts for days 1-30 in the month.
100     FORMAT(A,I4)
        DO IDAY = 1,30
          READ(5,100)WEATHER(IDAY),RAWDATA(IDAY)
        END DO

C       For each day of the month, the program checks to see if
C       the weather is recorded as being sunny, cloudy or rainy.
C       For the appropriate weather array, sunny, cloudy or rainy,
C           - The count for the number of days in the weather
C             category is incremented.
C           - The bacteria count is stored in the subset array
C             for the appropriate weather.
C           - The day of the month for which the weather for
C             this category was recorded in stored in a date array.
C           - The cumulative total for the bacteria counts for
C             each category are kept to provide a total for
C             calculating an average value for each category.
        DO IDAY = 1,30
          IF (WEATHER(IDAY) .EQ. 'SUN') THEN
             KNTSUN = KNTSUN + 1
             SUNDATA(KNTSUN) = RAWDATA(IDAY)
             SUNDATE(KNTSUN) = IDAY
             TOTSUN = TOTSUN + RAWDATA(IDAY)
          ELSE IF (WEATHER(IDAY) .EQ. 'CLOUD') THEN
             KNTCLOUD = KNTCLOUD + 1
             CLOUDDATA(KNTCLOUD) = RAWDATA(IDAY)
             CLOUDDATE(KNTCLOUD) = IDAY
             TOTCLOUD = TOTCLOUD + RAWDATA(IDAY)
          ELSE IF (WEATHER(IDAY) .EQ. 'RAIN') THEN
             KNTRAIN = KNTRAIN + 1
             RAINDATA(KNTRAIN) = RAWDATA(IDAY)
             RAINDATE(KNTRAIN) = IDAY
             TOTRAIN = TOTRAIN + RAWDATA(IDAY)
          ELSE
             WRITE(6,*)' ERROR IN DATA'
          END IF
        END DO


200     FORMAT(' ',2I10)
300     FORMAT(/,' ',10X,F10.0,'        AVERAGE,//)
        WRITE(6,*)'        DATE    SUNNY DAY DATA'
        WRITE(6,200)(SUNDATE(I),SUNDATA(I),I=1,KNTSUN)
        WRITE(6,300)TOTSUN/KNTSUN
        WRITE(6,*)'        DATE    CLOUDY DAY DATA'
        WRITE(6,200)(CLOUDDATE(I),CLOUDDATA(I),I=1,KNTCLOUD)
        WRITE(6,300)TOTCLOUD/KNTCLOUD
```

```
        WRITE(6,*)'      DATE    RAINY DAY DATA'
        WRITE(6,200)(RAINDATE(I),RAINDATA(I),I=1,KNTRAIN)
        WRITE(6,300)TOTRAIN/KNTRAIN
        STOP
        END
$ FORTRAN BACTERIA
$ LINK BACTERIA
$ RUN BACTERIA
```

Example 10.1
Output

DATE	SUNNY DAY DATA
2	200
7	200
8	300
9	300
17	300
18	200
19	100
20	200
21	400
22	300
23	400
26	900
30	400

```
        323.    AVERAGE
```

DATE	CLOUDY DAY DATA
1	400
5	400
6	500
10	400
11	500
16	700
24	500
25	600
29	800

```
        533.    AVERAGE
```

DATE	RAINY DAY DATA
3	500
4	800
12	900
13	800
14	700
15	800
27	800
28	900

```
        775.    AVERAGE
```

Description of Example 10.1.   Observing the input data, the program, and the output for the program, you can determine the way that the subset arrays are created.

The DATA statement in this program is used to initialize values. The DATA declaration in the program specifies that the six memory locations specified, KNTSUN ... TOTRAIN, be assigned the value zero at the time that the program begins execution. A DATA declaration, which must appear before any executable statements, assigns initial values to the memory locations, but the values can change as the program executes.

```
DATA KNTSUN,KNTCLOUD,KNTRAIN,TOTSUN,TOTCLOUD,TOTRAIN/6*0/
```

This DATA declaration has the same meaning as assigning the value of zero to each memory location in an assignment statement, as follows:

```
KNTSUN = 0
   :        :
TOTRAIN = 0
```

■ **Example 10.2: Selecting a Random Subset of Data**

In real applications, you may have very large sets of data. A good place to start in using data stored in machine-readable form is to go through and make sure that the data are indeed all readable, your formats are correct, and the ranges for data are what you expect them to be. If there is a very large amount of data, you probably do not want to print all the data, but you might select some values at random to print in order to visually check the data. This example could be used simply to read a set of data values, to count the number of values, to determine the minimum and maximum values, and to select at random some of the values to print for visual verification.

Another objective of this example is to demonstrate a method for selecting a subset of values for testing a program. In general, when you are writing a computer program to perform some data processing or data analysis, you need to use a small amount of the data for testing the program. You could select the first ten elements of data, but if you do that, you may not include a reasonable set of the possibilities that the data might introduce. This program prints the subset of values selected at random from the complete set of data and, in addition, WRITEs the subset of values to a disk file. The subset of data on a disk file could then be used as test data for an applications program.

The program READs all the data and finds the maximum and minimum values for the set of data. The maximum and minimum values can be compared with the range of values that the person who collected the data thinks should be in the set of data. The program counts the number of values in the file.

Then the program selects at random a subset of five values from the complete set of data values. There is a RANdom intrinsic function in FORTRAN that returns a value between 0 inclusive and 1.0 exclusive. The RANdom function requires a large, odd, integer seed value. The random value is actually generated based on a calculation with the seed number.

randomvalue   =   RAN(integerseed)

(a value between 0 and 1.0)   (a large, odd, integer value)

The RANdom function modifies the seed value by the following formula:

integerseed = 69069 * integerseed + 1 MOD (2**32)

Since the RANdom function modifies the seed value each time that a random number is generated, you need only provide a seed value for the first computation. If you provide a constant for the seed, you will get identical values with the RANdom function each time that the program is run, because there is a predefined formula for calculating the number. One way to provide a varying seed value that will in turn produce a more random place to start generating random numbers is to use the function SECoNDS to return a number of seconds based on the number of seconds since midnight.

seconds = SECNDS(realnumberofseconds)

The function returns the number of seconds since midnight minus the number of seconds in the parameter. The parameter must be a real number. If the parameter is 0.0, then the function returns the number of seconds since midnight.

Example 10.2
Input

```
$ EDIT LARGE.DAT
 23
 79
  8
 34
  4
  9
  2
  1
 34
 56
 78
 89
 99
 76
 55
  4
  5
 88
 32
 31
```

For the example, this data file is called a large file. A large data file might actually contain 1000 records or 20,000 records. Since it would be difficult to print 20,000 records here, this file contains 20 records.

```
$ EDIT SELECTRAN.FOR                                        Example 10.2
        DIMENSION N(20),KEEP(5)
        OPEN(11,FILE='LARGE.DAT',STATUS='OLD')
        OPEN(12,FILE='SUBSET.DAT',STATUS='NEW')
C       Read one value per record until the End Of File.
C       Kount the number of records and find the mininum  and
C       maximum values for the set of data.
        KOUNT = 0
        READ(11,100,IOSTAT=IEND)N(1)
        MIN=N(1)
        MAX=N(1)
        DO WHILE(IEND.EQ.0)
           KOUNT = KOUNT +1
           IF ( N(KOUNT).LT.MIN ) MIN = N(KOUNT)
           IF ( N(KOUNT).GT.MAX ) MAX = N(KOUNT)
           READ(11,100,IOSTAT=IEND) N(KOUNT +1)
        END DO

C       Store in an array named KEEP five randomly generated index
C       numbers for locations in the array named N
        ISEED = SECNDS(0.0)
        DO INDEX = 1,5
           FRACTION = RAN(ISEED)
           KEEP(INDEX) = NINT(FRACTION * KOUNT)
        END DO
C     Print the index number which was randomly generated and
C       the value in the array N pointed to by the index.
C       Write the value to a disk file.
        DO INDEX = 1,5
           WRITE(6,200) INDEX, KEEP(INDEX), N(KEEP(INDEX))
           WRITE(12,100) N(KEEP(INDEX))
        END DO

100     FORMAT(I3)
200     FORMAT(' ',3I5)
        STOP
        END
$ FORTRAN SELECTRAN
$ LINK SELECTRAN
$ RUN SELECTRAN                                            Example 10.2
     1    18    88                                         Output
     2     1    23
     3     2    79
     4    10    56
     5     9    34
```

In addition to the printed output, the data values would be stored in the file named SUBSET.DAT.

```
$ TYPE SUBSET.DAT
88
23
79
56
34
```

Description of Example 10.2. If you run this program, you will get a different set of output values, because your RANdom seed value for the number of seconds since midnight will be different.

There is nothing in the program to prevent an index value from being generated more than once or an index value of zero being generated. In a small set of data such as the one in this example, it is likely that a zero or multiple index values would be generated. However, in a large set of data, it is unlikely that the same index value would be generated more than once; but you could add code to the program to check for redundancy or zero index values.

Look at the section of code that generates the indexes into the array N to select a subset of data. First the value of ISEED is set to be the number of seconds since midnight. Then the loop begins to generate five index values, which can be later used to access the array N.

```
ISEED = SECNDS(0.0)
DO  INDEX = 1,5
    FRACTION = RAN(ISEED)
    KEEP(INDEX) = NINT(FRACTION * KOUNT)
END  DO
```

Using the RANdom intrinsic function, the statement FRACTION = RAN(ISEED) generates and stores a value between 0 inclusive and 1.0 exclusive into the memory location named FRACTION.

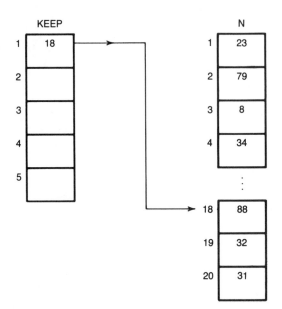

FIGURE 10.1

To generate a random index number into the array N, the FRACTION between 0 and 1.0 is multiplied times the KOUNT for the number of elements. There are 20 elements in this example program, and if the FRACTION generated were 0.8871, then the generated number would be 17.742. To produce an integer value that can be used as an index into an array, the NINT function is used to round the value to the nearest integer.

```
NINT(FRACTION * KOUNT)
NINT( 0.8871 * 20 )
    18
```

Now the value 18 is stored in the array named KEEP. Through the array named KEEP, the value 18 can be used as an index value into the array named N. (See Figure 10.1.)

The DO loop writes output to file 6, which is the terminal by default, and in addition writes the subset of data to a disk file named SUBSET.DAT for this example.

```
DO INDEX = 1,5
    WRITE(6,200) INDEX, KEEP(INDEX), N(KEEP(INDEX))
    WRITE(12,100) N(KEEP(INDEX))
END DO
```

Notice in the WRITE statements that a subscript for an array can be a value in another array. In the expression N(KEEP(INDEX)), the location in

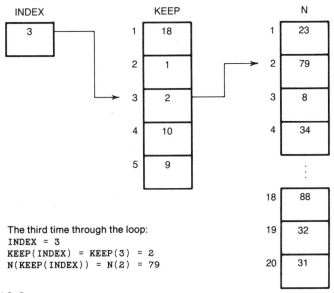

FIGURE 10.2

the array N is specified in the array named KEEP in the location pointed to by the current value of INDEX. The third time through this DO loop, the value of INDEX will be 3. For the values generated randomly in the array KEEP, the element in the array N is shown in Figure 10.2.

The third time through the loop

```
INDEX = 3
KEEP(INDEX) = KEEP(3) = 2
N(KEEP(INDEX)) = N(2) = 79
```

■ Example 10.3: Selection and Analysis

Assume that for some problem you need to store three years of rainfall data in a one-dimensional array. The purpose of this example is to demonstrate a method for accessing certain elements of the rainfall array.

Data for three years of rainfall are stored in a data file named RAIN.DAT. The first record contains a three-character abbreviation for the months in the year. The following three records contain the year, followed by the rainfall for each month. The program reads the month names into a singly dimensioned array named MONTHNAME. Then the program reads all 36 rainfall values into a singly dimensioned array named RAINFALL.

For each of the 12 months in the year, January through December, the program calculates and prints the average rainfall over the three years. The approach to moving through an array, selecting appropriate elements in the array, is used often in programming.

```
$ EDIT RAIN.DAT                                      Example 10.3
                                                     Input
       JAN  FEB  MAR  APR  MAY  JUN  JUL  AUG  SEP  OCT  NOV  DEC
 1981  6.5  5.8  6.2  5.3  4.9  4.7  3.8  3.2  4.7  4.6  5.4  5.9
 1982  7.1  5.4  5.2  6.1  4.6  5.2  4.8  3.0  2.9  5.5  6.2  6.6
 1983  6.3  6.6  5.4  5.0  4.8  3.9  3.3  4.8  4.8  5.9  4.0  6.1

$ EDIT RAINMONTH.FOR                                 Example 10.3
       DIMENSION RAINFALL(36),RAINMONTH(12)
       DATA RAINMONTH/12*0/
       CHARACTER MONTHNAME(12)*3
       OPEN(5,FILE='RAIN.DAT',STATUS='OLD')
100    FORMAT(4X,12(2X,A))
200    FORMAT(4X,12F5.1)
300    FORMAT(' ',12(1X,A),/,' ',12F4.1)

C      Read a three character  abbreviation  name for each month
C      from first record.
       READ(5,100)(MONTHNAME(I),I=1,12)

C      The format for reading the numeric data defines 12 fields.
C      In order to read values into each of the 36 locations
C      specified in the READ statement, values are read from 3
```

```
C      records.  The twelve values are read from the first record
C      of numeric data.  Since the count for I in the READ state-
C      ment is only 12, after reading the first record, the program
C      moves to the next record to input data and finally to the last
C      record  to input all 36 values specified in READ statement.
       READ(5,200)(RAINFALL(I),I=1,36)

C      Using the nested DO loops, the counter KNTALL is
C      incremented 36 times to access each element in the
C      RAINFALL  array.  The counter MONTH in the inside DO loop
C      is used to step through the months in each of the 3 years
C      adding the rainfall value to the total for the appropriate
C      month.
       KNTALL = 0
       DO IYEAR = 1,3
          DO MONTH = 1,12
             KNTALL = KNTALL + 1
             RAINMONTH(MONTH) = RAINMONTH(MONTH) + RAINFALL(KNTALL)
          END DO
       END DO

C      Calculate the average rainfall for each month.
       DO MONTH = 1,12
          RAINMONTH(MONTH) = RAINMONTH(MONTH)/3.0
       END DO

C      Write the average rainfall for each month.
       WRITE(6,300)(MONTHNAME(I),I=1,12),(RAINMONTH(I),I=1,12)

       STOP
       END
$ FORTRAN RAINMONTH
$ LINK RAINMONTH
$ RUN RAINMONTH
```

Example 10.3
Output

```
JAN FEB MAR APR MAY JUN JUL AUG SEP OCT NOV DEC
6.6 5.9 5.6 5.5 4.8 4.6 4.0 3.7 4.1 5.3 5.2 6.2
```

Description of Example 10.3.   Notice the way that the nested DO loops access and total the elements in the array.

```
DO IYEAR = 1,3
   DO MONTH = 1,12
      KNTALL = KNTALL + 1
      RAINMONTH(MONTH) = RAINMONTH(MONTH) +
      RAINFALL(KNTALL)
   END DO
END DO
```

For each of the three years, the inside DO loop goes through the 12 months. Since the counter KNTALL is incremented by 1 each of the 36 times the statements in the inside DO loop are executed, the value KNTALL provides an index for each of the 36 elements in the array named RAINFALL.

The index into the array named RAINMONTH is the counter MONTH for the inside DO loop. At the beginning of each new year, the month is again 1 and that corresponds with the rainfall for January. All 12 months of data are added to the monthly totals, and again the month is back to January, corresponding to the way that the data are stored.

10.2
SORTING

Sorting is one of the processes performed extremely well by a computer. Numbers can be sorted into ascending or descending order. Alphanumeric character strings can be sorted into ascending or descending order. This is a very time-consuming and tedious task for a person to perform, and it is a relatively time-consuming task for the computer to perform.

There are many algorithms for sorting values. The algorithm used in this section is called a bubble sort. The bubble sort is easy to understand after you study it. If a bubble sort contains a flag to indicate when the elements in an array are arranged in order, the bubble method is fairly efficient for sorting arrays that are nearly in the correct order. Other techniques are more efficient for general sorting. Sorting very large sets of data requires large amounts of CPU (central processing unit) time, and the algorithm used can make vast amounts of difference in processing time. Efficient code for sorting can be developed from the algorithm for the quick sort. The quick sort and the shell sort methods for sorting are covered in Chapter 14.

■ Example 10.4: Bubble Sort

For an array of data to be arranged in descending order, the smallest value should be stored at the bottom of the array. The bubble sort provides a method for moving the smallest value down through the array like a bubble that finally settles at the bottom. Then the second smallest value is moved down through the array like a bubble settling next to the last array element. An array could also be sorted into ascending order. The order of sort is determined by the relational operator used for comparing numbers.

UNSORTED DATA	DATA SORTED IN DESCENDING ORDER
9	11
2	9
11	7
4	4
7	2

The input data might be stored in an array named N. (See Figure 10.3.) The way that a bubble sort works is that the first value is compared with

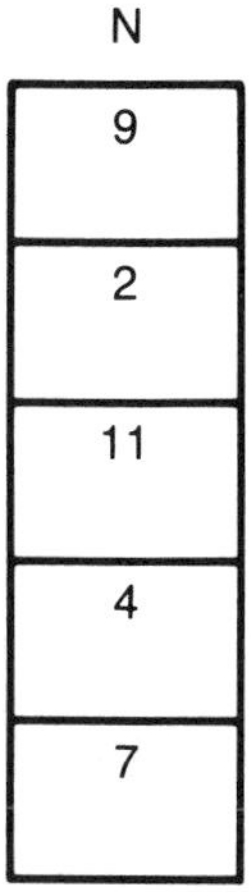

N

| 9 |
| 2 |
| 11 |
| 4 |
| 7 |

FIGURE 10.3

the next value to see if the first value is less than the succeeding value. If the first value is indeed less than the succeeding value, those two values are interchanged. The index is moved to the second element in the array and the second two values are compared and interchanged if the first value is less than the second value.

First Pass through Array. Compare each succeeding pair of elements up to the last element and interchange elements if the first element is less than the succeeding elements. Notice that the comparison ends with the comparison of the next to the last element with the last element. If you try to compare the last element with the succeeding element, you will go beyond the elements to be sorted.

NO INTER-CHANGE	INTER-CHANGE	INTER-CHANGE	INTER-CHANGE	RESULT OF FIRST PASS THROUGH ARRAY
9	9	9	9	9
2	2	11	11	11
11	11	2	4	4
4	4	4	2	7
7	7	7	7	2

Second Pass through Array. Start with the top element. Compare each succeeding pair of elements up to the next to the last element, and interchange elements if the first element is less than the succeeding element. Since the smallest value will always end up on the bottom in the first pass, you need only go to two elements from the end and compare with the next to the last element. The indexes for the comparisons to be made and the stopping points for comparisons are controlled in DO loops.

INTERCHANGE	NO INTERCHANGE	INTERCHANGE	RESULT OF SECOND PASS THROUGH ARRAY
9 ⌐	11	11	11
11 ⌐	9 ⌐	9	9
4	4 ⌐	4 ⌐	7
7	7	7 ⌐	4
2	2	2	2

Final Passes through Array. In fact, at this point the array is sorted into descending order. Two more passes through the array would be made in this approach. Each pass through the array goes one element fewer toward the end of the array, because one more value is always put in the appropriate location in each pass.

NO INTERCHANGE	NO INTERCHANGE	RESULT OF THIRD PASS THROUGH ARRAY
11 ⌐	11	11
9 ⌐	9 ⌐	9
7	7 ⌐	7
4	4	4
2	2	2

NO INTERCHANGE	RESULT OF FOURTH PASS THROUGH ARRAY
11 ⌐	11
9 ⌐	9
7	7
4	4
2	2

A *flag* could be inserted in the program to record if interchanges are made in a pass through the array. If there are no interchanges, then the array is in order, and no more passes through the array need be made. If this procedure is followed, one pass will be made through the array after the array is in order to detect that no more changes are made. If the flag is included in the program sorting the preceding data, the fourth pass through the array would not be made.

The program to implement the sorting routine reads in the data to be sorted. Then the program goes through the array one pass after another, each time comparing adjacent elements and switching those elements not in the correct order. The details of the passes and the comparisons have been shown. Each pass through the array, the last element accessed is one closer to the top of the array, because one more element is definitely in place at the bottom of the array. In addition, a flag is checked to see if an interchange was made on the last pass. Whenever there are no interchanges made, the array is in order.

The implementation of these comparisons and interchanges occurs in nested DO loops. Notice that the outside loop accesses the elements in the array up to the NUMBER__ARRAY__ELEMENTS – 1. The variable LAST__BUBBLE is set equal to NUMBER__ARRAY__ELEMENTS prior to beginning the loop and is then decremented each time through the loop to control the access into the array. The first decrement of the array LAST__BUBBLE prevents the comparison with the succeeding element at the end of the array, thus going beyond the end of the array and causing an error. Since at each pass through the array one more value is put in place coming from the bottom, the inside DO loop can be used to access the elements in the array only to the element represented by LAST__BUBBLE, which is the NUMBER__ARRAY__ELEMENTS minus the number of passes that have been made.

Example 10.4
Input

```
5
  9  2 11  4  7
```

Example 10.4

```
$ EDIT BUBBLE.FOR
        CHARACTER INTERCHANGE*9
        DIMENSION N(20)
        INTEGER THISVALUE

100     FORMAT(15I3)
200     FORMAT(' ','INPUT NUMBERS TO BE SORTED ',15I3)
300     FORMAT(' ','PASS NUMBER ',I3,12X,15I3)

C       Read the number of values to be input for the sort.
        READ(5,*) NUMBER_ARRAY_ELEMENTS
C       Read the elements into the array named N.
        READ(5,100) (N(I),I= 1,NUMBER_ARRAY_ELEMENTS)
C       Print the values accross an output line.
        WRITE(6,200) (N(I),I= 1,NUMBER_ARRAY_ELEMENTS)

C       The outside loop controls the number of elements in array
C       to be compared.  Each time through the array, one more
C       value is stored in order from the bottom of the array.
C       The variable LAST_BUBBLE is decremented each time through
C       the loop to control the number of elements in the inside
C       loop to be compared.   The flag, INTERCHANGE,
C       records if a change is made in a pass through the array.
C       The first time that a pass is made through the array with
C       no changes made, the DO WHILE loop terminates.
        NUMPASS = 0
        LAST_BUBBLE = NUMBER_ARRAY_ELEMENTS
        INTERCHANGE = 'CHANGED  '
```

```
          DO WHILE (LAST_BUBBLE.GT.1 .AND. INTERCHANGE.EQ.'CHANGED  ')
             LAST_BUBBLE = LAST_BUBBLE - 1
             INTERCHANGE = 'NO CHANGE'
C            Go through the array making comparisons
             DO THISVALUE = 1, LAST_BUBBLE
C               If this value is less than the next value in array,
C               then switch the values and reset interchange flag.
                IF (N(THISVALUE) .LT. N(THISVALUE+1)) THEN
                   NTEMPORARY_HOLD = N(THISVALUE)
                   N(THISVALUE) = N(THISVALUE + 1)
                   N(THISVALUE + 1) = NTEMPORARY_HOLD
                   INTERCHANGE = 'CHANGED  '
                END IF
             END DO
C            Write out the array for each pass to observe the order.
             NUMPASS = NUMPASS + 1
             WRITE(6,300)NUMPASS,(N(I),I=1,NUMBER_ARRAY_ELEMENTS)
          END DO
          STOP
          END
$ FORTRAN BUBBLE
$ LINK BUBBLE
$ RUN BUBBLE
INPUT NUMBERS TO BE SORTED     9  2 11  4  7
PASS NUMBER    1               9 11  4  7  2
PASS NUMBER    2              11  9  7  4  2
PASS NUMBER    3              11  9  7  4  2
```

Example 10.4
Output

Run the program again with another set of data. This set of data is almost in order. Observe that the INTERCHANGE flag terminates the DO WHILE loop after the pass through the array with no change. The array correctly ordered is printed twice, because the next to the last time through the loop the values are put in order, and then one time through is made with no change.

```
10
 99 88 77 66 55 44 22 33 11   0
```

Example 10.4
Input

```
$ RUN BUBBLE
```

Example 10.4
Output for second run

```
INPUT NUMBERS TO BE SORTED  99 88 77 66 55 44 22 33 11   0
PASS NUMBER 1               99 88 77 66 55 44 33 22 11   0
PASS NUMBER 2               99 88 77 66 55 44 33 22 11   0
```

Description of Example 10.4. The outside DO WHILE loop controls the number of passes through the array by checking the count for the variable LAST__BUBBLE, which is moving toward the top of the array, and by checking the interchange flag.

```
LAST__BUBBLE = NUMBER__ARRAY__ELEMENTS
INTERCHANGE = 'CHANGED '
DO WHILE (LAST__BUBBLE.GT.1 .AND. INTERCHANGE.EQ.'CHANGED ')
     LAST__BUBBLE = LAST__BUBBLE – 1
```

The inside DO loop moves through the array, comparing succeeding values and switching the values if the first value is less than the succeeding value. To make the switch, a temporary memory location must be used to prevent losing one of the values during the switch. (See Figure 10.4.)

```
DO THISVALUE = 1, LAST_BUBBLE
   IF (N(THISVALUE) .LT. N(THISVALUE+1)) THEN
```

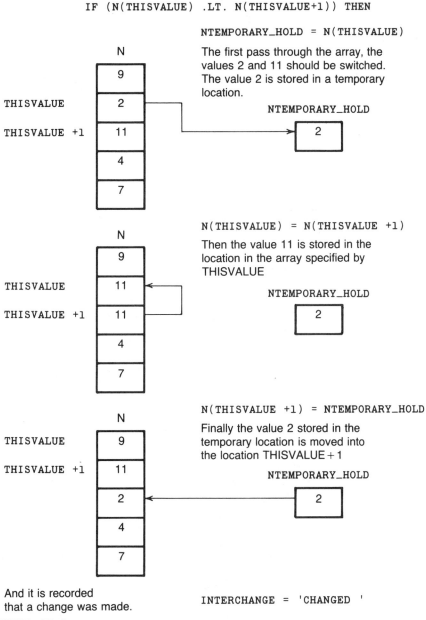

NTEMPORARY_HOLD = N(THISVALUE)

The first pass through the array, the values 2 and 11 should be switched. The value 2 is stored in a temporary location.

N(THISVALUE) = N(THISVALUE +1)

Then the value 11 is stored in the location in the array specified by THISVALUE

N(THISVALUE +1) = NTEMPORARY_HOLD

Finally the value 2 stored in the temporary location is moved into the location THISVALUE + 1

And it is recorded that a change was made.

INTERCHANGE = 'CHANGED '

FIGURE 10.4

■ Example 10.5: Keeping Associated Values Together in a Sort

The data for this example contain the names and estimated intelligence quotients (IQs) for noted celebrities. When the IQ data are sorted, the corresponding name should remain with the IQ. This program reads the names and IQs until the end of file is reached and then uses the bubble sort with a flag to sort the IQ data in ascending order.

Example 10.5
Input

```
SUPERMAN        170
CLARK KENT      110
LOIS LANE       102
MARY CLEAVE     180
WONDER WOMAN    170
RHETT BUTLER    145
E. T.           120
SCARLET OHARA   100
```

Example 10.5

```
$ EDIT SORTIQ.FOR
        DIMENSION IQ(10)
        CHARACTER NAME(10)*15,NAME_HOLD*15,CHANGE*3
        INTEGER THISVALUE

100     FORMAT(A,I3)
200     FORMAT(' ',I2,3X,A,I4)

C       Read the name and IQ values into arrays
C       and print the input data
        WRITE(6,*)' THE INPUT DATA'
        NUMBER = 0
        READ(5,100,IOSTAT=IEND)NAME(1),IQ(1)
        DO WHILE (IEND.EQ.0)
           NUMBER = NUMBER + 1
           WRITE(6,200)NUMBER,NAME(NUMBER),IQ(NUMBER)
           READ(5,100,IOSTAT=IEND)NAME(NUMBER+1),IQ(NUMBER+1)
        END DO

C       Sort into ascending order by IQ.  Whenever the IQ value
C       is switched in the array, the name is also switched.
        LAST_BUBBLE = NUMBER
        CHANGE = 'YES'
        DO WHILE (LAST_BUBBLE .GT. 1 .AND. CHANGE .EQ. 'YES')
           LAST_BUBBLE = LAST_BUBBLE - 1
           CHANGE = 'NO'
           DO THISVALUE = 1, LAST_BUBBLE
              IF (IQ(THISVALUE) .GT. IQ(THISVALUE+1)) THEN
                 IQ_HOLD = IQ(THISVALUE)
                 IQ(THISVALUE) = IQ(THISVALUE +1)
                 IQ(THISVALUE + 1) = IQ_HOLD
                 NAME_HOLD = NAME(THISVALUE)
                 NAME(THISVALUE) = NAME(THISVALUE +1)
                 NAME(THISVALUE + 1) = NAME_HOLD
                 CHANGE = 'YES'
```

```
          END IF
       END DO
    END DO

    WRITE(6,*)
    WRITE(6,*)' DATA SORTED IN ASCENDING ORDER BY IQ'
    WRITE(6,200)(I,NAME(I),IQ(I),I=1,NUMBER)

    STOP
    END
```

```
$ FORTRAN SORTIQ
$ LINK SORTIQ
$ RUN SORTIQ                                         Example 10.5
THE INPUT DATA                                       Output
SUPERMAN        170
CLARK KENT      110
LOIS LANE       102
MARY CLEAVE     180
WONDER WOMAN    170
RHETT BUTLER    145
E. T.           120
SCARLET OHARA   100

 DATA SORTED IN ASCENDING ORDER BY IQ
SCARLET OHARA   100
LOIS LANE       102
CLARK KENT      110
E. T.           120
RHETT BUTLER    145
SUPERMAN        170
WONDER WOMAN    170
MARY CLEAVE     180
```

■ **Example 10.6: Sorting Alphanumeric Data and Keeping Associated Values Together in the Sort**

Using the same data and sort algorithm as that in Example 10.5, this example sorts the names alphabetically in ascending order and keeps the IQ of each celebrity with the name in the sort. Notice that the only difference between this program and the previous program is that the values of the NAMES are compared in the IF statement in this program instead of the IQ's, which are compared in the previous program.

```
SUPERMAN        170                                  Example 10.6
CLARK KENT      110                                  Input
LOIS LANE       102
MARY CLEAVE     180
WONDER WOMAN    170
RHETT BUTLER    145
E. T.           120
SCARLET OHARA   100
```

```
$ EDIT SORTIQ.FOR                                        Example 10.6
        DIMENSION IQ(10)
        CHARACTER NAME(10)*15,NAME_HOLD*15,CHANGE*3
        INTEGER THISVALUE

100     FORMAT(A,I3)
200     FORMAT(' ',I2,3X,A,I4)

C       Read the name and IQ values into arrays
C       and print the input data
        WRITE(6,*)' THE INPUT DATA'
        NUMBER = 0
        READ(5,100,IOSTAT=IEND)NAME(1),IQ(1)
        DO WHILE (IEND.EQ.0)
           NUMBER = NUMBER + 1
           WRITE(6,200)NUMBER,NAME(NUMBER),IQ(NUMBER)
           READ(5,100,IOSTAT=IEND)NAME(NUMBER+1),IQ(NUMBER+1)
        END DO

C       Sort into ascending order by name.  Whenever the name
C       is switched in the array, the IQ is also switched.
        LAST_BUBBLE = NUMBER
        CHANGE = 'YES'
        DO WHILE (LAST_BUBBLE .GT. 1 .AND. CHANGE .EQ. 'YES')
           LAST_BUBBLE = LAST_BUBBLE - 1
           CHANGE = 'NO'
           DO THISVALUE = 1, LAST_BUBBLE
              IF (NAME(THISVALUE).GT. NAME(THISVALUE+1))THEN
                 IQ_HOLD = IQ(THISVALUE)
                 IQ(THISVALUE) = IQ(THISVALUE +1)
                 IQ(THISVALUE + 1) = IQ_HOLD
                 NAME_HOLD = NAME(THISVALUE)
                 NAME(THISVALUE) = NAME(THISVALUE +1)
                 NAME(THISVALUE + 1) = NAME_HOLD
                 CHANGE = 'YES'
              END IF
           END DO
        END DO

        WRITE(6,*)
        WRITE(6,*)' DATA SORTED IN ASCENDING ORDER BY NAME'
        WRITE(6,200)(I,NAME(I),IQ(I),I=1,NUMBER)

        STOP
        END
$ FORTRAN SORTIQ
$ LINK SORTIQ
$ RUN SORTIQ                                             Example 10.6
THE INPUT DATA                                           Output
SUPERMAN         170
CLARK KENT       110
LOIS LANE        102
MARY CLEAVE      180
WONDER WOMAN     170
RHETT BUTLER     145
E. T.            120
SCARLET OHARA    100
```

```
DATA SORTED IN ASCENDING ORDER BY NAME
CLARK KENT      110
E. T.           120
LOIS LANE       102
MARY CLEAVE     180
RHETT BUTLER    145
SCARLET OHARA   100
SUPERMAN        170
WONDER WOMAN    170
```

10.3
BUSINESS APPLICATIONS
AND PLOTTING

Computer programs for business applications often involve incomes and expenses. Accumulating amounts of income and expenditures over a period of time, as demonstrated in this example, is commonly included in programs. A bar chart is often used in a report to display business information graphically.

■ Example 10.7: Business Report
and Bar Chart

The logic of each problem must be developed individually, but this example provides one approach to setting up and accessing typical arrays containing financial data.

The program sums the income and the expenses for each of three years. For the accumulated incomes and expenses, the program produces income and expense amounts over the years 1981, 1982, and 1983. The data are arranged in order by years, but the data could be arranged in any order for the problem. The word END in the INCOME/EXPENSE field for the data provides a flag to indicate when the end of data has been reached.

Example 10.7
Input

```
INCOME  81  8000
EXPENSE 81  5000
EXPENSE 81  1000
INCOME  81  5000
EXPENSE 81  4000
INCOME  82 14500
EXPENSE 82  9000
INCOME  83 12500
EXPENSE 83  8000
INCOME  83  1500
EXPENSE 83  4000
END      0     0
```

Example 10.7

```
$ EDIT BAR.FOR
        CHARACTER IE*7,LINEINCOME(45)*1,LINEEXPENSE(45)*1
        INTEGER INCOME(3),EXPENSE(3),YEAR,AMOUNT
100     FORMAT(A,1X,I2,1X,I6)

        DO IYEAR = 1,3
           INCOME(IYEAR) = Ø
           EXPENSE(IYEAR) = Ø
        END DO

C       Input the data.
C       By subtracting 8Ø from the input YEAR, a subscript
C       of 1,2, or 3 is created for the arrays.  (YEAR-8Ø)
C                                                 ( 81 -8Ø)=1
C                                                 ( 82 -8Ø)=2,etc.
C       Accumulate the income and expenses for each of the three
C       years 1981, 82 and 83.
        READ(5,100)IE,YEAR,AMOUNT
        DO WHILE (IE .NE. 'END')
           IF(IE.EQ.'INCOME')INCOME(YEAR-8Ø)=INCOME(YEAR-8Ø)+AMOUNT
           IF(IE.EQ.'EXPENSE')EXPENSE(YEAR-8Ø)=EXPENSE(YEAR-8Ø)+AMOUNT
           READ(5,100)IE,YEAR,AMOUNT
        END DO

C       Generate a report of the accumulated income and expenses.
        WRITE(6,200)
200     FORMAT(///,' ',10X,'COMPARISON OF INCOME AND EXPENSE',//,
       -  ' ',15X,'INCOME          EXPENSE',//)
        DO IYEAR = 1,3
           WRITE(6,300)IYEAR,INCOME(IYEAR),EXPENSE(IYEAR)
        END DO
300     FORMAT('  198',I1,10X,I6,9X,I6,/)

C       Create a bar chart of the accumulated income and expenses.
C       Label the axes.
        WRITE(6,1000)
1000    FORMAT(///,' ',10X,'COMPARISON OF INCOME AND EXPENSE',//,
       -       ' ',10X,'    THOUSANDS OF DOLLARS',/)
        WRITE(6,1100)
1100    FORMAT(' ',6X,' 1  2  3  4  5  6  7  8  9 10 11 12 13 14 15',/,
       -  ' ',5X,'.',15('..1'))

C       Store an I in each location in the line for plotting Income.
C       Store an E in each location in the line for plotting Expenses.
        DO L = 1,45
           LINEINCOME(L)='I'
           LINEEXPENSE(L)='E'
        END DO

1200    FORMAT(' ',5X,'.',45A1)
1300    FORMAT(' ',5X,'.',//,' 198',I1,' .')
C       For each of the three years of data, store the length
C       of the line to be plotted for income and expenses.
C       The amount is scaled by dividing the amount of income
C       and expense by 1ØØØ.  The bar chart is labeled as
C       thousands of dollars.  Then to increase precision, that
```

```
C       value is multiplied times 3 to spread the chart over 45
C       plot positions instead of over the 15 positions which is
C       the maximum number of thousands of dollars.  Each line
C       is printed twice to strengthen the visual impact of the
C       plot.
        DO I = 1,3
           LENGTHINCOME = (INCOME(I)/1000.0) * 3
           LENGTHEXPENSE = (EXPENSE(I)/1000.0) * 3
           WRITE(6,1300) I
           WRITE(6,1200)(LINEINCOME(K),K=1,LENGTHINCOME)
           WRITE(6,1200)(LINEINCOME(K),K=1,LENGTHINCOME)
           WRITE(6,1200)(LINEEXPENSE(K),K=1,LENGTHEXPENSE)
           WRITE(6,1200)(LINEEXPENSE(K),K=1,LENGTHEXPENSE)
        END DO
        STOP
        END
$ FORTRAN BAR
$ LINK BAR
$ RUN BAR
```

Example 10.7
Output

```
        COMPARISON OF INCOME AND EXPENSE

                INCOME          EXPENSE

1981            13000           10000

1982            14500            9000

1983            14000           12000


        COMPARISON OF INCOME AND EXPENSE

           THOUSANDS OF DOLLARS

        1  2  3  4  5  6  7  8  9 10 11 12 13 14 15
       ...1..1..1..1..1..1..1..1..1..1..1..1..1..1..1
       .
1981   .
       .IIIIIIIIIIIIIIIIIIIIIIIIIIIIIIIIIIIIIIII
       .IIIIIIIIIIIIIIIIIIIIIIIIIIIIIIIIIIIIIIII
       .EEEEEEEEEEEEEEEEEEEEEEEEEEEEEE
       .EEEEEEEEEEEEEEEEEEEEEEEEEEEEEE
       .
1982   .
       .IIIIIIIIIIIIIIIIIIIIIIIIIIIIIIIIIIIIIIIIIIII
       .IIIIIIIIIIIIIIIIIIIIIIIIIIIIIIIIIIIIIIIIIIII
       .EEEEEEEEEEEEEEEEEEEEEEEEEEE
       .EEEEEEEEEEEEEEEEEEEEEEEEEEE
       .
1983   .
       .IIIIIIIIIIIIIIIIIIIIIIIIIIIIIIIIIIIIIIIIII
       .IIIIIIIIIIIIIIIIIIIIIIIIIIIIIIIIIIIIIIIIII
       .EEEEEEEEEEEEEEEEEEEEEEEEEEEEEEEEEEEE
       .EEEEEEEEEEEEEEEEEEEEEEEEEEEEEEEEEEEE
```

Description of Example 10.7. The program reads input data until the value of END is read into the variable IE from the INPUT/EXPENSE field. After a code for either INCOME or EXPENSE is read into the IE field, a two-digit value for YEAR is read, and the amount of input or expense is read; the program then checks to see if the code is income or expense.

```
READ(5,100)IE,YEAR,AMOUNT
DO WHILE (IE .NE. 'END')
    IF(IE.EQ.'INCOME')INCOME(YEAR-80) = INCOME(YEAR-80) +
-   AMOUNT
    IF(IE.EQ.'EXPENSE')EXPENSE(YEAR-80) = EXPENSE(YEAR-80)
-   + AMOUNT
    READ(5,100)IE,YEAR,AMOUNT
END DO
```

The two arrays for accumulating totals are the INCOME array and the EXPENSE array. Each array has three locations, one for each year, 1981, 1982, and 1983. The subscript into the array is actually a 1, 2, or 3. Since the input values for the year are 81, 82, and 83, subtracting the value 80 from the input YEAR provides a subscript into the array. (See Figure 10.5.)

If the IE code is INCOME, the input AMOUNT is added to the current value stored in the array named INCOME in the location specified by the subscript (YEAR-80). If the IE code is EXPENSE, the input AMOUNT is added to the current value stored in the array named EXPENSE in the location specified by the subscript (YEAR-80).

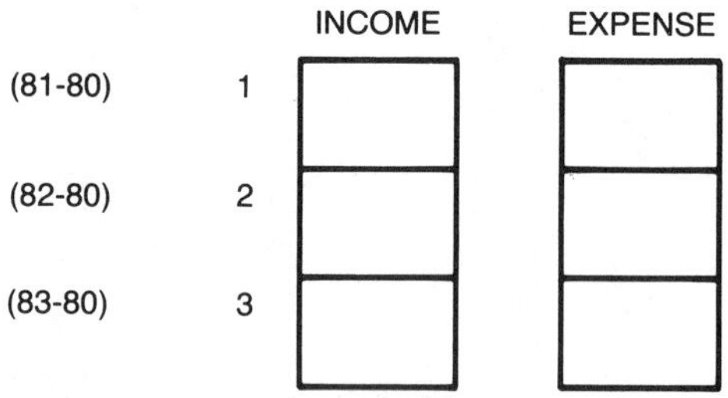

```
IF (IE.EQ.'INCOME')INCOME(YEAR-80)=INCOME(YEAR-80)+AMOUNT
IF (IE.EQ.'EXPENSE')EXPENSE(YEAR-80)=EXPENSE(YEAR-80)+AMOUNT
```

FIGURE 10.5

10.4
RESEARCH APPLICATIONS
AND PLOTTING

Many kinds of analyses can be performed on a set of data. Determination of a correlation coefficient and a simple regression line is often used in the analysis of research data. Plots that can be produced on a terminal screen or a line printer are used to provide a visual overview of the data. Example 10.8 is an example of writing a program to generate a correlation coefficient, a simple regression analysis, and a plot of the results.

■ Example 10.8: Statistical Data Analysis

A *correlation coefficient* is one measure of the strength of a relationship between sets of data. Often, one set of values is the independent set of data, and the other set of values is the dependent set of data. In general, there is a strong correlation between independent and dependent values if the dependent values become increasingly large as the independent values get increasingly large. There is a strong inverse correlation between the two sets of data if the dependent values become increasingly small as the independent values become increasingly large. (See Figure 10.6.)

Strong correlation				No correlation		
	X	Y			X	Y
	1	2.1			1	13.5
L	2	2.8	L	L	2	100.2	N O
A	3	5.7	A	A	3	28.0	O R
R	4	7.5	R	R	4	1.3	D
G	5	8.0	G	G	5	0.5	E
E	6	9.5	E	E	6	500.7	R
R	7	9.6	R	R	7	999.9	
	8	11.2			8	0.2	
	9	13.8			9	5.1	
	10	14.1			10	2.2	

FIGURE 10.6

A correlation coefficient is a number between 0.0 and 1.0 calculated from a formula using the sums of the x and y values, the sums of squares of the values, and adjusted sums of squares of the values in the data sets. Correlation coefficients with values near 1.0 indicate a strong correlation between sets of data.

A *simple regression line* is the straight line that can be drawn through the set of data points to most accurately represent the data with one line.

The calculation of the correlation coefficient and the regression line are based on minimizing the squares of the distances of values from the line of best fit. This is called the *least-squares method*. (See Figure 10.7.)

The simple regression line has the form

$$Y = B0 + B1(X)$$

where $B0$ is the intercept of the line on the Y axis and $B1$ is the slope of the line. The equation for the regression line is often used for predicting values. (See Figure 10.8.)

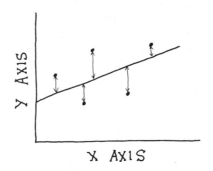

FIGURE 10.7

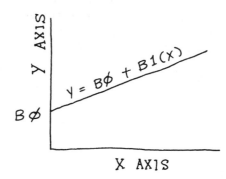

FIGURE 10.8

For an independent value, often referred to as an X value, a value of Y can be predicted based on the equation for the regression line. The validity of the prediction depends on many factors, but the correlation coefficient is one measure of the confidence that should be placed in the prediction equation.

This example program calculates the correlation coefficient and the equation for the regression line to provide a numerical description of the data and a simple plot to provide a pictorial representation of the data. The segments of the program that generate the correlation coefficient and the regression line are general and could be used with almost any data. The segment of the program producing the plot does not include scaling and was developed for these data in particular. A more general plotting routine is given in Chapter 14.

The problem for this example is to determine the relationship between the number of years that a plant has been growing and the height of the plant in feet at the end of each year of growth. The following are the data for the problem.

Years	1.	2.	3.	4.	5.	6.	7.	8.	9.	10.
Height in feet	2.1	2.8	5.7	7.5	8.0	9.5	9.6	11.2	13.8	14.1

This example program reads in the raw data, the X and Y values, and then the program calculates the values that are the elements necessary for calculating the correlation coefficient and the equation for the regression line. To generate these values, several values must be calculated, such as the sum of the data values squared and the adjusted sums of squares. The following are the formulas for calculating the correlation coefficient and the equation for the regression line, followed by the values that are included in the calculations for this example.

$$\text{Correlation Coefficient} = \frac{xy}{\sqrt{x^2 y^2}}$$

where the raw X and Y data values are represented by the uppercase letters X and Y. The calculated values, represented by the lowercase letters x and y, and referred to as adjusted values.

The adjusted sums of squares and xy values are calculated in the following way.

$$x^2 = X^2 - \frac{(X)^2}{n} \qquad x^2 = \sum X^2 - \frac{(\sum X)^2}{n}$$

$$y^2 = Y^2 - \frac{(Y)^2}{n}$$

$$xy = XY - \frac{XY}{n}$$

The values that need to be generated for this problem are the following:

X	Y	X^2	Y^2	XY
1.0	2.1	1.0	4.41	2.1
2.0	2.8	4.0	7.34	5.6
3.0	5.7	9.0	32.49	17.1
4.0	7.5	16.0	56.25	30.0
5.0	8.0	25.0	64.00	40.0
6.0	9.5	36.0	90.25	57.0
7.0	9.6	49.0	92.16	67.2
8.0	11.2	64.0	125.44	89.6
9.0	13.8	81.0	190.44	124.2
10.0	14.1	100.0	198.81	141.0
Sums 55.0	84.3	385.0	861.59	573.8

$$x^2 = 385.0 - \frac{(55.0)^2}{10} = 82.5$$

(Continued)

$$y^2 = 861.59 - \frac{(84.3)^2}{10} = 151.44$$

$$xy = 573.8 - \frac{(55.0)\,(84.3)}{10} = 110.15$$

$$\text{Correlation coefficient} = \frac{110.15}{\sqrt{(82.5)\,(151.44)}} = 0.98545$$

The calculation for the equation for the regression line is the following:

$$B1 = \frac{xy}{x^2} = \frac{110.15}{82.5} = 1.34$$

$$B0 = \frac{Y}{n} - B1\,\frac{X}{n} = \frac{84.3}{10} - 1.34\,\frac{55.0}{10} = 1.09$$

$$\text{Regression equation} = 1.09 + 1.34X$$

As usual, once you understand a problem completely and organize the approach to solving the problem, the code to generate the results can be developed. It is usually necessary to spend a great deal of time developing the approach to solving a problem.

Example 10.8
Input

```
10
 1.    2.    3.    4.    5.    6.    7.    8.    9.   10.
 2.1   2.8   5.7   7.5   8.0   9.5   9.6  11.2  13.8  14.1

$ EDIT REGRESS.FOR                    PD           NYRS.    Example 10.8
        DIMENSION X(10),Y(10),PREDICT(10),NUMYEAR(10)
        CHARACTER LINE(45)*1,LABEL(10)*1
        DATA LABEL/' ','Y',' ','E',' ','A',' ','R',' ',' '/
        DATA NUMYEAR/1,2,3,4,5,6,7,8,9,10/

C       Input data for analysis
        READ (5,*) N
        READ(5,100)(X(I),I=1,N)
        READ(5,100)(Y(I),I=1,N)
100     FORMAT(10F5.1)

C       Calculate the raw sum of XY, sum of X, sum of Y,
C       and the raw sum of X squared and sum of Y squared
        DO I = 1, N
        XY = XY + X(I)*Y(I)
        SUMX = SUMX + X(I)
        SUMY = SUMY + Y(I)
        XSQUARE = XSQUARE + X(I)*X(I)
        XSS = XSS
```

```
              YSQUARE = YSQUARE + Y(I)*Y(I)
           END DO

C      Calculate the adjusted sums of squares and the
C      adjusted sum of xy
       SUMXSQUARE = XSQUARE - SUMX*SUMX/N
       SUMYSQUARE = YSQUARE - SUMY*SUMY/N
       SUMXY = XY - SUMX*SUMY/N

C      Calculate and print the correlation coefficient
       CORRELATION = SUMXY/SQRT(SUMXSQUARE*SUMYSQUARE)
       WRITE(6,*)'CORRELATION COEFFICIENT ',CORRELATION

C      Calculate and print the equation for the regression line
       B1 = SUMXY/SUMXSQUARE
       BØ = SUMY/N - B1*SUMX/N
       WRITE(6,300)BØ,B1
300    FORMAT(' REGRESSION LINE =',F6.2,' + ',F6.2,'X')

C      Calculate and print the predicted values
       WRITE(6,400)
400    FORMAT(//,'     X          Y       PREDICTED Y VALUE')
500    FORMAT(' ',F6.1,5X,F6.1,10X,F6.1)
       DO I = 1,N
          PREDICT(I) = BØ + B1 * X(I)
          WRITE(6,500)X(I),Y(I),PREDICT(I)
       END DO



C      Generate a plot of the regression analysis
C      First, put the Y axis label on the plot
       WRITE (6,1000)
1000   FORMAT(///,' ',10X,'H E I G H T    I N    F E E T',/,' ',
      '  0  1  2  3  4  5  6  7  8  9 10 11 12 13 14 15')
       WRITE(6,1100)
1100   FORMAT('        ',15('..1'),'   Y AXIS')
1200   FORMAT(' ',A1,I2,1X,'.',45A1)
       DO I = 1,45
          LINE(I) = ' '
       END DO
       DO I = 1, 10
          NSTAR = (NINT(3*(Y(I))))
          LINE(NSTAR) = '*'
          L = NINT( 3 * (BØ + B1*I))
          LINE(L) = '.'
          WRITE(6,1200)LABEL(I),NUMYEAR(I),LINE
          LINE(L) = ' '
          LINE(NSTAR) = ' '
       END DO
       WRITE(6,1300)
1300   FORMAT(' X AXIS',/,'                    *  MEASURED',/,
      '                    .  PREDICTED')
       STOP
       END
$ FORTRAN REGRESS
$ LINK REGRESS
$ RUN REGRESS
```

Example 10.8
Output

```
CORRELATION COEFFICIENT    0.9854532
REGRESSION LINE =  1.09 +   1.34X
```

X	Y	PREDICTED Y VALUE
1.0	2.1	2.4
2.0	2.8	3.8
3.0	5.7	5.1
4.0	7.5	6.4
5.0	8.0	7.8
6.0	9.5	9.1
7.0	9.6	10.4
8.0	11.2	11.8
9.0	13.8	13.1
10.0	14.1	14.4

```
        H E I G H T   I N   F E E T
    0  1  2  3  4  5  6  7  8  9 10 11 12 13 14 15
    ..1..1..1..1..1..1..1..1..1..1..1..1..1..1..1    Y AXIS
    1 .    *.
Y   2 .       *   .
    3 .              .  *
E   4 .                  .    *
    5 .                     .*
A   6 .                        .  *
    7 .                         *  .
R   8 .                             *.
    9 .                                .    *
   10 .                                   *.
X AXIS
        *     MEASURED
        .     PREDICTED
```

Description of Example 10.8.   The DATA statements at the beginning of the program declare the values of memory locations at the beginning of the program. The array declarations for the CHARACTER array named LABEL and the numeric array named NUMYEAR precede the DATA declaration. The character data are enclosed in single quotation marks and separated by commas, and the numeric data are simply separated by commas. When data declarations for arrays are used, the exact number of elements in the array must be provided.

```
DIMENSION X(10),Y(10),PREDICT(10),NUMYEAR(10)
CHARACTER LINE(45)*1,LABEL(10)*1
DATA LABEL/' ','Y',' ','E',' ','A',' ','R',' ',' '/
DATA NUMYEAR/1,2,3,4,5,6,7,8,9,10/
```

The program statements to generate a correlation coefficient and an equation for a regression line are based on the calculations shown in the example prior to the listing of the program.

The program statements used to develop the plot include formats for inserting headings for this plot in particular. The maximum Y value is 15, but an array of 45 elements is used for plotting to increase plotting precision. First, blanks are stored in all 45 positions. Then for each year an asterisk and a period are inserted in the array named LINE for the measured and predicted values for the Y axis, and the LINE is printed for each year. To spread the line over the 45 positions to be printed across the page, the Y value to be plotted is multiplied times 3 and an asterisk is placed in the array LINE. The predicted Y value is calculated and multiplied by 3, and a period is stored in the array LINE.

```
DO I = 1, 10
    NSTAR = (NINT(3*Y(1))
    LINE(NSTAR) = '*'
    L = NINT( 3 * (B0 + B1*I))
    LINE(L) = '.'
    WRITE(6,1200)LABEL(I),NUMYEAR(I),LINE
    LINE(L) = ' '
    LINE(NSTAR) = ' '
END DO
```

An introduction to plotting with one-dimensional arrays is given in Section 9.7. A general routine for generating scaled scatter plots is given in Chapter 14.

10.5
SUMMARY

Selection of elements is one of the primary processes used in computer programs.

■ An element might be selected based on a condition that may or may not exist.

```
IF (condition) THEN
    index = somevalue
```

■ An element can be selected with the RANDOM function.

```
index = (RAN(integerseed) * range)
```

■ An element can be selected based on access to elements in the array according to the logic of the problem to be solved.

Sorting values into ascending or descending order can be performed with numeric and character data. The BUBBLE SORT is simple to write but is efficient only for sets of data that are nearly in order.

Plotting can be performed by storing characters in an array at locations to represent a value or magnitude and then printing the array. Programs to produce plots should include scaling and labeling for the axes.

10.6
EXERCISES

10.1. For the input data shown, what is the output for the following FORTRAN program?

```
Input
5,    4
3,    2
1,    6
2,    2
```

```
DIMENSION NO(5), SUM(3)
DO I = 1,4
    READ(5,*)J,NO(J)
END DO
NO(4) = (NO(1) + NO(2)) * NO(5)
DO J = 1,3
    SUM(J) = 0
END DO
DO K = 2,3
    SUM(2) = SUM(2) + NO(K)
END DO
DO I = 1,5
    WRITE(6,*)I,NO(I)
END DO
DO I = 1,3
    WRITE(6,*)I,SUM(I)
END DO
STOP
END
```

10.2. What would the following program do?

```
DIMENSION A(10), B(10)
READ(5,*) (A(I),I = 1,10)
MAX = 10
KNT = MAX + 1
DO 10 I = 1, MAX
    KNTB = KNT - I
```

```
      B(KNTB) = A(I)
END DO
STOP
END
```

10.3. The following statements store 75 values in the array X and 75 values in the array Y. Write the statements that will cause the values stored in the array X to be stored in array Y and the values stored in the array Y to be stored in the array X.

```
DIMENSION X(75), Y(75)
READ(5,*) (X(I),Y(I),I = 1,75)
```

10.4. Write a FORTRAN program to read 10 values into a one-dimensional array named IFIND. The program should find and print the smallest value in the array and the location in the array for the smallest value.

10.5. Assume that the following statements store exactly 500 data values in array A.

```
DIMENSION A(500)
READ(5,*) (A(I),I = 1,500)
```

Write the FORTRAN statements to calculate and print all the values in the array A that are greater than the average value in the array. And write the statements necessary to find and print the smallest value in the array A that is greater than the average value in the array.

10.6. Write a FORTRAN program that will read a set of three values into an integer array and will determine the largest of the three values in the set and write out the largest value. The program should read and then find the maximum for five sets of data.

10.7. There is an array A with 150 locations and an array B with 30 locations. Assume that data are stored in the arrays or generate some data

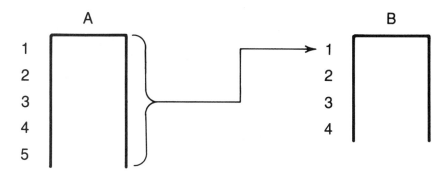

FIGURE 10.9

to store in the arrays. Write a FORTRAN program segment that will add together the first five elements of array A and store them in the first location of array B; then add together the next five elements of array A and store them in the second location of array B; and so on. All 30 locations in array B should be filled. (See Figure 10.9.)

10.8. The way that words are used in a sentence has in important effect on the reader. The four adjectives refreshing, sparkling, cool, and bubbly could be arranged in 24 ways. After storing the words in four fields in the character array named WORDS, write the FORTRAN code to print all the combinations of the four words.

```
CHARACTER WORDS(4)*10
WORDS(1) = 'REFRESHING'
WORDS(2) = 'SPARKLING'
WORDS(3) = 'COOL'
WORDS(4) = 'BUBBLY'
```

Example output:

REFRESHING	SPARKLING	COOL	BUBBLY
REFRESHING	SPARKLING	BUBBLY	COOL
REFRESHING	BUBBLY	SPARKLING	COOL

10.9. Write a program that will generate the first 50 elements of the sequence $1, 1, \frac{1}{2}, \frac{1}{3}, \frac{1}{5}, \frac{1}{8}, \frac{1}{13}$, . . . , and store the elements in an array called SEQENCE. After the first two elements, the denominator of each fraction is the sum of the denominators of the previous two fractions. Of course, the numbers are stored as decimal values and not actually as fractions.

10.10. This problem requires calculating the total of some values, and Problem 10.11 requires calculating the total for some values. This problem does not require an array, and you should write the code without an array in order to be aware of the times when an array is not necessary. Problem 10.11 does require an array. Notice the difference in the problems.

A company has seven districts. Each district has five stores. Write a FORTRAN program to read sales and calculate and print the average sales for each district. The sales for one store are contained in one record and all the records for one district are placed one after another.

```
Input ⎤
40000. |
50000. |  five
30000. ⎬  stores in
20000. |  district 1
10000. ⎦
60000. ⎤
40000. |  five                          Output
30000. ⎬  stores in    DISTRICT 1   AVERAGE   30000
10000. |  district 2    DISTRICT 2   AVERAGE   40000
60000. ⎦                     ⋮                    ⋮
```

10.11. A company has ten employees. Each employee has an employee number from 1 to 10. You should write a payroll program for the company. All employees are paid $4 an hour. Each record of data will contain an employee number from 1 to 10 and a number of hours worked. There may be no records for an employee or several records for an employee, and the records are in no particular order.

Calculate the total pay for each employee. Write out the employee number from 1 to 10 and the calculated pay.

```
Input
 4    37
 2    19
 7    28
 3    40
 1    40
 4    40
 9    30
10     3
 3    35
```

10.12. Write a FORTRAN program to read 20 elements into an array X, sort the elements into ascending order, and print the sorted array. In addition, sort the elements in the array into descending order and print the array.

10.13. There are seven students in a class. For each student, a record contains the student name and two scores. Write a FORTRAN program to input the student names and scores, calculate the average of two scores for each student, and sort the student information in descending order by the calculated scores. Print the sorted information, including the student names, the average, and the two scores.

Input

Auxley	79	77
Bevins	94	96
Canon	86	88
Daron	77	75
Freman	80	70
Gesel	65	69
Hardy	93	91

Output

Bevins	95	94	96
Hardy	92	93	91
Canon	87	86	88
Auxley	78	79	77
Daron	76	77	75
Freman	75	80	70
Gesel	67	65	69

10.14. Read 15 data cards with a Format(I2,I3). Each data card contains the index number for a location in an array and the age of the person that will be the value of that location in the array. Follow the READ statement immediately by a WRITE statement to echo the input. Store the data in the specified indexed location in an array named AGE.

Next, sequentially step through the array AGE and write out the index number and value for each location in the array.

Find and print the index numbers and ages for all those people between 18 and 22 inclusive.

Divide the ages into four categories, and store the count for the number of people in each age category in an array called GROUP.

GROUP(1) should contain the count for the number of people under 18.

GROUP(2) should contain the count for the number of people who are 18 to 30 inclusive.

GROUP(3) should contain the count for the number of people who are 31 to 50 inclusive.

GROUP(4) should contain the count for the number of people over 50.

Write the index numbers and contents for the GROUP array.

Each section of the output should be given descriptive headings. Test the program with the following input. Write the programs so that the right-hand data value, the integer age value, will be stored in the array in the index location that is the left-hand data integer (i.e., the first data value of 19 should be stored in the fourth location in the array named AGE). The 15 input records should be arranged in the order shown.

Input
4 19
7 21
1 24
11 57
15 22
12 18
8 21
13 19
2 22
3 17
6 36
14 20
10 31
5 54
9 35

Output
The output should include the following.
The output should be one section after another instead of across the page as shown here.

Input echo		AGE array		18 to 22 years		Age GROUPs	
4	19	1	24	2	22	1	1
7	21	2	22	4	19	2	9
1	24	3	17	7	21	3	3
11	57	4	19	8	21	4	2
15	22	5	54	12	18		
12	18	6	36	13	19		
8	21	7	21	14	20		
13	19	8	21	15	22		
2	22	9	35				
3	17	10	31				
6	36	11	57				
14	20	12	18				
10	31	13	19				
5	54	14	20				
9	35	15	22				

11

Introduction to Two-Dimensional Arrays

It is often advantageous to store a set of data in an array structure in the FORTRAN language in order to be able to access the elements systematically with the features of the language. A one-dimensional array is used to store a set of data that can be defined as a column of data. A two-dimensional array is used to store a set of data that requires both a row and column specification to define a variable.

11.1
DESCRIPTION OF A
TWO-DIMENSIONAL ARRAY

Data for a two-dimensional array might be grades for students in a class. The student might be defined by the row and seat occupied in the class.

	SEAT 1	SEAT 2	SEAT 3	SEAT 4
Row 1	60	70	50	80
Row 2	60	50	40	80
Row 3	70	90	60	50

A two-dimensional array is a group of memory locations that have a common name and are accessed by specifying a row number and a column number in the group of memory locations. To store data in a two-dimensional array, a declaration must appear before any executable statements in the program.

DIMENSION two__d__array__name(n,m)

where (n,m) must be specific numbers for setting aside a particular number of memory locations.

The number of memory locations set aside for storage for an array is n multiplied by m. FORTRAN requires that the number of memory locations used in the program be absolutely defined at the beginning of execution.

Accessing a particular element in the array then requires one subscript that specifies the row number and another subscript that specifies the column number. The subscripts for row numbers and column numbers can be specific numbers, or they can be variable names that take on values as a program executes.

two__d__array__name(irow,icol)

Two-dimensional arrays can also be declared with an INTEGER or REAL declaration followed by the number of elements in the array.

INTEGER two__d__array__name(n,m)
REAL two__d__array__name(n,m)

Example 11.1 demonstrates in absolute terms without an array the way that values are stored in memory locations and then accessed to be printed. Example 11.2 performs exactly the same function as Example 11.1 using a two-dimensional array for storing and accessing values. Examples 11.3 and 11.4 READ the data as input to a two-dimensional array, statement by statement. Example 11.5 is a realistic approach to using DO loops to store and access data in a two-dimensional array in a systematic way using only a few statements.

■ Example 11.1: Program That Needs a Two-Dimensional Array

The grades for students occupying positions specified by row and seat numbers are used for this example and Examples 11.2 to 11.7.

	SEAT 1	SEAT 2	SEAT 3	SEAT 4
Row 1	60	70	50	80
Row 2	60	50	40	80
Row 3	70	90	60	50

Storing and printing the grades for the students in all the seats in all the rows in the class could be very tedious without arrays, as this example shows. If there were 20 rows with 10 seats each, 200 assignment statements would be required to store all the values. The purpose for this example is to demonstrate in absolute terms the way that values are stored in memory locations and then accessed to be printed. Example 11.2 performs exactly the same function as this example using a two-dimensional array for storing values. Examples 11.3 to 11.5 build the concepts of using two-dimensional arrays.

Example 11.1

```
$ EDIT TEDIOUS.FOR
        IROW1SEAT1 = 60
        IROW1SEAT2 = 70
        IROW1SEAT3 = 50
        IROW1SEAT4 = 80
        IROW2SEAT1 = 60
        IROW2SEAT2 = 50
        IROW2SEAT3 = 40
        IROW2SEAT4 = 80
        IROW3SEAT1 = 70
        IROW3SEAT2 = 90
        IROW3SEAT3 = 60
        IROW3SEAT4 = 50
        WRITE(6,*) IROW1SEAT1
        WRITE(6,*) IROW1SEAT2
        WRITE(6,*) IROW1SEAT3
        WRITE(6,*) IROW1SEAT4
        WRITE(6,*) IROW2SEAT1
        WRITE(6,*) IROW2SEAT2
        WRITE(6,*) IROW2SEAT3
        WRITE(6,*) IROW2SEAT4
        WRITE(6,*) IROW3SEAT1
        WRITE(6,*) IROW3SEAT2
        WRITE(6,*) IROW3SEAT3
        WRITE(6,*) IROW3SEAT4
        STOP
        END
$ FORTRAN TEDIOUS
$ LINK TEDIOUS
$ RUN TEDIOUS                              Example 11.1
60                                         Output
70
50
80
60
50
40
80
70
90
60
50
```

Description of Example 11.1.

IROW1SEAT1 = 60
IROW1SEAT2 = 70
IROW1SEAT3 = 50
IROW1SEAT4 = 80
IROW2SEAT1 = 60
IROW2SEAT2 = 50
IROW2SEAT3 = 40
IROW2SEAT4 = 80
IROW3SEAT1 = 70
IROW3SEAT2 = 90
IROW3SEAT3 = 60
IROW3SEAT4 = 50

For each variable in the program, there is a memory location with a unique symbolic name for storing the value assigned.

IROW1SEAT1	IROW1SEAT2	IROW1SEAT3	IROW1SEAT4
60	70	50	80

IROW2SEAT1	IROW2SEAT2	IROW2SEAT3	IROW2SEAT4
60	50	40	80

IROW3SEAT1	IROW3SEAT2	IROW3SEAT3	IROW3SEAT4
70	90	60	50

To access a memory location, it is necessary to specify the particular variable name.

■ Example 11.2: Declaring and Using a Two-Dimensional Array

For student grades stored by row and seat numbers, it is appropriate to store the data in a two-dimensional array.

	SEAT 1	SEAT 2	SEAT 3	SEAT 4
Row 1	60	70	50	80
Row 2	60	50	40	80
Row 3	70	90	60	50

This example simply shows the array declaration at the beginning of the program and the use of subscripts to define the row and column numbers in accessing the array. This example performs exactly the same function as Example 11.1. Observe that the subscripts for the array correspond to the row and seat numbers for the associated grades.

```
$ EDIT TWOD.FOR                              Example 11.2
      DIMENSION ISTUDENT_GRADE(3,4)
      ISTUDENT_GRADE(1,1) = 60
      ISTUDENT_GRADE(1,2) = 70
      ISTUDNET_GRADE(1,3) = 50
      ISTUDENT_GRADE(1,4) = 80
      ISTUDENT_GRADE(2,1) = 60
      ISTUDENT_GRADE(2,2) = 50
      ISTUDENT_GRADE(2,3) = 40
```

```
          ISTUDENT GRADE(2,4) = 80
          ISTUDENT GRADE(3,1) = 70
          ISTUDENT GRADE(3,2) = 90
          ISTUDENT GRADE(3,3) = 60
          ISTUDEND GRADE(3,4) = 50
          WRITE(6,*)   ISTUDENT GRADE(1,1)
          WRITE(6,*)   ISTUDENT GRADE(1,2)
          WRITE(6,*)   ISTUDENT GRADE(1,3)
          WRITE(6,*)   ISTUDENT GRADE(1,4)
          WRITE(6,*)   ISTUDENT GRADE(2,1)
          WRITE(6,*)   ISTUDENT GRADE(2,2)
          WRITE(6,*)   ISTUDENT GRADE(2,3)
          WRITE(6,*)   ISTUDENT GRADE(2,4)
          WRITE(6,*)   ISTUDENT GRADE(3,1)
          WRITE(6,*)   ISTUDENT GRADE(3,2)
          WRITE(6,*)   ISTUDENT GRADE(3,3)
          WRITE(6,*)   ISTUDENT GRADE(3,4)
          STOP
          END
$ FORTRAN TWOD
$ LINK TWOD
$ RUN TWOD
60
70
50
80
60
50
40
80
70
90
60
50
```

Example 11.2
Output

Description of Example 11.2. The DIMENSION statement sets aside an array of memory locations to be accessed by the name ISTUDENT_GRADE. The number of memory locations set aside is 12. The 12 memory locations include the 3 rows and 4 columns declared in the parentheses (3,4) following the symbolic name of the array.

DIMENSION ISTUDENT_GRADE(3,4)

When the program executes, the values in the assignment statements are stored in the array of storage locations defined by the array name and the particular location specified by the subscripts.

The first assignment statement in the program assigns the value 60 to be stored in the array named ISTUDENT_GRADE in the location (1,1), that is row 1, column 1. The row and column numbers for the array are shown at the upper left of each memory location sketched in the array. (See Figure 11.1.)

ISTUDENT_GRADE(1,1) = 60

The remainder of the scores for row 1 are stored with the following assignment statements.

ISTUDENT_GRADE(1,2) = 70
ISTUDENT_GRADE(1,3) = 50
ISTUDENT_GRADE(1,4) = 80

The first subscript for each value specifies the row number, and the second subscript specifies the column number.

The first score for row two is assigned to the location specified by the subscript of (2,1).

ISTUDENT_GRADE(2,1) = 60

The meaning of this assignment statement is that the value 60 will be stored in the array named ISTUDENT_GRADE in the location of row 2, column 1.

After all the assignment statements in the program have been executed, a grade is stored in each memory location in the array.

ISTUDENT_GRADE(2,2) = 50
ISTUDENT_GRADE(2,3) = 40
ISTUDENT_GRADE(2,4) = 80
ISTUDENT_GRADE(3,1) = 70
ISTUDENT_GRADE(3,2) = 90
ISTUDENT_GRADE(3,3) = 60
ISTUDENT_GRADE(3,4) = 50

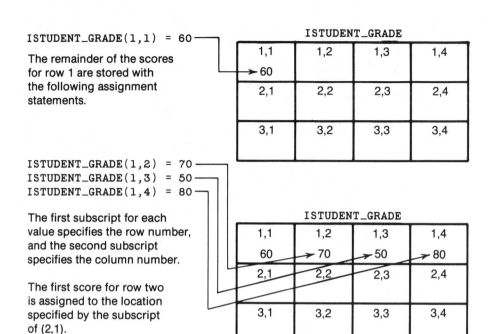

FIGURE 11.1

276

In this program, after all the grades are stored in the array named ISTUDENT_GRADE, the elements in the array are accessed in the WRITE statements. (See Figure 11.1A.)

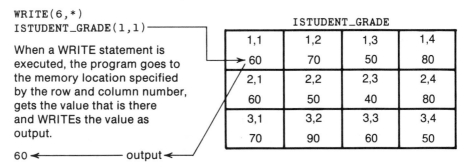

```
WRITE(6,*)
ISTUDENT_GRADE(1,1)
```

When a WRITE statement is executed, the program goes to the memory location specified by the row and column number, gets the value that is there and WRITEs the value as output.

60 ← ———— output ←

FIGURE 11.1A

■ Example 11.3: Input for a Two-Dimensional Array

This example demonstrates entering data one value per record to be read into a two-dimensional array. The location in the array where the value will be stored is specified by the subscripts to the variable representing the row number and column number. The values are output a row at a time.

```
60                                                          Example 11.3
70                                                          Input
50
80
60
50
40
80
70
90
60
50
$ EDIT READDOWN.FOR                                        Example 11.3
        INTEGER GRADE(3,4)
        READ(5,*) GRADE(1,1)
        READ(5,*) GRADE(1,2)
        READ(5,*) GRADE(1,3)
        READ(5,*) GRADE(1,4)
        READ(5,*) GRADE(2,1)
        READ(5,*) GRADE(2,2)
        READ(5,*) GRADE(2,3)
        READ(5,*) GRADE(2,4)
        READ(5,*) GRADE(3,1)
        READ(5,*) GRADE(3,2)
        READ(5,*) GRADE(3,3)
        READ(5,*) GRADE(3,4)
```

```
        WRITE(6,*)   GRADE(1,1), GRADE(1,2), GRADE(1,3), GRADE(1,4)
        WRITE(6,*)   GRADE(2,1), GRADE(2,2), GRADE(2,3), GRADE(2,4)
        WRITE(6,*)   GRADE(3,1), GRADE(3,2), GRADE(3,3), GRADE(3,4)
        STOP
        END
$ FORTRAN READDOWN
$ LINK READDOWN
$ RUN READDOWN
     6Ø       7Ø       5Ø       8Ø
     6Ø       5Ø       4Ø       8Ø
     7Ø       9Ø       6Ø       5Ø
```

Example 11.3
Output

Description of Example 11.3. Since the symbolic name GRADE would usually store real values, the INTEGER declaration is used to declare that a two-dimensional array named GRADE will contain 12 locations, 3 rows and 4 columns.

INTEGER GRADE(3,4)

The input data are provided one value per record, and the READ statements are one after another in the program to match the input data. The input data are stored by the READ statements in the array named GRADE in the location specified by the row and column numbers in the subscript.

The first data value to be input is 60. (See Figure 11.2.)

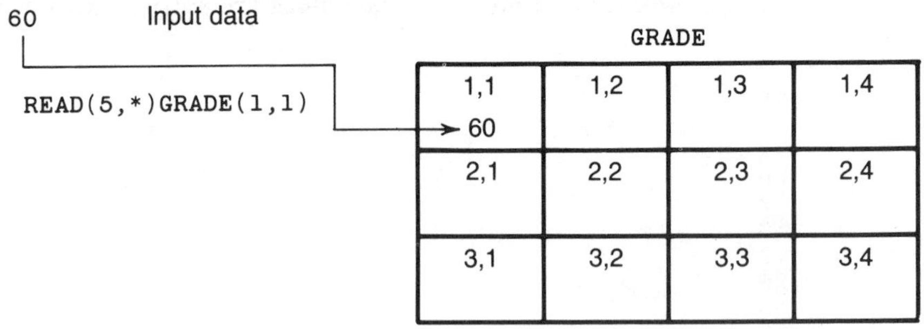

FIGURE 11.2

The first READ statement causes the first data value, which is 60, to be stored in the array named GRADE in the location specified by the subscripts of row 1 and column 1.

Each succeeding READ statement causes the succeeding input data value to be stored in the array named GRADE in the location specified by the subscript numbers for row and column.

When the first WRITE statement is executed, the values in the first row of the array named GRADE are printed. In the first WRITE statement, row number 1 is specified in the first subscript for each value to be output. Each of the columns 1 to 4 is specified. (See Figure 11.3.).

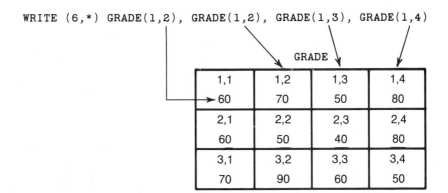

```
WRITE (6,*) GRADE(1,2), GRADE(1,2), GRADE(1,3), GRADE(1,4)
```

FIGURE 11.3

When the second WRITE statement is executed, the values in the second row of the array are printed.

When the third WRITE statement is executed, the values in the third row of the array are printed.

■ Example 11.4: Input by Row for a Two-Dimensional Array

This example demonstrates entering data with all the data for one row of the array stored in one record. There is then one READ statement per row in the array. The location in the array where the value will be stored is specified by the subscripts to the variable representing the row number and column number. The values are output by row across the row.

```
60,70,50,80                                             Example 11.4
60,50,40,80                                             Input
70,90,60,50
$ EDIT READACROS.FOR                                    Example 11.4
      INTEGER GRADE(3,4)
      READ(5,*) GRADE(1,1), GRADE(1,2), GRADE(1,3), GRADE(1,4)
      READ(5,*) GRADE(2,1), GRADE(2,2), GRADE(2,3), GRADE(2,4)
      READ(5,*) GRADE(3,1), GRADE(3,2), GRADE(3,3), GRADE(3,4)
      WRITE(6,*)  GRADE(1,1), GRADE(1,2), GRADE(1,3), GRADE(1,4)
      WRITE(6,*)  GRADE(2,1), GRADE(2,2), GRADE(2,3), GRADE(2,4)
      WRITE(6,*)  GRADE(3,1), GRADE(3,2), GRADE(3,3), GRADE(3,4)
      STOP
      END
$ FORTRAN READACROS
$ LINK READACROS
$ RUN READACROS                                         Example 11.4
      60       70       50       80                     Output
      60       50       40       80
      70       90       60       50
```

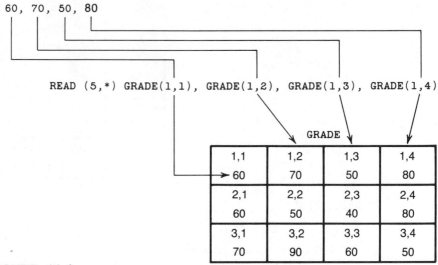

FIGURE 11.4

Description of Example 11.4. The input data are provided one record per row of the array, so there is one READ statement for each of the three rows of the array. The input data are stored by the READ statements in the array named GRADE in the location specified by the row and column numbers in the subscript.

The first record of input data is stored in the first row of the array. (See Figure 11.4.)

When the second READ statement is executed, the values in the second row of the array are input.

When the third READ statement is executed, the values in the third row of the array are input.

The WRITE statements output the values in the array row by row using the subscripts to the array named GRADE to indicate the particular memory location to be accessed.

■ Example 11.5: Accessing Elements of a Two-Dimensional Array with DO Loops

Examples 11.1 to 11.4 are intended to introduce a way to understand two-dimensional arrays and the programs are not realistic. The primary advantage to using arrays is in the capability of accessing the elements in an array in a systematic way using DO loops. With DO loops all the elements in an array can be accessed with only a few statements, whether there are 10 elements in the array or 10,000. Nested DO loops are often used to access all the elements in a two-dimensional array.

Refer again to the data that represents grades for students identified by a location in the class using a row number and a column number.

	SEAT 1	SEAT 2	SEAT 3	SEAT 4
Row 1	60	70	50	80
Row 2	60	50	40	80
Row 3	70	90	60	50

For this program, the input data are stored one value per record, with all the values for row 1, followed by all the values for row 2, and then all the values for row 3. The output for the program prints the values one after another and then prints the values one row after another.

Example 11.5
Input

```
60
70
50
80
60
50
40
80
70
90
60
50
```

```
$ EDIT DO2D.FOR                                        Example 11.5
      INTEGER GRAD(3,4), ROW, SEAT

C     Input the data which is stored one value after another,
C     with all the seats in row one first, then all row 2, etc.
      DO ROW = 1,3
         DO SEAT = 1,4
            READ(5,*) GRAD(ROW,SEAT)
         END DO
      END DO

C     Write the GRADes one after another down the page.
      WRITE(6,*)'GRADES WRITTEN ONE AFTER ANOTHER DOWN THE PAGE'
100   FORMAT(' ','ROW= ',I1,'   SEAT= ',I1,'   GRADE=',I3)
      DO ROW = 1,3
         DO SEAT = 1,4
            WRITE(6,100)ROW, SEAT, GRAD(ROW,SEAT)
         END DO
      END DO

C     Write the GRADes by row.
      WRITE(6,*)
      WRITE(6,*)'          GRADES WRITTEN BY ROW'
      WRITE(6,*)'        SEAT1  SEAT2  SEAT3  SEAT4'
200   FORMAT(' ROW= ',I1,4I7)
      DO ROW = 1,3
      WRITE(6,200)ROW,GRAD(ROW,1),GRAD(ROW,2),GRAD(ROW,3),GRAD(ROW,4)
```

```
        END DO
        STOP
        END
$ FORTRAN DO2D
$ LINK DO2D
$ RUN DO2D
```
Example 11.5
Output

```
GRADES WRITTEN ONE AFTER ANOTHER DOWN THE PAGE
ROW= 1    SEAT= 1    GRADE=  60
ROW= 1    SEAT= 2    GRADE=  70
ROW= 1    SEAT= 3    GRADE=  50
ROW= 1    SEAT= 4    GRADE=  80
ROW= 2    SEAT= 1    GRADE=  60
ROW= 2    SEAT= 2    GRADE=  50
ROW= 2    SEAT= 3    GRADE=  40
ROW= 2    SEAT= 4    GRADE=  80
ROW= 3    SEAT= 1    GRADE=  70
ROW= 3    SEAT= 2    GRADE=  90
ROW= 3    SEAT= 3    GRADE=  60
ROW= 3    SEAT= 4    GRADE=  50

             GRADES  WRITTEN  BY  ROW
          SEAT1   SEAT2   SEAT3   SEAT4
ROW= 1     60      70      50      80
ROW= 2     60      50      40      80
ROW= 3     70      90      60      50
```

Description of Example 11.5.   Look at the DO loop that stores the input values into the array named GRAD. The first time through the outside DO loop, the value stored in the memory location named ROW is a 1. While the value of ROW remains 1, the inside DO loop is executed 4 times, with the value of SEAT becoming first 1, then 2, and so on. The READ statement is executed a total of 12 times.

```
DO ROW = 1,3
   DO SEAT = 1,4
      READ(5,*) GRAD(ROW,SEAT)
   END DO
END DO
```

The first time that the READ statement is executed, the value in the memory location named ROW is 1, and the value in the memory location named SEAT is 1, making the subscripts for the array (1,1); so the first input value is stored in the first row in column 1 of the array. (See Figure 11.5.) The first READ statement causes the first data value, which is 60, to be stored in the array named GRADE in the location specified by the subscripts of row 1 and seat 1.

As the subscripts change with the DO loops, the READ statement stores the next input data value into the location specified by the subscripts ROW and SEAT.

After all the data values are stored in the array, the values are written

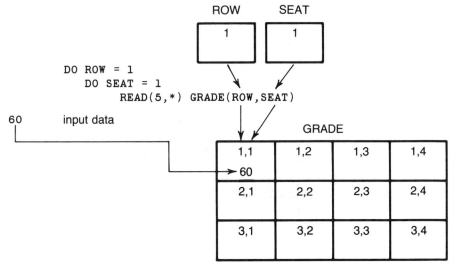

FIGURE 11.5

out. First the values are written one after another down the page. Notice that in the statements to WRITE the values one after another down the page the nested DO loops cause the WRITE statement to be executed 12 times, once for each value in the array.

```
DO ROW = 1,3
    DO SEAT = 1,4
        WRITE(6,100)ROW, SEAT, GRAD(ROW,SEAT)
    END DO
END DO
```

Then the values in the array are written out by rows. Notice that there is only one DO loop and the WRITE statement is executed only three times. Each element across the row is specified by the value in the variable ROW and a constant number of 1, 2, 3, or 4.

```
DO ROW = 1,3
WRITE(6,200)ROW,GRAD(ROW,1),GRAD(ROW,2),GRAD(ROW,3),GRAD
(ROW,4)
END DO
```

■ Example 11.6: Ordering Data Input to a Two-Dimensional Array

Refer again to the grades for each of the 12 students who are identified by the seating position in the class.

	SEAT 1	SEAT 2	SEAT 3	SEAT 4
Row 1	60	70	50	80
Row 2	60	50	40	80
Row 3	70	90	60	50

Perhaps in the class, the students turn in their papers in an undetermined order, not necessarily one after another, all of row 1 followed by all of row 2, then all of row 3. Perhaps the person in row 3, seat 2 turns in the first paper. The person in row 1, seat 3 might turn in the second paper.

This example program is written to allow the row and seat numbers to be read as input data and to be used to store the grade in the correct location. The input data are printed as they are input to observe the order of the input data. Then the contents of the array are printed to demonstrate that the values were indeed stored correctly.

```
3 2 90                                                    Example 11.6
1 3 50                                                    Input
1 4 80
2 1 60
3 3 60
2 2 50
2 3 40
1 1 60
1 2 70
2 4 80
3 1 70
3 4 50
```

```
$ EDIT ARRANGE2D.FOR                                      Example 11.6
      INTEGER GRAD(3,4), ROW, SEAT
100   FORMAT(' ','ROW= ',I1,'   SEAT= ',I1,'   GRADE=',I3)
200   FORMAT(' ROW= ',I1,4I7)

      WRITE(6,*)' ECHO THE INPUT AS IT IS READ'
C     Input the data.  For each record, the row number is stored
C     and the seat number is stored preceding the grade.  The
C     row number and seat number are then used to store the grade
C     in the appropriate location in the array named GRAD.  The
C     DO loop in this example provides a loop for the execution
C     of the read statement the correct number of times, but the
C     counter in the DO loop is not used as a subscript.
      DO NUMBER_GRADES = 1,12
         READ(5,*) ROW, SEAT, GRAD(ROW,SEAT)
         WRITE(6,100)ROW, SEAT, GRAD(ROW,SEAT)
      END DO

C     Write the GRADes by row.
      WRITE(6,*)
      WRITE(6,*)'             GRADES WRITTEN BY ROW'
      WRITE(6,*)'         SEAT1   SEAT2   SEAT3   SEAT4'
      DO ROW = 1,3
      WRITE(6,200)ROW,GRAD(ROW,1),GRAD(ROW,2),GRAD(ROW,3),GRAD(ROW,4)
      END DO
      STOP
      END
```

```
$ FORTRAN ARRANGE2D
$ LINK ARRANGE2D
$ RUN ARRANGE2D
  ECHO THE INPUT AS IT IS READ
ROW= 3    SEAT= 2    GRADE=  90
ROW= 1    SEAT= 3    GRADE=  50
ROW= 1    SEAT= 4    GRADE=  80
ROW= 2    SEAT= 1    GRADE=  60
ROW= 3    SEAT= 3    GRADE=  60
ROW= 2    SEAT= 2    GRADE=  50
ROW= 2    SEAT= 3    GRADE=  40
ROW= 1    SEAT= 1    GRADE=  60
ROW= 1    SEAT= 2    GRADE=  70
ROW= 2    SEAT= 4    GRADE=  80
ROW= 3    SEAT= 1    GRADE=  70
ROW= 3    SEAT= 4    GRADE=  50


          GRADES WRITTEN BY ROW
         SEAT1   SEAT2   SEAT3   SEAT4
ROW= 1    60      70      50      80
ROW= 2    60      50      40      80
ROW= 3    70      90      60      50
```

Example 11.6
Output

Description of Example 11.6.   The READ statement in this program is executed 12 times, transferring 12 values into the array named GRAD. In order for the value for the grade to be stored in the correct position in the array, the row number and seat number are also input as data values. The data values input as ROW and SEAT are then used as subscripts to specify the location in which the grade, that is, the third value, should be stored.

```
DO NUMBER_GRADES = 1,12
    READ(5,*) ROW, SEAT, GRAD(ROW,SEAT)
    WRITE(6,100)ROW, SEAT, GRAD(ROW,SEAT)
END DO
```

For the first input record, the values are 3   2   90. The 3 is stored in the memory location named ROW. The 2 is stored in the memory location named

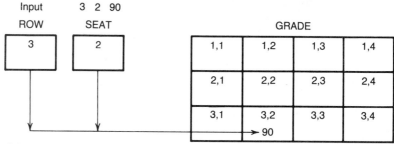

FIGURE 11.6

SEAT. The values stored in the memory locations ROW and SEAT are then used as subscripts to specify the location in the array named GRAD where the value 90 should be stored. (See Figure 11.6.)

The next input record contains the data 1   3   50. The value 1 is stored in the memory location named ROW. The value 3 is stored in the memory location named SEAT. Then the value 90 is stored in the array named GRAD in the location specified by the subscripts (ROW,SEAT). (See Figure 11.7.)

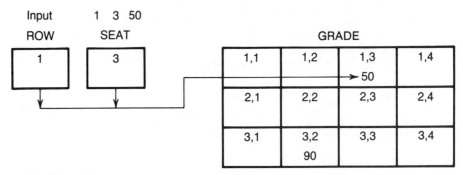

FIGURE 11.7

The remainder of the values in the array are stored similarly by first reading the row number and the seat number and then using those values to specify the location in the array named GRAD where the grade should be stored. Once the data are stored in the array, they can be accessed using DO loops to step through the array sequentially, because all the data values are stored in the correct positions.

■ Example 11.7: A Realistic Program with Two-Dimensional Arrays

The program inputs the names and three test grades for each of six students. The names are stored in a one-dimensional character array, and the test grades are stored in a two-dimensional array. The program calculates and prints the average for each student, the average for each of the three tests, and the class average for all the grades for all the students.

Example 11.7
Input

ADAMS	65.	75.	85.
BOX	64.	62.	60.
CARNES	80.	85.	90.
DAVIS	92.	90.	88.
EDSON	65.	55.	60.
FRANCO	84.	86.	88.

```
$ EDIT ARAYACESS.FOR                                    Example 11.7
      CHARACTER NAME(6)*10
      DIMENSION GRAD(6,3)
      INTEGER STUD
100   FORMAT(A,3F5.0)
200   FORMAT(' ',A,'   AVERAGE= ',F5.1)
C     Input data
      DO STUD = 1,6
         READ(5,100)NAME(STUD),GRAD(STUD,1),GRAD(STUD,2),GRAD(STUD,3)
      END DO

C     Calculate and print the average for each student
      DO STUD = 1,6
         TOTAL = 0
         DO ITEST = 1,3
            TOTAL = TOTAL + GRAD(STUD,ITEST)
         END DO
         WRITE(6,200)NAME(STUD),TOTAL/3.0
      END DO

C     Calculate and print the average for each of the three tests
      DO ITEST = 1,3
         TOTAL = 0
         DO STUD = 1,6
            TOTAL = TOTAL + GRAD(STUD,ITEST)
         END DO
         WRITE(6,*)'FOR TEST',ITEST,'  THE AVERAGE=',TOTAL/6.0
      END DO

C     Calculate and print the average for the class
      TOTAL = 0
      DO STUD = 1,6
         DO ITEST = 1,3
            TOTAL = TOTAL + GRAD(STUD,ITEST)
         END DO
      END DO
      WRITE(6,*)'FOR THE CLASS, THE AVERAGE=',TOTAL/18.0

      STOP
      END
$ FORTRAN ARAYACESS
$ LINK ARAYACESS
$ RUN ARAYACESS
```

```
ADAMS        AVERAGE=   75.0                    Example 11.7
BOX          AVERAGE=   62.0                    Output
CARNES       AVERAGE=   85.0
DAVIS        AVERAGE=   90.0
EDSON        AVERAGE=   60.0
FRANCO       AVERAGE=   86.0
FOR TEST          1    THE AVERAGE=    75.00000
FOR TEST          2    THE AVERAGE=    75.50000
FOR TEST          3    THE AVERAGE=    78.50000
FOR THE CLASS, THE AVERAGE=    76.33334
```

Description of Example 11.7. To calculate the average for each student, the outside DO loop contains the counter used for the subscript for the rows.

GRAD

1,1	1,2	1,3
65	75	85
2,1	2,2	2,3
64	62	60

STUD	TOTAL	ITEST
1	0	1

TOTAL=TOTAL+GRAD(STUD,ITEST)
That is add the value in the array named
GRAD in location (1,1) to the TOTAL.

FIGURE 11.8

Each row corresponds to a record for a student. The subscript for the student is held constant then while the inside DO loop is changing the subscript for the three tests for the student. Notice that the TOTAL is set to zero at the beginning of the summation for each new student.

```
C    Calculate and print the average for each student.
     DO  STUD = 1,6
         TOTAL = 0
         DO ITEST = 1,3
             TOTAL = TOTAL + GRAD(STUD,ITEST)
         END DO
         WRITE(6,*)NAME(STUD),'AVERAGE = ',TOTAL/3.0
     END DO
```

See Figure 11.8.

The execution continues in the inside DO loop. The value of STUD stays the same. The value of ITEST is incremented in the inside DO loop. The value of TOTAL now contains the addition of the first element in the first row of the array named GRAD. (See Figure 11.9.)

GRAD

1,1	1,2	1,3
65	75	85
2,1	2,2	2,3
64	62	60

STUD	TOTAL	ITEST
1	65	2

TOTAL=TOTAL+GRAD(STUD,ITEST)
That is add the value in the array named
GRAD in location (1,2) to the TOTAL.

FIGURE 11.9

The value 75 was added to the value of 65 already stored in the memory location named TOTAL, making the current value of TOTAL 140. The counter ITEST for the inside DO loop is still causing the elements across the first row of the array named GRAD to be accessed. The value of STUD remains 1. (See Figure 11.10.)

GRAD		
1,1	1,2	1,3
65	75	85
2,1	2,2	2,3
64	62	60

STUD	TOTAL	ITEST
1	140	3

TOTAL=TOTAL+GRAD(STUD,ITEST)
That is add the value in the array named
GRAD in location (1,3) to the TOTAL.

FIGURE 11.10

The first pass through the inside DO loop has completed. The TOTAL
for the first row of values in the array has been calculated. In the context of
this example, the total for the first student has been calculated. Now the
average of the three scores is calculated and printed along with the name.
(See Figure 11.11.)

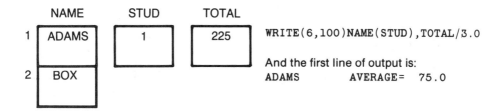

WRITE(6,100)NAME(STUD),TOTAL/3.0

And the first line of output is:
ADAMS   AVERAGE=   75.0

FIGURE 11.11

Now the outside DO loop is executed again. This time the value of STUD
will be 2 while the value of ITEST changes from 1 to 3, moving across the
second row in the array. (See Figure 11.12.)

The calculation of the total and subsequently the average for each student demonstrated previously is accomplished by setting the TOTAL to zero
at the beginning of the calculation for a row and holding the subscript for the
row number constant in the outside DO loop while the subscript moves
across the row in the inside DO loop.

GRAD		
1,1	1,2	1,3
65	75	85
2,1	2,2	2,3
64	62	60

STUD	TOTAL	ITEST
2	0	1

TOTAL=TOTAL+GRAD(STUD,ITEST)
That is add the value in the array named
GRAD in location (2,1) to the TOTAL.

FIGURE 11.12

GRAD

1,1	1,2	1,3
65	75	85
2,1	2,2	2,3
64	62	60
3,1	3,2	3,3
80	85	90
4,1	4,2	4,3
92	90	88
5,1	5,2	5,3
65	55	60
6,1	6,2	6,3
84	86	88

STUD	TOTAL	ITEST
1	0	1

`TOTAL=TOTAL+GRAD(STUD,ITEST)`
That is add the value in the array named GRAD in location (1,1) to the TOTAL.

In this section of code, the row number is being changed in the inside DO loop and the TOTAL is being calculated going down column 1.

GRAD

1,1	1,2	1,3
65	75	85
2,1	2,2	2,3
64	62	60
3,1	3,2	3,3
80	85	90

STUD	TOTAL	ITEST
2	65	1

`TOTAL=TOTAL+GRAD(STUD,ITEST)`
That is add the value in the array named GRAD in location (2,1) to the TOTAL. Add the value 64 to the current TOTAL.

GRAD

1,1	1,2	1,3
65	75	85
2,1	2,2	2,3
64	62	60
3,1	3,2	3,3
80	85	90
4,1	4,2	4,3
92	90	88
5,1	5,2	5,3
65	55	60
6,1	6,2	6,3
84	86	88

STUD	TOTAL	ITEST
3	129	1

`TOTAL=TOTAL+GRAD(STUD,ITEST)`
That is add the value in the array named GRAD in location (3,1) to the TOTAL. Add the value 80 to the current TOTAL.

The total for column one is being generated. The subscripts in the variable named STUD continue to change accessing locations (4,1), (5,1), and (6,1).

After the total for the column is generated, the average is calculated and printed. Then the average for column two is calculated and printed.

FIGURE 11.13

The calculation of the total and subsequently the average for each test demonstrated in the following is accomplished by setting the TOTAL to zero at the beginning of the calculation for a column and holding the subscript for the column number constant in the outside DO loop while the subscript moves down the column in the inside DO loop.

```
C   Calculate and print the average for each of the three tests.
    DO ITEST = 1,3
        TOTAL = 0
        DO STUD = 1,6
            TOTAL = TOTAL + GRAD(STUD,ITEST)
        END DO
        WRITE(6,*)'FOR TEST',ITEST,' THE AVERAGE = ',TOTAL/6.0
    END DO
```

See Figure 11.13.

When the average for all the scores for all the students is calculated, the TOTAL is set to zero outside both DO loops, because the total should include every grade in every row and every column. The DO loops in this case can be arranged to move across the rows first or down the columns first, because the order is not important in accessing every element in the array.

```
C   Calculate and print the average for the class.
    TOTAL = 0
    DO STUD = 1,6
        DO ITEST = 1,3
            TOTAL = TOTAL + GRAD(STUD,ITEST)
        END DO
    END DO
    WRITE(6,*)'FOR THE CLASS, THE AVERAGE = ',TOTAL/18.0
```

11.2
INPUT AND OUTPUT
WITH IMPLIED DO LOOPS

An implied DO loop used with a two-dimensional array provides a structure for defining systematic ways to input data stored in a variety of ways and to output data with various formats. For some kinds of input and output, there are no practical methods for the process other than using implied DO loops. An implied DO loop can be used only for input and output and cannot be used in association with other processing in a program. The following are some forms of an implied DO loop for a two-dimensional array.

For the following READ statement and WRITE statement, there is an implied DO loop contained inside a DO loop. In each structure shown, the outside DO loop controls the access to rows, and the implied DO loop accesses the elements across the columns.

```
DO NROW = N1,N2
    READ(unit,format) (array(nrow,mcol),mcol = m1,m2)
END DO

DO NROW = N1,N2
    WRITE(unit,format) (array(nrow,mcol),mcol = m1,m2)
END DO
```

The following READ statement and WRITE statement contain nested implied DO loops. The inside implied DO loop behaves as an inside DO loop in standard nested DO loops.

```
READ(unit,format)((array(nrow,mcol),mcol = m1,m2),nrow = n1,n2)
WRITE(unit,format)((array(nrow,mcol),mcol = m1,m2),nrow = n1,n2),
                            ↑                         ↑
                    performs first           performs last
```

The value for NROW is held constant while each element of the array specified by MCOL is accessed from M1 through M2. Then the value for NROW is incremented and every element of MCOL from M1 through M2 is accessed.

The combination of the READ and WRITE statements and the format statements actually determines the way that input and output will be performed. The following example indicates some of the possibilities for input and output.

■ **Example 11.8: Two-Dimensional Implied DO Loops**

The example provides various ways to input and output data.

```
60                                              Example 11.8
70                                              Input
50
80
60
50
40
80
70
90
60
50
65  75  55  85
65  55  45  85
75  95  65  55
```

```
$ EDIT IMPLIED2D.FOR                                    Example 11.8
      INTEGER N(3,4), M(3,4)
100   FORMAT(I3)
200   FORMAT(' ',I3)
300   FORMAT(' ',4I3)
400   FORMAT(4I3)
C     Read twelve values into the array N, one value per
C     record using FORMAT 100.
      READ(5,100)((N(IROW,ICOLUMN),ICOLUMN=1,4),IROW=1,3)

      WRITE(6,*)'The N array one value per record - FORMAT 200'
      WRITE(6,200)((N(IROW,ICOLUMN),ICOLUMN=1,4),IROW=1,3)

      WRITE(6,*)'The N array by row using FORMAT 300'
      WRITE(6,300)((N(IROW,ICOLUMN),ICOLUMN=1,4),IROW=1,3)

C     Now read the data which is stored by rows using FORMAT 400.
      READ(5,400)((M(IROW,ICOLUMN),ICOLUMN=1,4),IROW=1,3)

      WRITE(6,*)'The M array one value per record - FORMAT 200'
      WRITE(6,200)((M(IROW,ICOLUMN),ICOLUMN=1,4),IROW=1,3)

      WRITE(6,*)'The M array  by row using FORMAT 300'
      WRITE(6,300)((M(IROW,ICOLUMN),ICOLUMN=1,4),IROW=1,3)
      STOP
      END
$ FORTRAN IMPLIED2D
$ LINK IMPLIED2D
$ RUN IMPLIED2D
The N array one value per record - FORMAT 200
  60
  70
  50
  80
  60
  50
  40
  80
  70
  90
  60
  50
The N array by row using FORMAT 300
  60 70 50 80
  60 50 40 80
  70 90 60 50
The M array one value per record - FORMAT 200
  65
  75
  55
  85
  65
  55
  45
  85
  75
  95
  65
  55
```

Example 11.8
Output

(Continued)

(Continued)

```
The M array  by row using FORMAT 300
    65 75 55 85
    65 55 45 85
    75 95 65 55
```

11.3
GENERAL APPROACH TO WRITING
PROGRAMS WITH ARRAYS

The first goal in writing a computer program is to make the program work. In addition to making it work, it is advisable to consider the future use of the program. It is important in writing computer programs to make the code clear to someone who is trying to understand the program and to make the code easy to modify to meet changing needs for the program. Using arrays in programs allows you to divide the program into definable tasks and to document the tasks in the program so that the code is understandable and easy to modify. Another help in writing modifiable code is to make the limits for counters in DO loops variable names so that the program can be run for any number of records.

■ **Example 11.9: Program**
Using General Concepts
for Two-Dimensional Arrays

There is a chain of department stores with sales information for one day of sales. In this chain of stores at this time, there are five stores, each with four departments. An expansion is expected, however, and the program should be written to allow additional stores or departments to be added to the analysis.

The program dimensions the array for sales named ISALE to allow for 10 stores and 20 departments. The department names are assigned in a DATA statement and represent an absolute value that would have to change if the number of departments expanded.

The program first inputs the count for the number of stores and the number of departments per store. These values will then be used throughout the program to control the access into arrays.

The program performs the following tasks, each of which is coded in a set of instructions and documented.

Read the data for all the departments for every store.

Print the input data.

Calculate and print the sum of the total sales for all the stores.

Calculate and print the total sales for each store.

Calculate and print the total sales for each department over all the stores. That is, calculate the total sales in the children's department over all the stores, in the women's department over all the stores, etc.

For each store, find the department that has the maximum sales.

For each department, find the store with the minimum sales. Find the store that has sold the least amount in the children's department, the least amount in the women's department, and so on.

Over all the stores, find the maximum sale and the store and the department in which the maximum sale occurred.

```
5 4     Number of stores and departments
CHILDRENS
WOMENS
MENS
SPORTS
 3200 1600 4100 3800
 1200  900 3300 1700
 1400  600 2200  800
 3900 2300 2100 3000
  200  100  300  400
```

Example 11.9
Input

```
$ EDIT GENERAL2D.FOR
        DIMENSION ISALE(10,20)
        INTEGER TOTAL
        CHARACTER DEPT_NAME(10)*9

C       Read the number of stores and the number of departments.
        READ(5,*)NUMSTOR,NUMDEPT
C       Read the names of the departments.
50      FORMAT(A)
        READ(5,50)(DEPT_NAME(IDEPT),IDEPT=1,NUMDEPT)

C       Read the data for all the departments for every store.
C       For this data, each record contains the data for all the
C       departments in one store.
        DO ISTORE = 1, NUMSTOR
           READ(5,100)(ISALE(ISTORE,IDEPT),IDEPT=1,NUMDEPT)
        END DO
100     FORMAT(4I5)

C       Print the input data.  The names of the departments are
C       stored with the DATA declaration at the beginning of program
200     FORMAT(' ',12X,4(4X,A))
300     FORMAT(' STORE #',I2,10X,4(I5,9X))
        WRITE(6,200)DEPT_NAME
        DO ISTORE = 1,NUMSTOR
           WRITE(6,300)ISTORE,(ISALE(ISTORE,IDEPT),IDEPT=1,NUMDEPT)
        END DO

C       Calculate overall total sales for all stores
400     FORMAT(/,' TOTAL SALE FOR ALL STORES = ',I8,/)
        TOTAL = 0
```

Example 11.9

```
      DO ISTORE = 1,NUMSTOR
         DO IDEPT = 1,NUMDEPT
            TOTAL = TOTAL + ISALE(ISTORE,IDEPT)
         END DO
      END DO
      WRITE(6,400)TOTAL

C     Calculate the total sales for each store
500   FORMAT(' TOTAL SALES FOR STORE #',I2,' =',I8)
      DO ISTORE = 1, NUMSTOR
         TOTAL = 0
         DO IDEPT = 1,NUMDEPT
            TOTAL = TOTAL + ISALE(ISTORE,IDEPT)
         END DO
         WRITE(6,500)ISTORE,TOTAL
      END DO

      WRITE(6,*)                              !Blank Line
C     Calculate and print the total sales for each department
C     over all the stores.  That is calculate the total sales
C     in the children's departments for all stores, in the
C     women's department for all stores, etc.
600   FORMAT(' ','TOTAL SALES FOR THE ',A,' DEPARTMENT ARE',I8)
      DO IDEPT = 1,NUMDEPT
         TOTAL = 0
         DO ISTORE = 1, NUMSTOR
            TOTAL = TOTAL + ISALE(ISTORE,IDEPT)
         END DO
         WRITE(6,600)DEPT_NAME(IDEPT),TOTAL
      END DO

      WRITE(6,*)                              !Print Blank Line
700   FORMAT(' ',A,' DEPARTMENT MAXIMUM SALE IN STORE #',I2)
C     For each store, find the department with the maximum sales
      DO ISTORE = 1, NUMSTOR
         MAX = 0
         DO IDEPT = 1,NUMDEPT
            IF (ISALE(ISTORE,IDEPT).GT.MAX) THEN
               MAX = ISALE(ISTORE,IDEPT)
               MAXDEPT = IDEPT
            END IF
         END DO
         WRITE(6,700)DEPT_NAME(MAXDEPT),ISTORE
      END DO

      WRITE(6,*)                              !Print blank line
800   FORMAT(' ',A,' DEPARTMENT MINIMUM SALE IN STORE #',I2)
C     For each department, find the store with the minimum sales.
C     Find the store which has sold the least amount in the
C     children's department, the least in the women's dept, etc.
      DO IDEPT = 1,NUMDEPT
         MIN = ISALE(1,IDEPT)
         MIN_STORE = 1
         DO ISTORE = 2, NUMSTOR
            IF (ISALE(ISTORE,IDEPT) .LT. MIN) THEN
               MIN = ISALE(ISTORE,IDEPT)
               MIN_STORE = ISTORE
            END IF
```

```
         END DO
         WRITE(6,800)DEPT_NAME(IDEPT),MIN_STORE
      END DO

C     Find the maximum sale and the store and the department in
C     which the maximum sale occured.
900   FORMAT(/,' OVERALL MAXIMUM SALE= ',I5,/,
     - ' SALE WAS IN STORE #',I2, 'IN THE ',A,' DEPARTMENT')
      MAX = 0
      DO ISTORE = 1,NUMSTOR
         DO IDEPT = 1,NUMDEPT
            IF (ISALE(ISTORE,IDEPT) .GT. MAX) THEN
               MAX = ISALE(ISTORE,IDEPT)
               MAXSTORE = ISTORE
               MAXDEPT = IDEPT
            END IF
         END DO
      END DO
      WRITE(6,900)MAX,MAXSTORE,DEPT_NAME(MAXDEPT)
      STOP
      END
$ FORTRAN GENERAL2D
$ LINK GENERAL2D
$ RUN GENERAL2D
```

Example 11.9
Output

```
                CHILDRENS        WOMENS          MENS        SPORTS

STORE #1           3200           1600          4100          3800
STORE #2           1200            900          3300          1700
STORE #3           1400            600          2200           800
STORE #4           3900           2300          2100          3000
STORE #5            200            100           300           400

TOTAL SALE FOR ALL STORES =    37100

TOTAL SALES FOR STORE #1 =   12700
TOTAL SALES FOR STORE #2 =    7100
TOTAL SALES FOR STORE #3 =    5000
TOTAL SALES FOR STORE #4 =   11300
TOTAL SALES FOR STORE #5 =    1000

TOTAL SALES FOR THE CHILDRENS DEPARTMENT ARE    9900
TOTAL SALES FOR THE   WOMENS DEPARTMENT ARE    5500
TOTAL SALES FOR THE     MENS DEPARTMENT ARE   12000
TOTAL SALES FOR THE   SPORTS DEPARTMENT ARE    9700

MENS      DEPARTMENT MAXIMUM SALE IN STORE # 1
MENS      DEPARTMENT MAXIMUM SALE IN STORE # 2
MENS      DEPARTMENT MAXIMUM SALE IN STORE # 3
CHILDRENS DEPARTMENT MAXIMUM SALE IN STORE # 4
SPORTS    DEPARTMENT MAXIMUM SALE IN STORE # 5

CHILDRENS DEPARTMENT MINIMUM SALE IN STORE #5
   WOMENS DEPARTMENT MINIMUM SALE IN STORE #5
     MENS DEPARTMENT MINIMUM SALE IN STORE #5
   SPORTS DEPARTMENT MINIMUM SALE IN STORE #5

OVERALL MAXIMUM SALE=  4100
SALE WAS IN STORE #1 IN THE       MENS DEPARTMENT
```

11.4
SUMMARY

A *two-dimensional array* is a set of memory locations defined by one symbolic name. An element in a two-dimensional array is specified by a row and column number. The array can be defined with a DIMENSION, INTEGER or REAL declaration.

```
DIMENSION arrayname(numrow,numcol)
INTEGER arrayname(numrow,numcol)
REAL arrayname(numrow,numcol)
```

Each element in a two-dimensional array can be accessed systematically with a nested DO loop.

```
DO irow = 1, num_of_rows
    DO icolumn = 1, num_of_columns
        arrayname(irow,icolumn)
    END DO
END DO
```

Input and output for two-dimensional arrays is often controlled with implied DO loops. In the following structures, the outside DO loop controls the access to rows and the implied DO loop controls the access to the elements across the columns.

```
DO nrow = 1, numrows
    READ(unit,format) (array(nrow,ncolumn),ncolumn = 1,numcol)
    WRITE(unit,format) (array(nrow,ncolumn),ncolumn = 1,numcol)
END DO
```

The inside DO loop in the following structures behaves as an inside DO loop in a standard DO loop structure.

```
READ(unit,formt) ((aray(irow,icol),icol = 1,numcol),irow = 1,numrow)
WRITE(unit,formt) ((aray(irow,icol),icol = 1,numcol),irow = 1,numrow)
```

In writing most programs, each time through an array, some definable task is performed. It is important to delimit and document each task.

The absolute size of an array must be specified in an array declaration; however, it is important to use symbolic names as limits in DO loops accessing arrays, because then the program can be used at various times for different numbers of rows and columns.

11.5
EXERCISES

Stepping through the code that you write is the way to initially verify that a program is correct. Stepping through the code in Exercises 11.1 through 11.5 can aid in your understanding of two-dimensional arrays, as well as reemphasize the value of the technique for determining what a program is actually doing.

As usual, the way to step through code is to draw a box for each memory location and write in each box the value stored in that memory location as the program executes. As a value changes in a memory location, strike through the old value and write the new value.

11.1.   What is the output for the following FORTRAN program?

```
DIMENSION  N1(3,2),  N2(3,2)
N1(1,1) = 55
N1(1,2) = 65
N1(2,1) = 60
N1(2,2) = 65
N1(3,1) = 75
N1(3,2) = 80
DO I = 1,3
    DO J = 1,2
        N2(I,J) = N1(I,J) + 10
    END DO
END DO
DO I = 1,3
    WRITE(6,*)I,N1(I,1),N1(I,1)
END DO
DO I = 1,3
    WRITE(6,*)I,N2(I,1),N2(I,1)
END DO
DO I = 1,3
    DO J = 1,2
        WRITE(6,*)I,J,N1(I,J),N2(I,J)
    END DO
END DO
STOP
END
```

11.2.   What is the output for the following FORTRAN program with the input data shown on the following page?

```
            DIMENSION  N(3,2)                     Input data for
    100     FORMAT(' ',2I5)                       the program
            DO I = 1, 3                                4
                DO J = 1,2                             7
                    READ(5,*)N(I,J)                    3
                END DO                                 2
            END DO                                     9
            DO I = 1,3                                 8
                WRITE(6,100) (N(I,J),J = 1,2)
            END DO
            DO J = 1,2
                TOTAL = 0
                DO I = 1,3
                    TOTAL = TOTAL + N(I,J)
                END DO
                WRITE(6,*)'COLUMN',J,TOTAL
            END DO
            STOP
            END
```

11.3. What is the output for the following FORTRAN program with the input data shown?

```
            DIMENSION  VALUE(5,5)              Input data for
    100     FORMAT(5F4.0)                      the program
            DO I = 1,5                         20  30  20  10  40
                READ(5,100) (VALUE(I,J),J = 1,5)   14  12  11  21  14
            END DO                              2   4   1   3   1
            DO 10 I = 1,5                      10  10  10  10  10
                TOTAL = 0                       4   3   9   1   2
                DO 20 J = 1,5
                    TOTAL = TOTAL + VALUE(I,J)
    20          CONTINUE
                WRITE(6,*)'ROW',I,TOTAL
    10      CONTINUE
            STOP
            END
```

11.4. What is the output for the following program? It is important to draw a box to represent each memory location and to step through the program like the computer would do, showing what would be in each memory location as the program executes. There is no input for the program.

```
            INTEGER   SUM(5,5)
            DO 5 I = 1,5
                DO 6 J = 1,5
```

```
                    SUM(I,J) = 0
6           CONTINUE
5       CONTINUE
        DO 10 I = 2, 4
            MAX = I
            DO 20 J = 1, 5
                DO 30 K = 1, MAX
                SUM(I,J) = SUM(I,J) + I
30              CONTINUE
20          CONTINUE
10      CONTINUE

        DO 40 I = 1, 5
            WRITE(6,*) (SUM(I,J),J = 1,5)
40      CONTINUE
        STOP
        END
```

11.5. What is the output for the following program with the input data shown?

```
        DIMENSION ISTORE(2,3)                        Input data for
100     FORMAT(' ',3I3)                              the program
        DO I = 1,2                                        2  2  4
            DO J = 1,3                                    1  3  3
                READ(5,*)IROW,ICOL,ISTORE(IROW,ICOL)     1  1  6
            END DO                                        2  3  2
        END DO                                            1  2  5
        DO IROW = 1, 2                                    2  1  7
            WRITE(6,100) (ISTORE(IROW,ICOL),ICOL = 1,3)
        END DO
        STOP
        END
```

11.6. The following statements listed set up a two-dimensional array and allow values to be input to the array. Generate your own input data.

```
        DIMENSION NUMBER(50,3)
100     FORMAT(3I5)
        DO I = 1, 50
            READ(5,100) (NUMBER(I,J),J = 1,3)
        END DO
```

Write the remaining statements in the program to perform the following procedures and print the results. Provide headings for all output.

a. Find the sum of all the values in the array.

b. Find the sum of each column in the array.

   c. Find the sum of each row in the array.

   d. Find the average of all the positive values in the array.

   e. Find the average of all the negative values in each row.

   f. Find the maximum value in the array.

   g. Find the maximum value for each column of the array.

   h. Find the minimum value for each row of the array.

11.7. Write a FORTRAN program to generate values for three arrays with the random (RAN) function. The random function is described in Example 10.2.

DIMENSION ONE(20,3)   Generate real integer values between 0.1 and 9.9

DIMENSION TWO(10,5)   Generate integer values between 100 and 1000

DIMENSION THREE(3,5)   Generate integer values between −25 and 0

11.8. Write a program to create a one-dimensional array that contains the average of all the positive numbers in each row of a two-dimensional array. The program should work for a two-dimensional array up to 100 by 8. Make the program general so that the actual numbers of rows and columns are read as data from the first record of input.

2	−3	6	Ø
Ø	1	3	−3

-->

4
2

11.9. Set up three arrays with a dimension statement. Arrays 1 and 2 have some values stored in them. Multiply each element in array 1 times the corresponding element in array 2 and store the calculated value in the corresponding location in array 3.

```
THREE(1,1)  = ONE(1,1)*TWO(1,1)
THREE(1,2)  = ONE(1,2)*TWO(1,2)
```

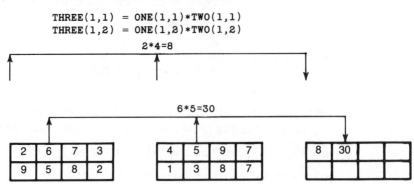

11.10. Using a systematic approach to accessing the elements in a two-dimensional array, store an asterisk character in each of the elements of an array as shown. Then print the contents of the array.

The program should generate this pattern in various sizes. Generate one pattern 7 by 7, as shown here. Generate another pattern 21 by 21. The program should be general to allow the user to select the size at run time.

```
*******
***  ***
**    **
*      *
**    **
***  ***
*******
```

11.11. Write a FORTRAN program for the following problem. There are four colleges administered by the regents of the Middle Mountain Region. The following data are available.

MIDDLE MOUNTAIN REGION

	NUMBER OF STUDENTS	TUITION COST PER STUDENT	HOUSING FEE PER STUDENT
Mid State College	1012	1550	2100
Mountain College	2300	1280	2800
Ivy Covered College	985	3800	4000
Nearby Skiing College	9800	1100	1800

In the program, read the name of the region and the names of the colleges as data. Then read the numerical data into a two-dimensional array.

For each college, generate a report including the total funds for the college provided by tuition and housing. For the entire region, generate a report including the total funds for tuition and housing. Label all output in a report form.

11.12. Write a program with three two-dimensional arrays. Dimensions for the arrays should be the following. Each element of the arrays is a one-digit number.

DIMENSION ARRAY1(3,10), ARRAY2(3,10),ARRAY3(3,20)

Generate data values for arrays 1 and 2. Array 3 should be the elements in arrays 1 and 2 concatenated with all imbedded zeros removed. Print the values in array 3.

ARRAYONE	ARRAYTWO	ARRAYTHREE
345000000	6893400000	34568934000000000000
293490000	5547826500	29349554782650000000
300502599	5050440000	35259955440000000000

12

Subprograms:
An Introduction
to Functions

In writing computer programs, it is important to make the program easy to understand by a person trying to read or modify the program. The SUBROUTINE and FUNCTION subprogram structures in the FORTRAN language provide boundries for beginning and ending a section of code to perform a specific task. Every nontrivial program should be written with subprograms performing definable tasks, each of which is easily understandable. SUBROUTINES are covered in Chapter 13.

12.1
DESCRIPTION OF A FUNCTION
AND ACCESSING A FUNCTION

A FUNCTION is a set of code written as a separate program unit and accessed by a function name to perform some manipulations and to return one value from the operation. The intrinsic library functions that are a part of the FORTRAN language include procedures that are commonly used by programmers. In addition to the library functions, a user can write functions.

The form of the *intrinsic library functions* covered in Chapter 2 is:

$$M = MIN(23,16,39)$$

The example means that the function named MIN will be executed. The set of code in the intrinsic library function stored as part of the FORTRAN language to find the minimum value of a set of numbers will be accessed and executed. The values 23, 16, and 39 are called *parameters* or *arguments* for the function. The argument values of 23, 16, and 39 are used as data for the instructions in the function. When the function is executed, the minimum value of 16 is returned from the function and stored in the memory location named M.

DEFINITION: A *function* is a series of statements that performs some operation(s) and returns *one* value to the calling routine. The series of statements begins wth the word FUNCTION and ends with the word RETURN and then the word END on the last line.

To invoke a function in a program, the following statement is used:

Symbolic_name = function_name(argument list)

When the statement to invoke a function is executed, control in the program goes to the set of instructions with the specified function_name to perform some operation. The values named in the argument list are data values passed into the function for performing the operation.

The general form of a user-written function is the following:

```
FUNCTION function_name(argument list)
     any number of statements to perform some operation
RETURN
END
```

When the function is invoked, values that can be used for data in the operation are passed into the function through the argument list. The statements in the function are executed, and the one value to be returned to the calling routine should be stored in the memory location with the symbolic name of the function_name. When the RETURN statement is executed, the value stored in the memory location specified by the function_name will be returned to the memory location on the left of the equals sign in the statement invoking the function.

A function name may be any valid symbolic name with 31 or fewer characters containing letters, numbers, and the underline character. Function names should be the correct type, that is, integer or real, to store the value. Function names beginning with the characters I, J, K, L, M, or N store integer values, and function names beginning with other characters store real values.

The best way to understand functions is to look at a simple example.

■ Example 12.1: Program
with a Function

Example 12.1

```
$ EDIT AVETHREE.FOR
C     Program with Function to Calculate the Average of 3 Numbers
C
C     The MAIN PROGRAM is this section of the program which
C     terminates with the STOP followed by the END.
C
C     The main program stores a value in locations A, B and C.
C     Then the main program invokes a function to calculate
C     the average of the three values, A, B and C.
C     The main program prints the calculated average which
C     is stored in the memory location named D.
C
C     Store three numbers.  The values would normally be
C     be input as data.
      A = 100
      B = 200
      C = 300

C     Invoke the function AVERAGE.
      D = AVERAGE(A,B,C)

C     Print the value of D which is returned from the function.
      PRINT *, D
      STOP
      END

      FUNCTION AVERAGE(A,B,C)
C     The function calculates the average of the three values.
      TOT = A + B + C
      AVERAGE = TOT / 3.0
      RETURN
      END

$ FORTRAN AVETHREE
$ LINK AVETHREE
$ RUN AVETHREE
200.0000
```

Example 12.1
Output

Description of Example 12.1.   FORTRAN determines that the statement D=AVERAGE(A,B,C) is invoking a function by recognizing the set of parentheses associated with the symbolic name AVERAGE, and checking to see if a user-written function by that name exists.

When the statement D= AVERAGE(A,B,C) is executed in the MAIN PROGRAM, execution is transferred to the set of instructions in the subprogram set off between the FUNCTION AVERAGE (A,B,C) and the RETURN/END statements. After the instructions in the function subprogram are executed, control is transferred back to the MAIN program to the statement following the call to the function.

```
        A = 100
        B = 200
        C = 300

   C    Invoke the function AVERAGE.
        D = AVERAGE(A,B,C) ─────────┐        Transfers control to the func-
                                    │        tion named AVERAGE.
   C    Print returned value of D.
        PRINT *, D          ◄──────────────┐
        STOP                │              │
        END                 │              │
                            │              │    When the instructions in the
        FUNCTION AVERAGE(A,B,C) ◄───┘       │    function are executed, the
   C    Calculate the average.              │    one value to be returned to
        TOT = A + B + C                     │    the calling program must be
        AVERAGE = TOT / 3.0                 │    stored in the memory loca-
        RETURN                              │    tion named AVERAGE.
        END ────────────────────────────────┘
```

When the RETURN and END are executed in the function, the value stored in location AVERAGE is copied into location D, and the execution of the program returns to the statement immediately following the call to the function. So, the execution returns to the PRINT statement, where the calculated average stored in the memory location named D is printed.

When the STOP and the END statements in the main program are executed, the execution of the program terminates. The only way that statements in the function can be executed is by a call from another routine. Execution cannot proceed down through the STOP and END statements in the main program into the function.

12.2
PROVIDING PARAMETERS
FOR A FUNCTION AND RETURNING
A FUNCTION VALUE

In Example 12.1, the symbolic names in the argument list in the calling routine and in the function are the same.

```
D = AVERAGE(A,B,C)

FUNCTION AVERAGE(A,B,C)
```

The symbolic names in the argument list in the calling routine and the symbolic names in the argument list in the function do not need to be the same names.

A = SOMEFUNCTION(TOT,AMIN,ANUM,CALCULATED_AMOUNT)

FUNCTION SOMEFUNCTION(TOTAL,ALEAST,ANUMBER,AMOUNT)

The symbolic names in the argument list are not important. There are three things that are important.

1. There should be the same number of parameters in the calling argument list and in the function argument list.

(X,Y,Z)
↑ ↑ ↑
(A,B,C)

2. If a symbolic name represents an array in the calling argument list, the paired symbolic name should represent an array in the function's argument list.

3. All pairs of arguments should be matching types, either real or integer.

(TOT,MAX,KNT)
 ↑   ↑   ↑
(SUM,MAX,NUMBER)

■ Example 12.2: Passing Parameters for a Function

```
$ EDIT MAXABC.FOR                                     Example 12.2

C       The program allows a user to enter three numbers each of
C       the four times through the DO loop.  Each time, the
C       FUNCTION THREEMAX is invoked to determine the maximum
C       value of the three values.

        DO LOOP = 1,4                                  !Execute 4 times
           WRITE(6,*)'ENTER THREE NUMBERS'             !Prompt user
           READ(5,*)X,Y,Z                              !Input 3 numbers
           XYZMAX = THREEMAX(X,Y,Z)                    !Invoke FUNCTION
           WRITE(6,*)'MAXIMUM VALUE IS ',XYZMAX        !Print max value
        END DO
        STOP
        END

        FUNCTION THREEMAX(A,B,C)                       !Pass arguments
        THREEMAX = A                                   !Find max
        IF (B.GT.THREEMAX) THREEMAX = B                !Find max
        IF (C.GT.THREEMAX) THREEMAX = C                !Find max
        RETURN                                         !Return max value
        END
```

```
$ FORTRAN MAXABC
$ LINK MAXABC
$ RUN MAXABC
```

Example 12.2
Input
Output

Messages are printed at the terminal to
prompt you to enter values. The program
stops and waits for you to enter three
values. The maximum of the three values is
calculated and printed. The program goes
through this process four times.

The program prompts you to enter numbers.

ENTER THREE NUMBERS

The program waits for you to enter 3 numbers.

25.5,68,0.05

The program goes to the FUNCTION and determines
the max value. Control returns to the main program
and prints the maximum value.

MAXIMUM VALUE IS 68.0000

Prompt user to enter three more numbers.

ENTER THREE NUMBERS

Stop and wait for user to enter three numbers.

-7.2,-2058.7,-1058

The program goes to the FUNCTION and determines
the max value. Control returns to the main program
and prints the maximum value.

MAXIMUM VALUE IS -7.2000

Prompt user to enter three numbers.

ENTER THREE NUMBERS

Stop and wait for user to enter three numbers.

34,58,134

The program goes to the FUNCTION and determines
the max value. Control returns to the main program
and prints the maximum value.

MAXIMUM VALUE IS 134.0000

The program prompts the user to enter three numbers.

ENTER THREE NUMBERS

Stop and wait for user to enter three numbers.

0.9,0.0,0.9

The program goes to the FUNCTION and determines
the max value. Control returns to the main program
and prints the maximum value.

MAXIMUM VALUE IS 0.9000

The statements in the DO loop have been executed
four times and the program stops.

Description of Example 12.2.   The statements inside the DO loop are executed four times. One of the statements in the loop is the statement to invoke the function named THREEMAX. When the function is invoked, control of the program transfers to the set of statements between the word FUNCTION and the RETURN/END. After the statements in the FUNCTION have been executed, control returns to the statement in the main program immediately following the statement to invoke the function.

Notice that the three parameters in the call to the function in the main program are X, Y, and Z. The parameters in the function are A, B, and C. When the main program invokes the function, the value stored in location X will be used whenever the symbolic name A is referenced. When the symbolic name B is referenced in the function, the value stored in the memory location named Y will be used. When the FUNCTION references the symbolic name C, the value stored in the memory location named Z will be used. The value returned from the function will be returned in the memory location named THREEMAX and subsequently stored in the memory location named XYZ-MAX. (See Figure 12.1.)

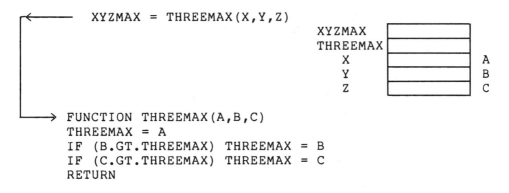

```
XYZMAX = THREEMAX(X,Y,Z)
```

```
FUNCTION THREEMAX(A,B,C)
THREEMAX = A
IF (B.GT.THREEMAX) THREEMAX = B
IF (C.GT.THREEMAX) THREEMAX = C
RETURN
```

FIGURE 12.1

12.3
PASSING ARRAYS AS ARGUMENTS FOR A FUNCTION

An argument for a FUNCTION may be an array. If an argument is an array, the array must be DIMENSIONed in the calling routine or in the original DIMENSION statement with the specific number of storage locations to be set aside. If the array is passed as a parameter for the function, the array must also be dimensioned in the subprogram. The array in the function subprogram is called a *dummy array*.

The dimension statement in the main program must declare the exact number of memory locations to be set aside.

DIMENSION SCOR(50)

The dimension statement in the function can be a specific number equal to or less than the actual size of the array declared in the calling program.

FUNCTION ONE(SCOR)
DIMENSION SCOR(50)

The size of the array declared in the dimension statement in the function could be passed as a variable. The size of the dummy array is then determined at the time of reference to the subprogram.

FUNCTION A(SCOR,K)
DIMENSION SCOR(K)

An asterisk can be used in the dimension statement for the dummy array to indicate that the dummy array size should be the same size as the completely defined array.

FUNCTION ONE(SCOR)
DIMENSION SCOR(*)

If an array has multiple dimensions, the array must be completely dimensioned in the main program.

DIMENSION X(20,30)

For a multiply dimensioned array, only the rightmost dimension specification can be treated as a variable.

FUNCTION SOME(X)
DIMENSION X(20,*)

■ **Example 12.3: Function with an Array**

Example 12.3
Input

```
$ TYPE GRADES.DAT
254655654 86 74 80 ADAMS, ALFRED
579690650 75 90 95 BEX, BENNIE
325869322 54 65 71 AMELIA, ANDY
456768910 93 87 90 CARR, CANDY
444552133 59 58 69 DAVISON, DANNY
404325431 77 65 81 DANIELS, DAVE
567894319 88 94 82 DENNISON, DEB
345663244 82 83 84 EDWARDS, ED
476345222 77 81 79 FOX, FRED
```

Example 12.3

```
$ EDIT MAXFUNCTN.FOR
C     Program to find the student with the highest
C     score on the first exam.

C     The program reads the first score for each student from
C     the disk data file named GRADES.DAT.  Then the program
C     calls a function to determine the subscript for the
C     student who has the highest score on the first exam.

C     After the subscript for the highest score is determined,
C     the main program writes the subscript number and the
C     corresponding score.
```

```
      DIMENSION SCOR(50)
      OPEN(1,FILE='GRADES.DAT',STATUS='OLD')
100   FORMAT(9X,F3.0)
200   FORMAT(' STUDENT NUMBER',I2,' HAS THE HIGHEST SCORE',
     -/,' ON THE FIRST EXAM WITH A SCORE OF ',F4.0)


C     Input the data and count the number of students.
      READ(1,100,IOSTAT=IEND)SCOR(1)
      NUM=0
      DO WHILE (IEND.EQ.0)
         NUM = NUM + 1
         READ(1,100,IOSTAT=IEND) SCOR(NUM+1)
      END DO


C     Invoke a function to find the subscript for the largest
C     value in the array SCOR.
      NUM_OF_STUDENT = INDEX_FOR_LARGEST(SCOR,NUM)

      WRITE(6,200) NUM_OF_STUDENT, SCOR(NUM_OF_STUDENT)
      STOP
      END


      FUNCTION INDEX_FOR_LARGEST(SCOR,NUM)
C     The function returns the subscript for the
C     largest value in the array named SCOR.
      DIMENSION SCOR(NUM)
      INDEX_FOR_LARGEST = 1
      SCORMAX = SCOR(1)
      DO LOOP = 2, NUM
         IF (SCORMAX.LT.SCOR(LOOP)) THEN
            INDEX_FOR_LARGEST = LOOP
            SCORMAX = SCOR(LOOP)
         END IF
      END DO
      RETURN
      END
$ FORTRAN MAXFUNCTN
$ LINK MAXFUNCTN
$ RUN MAXFUNCTN
```

Example 12.3
Output

```
STUDENT NUMBER 4 HAS THE HIGHEST SCORE
ON THE FIRST EXAM WITH A SCORE OF 93.
```

Description of Example 12.3.   In this example, the value stored in the memory location named NUM represents the number of students. The value of NUM is determined by the number of records read from disk. The value NUM is used as an argument for the subprogram and can then be used as an adjustable dimension size.

NUM__OF__STUDENT = INDEX__FOR__LARGEST(SCOR,NUM)

FUNCTION INDEX__FOR__LARGEST(SCOR,NUM)
DIMENSION SCOR(NUM)

For the data file in this example, there are nine students and NUM will have the value of 9. At another time, the data file might contain 35 student records and NUM would have the value 35.

12.4
APPLICATION

■ Example 12.4: Finding the Area of a Polygon

The area of a polygon can be estimated with the following formula.

$$\text{Area} = \frac{(x_1 + x_2) * (y_1 + y_2) + (x_2 + x_3) * (y_2 - y_3) + \ldots + (x_n + x_1) * (y_n - y_1)}{2}$$

where n = number of vertices. The accuracy of the calculation increases with the number of vertices that are defined.

For the example, the following vertices are defined for the azalea garden in the Cookeville Creek Park. Estimate the size of the azalea garden. (See Figure 12.2.)

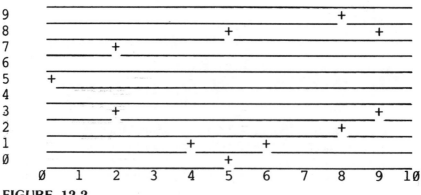

FIGURE 12.2

Example 12.4
Input

```
0,5
2,7
5,8
8,9
9,8
9,3
8,2
6,1
5,0
4,1
2,3
```

Example 12.4

```
$ EDIT AREASIZE.FOR
      DIMENSION X(1000), Y(1000)
C     The program calculates the estimated area of a polygon.



C     Input the data and count the number of data values.
      READ(5,*,IOSTAT=IEND) X(1), Y(1)
      KOUNT = 0
      DO WHILE (IEND.EQ.0)
         KOUNT = KOUNT + 1
         READ(5,*,IOSTAT=IEND) X(KOUNT+1), Y(KOUNT+1)
      END DO



C     Invoke the function SIZE to calculate the area.
      AREA = SIZE(X,Y,KOUNT)
      WRITE(6,*)'AREA=',AREA
      STOP
      END



      FUNCTION SIZE(X,Y,KOUNT)
C     Function to estimate the size of a polygon.
      DIMENSION X(*),Y(*)
C     Set up the last vertex to connect to the first vertex.
      X(KOUNT+1) = X(1)
      Y(KOUNT+1) = Y(1)
      SIZE = 0
      DO K = 1, KOUNT
         SIZE = SIZE + (X(K)+X(K+1))*(Y(K)-Y(K+1))
      END DO
      SIZE = SIZE / 2.0
      RETURN
      END
$ FORTRAN AREASIZE
$ LINK AREASIZE
$ RUN AREASIZE
AREA=   22.00000
```

Example 12.4
Output

12.5
SUMMARY

Developing a computer program as a series of definable tasks is extremely important in developing a correct and usable program. The *function* and *subroutine* subprogram structures are the tools for developing the top level of structure for a program. A FUNCTION is a set of code written as a unit with one way into the code and one way out; therefore a function is appropriate for performing a definable task.

A function is invoked with the following statement:

symbolic__name = function__name(argument list)

The argument list can contain constants and symbolic names. These are the values that are to be used inside the function. Only those values passed into the function are available to the function. Arguments are also called parameters.

When the function is invoked in the calling program, execution transfers to the function specified. The statements in the function are executed and when the RETURN END statements are encountered, execution returns to the calling program and the one value represented by the function name is stored in the symbolic__name to the left of the equal sign in the statement that invoked the function.

Many intrinsic functions are included as a part of the FORTRAN language and can be invoked by using the name of the function and providing the appropriate parameters. A few of the intrinsic functions available are the following:

SQRT   LOG10   ABS   INT   REAL   MAX   SIN
LOG   EXP   INT   NINT   MOD   MIN   COS

The following structure is used for writing functions to be included in a FORTRAN program.

FUNCTION function__name(argument list)
    any number of statements to perform some operation
RETURN
END

12.6
EXERCISES

12.1. What is the output for the following programs with functions?

a.
```
L = 20
M = 10
LMTOT = ITOTAL(L,M)
WRITE(6,*)LMTOT
STOP
END

FUNCTION ITOTAL(L,M)
ITOTAL = L + M
RETURN
END
```

b.
```
L = 20
M = 10
LMDIFER = IDIFER(L,M)
WRITE(6,*)LMDIFER
STOP
END

FUNCTION IDIFER(I,J)
IDIFER = I − J
RETURN
END
```

c.
```
DIMENSION X(10)
DO I = 1,10
    X(I) = I
END DO
XTOTAL = TOTAL(X)
WRITE(6,*) XTOTAL
STOP
END

FUNCTION TOTAL(X)
DIMENSION X(10)
TOTAL = 0
DO I = 1,10
    TOTAL = TOTAL + X(I)
END DO
RETURN
END
```

```
d.  DIMENSION Y(10)
    KOUNT = 4
    DO I = 1,KOUNT
        Y(I) = Y(I) * 2
    END DO
    YTOTAL = TOTAL(Y,KOUNT)
    WRITE(6,*)YTOTAL
    END

    FUNCTION TOTAL(Y,KOUNT)
    DIMENSION Y(*)
    TOTAL = 0
    DO I = 1,KOUNT
        TOTAL = TOTAL + Y(I)
    END DO
    RETURN
    END
```

12.2. Write a FORTRAN program with a function to calculate the sum of all the even numbers between zero and 100.

12.3. Data could be input and stored with the following partial program.

```
DIMENSION X(50)
READ (5,*,IOSTAT = IEND) X(1)
NUM = 0
DO WHILE (IEND.EQ.0)
    NUM = NUM + 1
    READ (5,*,IOSTAT = IEND) X(NUM + 1)
END DO
```

Write the remainder of the main program and the following functions.

a. Write a function to find the maximum value in the data.

b. Write a function to find the index for the maximum value.

c. Write a function to find the smallest value that is greater than zero.

12.4. A manufacturing company makes three television models. Model 1 costs \$90. Model 2 costs \$250. Model 3 costs \$500. An order placed for a television contains the model number for the televisions being ordered along with the quantity being ordered and the name of the firm placing the order. The following are sample records:

2	12	Center Hill Studios
1	14	Systems Services
3	5	Lorens Showcase
1	10	Pops TV and Appliance

Write a FORTRAN program that inputs the data in a main program. For each firm placing an order, the main program should invoke a function to calculate the cost of the shipment. After the cost of the shipment is returned to the main program, the cost should be printed.

13

Subroutines

A computer program should be developed and written as a series of subprograms performing definable tasks. The subroutine structure is the most commonly used subprogram structure.

13.1
DESCRIPTION OF A SUBROUTINE
AND ACCESSING A SUBROUTINE

DEFINITION: A *subroutine* is a subprogram written as a separate unit that can be accessed by a subroutine name to perform some manipulations and may transfer data values back and forth between the calling routine and the subroutine.

A CALL statement invokes a subroutine.

CALL subroutine__name (argument list)

When the CALL statement is executed, control transfers to the set of instructions with the specified subroutine name to perform some task. The values named in the argument list are data values passed into the subroutine for performing the task.

The general form of a subroutine is the following:

SUBROUTINE subroutine_name (argument list)
  statements to perform some task
RETURN
END

When the subroutine is invoked, values that can be used for data are passed into the subroutine through the argument list. Then the statements in the subroutine are executed. When the RETURN statement is executed, each value in the argument list is passed back into the calling routine. Any or all of the values in an argument list may be changed as a subroutine executes, and all the changes will be returned to the calling routine.

The symbolic name for a subroutine may be any valid symbolic name with 31 or fewer characters containing letters, numbers, and the underline character. A subroutine may be invoked with the CALL statement from a main program, a function, or another subroutine.

The best way to understand subroutines is to study some examples.

■ Example 13.1: Program with a Subroutine

```
$ EDIT MINVALUE.FOR                                      Example 13.1
C    Program with a subroutine to determine the minimum
C    value among five values.

C   The program stores 5 values in locations P,Q,R,S,T.
C    Then the program calls a subroutine to find the smallest
C    value among the 5 values.  The program prints the
C    smallest value in the main program after the smallest
C    value is returned from the subroutine.

C    Store five values.  The data would usually be input,
C    but the values are simply assigned to memory locations
C    for this example.
     P = 23.5
     Q = 17.98
     R = 1.023
     S = 37.08
     T = 31.0

C    Call a subroutine to find the smallest of the five values.
     CALL MINIMUM(P,Q,R,S,T,FIVEMIN)

C    Print the returned smallest value.
     WRITE(6,*)' MINIMUM VALUE ',FIVEMIN
     STOP
     END
```

```
      SUBROUTINE MINIMUM(P,Q,R,S,T,FIVEMIN)
C     Subroutine to find the minimum of the five values passed
C     as parameters in values P,Q,R,S;T and to return the minimum
C     value in the memory location named FIVEMIN.
      FIVEMIN = P
      IF (Q.LT.FIVEMIN) FIVEMIN = Q
      IF (R.LT.FIVEMIN) FIVEMIN = R
      IF (S.LT.FIVEMIN) FIVEMIN = S
      IF (T.LT.FIVEMIN) FIVEMIN = T
      RETURN
      END
```

```
$ FORTRAN MINVALUE
$ LINK MINVALUE
$ RUN MINVALUE
MINIMUM VALUE 1.02300
```

Example 13.1
Output

Description of Example 13.1.   When the CALL statement in the main program is executed, program control transfers to the subroutine set off between the SUBROUTINE and the RETURN/END statements. After the instructions in the subroutine are executed, control is transferred back to the main program to the statement following the call to the subroutine.

P = 23.5
Q = 17.98
R = 1.023
S = 37.08
T = 31.0

When the CALL statement is executed, control transfers to the top of the SUBROUTINE subprogram. The values P, Q, R, S, and T will be available to be used or changed in the subroutine. In addition, the memory location named FIVEMIN will be available to move the determined minimum value back to the main program for printing.

```
CALL MINIMUM(P,Q,R,S,T,FIVEMIN)
WRITE(6,*)' MINIMUM VALUE',FIVEMIN
END
```

Control returns to the WRITE after the subroutine executes.

```
SUBROUTINE MINIMUM(P,Q,R,S,T,FIVEMIN)
FIVEMIN = P
IF (Q.LT.FIVEMIN) FIVEMIN = Q
IF (R.LT.FIVEMIN) FIVEMIN = R
IF (S.LT.FIVEMIN) FIVEMIN = S
IF (T.LT.FIVEMIN) FIVEMIN = T
RETURN
END
```

When the RETURN/END is executed, the current value for each element in the argument list is passed to the MAIN program. In this example, the values in P, Q, R, S, and T are unchanged. The value in FIVEMIN is calculated in the subroutine and is returned to the calling routine, which is the main program in this case.

When execution returns to the main program, the value in FIVEMIN will be printed and the program will END. There is no way that execution can proceed down through the subroutine following the END statement in the main program. The only way that a subroutine can be executed is through the CALL statement.

13.2

PROVIDING PARAMETERS FOR A SUBROUTINE AND RETURNING VALUES TO THE CALLING PROGRAM

In Example 13.1, the symbolic names in the argument list in the CALL statement and in the SUBROUTINE are the same.

```
CALL MINIMUM(P,Q,R,S,T,FIVEMIN)

SUBROUTINE MINIMUM(P,Q,R,S,T,FIVEMIN)
```

The symbolic names in the argument list in the calling routine and the symbolic names in the argument list in the subroutine do not need to be the same names.

```
CALL SOMESUB(TOT,AMIN,ANUM,CALCULATED__AMOUNT)

SUBROUTINE SOMESUB(TOTAL,ALEAST,ANUMBER,AMOUNT)
```

The symbolic names in the argument list are not important. There are three things that are important.

1. There should be the same number of parameters in the calling and in the subroutine argument list.

```
(X,Y,Z)
 ↑ ↑ ↑
(A,B,C)
```

2. If a symbolic name represents an array in the calling argument list, the paired symbolic name should represent an array in the function's argument list.

3. All pairs of arguments should be matching types, either real or integer.

(TOT,MAX,KNT)

(SUM,MAX,NUMBER)

If an argument for a subroutine is an array, then the array must be *dimensioned* in both the calling routine and the subroutine. The array in the subroutine is called a *dummy array*. The first time that an array is declared in a program, the exact dimensions of the array must be specified to set aside a particular number of memory locations. Thereafter, in subprograms in which an array is a part of the argument list, the array can be dimensioned with a variable size that is always less than or equal to the original size.

The dimension statement in the calling program must declare the exact number of memory locations to be set aside.

DIMENSION SCOR(50)

The dimension statement in the subroutine can be a specific number equal to or less than the actual size of the array.

SUBROUTINE ONE(SCOR)
DIMENSION SCOR(50)

The size of the array declared in the dimension statement in the subroutine could be passed as a variable. The size of the dummy array is then determined at the time of reference to the subprogram.

SUBROUTINE TWO(SCOR,KNT)
DIMENSION SCOR(KNT)

An asterisk can be used in the dimension statement for the dummy array to indicate that the dummy array size is the same size as the completely defined array.

SUBROUTINE ONE(SCOR)
DIMENSION SCOR(*)

If an array has multiple dimensions, the array must be completely dimensioned in the main program.

DIMENSION X(20,30)

For a multiply dimensioned array, only the rightmost dimension specifications can be treated as a variable.

SUBROUTINE SOME(X)
DIMENSION X(20,*)

■ **Example 13.2: Passing Values into and from a Subroutine**

The grades for a class are stored in a data file named GRADES.DAT. The final exam score is the third score in each record. The example program reads the final exam score for each of the students in the class and then calls a subroutine to add a bonus of three points to each grade that is higher than 80.

<table>
<tr><td>

```
$ TYPE GRADES.DAT
254655654 86 74 80 ADAMS, ALFRED
579690650 75 90 95 BEX, BENNIE
325869322 54 65 71 AMELIA, ANDY
456768910 93 87 90 CARR, CANDY
444552133 59 58 69 DAVISON, DANNY
404325431 77 65 81 DANIELS, DAVE
567894319 88 94 82 DENNISON, DEB
345663244 82 83 84 EDWARDS, ED
476345222 77 81 79 FOX, FRED
```
</td><td>Example 13.2
Input</td></tr>
</table>

```
$ EDIT ONESUB.FOR
C     BONUS PROGRAM

C     The main program reads the final exam score, that is the
C     third score, for each student from the file GRADES.DAT.
C     The main program writes each of the input final exam scores.
C     The main program calls a subroutine to add a bonus of three
C     points to each score which is greater than 80.
C     The main program writes out the adjusted final exam score
C     which includes the bonus points added.

      DIMENSION SCOR(50)
      OPEN(1,FILE='GRADES.DAT',STATUS='OLD')

C     Input format skips social security num, score1 and score2
100   FORMAT(15X,F3.0)
C     Input data
      READ(1,100,IOSTAT=IEND) SCOR(1)
      KNT = 0
      DO WHILE (IEND.EQ.0)
         KNT = KNT + 1
         READ(1,100,IOSTAT=IEND) SCOR(KNT+1)
      END DO

C     Write out scores which were input along with student number
      WRITE(6,*)' INPUT FINAL EXAM SCORES'
      WRITE(6,*)' STUDENT NUMBER    SCORE'
      DO ISTUD = 1,KNT
         WRITE(6,*)ISTUD,SCOR(ISTUD)
      END DO

C     Invoke the subroutine BONUS and add 3 points to each score
C     which is greater than 80.
      CALL BONUS(SCOR,KNT)
```

Example 13.2

```
C       Write out the scores along with the student number.  Scores
C       greater than 80 have been adjusted by adding 3 points.
        WRITE(6,*)' ADJUSTED FINAL EXAM SCORES'
        WRITE(6,*)' STUDENT NUMBER    SCORE'
        DO ISTUD = 1,KNT
           WRITE(6,*)ISTUD,SCOR(ISTUD)
        END DO
        STOP
        END

        SUBROUTINE BONUS(EXAM,NUM_STUD)
C       The subroutine adds 3 points to each element of the array
C       named EXAM which has a value greater than 80.
        DIMENSION EXAM(NUM_STUD)
        DO ISTUD = 1,NUM_STUD
           IF (EXAM(ISTUD).GT.80.0) EXAM(ISTUD)=EXAM(ISTUD)+3.0
        END DO
        RETURN
        END
```

```
$ FORTRAN ONESUB
$ LINK ONESUB
$ RUN ONESUB                                        Example 13.2
 INPUT FINAL EXAM SCORES                            Output
 STUDENT NUMBER    SCORE
            1        80.0000            These are the scores stored in
            2        95.0000            the array named SCOR as
            3        71.0000            they were input before the
            4        90.0000            subroutine named BONUS
            5        69.0000            was called.
            6        81.0000
            7        82.0000
            8        84.0000
            9        79.0000
 ADJUSTED FINAL EXAM SCORES
 STUDENT NUMBER    SCORE
            1        80.0000            These are the scores stored in
            2        98.0000            the array named SCOR after
            3        71.0000            three points were added in
            4        93.0000            the subroutine named BO-
            5        69.0000            NUS to each score greater
            6        84.0000            than 80.
            7        85.0000
            8        87.0000
            9        79.0000
```

Description of Example 13.2. When the statement CALL BONUS (SCOR,KNT) is executed, the program execution transfers to the SUBROUTINE named BONUS. At the time when the subroutine is called, the values stored in the array with the symbolic name SCOR will be made available to the subroutine, and those values will be called EXAM during the execution of the subroutine. When the subroutine returns to the calling routine, the values in the array called EXAM will be returned to the calling routine and will again be represented by the symbolic name SCOR.

At the time when the subroutine is called, the value stored in the location with the symbolic name KNT will be made available to the subroutine, and that value will be called NUM_STUD during the execution of the subroutine. When the subroutine returns to the calling routine, the value called NUM_STUD will be returned to the calling routine and will be referred to as KNT again.

```
      CALL BONUS(SCOR,KNT)
                    ↑    ↑
 SUBROUTINE  BONUS(EXAM,NUM_STUD)
```

The array EXAM must be dimensioned in the subroutine. Three possible ways to dimension the array are the following:

```
      DIMENSION EXAM(50)
   or DIMENSION EXAM(*)
   or DIMENSION EXAM(NUM_STUD)
```

13.3
SUBROUTINES AND STRUCTURED PROGRAMMING

It is often difficult to begin the process of writing a program. An easy way to begin is to write down the major things that need to be accomplished in a program. Often each of those major tasks can be written as one unit of a program in a structured form in a subroutine. If a task is still overwhelming, then that task can be further broken down until each task seems manageable. This procedure of starting at the top with the overall problem and breaking down the problem into parts that can be easily understood and coded is called *top down* programming.

In general, every program should be written as a series of subprograms, each of which performs a definable task. It is good practice to limit the number of lines in a subroutine to the number of lines that can be printed on one page or, more importantly, to the number of lines that can be easily understood by someone studying the program. Perhaps there could be 30 lines of simple code in a subroutine, whereas there might be only 10 lines of complex code in a subroutine. All subroutines should be well documented.

■ **Example 13.3: Dividing a Program into Subprograms to Make Program Writing and Program Understanding Easy**

Consider the following problem. The problem is the same as the problem for Example 13.2 except that student names are included in this example.

The final exam score and the name for each student should be read from the data file named GRADES.DAT. The input final exam score and the student name should be printed at the terminal along with the student number. Then a bonus of three points should be added to each score greater than 80. Finally, the student number, adjusted score, and name should be printed.

When you look at all the things that need to be done, you can see each of those parts as a definable task that might be written as a subroutine.

Read data from disk

Write out input scores and names

Add bonus

Write out adjusted scores and names

And when you think about it, you realize that printing the input data and the adjusted scores really would be the same task. The *main* program in a FOR-TRAN program is often only a set of calls to subroutines, which have descriptive names along with the DIMENSION statements to set aside space for arrays.

```
DIMENSION SCOR(50)
CALL READ_INPUT_DATA_FROM_DISK (SCOR,KNT,NAME)
CALL WRITE_RECORDS (SCOR,KNT,NAME)
CALL ADD_BONUS (SCOR,KNT)
CALL WRITE_RECORDS (SCOR,KNT,NAME)
```

Example 13.3
Input

```
$ TYPE GRADES.DAT
254655654 86 74 80 ADAMS, ALFRED
579690650 75 90 95 BEX, BENNIE
325869322 54 65 71 AMELIA, ANDY
456768910 93 87 90 CARR, CANDY
444552133 59 58 69 DAVISON, DANNY
404325431 77 65 81 DANIELS, DAVE
567894319 88 94 82 DENNISON, DEB
345663244 82 83 84 EDWARDS, ED
476345222 77 81 79 FOX, FRED
```

Example 13.3

```
$ EDIT EASYSUB.FOR
C                A STRUCTURED FORTRAN PROGRAM
C        WITH SUBROUTINES TO PERFROM DEFINABLE TASKS

C    The program reads the final exam score and the name for
C    each student in the class records in file GRADES.DAT.
C    The program writes the input data.
C    The program adds a bonus of three points to each score
C    which is greater than 80.
C    The program writes the updated data.

     DIMENSION SCOR(30)
     CHARACTER*50 NAME(30)
```

```
          CALL READ_INPUT_DATA (SCOR,KNT,NAME)
          CALL WRITE_STUDENT_RECORDS (SCOR,KNT,NAME)
          CALL ADD_BONUS (SCOR,KNT)
          CALL WRITE_STUDENT_RECORDS (SCOR,KNT,NAME)
          STOP
          END

C  -----------------------------------------------------
          SUBROUTINE READ_INPUT_DATA (EXAM,NUM_STUD,NAME)
C  -----------------------------------------------------
C The subroutine reads the final exam score and the name
C for each student whose record is stored in the disk file.
C The program counts the number of students.  The input data
C is returned to the main program through the argument list.

          DIMENSION EXAM(*)
          CHARACTER *50 NAME(*)
          OPEN(1,FILE='GRADES.DAT',STATUS='OLD')
100       FORMAT(15X,F3.0,A)

          READ(1,100,IOSTAT=IEND) SCOR(1), NAME(1)
          NUM_STUD = 0
          DO WHILE (IEND.EQ.0)
             NUM_STUD = NUM_STUD + 1
             READ(1,100,IOSTAT=IEND)SCOR(NUM_STUD+1),NAME(NUM_STUD+1)
          END DO
          CLOSE(1)
          RETURN
          END

C  -----------------------------------------------------------
          SUBROUTINE WRITE_STUDENT_RECORDS (SCOR,KNT,NAME)
C  -----------------------------------------------------------
C For each student, the subroutine writes the student
C number, the score and the name

          DIMENSION SCOR(KNT)
          CHARACTER *50 NAME(KNT)
200       FORMAT(' ',I2,F10.0,A)
          DO ISTUD = 1,KNT
             WRITE(6,200)ISTUD,SCOR(ISTUD),NAME(ISTUD)
          END DO
          RETURN
          END

C  -----------------------------------------------------------
          SUBROUTINE ADD_BONUS (EXAM,NUM_STUD)
C  -----------------------------------------------------------
C The subroutine adds a bonus of three points to
C each exam score which is greater than 80.

          DIMENSION EXAM(*)
          DO I = 1, NUM_STUD
             IF (EXAM(I).GT.80.0) EXAM(I)=EXAM(I) + 3.0
          END DO
          WRITE(6,*)'BONUS HAS BEEN ADDED'
          RETURN
          END
```

```
$ FORTRAN EASYSUB
$ LINK EASYSUB
$ RUN EASYSUB
  1        80.   ADAMS, ALFRED
  2        95.   BEX, BENNIE
  3        71.   AMELIA, ANDY
  4        90.   CARR, CANDY
  5        69.   DAVISON, DANNY
  6        81.   DANIELS, DAVE
  7        82.   DENNISON, DEB
  8        84.   EDWARDS, ED
  9        79.   FOX, FRED
BONUS HAS BEEN ADDED
  1        80.   ADAMS, ALFRED
  2        98.   BEX, BENNIE
  3        71.   AMELIA, ANDY
  4        93.   CARR, CANDY
  5        69.   DAVISON, DANNY
  6        84.   DANIELS, DAVE
  7        85.   DENNISON, DEB
  8        87.   EDWARDS, ED
  9        79.   FOX, FRED
```

Example 13.3
Output

13.4
COMMON DECLARATION

It is usually necessary to pass parameters into a subprogram and back from a subprogram. The formal argument list in the CALL and the SUB-ROUTINE statements is the best way to transfer values between the calling routine and the subprogram that is called. Another way of passing parameters is through the use of COMMON declarations. COMMON declarations can be very useful if sets of parameters are repeatedly passed into subprograms, but using the COMMON statement provides opportunity for creating problems.

DEFINITION: The COMMON statement declares that a variable in a subprogram is assigned to the same memory location as a variable in the routine that calls the subprogram.

> COMMON list of variable and array names
> or   COMMON /name/list of variable and array names

The COMMON statement sets up a sequence of memory locations that are then made available as global data to any subprogram with the associated COMMON declaration. One COMMON declaration may be un-named. Multiple COMMON statements must contain a name for identification of the COMMON BLOCK to be accessed.

The COMMON statement, like other declarations, must appear before all executable statements in a program or subprogram. The COMMON statement also serves as the declaration for arrays. It is allowable to have symbolic names that do not agree in type, integer or real, referring to the same memory location, and great care must be taken to prevent the problems associated with such mismatches. One solution is to have a separate COMMON declaration for real values and for integer values.

COMMON X, Y, Z

This could be the declaration in the main program or the calling program.

The COMMON statement in the subprogram could be one of the following:

COMMON X, Y, Z

Each memory location in the subprogram will have the same symbolic name as in the calling program

COMMON A, B, C

In the subprogram, the memory location called X in the calling program will be called A, the location named Y will be called B, etc.

COMMON D(3)

In the subprogram, the array of three memory locations named D occupy the same memory locations as the variables X, Y, and Z in the calling routine.

COMMON BLOCK variables can be assigned values at compile time with the use of the BLOCK DATA structure.

COMMON I, J, K
COMMON /THIS/X,Y,Z

These values are declared in the main program.

⋮   ⋮

END

BLOCK DATA
COMMON I, J, K
COMMON /THIS/X,Y,Z
DATA I,J,K/3,7,9/
DATA X,Y,Z,/2.5,3.4,9.9/
END

The BLOCK DATA is written as a unit of the program terminating with the word END.

■ Example 13.4: Using the
COMMON Statement

Example 13.4

```
$ EDIT COMMON1.FOR
C     The program assigns some values to memory locations
C     which are declared to be in COMMON storage with memory
C     locations in the subroutine.  The subroutine is called,
C     some calculations are made and the values in the COMMON
C     storage are returned to the main program and printed.

      COMMON COST, DISCOUNT, ITEMS, SALE
      COST = 20.00
      DISCOUNT = 0.25
      ITEMS = 10
      CALL CALCULATE
      WRITE(6,*) COST, DISCOUNT, ITEMS, SALE
      STOP
      END

      SUBROUTINE CALCULATE
      COMMON AMOUNT, REDUCTION, NUMBER, TOTAL
      AMOUNT = AMOUNT - AMOUNT*REDUCTION
      TOTAL = AMOUNT * NUMBER
      RETURN
      END
```

Example 13.4
Output

```
$ RUN COMMON1
15.00000        0.2500000        10        150.0000
```

Description of Example 13.4.   When the COMMON declaration is made in the main program, a sequence of storage locations is set up for global access in the program. The COMMON statement in the subroutine associates those memory locations with the variables that are being referenced in the subroutine.

COMMON COST, DISCOUNT, ITEMS, SALE

COMMON AMOUNT, REDUCTION, NUMBER, TOTAL

COST		AMOUNT
DISCOUNT		REDUCTION
ITEMS		NUMBER
SALE		TOTAL

Of course, any changes made in the memory location named AMOUNT in the execution of the subroutine will be available in the same memory location named COST in the main program.

■ Example 13.5: COMMON Storage
with Arrays

```
$ EDIT COMMON2.FOR                                      Example 13.5
C     With COMMON storage locations, the same locations are used
C     for different variables in separate parts of a program.

      COMMON /ONE/X, Y, Z(5)
      X = 5.0
      Y = 6.0
      DO I = 1,5
         Z(I) = FLOAT(I)
      END DO
      FIRST = 16.5
      CALL TRY(FIRST)
      WRITE(6,*)'VARIABLES IN THE MAIN PROGRAM AFTER'
      WRITE(6,*)'RETURN FROM THE SUBROUTINE TRY'
      WRITE(6,*)' X = ',X,' Y = ',Y
      WRITE(6,*)' Z ARRAY '
      WRITE(6,*) Z
      WRITE(6,*)' FIRST ',FIRST
      STOP
      END

      SUBROUTINE TRY(A)
      COMMON /ONE/W(3), G(3), D
      WRITE(6,*)'VARIABLES AT THE ENTRY TO SUBROUTINE TRY'
      WRITE(6,*)'W ARRAY ',W
      WRITE(6,*)'G ARRAY ',G
      WRITE(6,*)'D= ',D,'A= ',A
      DO J = 1,3
         W(J) = W(J) + 1.0
         G(J) = G(J) + 1.0
      END DO
      A = A + 1
      RETURN
      END

$ FORTRAN COMMON2
$ LINK COMMON2
$ RUN COMMON2                                           Example 13.5
VARIABLES AT THE ENTRY TO SUBROUTINE TRY                Output
 W ARRAY     5.000000        6.000000        1.000000
 G ARRAY     2.000000        3.000000        4.000000
 D=    5.000000     A=     16.50000
VARIABLES IN THE MAIN PROGRAM AFTER
RETURN FROM THE SUBROUTINE TRY
 X =    10.00000      Y =     12.00000
 Z ARRAY
  2.000000       3.000000       4.000000      5.00000      6.00000
 FIRST     17.50000
```

Description of Example 13.5. The COMMON statement in the main program sets aside seven locations with the COMMON BLOCK name of ONE. The COMMON statement in the subroutine assigns the same memory locations in the COMMON BLOCK named ONE to be accessed with different symbolic names.

ONE

X		W(1)
Y		W(2)
Z(1)		W(3)
Z(2)		G(1)
Z(3)		G(2)
Z(4)		G(3)
Z(5)		D

13.5
APPLICATION

■ Example 13.6: Sorting Data by Category – A Frequency Distribution

It might be necessary to generate a frequency distribution for any kind of data. It might be necessary to count the number of days of rain of various amounts, 0 to 0.1, 0.1 to 0.4, 0.4 to 0.7, and 0.7 to 1.0 inches of rain. Or it might be necessary to count the number of sales in various price ranges, 0 to $10, $10 to $50, and $50 to $100.

This example program generates a frequency distribution for a set of data that might represent ages. The age groups are 0 to 20, 20 to 40, and 40 to 100.

The program is written in a completely general way to allow a frequency distribution to be generated for almost any data. Notice that the number of categories for the distribution is input as data, as well as the boundaries for each category. Then the data to be sorted are input and counted until the end of file is reached. The count for the number of categories and the count for the number of data values are passed as arguments into the subroutines. The general subroutines in this program can be written as shown here and used in other programs that need a frequency distribution.

```
3
Ø,20
20,40
40,100
37
40
19
23
80
10
9
31
```

Example 13.6
Input

Example 13.6

```
$ EDIT BOUNDS.FOR
C The program generates a frequency distribution for a set of
C  data.  The maximum number of categories for the distribution
C  is set to be 10 in the DIMENSION declaration.  The maximum
C  number of values to be sorted is 100.

      DIMENSION BOUND(10,2),X(100)
      CALL INPUT(NUMCAT,BOUND,X,NUMX)
      CALL GENERATE_FREQUENCY(NUMCAT,BOUND,X,NUMX)
      STOP
      END

C -------------------------------------------------------
      SUBROUTINE INPUT(NUMCAT,BOUND,X,NUMX)
C -------------------------------------------------------
C The subroutine inputs the number of categories, the
C boundaries for the categories.  Then the subroutine
C inputs the data values to be sorted and counts the
C number of data values.

      DIMENSION BOUND(10,2),X(*)
C     Input the number of categories
      READ(5,*)NUMCAT
C     Input the boundaries for each category
      READ(5,*)(BOUND(I,1),BOUND(I,2),I=1,NUMCAT)
C     Input the data values to be sorted until the end of file
      READ(5,*,IOSTAT=IEND)X(1)
      NUMX=0
      DO WHILE (IEND.EQ.0)
         NUMX = NUMX + 1
         READ(5,*,IOSTAT=IEND) X(NUMX+1)
      END DO
      RETURN
      END
C ---------------------------------------------------------
      SUBROUTINE GENERATE_FREQUENCY(NUMCAT,BOUND,X,NUMX)
C ---------------------------------------------------------
C The subroutine generates a frequency distribution for
C the set of data to be sorted into the categories
C specified by the boundaries which were input.

      DIMENSION BOUND(10,2),X(*),IFREQ(10)

C     Initialize the count for each category to zero.
      DO ICATEGORY = 1, NUMCAT
         IFREQ(ICATEGORY) = 0
      END DO

C     Count the number of occurences of data values in each
C     category.
      DO IDATAVALUE = 1, NUMX
         DO ICATEGORY = 1, NUMCAT
            IF (X(IDATAVALUE) .GT. BOUND(ICATEGORY,1) .AND.
     -          X(IDATAVALUE). LE. BOUND(ICATEGORY,2)
     -          IFREQ(ICATEGORY) = IFREQ(ICATEGORY) + 1
         END DO
      END DO
```

```
C       Print the distribution for the categories
100     FORMAT('0  RANGE',T25,'FREQUENCY')
200     FORMAT('0',F5.1,' - ',F5.1,10X,I5)
        WRITE(6,100)
        WRITE(6,200)((BOUND(I,J),J=1,2),IFREQ(I),I=1,NUMCAT)

        RETURN
        END
$ FORTRAN BOUNDS
$ LINK BOUNDS
$ RUN BOUNDS
```

Example 13.6
Output

```
    RANGE                   FREQUENCY

    0.0 -    20.00              3

   20.0 -    40.00              4

   40.00 - 100.00               1
```

13.6
SUMMARY

Subroutines are the top level structure used for developing structured programs. A program should generally be a set of subroutines with each subroutine performing a major task.

A *subroutine* is a group of statements stored as a unit. Data values are passed back and forth between the subroutine and the calling program through a list of arguments. The statements in a subroutine are accessed by a CALL statement to the subroutine name.

    CALL subroutine_name(argument list)

Control transfers to the set of instructions with the specified subroutine_name when the CALL statement is executed.

The following is the structure of a subroutine.

    SUBROUTINE subroutine_name(argument list)
        statements to perform some task
    RETURN
    END

When the RETURN statement is executed, each of the values in the argument list is returned to the calling program. Any or all the values in the argument list may be changed during the execution of the subroutine.

If an argument for a subroutine is an array, then the size of the array must be declared in both the calling program and the subroutine.

13.7
EXERCISES

13.1. What is the output for the following FORTRAN programs?

a.
```
X = 15.2
Y = 12.3
CALL ADDIT(X,Y,Z)
WRITE(6,*)'Z = ',Z
END

SUBROUTINE ADDIT(X,Y,Z)
Z = X + Y
RETURN
END
```

b.
```
DIMENSION N(3)
DO I = 1,3
   N(I) = I*I
CONTINUE
CALL DIV(N,A)
WRITE(6,*)'A = ',A
END

SUBROUTINE DIV(NUM,AVE)
DIMENSION NUM(3)
AVE = 0.0
DO I = 1,3
    AVE = AVE + NUM(I)
END DO
AVE = AVE/3
RETURN
END
```

c.
```
DIMENSION Y(5)
DO I = 1,5
    Y(I) = 5.0 − I
END DO
CALL REV(Y,5)
WRITE(6,*) (Y(I),I = 1,5)
END

SUBROUTINE REV(X,MAX)
DIMENSION X(5),A(5)
KNT = MAX + 1
DO I = 1,MAX
    KNTA = KNT − I
    A(KNTA) = X(I)
END DO
DO I = 1, MAX
    X(I) = A(I)
END DO
RETURN
END
```

d.
```
COMMON D,E,F
D = 2.3
E = 1.2
CALL FINDTOTAL
WRITE(6,*)'F = ',F
END

SUBROUTINE FINDTOTAL
COMMON P,Q,R
R = P + Q
RETURN
END
```

13.2. Write a FORTRAN program with a main program that calls a subroutine to input 10 data values into a one-dimensional array and another subroutine to find and print the smallest value and the location of the smallest value in the array.

13.3. A firm has records which include sales data for 4 quarters for the last three years. The data might look like the following.

	Quarter 1	Quarter 2	Quarter 3	Quarter 4
Year 1	5000	4000	4000	6000
Year 2	6000	7000	3000	8000
Year 3	7000	9000	5000	8000

Write a FORTRAN program to store the sales data in a two-dimensional array and perform some analyses of the sales data. Each task listed should be performed in a separate subroutine. Label all output.

Determine the sales totals for each year.
Determine the sales totals for each quarter.
Determine in which quarter of the year the sales were the poorest.
Determine in which year the sales were the best.
Find the year and quarter with the best sale.

13.4. A forest has recently been designated as a wilderness area. The animal population for all species are expected to increase. The following data for each species is available in a file named FOREST.DAT. There is one record for each animal. It is not known how many records there are. The records have the following format.

Animal name	Current number	Expected number
Col 1–20	Col 21–30	Col 31–40
ANTELOPE	500	570
BROWN BEAR	600	685
:	:	:

The percentage increase for antelope would be (570–500)/500.

Write a program with subroutines to perform each of the major tasks in the program. The program should input the animal names into a character array and input the two columns of numeric data into a two-dimensional array. Read to the End of File with a control to continue execution of the program when the End of File is reached. Then calculate the percentage increase for each animal and the overall percentage increase. For each animal, print the name of the animal, the current and expected numbers, and the percentage increase. Print the overall totals and the overall increase at the end of the individual animal report.

13.5. Write a structured program with subroutines for each task to perform the following procedures. Input a set of data and store the data in a two-dimensional array. Then write the code to roll the elements in the array left, right, up, and down, producing results similar to that shown below. Make your array 10 by 10.

ARRAY	ROLLED LEFT	ROLLED RIGHT	ROLLED DOWN	ROLLED UP
1 2 3	2 3 1	3 1 2	7 8 9	4 5 6
4 5 6	5 6 4	6 4 5	1 2 3	7 8 9
7 8 9	8 9 7	9 7 8	4 5 6	1 2 3

13.6. A department store needs a program to aid cashiers in making change. The program should accept as input the cost of an item and the amount of money given by the customer. The program should include a subroutine to calculate and print the amount of change to be returned to the customer along with the exact currencies and coins to be returned to the customer minimizing the number of pieces of change returned. For instance, if a customer's purchase is $7.83 and the customer gives a $10 bill in payment, the program should print that the change is $1.17 and should be returned as 1 $1-bill, 1 10-cent coin, 1 5-cent coin and 2 1-cent coins.

13.7. It can be helpful to produce a graphical display of the layout of a computer room before actually placing furniture and equipment in the room. Using a 30 by 40 array to represent a room of size 30 by 40 feet, try graphically placing furniture and equipment in different positions.

Write a program that runs interactively and asks the user for a symbol to represent a piece of equipment, the size of the equipment in feet, and the coordinates of the lower left-hand corner of the piece. The program should put the piece of equipment in place on the screen and ask the user for the next entry. The following might be the prompt and a user response to display a terminal 2 feet by 2 feet placed at a location of 1 foot from the wall down the room 4 feet.

```
ENTER EQUIPMENT SYMBOL, SIZE IN FEET, LOCATION COOR-
DINATES IN FEET
T 2 2 1 4
```

Only a small portion of the graph is shown.

```
   TT
 | TT
 |_____
```

You might want to add a chair.

ENTER EQUIPMENT SYMBOL, SIZE IN FEET, LOCATION COOR-
DINATES IN FEET
C 2 2 1 6

| TTCC
| TTCC
|_____

Only a small portion of the graph is shown.

You could continue adding equipment.

13.8. Write a FORTRAN program to input five names from a disk file into a
masterfile array. Then interactively enter another set of names that
might be used for some transaction. For each name entered interactively, a search through the masterfile should be made for the name. If
the name is found, print the location in the array where the name was
found. If the name is not found, add the name to the array in the correct alphabetical location.

ADAMS ⎤
JONES ⎟   Names
SMITH ⎬   for
TEAL   ⎟   search
WALKER ⎦

WALKER ⎤   Names for
MATSON ⎬   search and update
JONES ⎦

14

Applications Programming

As you begin to write significant computer programs, you need to develop subroutines that will be useful to you. If you need a particular kind of data manipulation repeatedly, you should write a subroutine or a group of subroutines to perform that manipulation, test the subroutine(s) carefully, and then use the tested routines in any program needing that application. For many common problems, algorithms have been developed, and you can use a commonly available algorithm as the basis for a program or a subroutine. This chapter covers various topics to introduce you to concepts that you should consider in writing programs.

14.1
SORTING

Sorting is a common procedure and requires a great deal of processing time on a computer. Algorithms for sorting are available in computer science literature. The efficiency of various algorithms depends somewhat on the data to be sorted. The three sort procedures covered in this book, the bubble sort, the shell sort, and the quick sort, are probably the most common sort routines.

The *bubble sort,* which compares adjacent values and exchanges the values if necessary, is covered in Chapter 10. The bubble sort is, in general, not an efficient sorting routine; but if the records to be sorted are only slightly out of order, the bubble sort may be the most efficient algorithm to use.

The *shell sort* divides a list into halves and then continues to divide each sublist into halves, comparing values in the list and exchanging values. The method of division and comparison makes the shell sort more efficient than the bubble sort.

The *quick sort* is the most efficient algorithm for most sorts.

■ **Example 14.1: Quick Sort**

Implementing the quick sort algorithm requires that a structure called a *stack* be developed in the program. A description of a stack is necessary before going on with the quick sort.

DESCRIPTION OF A STACK: A *stack* is a structure that can be developed in a program and has as a part of the function of the structure a *pointer* to a particular element in the stack. A stack in a program is like a stack of books; you can add one book to a stack of books or take one book off the top, but you would never pull a book from the bottom or the middle of the stack. (See Figure 14.1.)

Increasing the value of the STACKELEMENT index into the array and storing a value in that location is called *pushing* a value onto the stack.

```
DIMENSION STACK(5)
STACKELEMENT = 0
STACKELEMENT = STACKELEMENT + 1
STACK(STACKELEMENT) = SOMEVALUE
STACKELEMENT = STACKELEMENT + 1
STACK(STACKELEMENT) = SOMEVALUE
STACKELEMENT = STACKELEMENT - 1
```

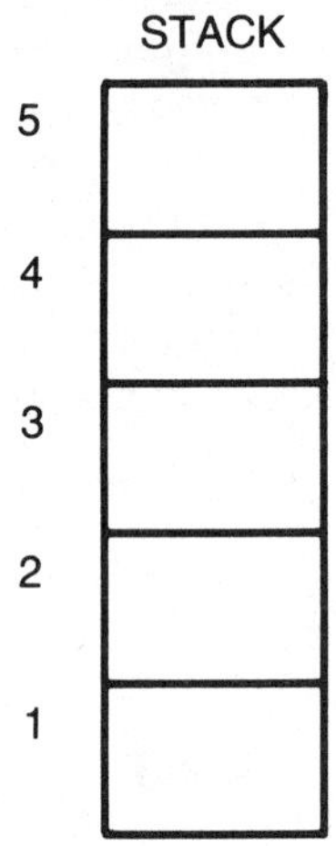

FIGURE 14.1

Decreasing the value of the STACKELEMENT index into the array is called *popping* an element from the STACK.

The algorithm for the quick sort places one data element in its correct position in the set of data elements to be sorted during each pass through the sorting routine. Because each time through the data an additional element is in place, one fewer comparison must be made in each entry into the sorting routine.

The algorithm begins with the first element in the set of data and proceeds to divide the data into subsets of data. The algorithm is based on separating the list of data elements into a set of data containing values less than or equal to some value and a set of data containing values greater than or equal to that value. (See Figure 14.2.)

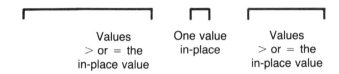

Values   One value   Values
> or = the   in-place   > or = the
in-place value   in-place value

FIGURE 14.2

Each subset of data is then further separated with one element in place and subsets to be arranged. (See Figure 14.3)

Must   In   Must   In   Must
be   place   be   place   be
sorted   sorted   sorted

FIGURE 14.3

In all the array programs in the text, you have been observing the use of pointers. The index into each array *points* to a particular element in an array. Pointers to the beginning and ending elements of each subset of data to be sorted are stored in a stack structure. (See Figure 14.4)

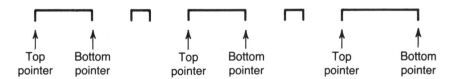

Top   Bottom   Top   Bottom   Top   Bottom
pointer   pointer   pointer   pointer   pointer   pointer

FIGURE 14.4

In evaluating each sublist, when the top pointer equals the bottom pointer, the one element in the sublist that can be put in place is exchanged to the correct location. As a subset is divided into more subsets, the top and bottom pointers to each of the subsets of data to be sorted are pushed onto the stack.

The entire list is determined to be sorted when there are no sublists on the stack to be evaluted.

This example demonstrates the quick sort. The quick sort is used in a general program in Chapter 15. A trace of the data as it is sorted with the quick sort follows the program.

Example 14.1
Input

11 34 23 54 78 65 99 76 44 32 43 54 63 12 2 4 56 78 54 20

$ EDIT QUICK.FOR   Example 14.1

```
C----------------------------------------------------------------
C       MAIN PROGRAM
C----------------------------------------------------------------
C       The main program inputs and echos data values to be sorted.
C       The main program calls the QUICK_SORT routine to sort the
C       data in ascending order and output the sorted list.

        REAL SCORES(20)

100     FORMAT(20F3.0)
200     FORMAT(' ',20F4.0)

        READ(5,100)(SCORES(I),I=1,20)
        WRITE(6,*)'INPUT DATA'
        WRITE(6,200)SCORES

        CALL QUICK_SORT(20,SCORES)

        WRITE(6,*)'DATA SORTED WITH QUICK SORT'
        WRITE(6,200)SCORES

        STOP
        END
```

!Example 14.1   Program QUICK.FOR
```
C----------------------------------------------------------------
        SUBROUTINE QUICK_SORT (NUM,SORTLIST)
C----------------------------------------------------------------
C       Sort numbers in ascending order
C----------------------------------------------------------------

        REAL SORTLIST(*)
        INTEGER TOPSTACK(20),BOTTOMSTACK(20),TOP,BOTTOM,B
C
```

```
C        Initialize stack to point to top of the list of data and the
C        bottom of the list of data to be sorted.
         POINTER = 1
         TOPSTACK(POINTER) = 1
         BOTTOMSTACK(POINTER) = NUM
C
C        As long as the pointer to the stacks is > 0, there are sets
C        of data to be sorted.

         DO WHILE (POINTER .GT. 0)

            IF (TOPSTACK(POINTER) .GE. BOTTOMSTACK(POINTER)) THEN

               POINTER = POINTER-1

            ELSE

C              Set the pointer to top and bottom of sublist to be processed.
               TOP = TOPSTACK(POINTER)
               BOTTOM = BOTTOMSTACK(POINTER)

C              Invoke the subroutine to divide the sublist to be processed
C              into two succeeding sublists with one element in place between
C              the sublists developed.
               CALL PARTITION_LIST (SORTLIST,TOP, BOTTOM, B)

C                  Put the two new sublists on the stack
                   TOPSTACK(POINTER) = TOP
                   BOTTOMSTACK(POINTER) = B - 1
                   POINTER = POINTER+1
                   TOPSTACK(POINTER) = B + 1
                   BOTTOMSTACK(POINTER) = BOTTOM

            END IF
         END DO

         RETURN
         END


!  Example 14.1                                    Program QUICK.FOR
C-----------------------------------------------------------------------
         SUBROUTINE PARTITION_LIST (SORTLIST,TOP,BOTTOM,B)
C-----------------------------------------------------------------------
C        Partitions the list of scores into a top sublist and a bottom
C        sublist.  Every element in the top sublist is less than every
C        element in the bottom sublist.
C-----------------------------------------------------------------------
         REAL SORTLIST(*)
         INTEGER TOP,BOTTOM,T,B

C        The value from the top of the stack is assumed to be the
C        VALUE_IN_PLACE for comparison.  The actual VALUE_IN_PLACE is
C        determined and put in place at the end of this subroutine.
         VALUE_IN_PLACE = SORTLIST(TOP)
C        Set pointers to the top and bottom of this sublist to be sorted.
         T = TOP
         B = BOTTOM+1
```

```
C       Go through the sublist comparing each element with the VALUE_IN_PLACE.
C       The bottom pointer will move from the bottom and the top pointer will
C       move from the top finding the one value that can be put in place.
C       Move through array until top (T) pointer reaches bottom (B) pointer.
        DO WHILE (T .LT. B)
          B = B-1

C       As long as the values in the sublist are > the comparison value, the
C       program continues to move up from the bottom of the list and compare.
        DO WHILE (SORTLIST(B) .GT. VALUE_IN_PLACE)
          B = B-1
        END DO
C.      When a value is found to be out of place coming from the bottom,
C       the program starts to make comparisons coming from the top.
        T = T+1

C       As long as the values in the sublist are < the comparison value, and
C       the top pointer is still above the bottom pointer in the list, the
C       program continues to move down from the top of the list and compare.
        DO WHILE((SORTLIST(T).LT.VALUE_IN_PLACE).AND.(T.LT.B))
          T = T+1
        END DO

C       If top pointer is still above bottom pointer, exchange top and bottom.
        IF (T .LT. B) THEN
          STEMP = SORTLIST(T)
          SORTLIST(T) = SORTLIST(B)
          SORTLIST(B) = STEMP
        END IF
      END DO

C       Put the new VALUE_IN_PLACE.
      SORTLIST(TOP) = SORTLIST(B)
      SORTLIST(B) = VALUE_IN_PLACE
      RETURN
      END


$ FORTRAN QUICK
$ LINK QUICK
$ RUN QUICK
```

Example 14.1
Output

```
INPUT DATA
  11. 34. 23. 54. 78. 65. 99. 76. 44. 32. 43. 54. 63. 12.  2.  4. 56. 78. 54. 20.
DATA SORTED WITH QUICK SORT
   2.  4. 11. 12. 20. 23. 32. 34. 43. 44. 54. 54. 54. 56. 63. 65. 76. 78. 78. 99.
```

The following is a trace of the data values for Example 14.1 as they are sorted. The arrow indicates the value that is moved into place during one partition and placement. The block marker under a line indicates the next subset of data to be partitioned with one value put in place. One element subsets are not sorted.

Example 14.1
Trace of Quick Sort

```
2   4  11  54  78  65  99  76  44  32  43  54  63  12  23  34  56  78  54  20
          ^

2   4  11  12  20  54  34  23  44  32  43  54  63  54  76  99  56  78  65  78

                                        ^

2   4  11  12  20  54  34  23  44  32  43  54  56  54  63  99  76  78  65  78

                                                          ^

2   4  11  12  20  54  34  23  44  32  43  54  56  54  63  78  76  78  65  99

                                                                          ^

2   4  11  12  20  54  34  23  44  32  43  54  56  54  63  65  76  78  78  99

                                                      ^

2   4  11  12  20  54  34  23  44  32  43  54  56  54  63  65  76  78  78  99

                                                  ^

2   4  11  12  20  54  34  23  44  32  43  54  54  56  63  65  76  78  78  99

                                          ^

2   4  11  12  20  54  34  23  44  32  43  54  54  56  63  65  76  78  78  99

              ^

2   4  11  12  20  54  34  23  44  32  43  54  54  56  63  65  76  78  78  99

              ^

2   4  11  12  20  43  34  23  44  32  54  54  54  56  63  65  76  78  78  99

                                  ^

2   4  11  12  20  32  34  23  43  44  54  54  54  56  63  65  76  78  78  99

                          ^

2   4  11  12  20  23  32  34  43  44  54  54  54  56  63  65  76  78  78  99

                  ^

2   4  11  12  20  23  32  34  43  44  54  54  54  56  63  65  76  78  78  99
```

■ Example 14.2: Shell Sort

The *shell sort* continually halves sublists and makes comparisons and exchanges between adjacent sublists. Comparisons are made between the corresponding elements in adjacent sublists. Elements are exchanged if necessary to put the elements 1 and HALF+1, 2 and HALF+2, and so on, into the correct order. The list is then halved again and comparisons and exchanges are made. The list is sorted when the length of the sublist of elements is 1.

Consider the following data, which will be sorted with the shell sort. (See Figure 14.5.)

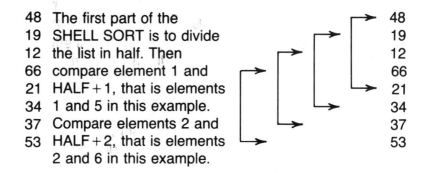

48	The first part of the	48
19	SHELL SORT is to divide	19
12	the list in half. Then	12
66	compare element 1 and	66
21	HALF + 1, that is elements	21
34	1 and 5 in this example.	34
37	Compare elements 2 and	37
53	HALF + 2, that is elements	53
	2 and 6 in this example.	

FIGURE 14.5

If the value in the upper list is greater than the value in the lower list, the two values are exchanged. Then each of these two lists is halved, and comparisons and exchanges between adjacent sublists are again made.

48	21	12	12
19	19	19	19
12	12	21	21
66	53	34	34
21	48	37	37
34	34	53	48
37	37	48	53
53	66	66	66

```
48                                              Example 14.2
19                                              Input
12
66
21
34
37
53
-99
```

```
$ EDIT SHELL.FOR                                Example 14.2
C
C       _____
C       MAIN PROGRAM
C
C       _____
C                       Inputs and echos data values to be sorted.
C                       Calls the SHELL SORT routine
C                       Outputs the sorted data.

        INTEGER VALUES(20)

100     FORMAT(' ',20I3)
C       Input data values until a flag data value of -99 is reached.
        READ (5,*) VALUES(1)
        NUMVALUES = 0
        DO WHILE (VALUES(NUMVALUES+1).NE. -99)
            NUMVALUES = NUMVALUES + 1
            READ(5,*)VALUES(NUMVALUES+1)
        END DO
        WRITE(6,*)'INPUT DATA'
        WRITE(6,100)(VALUES(J),J=1,NUMVALUES)


        CALL SHELLSORT(VALUES,NUMVALUES)


        WRITE(6,*)'DATA SORTED WITH THE SHELL SORT'
        WRITE(6,100)(VALUES(J),J=1,NUMVALUES)
        STOP
        END


C       Example 14.2                            Program SHELL.FOR
C
C       _____
        SUBROUTINE SHELLSORT(VALUES,NUMVALUES)
C
C       _____
C                       Sort an array of elements into
C                       ascending order.
        INTEGER VALUES(20)

C       Set the initial list length to the number of array elements.
        LISTLENGTH = NUMVALUES

C       Continue the sorting procedure as long as there are still
C       elements to be sorted.
        DO WHILE (LISTLENGTH .GT. 1)
```

```
C           Divide the list in half for comparisons.
            LISTLENGTH = LISTLENGTH/2

C           Compare values between adjacent sublists and exchange values
C           when appropriate.
            FLAG = 1
            DO WHILE (FLAG .NE. 0)
              FLAG = 0
              NUMBER_COMPARISONS = NUMVALUES - LISTLENGTH
              DO J=1,NUMBER_COMPARISONS
                IF (VALUES(J) .GT. VALUES(J+LISTLENGTH)) THEN
                    TEMP = VALUES(J)
                    VALUES(J) = VALUES(J+LISTLENGTH)
                    VALUES(J+LISTLENGTH) = TEMP
                  FLAG = 1
                END IF
              END DO
            END DO

          END DO
          RETURN
          END
```

```
$ FORTRAN SHELL
$ LINK SHELL
$ RUN  SHELL
```

Example 14.2
Output

```
  INPUT DATA
  48 19 12 66 21 34 37 53
 DATA SORTED WITH THE SHELL SORT
  12 19 21 34 37 48 53 66
```

A trace of the way the numbers are sorted is provided in the explanation of the Shell Sort preceding the program.

14.2
AN INTERACTIVE DATA BASE APPLICATION

There are many concepts to consider in writing a computer program. Obviously, the syntax and the logic must be correct, but beyond that there are many ways to approach any problem.

Example 14.3 is included to provide a look at using a set of data that is stored on disk as a master file and then interacting with a user at the terminal to access that data. This approach is often used in business applications and is being used more and more in research applications.

For business applications, a bank would have the financial records for its customers stored on disk. When a customer comes in to do some banking, a program can be executed to input customer records from disk and then to interact at the terminal to perform the customer's transaction.

For scientific applications, a natural resources group in the state would have vast amounts of information stored on disk about the water runoff in the state. A researcher could then use a terminal to interact with the computer to enquire about some data or to insert some data into the system.

■ Example 14.3: Accessing a Data Base

The program inputs records for a group of employees from a disk file named EMPMASTER.DAT. For each employee, a record on disk includes the name, pay rate, number of years of service, and age. After the records are available to the user in the program, a menu is printed on the screen requesting that the user select a column on which to sort.

Example 14.3
Input

```
$ EDIT EMPMASTER.DAT
EDGAR EDMONDS          4.59    22    47
CARIE FARREL          10.00    10    19
FUNNY HARPO            1.98     1    49
B. S. HSIEH           50.00     9    27
PAM PARSOL            12.00    52    88
M.B.A. BURNHAM        55.55     5    25
SUE SUPERSTAR         99.99    20    42
END
```

Example 14.3

```
$ EDIT EMPSORT.FOR
        CHARACTER*20 NAME(20)
        REAL ATTRIBUTE(20,3)
        INTEGER SORTCOLUMN

        OPEN(1,FILE='EMPMASTER.DAT',STATUS='OLD')

C       _____
C       MAIN PROGRAM
C
C       _____
C                     The program reads a set of employee records from
C                     the file named EMPMASTER.DAT.  For each employee,
C                     the data includes the name, pay rate, years of
C                     service and age.
C
C                     Then the program runs interactively requesting that
C                     the user enter at the terminal an attribute on
C                     which to sort.  The sort is performed and the
C                     records are displayed at the terminal in the
C                     order requested for the sort.
```

```
C                              The program loops requesting the attribute for
C                              the sort, performing the sort, and printing
C                              the result until the user selects the EXIT
C                              option for the attribute selection.

      CALL INPUT_MASTERFILE(NAME,NUMEMPLOY,ATTRIBUTE)

      CALL CHOOSE_SORT_ATTRIBUTE (SORTCOLUMN)
      DO WHILE (SORTCOLUMN.GT.0)
        CALL SHELL (NAME,ATTRIBUTE,NUMEMPLOY,SORTCOLUMN)
        CALL PRINT_SORTED_OUTPUT (NAME,ATTRIBUTE,NUMEMPLOY)
        CALL CHOOSE_SORT_ATTRIBUTE (SORTCOLUMN)
      END DO
      STOP
      END

C                                               Program EMPSORT.FOR
C
      SUBROUTINE INPUT_MASTERFILE(NAME,NUMEMPLOY,ATTRIBUTE)
C     _____
C                              Enter the employee master file information.
C                              Read employee records until the flag END
C                              for an employee name is encountered.

      CHARACTER*20 NAME(20)
      REAL ATTRIBUTE(20,3)

100   FORMAT(A,F5.2,2F5.0)
      READ (1,100) NAME(1), (ATTRIBUTE(1,J),J=1,3)
      NUMEMPLOY = 0
      DO WHILE (NAME(NUMEMPLOY+1).NE.'END')
        NUMEMPLOY = NUMEMPLOY + 1
        READ(1,100)NAME(NUMEMPLOY+1),(ATTRIBUTE(NUMEMPLOY+1,J),J=1,3)
      END DO
      RETURN
      END

C     _____
      SUBROUTINE CHOOSE_SORT_ATTRIBUTE (SORTCOLUMN)
C     _____
C                              Prompt user to pick a column in
C                              the attribute list on which to sort.
      INTEGER SORTCOLUMN
100   FORMAT(//,' ',  '        ENTER THE NUMBER OF THE FIELD',
     -  /,        ' ',  '       ON WHICH TO SORT (OR ZERO TO EXIT)',
     -  /,        ' ',  '       ------------------------------------',
     -  /,        ' ',  '       1   PAY RATE',
     -  /,        ' ',  '       2   YEARS OF SERVICE',
     -  /,        ' ',  '       3   AGE',
     -  /,        ' ',  '       0   EXIT',//)
      WRITE (6,100)
      READ (5,*) SORTCOLUMN
      IF (SORTCOLUMN.EQ.1) WRITE(6,*) 'SORT BY PAY RATE'
      IF (SORTCOLUMN.EQ.2) WRITE(6,*) 'SORT BY YEARS OF SERVICE'
      IF (SORTCOLUMN.EQ.3) WRITE(6,*) 'SORT BY AGE'
      IF (SORTCOLUMN.EQ.0) WRITE(6,*) 'EXIT'
      RETURN
      END
```

```
C                                              Program EMPSORT.FOR
C
C           _____

      SUBROUTINE SHELL(NAME,ATTRIBUTE,NUMEMPLOY,SORTCOLUMN)
C
C           _____
C                       Sort a 2-dimensional array of elements into
C                       ascending order using the column selected by
C                       the user as the column on which to sort.
C                       The name is kept with the attributes in the sort.

      CHARACTER*20 NAME(20), NAMEHOLD
      REAL ATTRIBUTE(20,3)
      INTEGER SORTCOLUMN

C     Set the initial list length to the number of array elements.
      LISTLENGTH = NUMEMPLOY

C     Continue the sorting procedure as long as there are still
C     elements to be sorted.
      DO WHILE (LISTLENGTH .GT. 1)

C        Divide the list in half for comparisons.
         LISTLENGTH = LISTLENGTH/2

C        Compare values between adjacent sublists and exchange values
C        when appropriate.
         FLAG = 1
         DO WHILE (FLAG .NE. 0)
           FLAG = 0
           NUMBER_COMPARISONS = NUMEMPLOY - LISTLENGTH
           DO J=1,NUMBER_COMPARISONS
             IF (ATTRIBUTE(J,SORTCOLUMN) .GT.
                 ATTRIBUTE(J+LISTLENGTH,SORTCOLUMN)) THEN
               NAMEHOLD = NAME(J)
               NAME(J) = NAME(J+LISTLENGTH)
               NAME(J+LISTLENGTH) = NAMEHOLD
               DO NCOLUMN=1,3
                 TEMP = ATTRIBUTE(J,NCOLUMN)
                 ATTRIBUTE(J,NCOLUMN) = ATTRIBUTE(J+LISTLENGTH,NCOLUMN)
                 ATTRIBUTE(J+LISTLENGTH,NCOLUMN) = TEMP
               END DO
               FLAG = 1
             END IF
           END DO
         END DO

      END DO
      RETURN
      END
C                                              Program EMPSORT.FOR
C
C     _____
      SUBROUTINE PRINT_SORTED_OUTPUT (NAME,ATTRIBUTE,NUMEMPLOY)
C
C     _____
C
C                       Print results of the sort on the specified
C                       attribute.
      CHARACTER*20 NAME(20)
      REAL ATTRIBUTE(20,3)
```

```
100      FORMAT(/,' ',29X,'PAY',10X,'YEARS OF',/,
   -     ' ',5X,'NAME',20X,'RATE',9X,'SERVICE',5X,'AGE',/)
200      FORMAT(' ',5X,A,F8.2,5X,F7.1,5X,F7.1)

         WRITE (6,100)
         DO N=1,NUMEMPLOY
           WRITE (6,200) NAME(N), (ATTRIBUTE(N,J),J=1,3)
         END DO
         RETURN
         END


$ FORTRAN EMPSORT
$ LINK EMPSORT
$ RUN EMPSORT
```

Example 14.3
Input and Output from
Terminal

```
        ENTER THE NUMBER OF THE FIELD
    ON WHICH TO SORT (OR ZERO TO EXIT)
    ------------------------------------

        1    PAY RATE
        2    YEARS OF SERVICE
        3    AGE
        0    EXIT
2                                               user entry

    SORT BY YEARS OF SERVICE


                            PAY          YEARS OF
        NAME                RATE         SERVICE     AGE

        FUNNY HARPO          1.98         1.0        49.0
        M.B.A. BURNHAM      55.55         5.0        25.0
        B. S. HSIEH         50.00         9.0        27.0
        CARIE FARREL        10.00        10.0        19.0
        SUE SUPERSTAR       99.99        20.0        42.0
        EDGAR EDMONDS        4.59        22.0        47.0
        PAM PARSOL          12.00        52.0        88.0

        ENTER THE NUMBER OF THE FIELD
    ON WHICH TO SORT (OR ZERO TO EXIT)
    ------------------------------------

        1    PAY RATE
        2    YEARS OF SERVICE
        3    AGE
        0    EXIT
3                                               user entry

    SORT BY AGE


                            PAY          YEARS OF
        NAME                RATE         SERVICE     AGE

        CARIE FARREL        10.00        10.0        19.0
        M.B.A. BURNHAM      55.55         5.0        25.0
        B. S. HSIEH         50.00         9.0        27.0
        SUE SUPERSTAR       99.99        20.0        42.0
        EDGAR EDMONDS        4.59        22.0        47.0
        FUNNY HARPO          1.98         1.0        49.0
        PAM PARSOL          12.00        52.0        88.0
```

```
        ENTER THE NUMBER OF THE FIELD
        ON WHICH TO SORT (OR ZERO TO EXIT)
        ------------------------------------
            1   PAY RATE
            2   YEARS OF SERVICE
            3   AGE
            Ø   EXIT
  Ø                                                   user entry
     EXIT
```

14.3
PLOTTING

Computers are widely used to display a set of data graphically. There are many graphical devices for plotting. A graphics device has the capability of drawing a line rather than printing a series of points. High-quality graphs must be created with a graphics device; however, simple plots to display some information can be created with a line printer. Creating plots with graphics devices requires that special commands recognized by the graphics devices be used. Example 14.4 creates a plot for a standard line printer using only the FORTRAN language.

■ Example 14.4: Creating a Plot
for a Line Printer

Completely general plotting routines that allow a user to plot any set of data can be very complex. The program in this example is a plotting program that plots most sets of integer data. The program requires that a file be created prior to running the program, which contains the title for the plot, the title for the y axis, and the title for the x axis, in addition to the data to be plotted.

Look at the plot that is produced at the end of the program. Then study the program to observe the steps that are necessary in creating a general plot. The axes must be scaled and the tick mark values must be determined for the scaled axes. The data itself must be scaled to fit on the plot.

Example 14.4
Input

```
$ EDT SPENDING.DAT
SPENDING BY COLLEGE STUDENTS
MONEY SPENT
CASH AVAILABLE IN POCKET
120, 90
230, 170
370, 210
60, 50
90, 90
140, 120
240, 150
-999,-999
```

Example 14.4

```
$ EDT SCATPLOT.FOR
C       _____
C       MAIN PROGRAM
C       _____
C       The program reads data to be plotted from a file.  The file
C       must contain a title for the plot, a title for the Y axis,
C       a title for the X axis and the data to be plotted.

C       The program determines and prints the minimum and maximum
C       data values for the x and y axes and prompts the user to
C       select a range for the axes and the program generates
C       scaling for the plot.

C       Then the program actually prints the plot with the titles
C       specified and the data scaled for the plot.

        INTEGER X(50),Y(50),XLABEL(11),YLABEL(11),XMAX,XMIN,YMAX,YMIN
        CHARACTER YAXISLABEL(30)*1, XAXISLABEL*40
        CHARACTER PLOT(0:30,0:50)*1,TITLE*40
        DATA YAXISLABEL/30*' '/

        CALL INPUT (TITLE,YAXISLABEL,XAXISLABEL,
     -             X,Y,XMIN,XMAX,YMIN,YMAX,KNT)
        CALL SCALE_AXES  (XMIN,XMAX,XINC,YMIN,YMAX,YINC,XRANGE,YRANGE,
     -             LENGTHXAXIS,LENGTHYAXIS,NUMXINC,NUMYINC)

        CALL MAKELABELS(XLABEL,XMIN,XMAX,XINC,NUMXINC,LENGTHXAXIS,'X')
        CALL MAKELABELS(YLABEL,YMIN,YMAX,YINC,NUMYINC,LENGTHYAXIS,'Y')

        CALL SCALE_DATA  (X,XMIN,XRANGE,LENGTHXAXIS,KNT,
     -             Y,YMIN,YRANGE,LENGTHYAXIS,PLOT)
        CALL DRAWPLOT(LENGTHXAXIS,NUMXINC,XLABEL,XAXISLABEL,LENGTHYAXIS,
     -             NUMYINC,YLABEL,YAXISLABEL,KNT,TITLE,PLOT)
        STOP
        END
```

```
C                                                Program SCATPLOT.FOR
C       _____
        SUBROUTINE INPUT(TITLE,YAXISLABEL,XAXISLABEL,
     -             X,Y,XMIN,XMAX,YMIN,YMAX,KNT)
C       _____
C                       The subroutine prompts a user to enter the name
C                       of the data file where the data to be plotted is
C                       stored and that file is opened.  Titles for the
C                       plot and plot data are input from the file.
C                       The program finds the minimum and maximum
C                       for the X and Y values.

        INTEGER X(*),Y(*),XMIN,XMAX,YMIN,YMAX
        CHARACTER FILENAME*20
        CHARACTER TITLE*40,YAXISLABEL(30)*1, XAXISLABEL*40

100     FORMAT(A)
200     FORMAT(15A)
300     FORMAT(2I5)
```

```
         WRITE(6,*)'ENTER THE NAME OF THE FILE'
         WRITE(6,*)'WHICH CONTAINS THE DATA TO PLOT'
         READ(5,100)FILENAME
         OPEN(11,FILE=FILENAME,STATUS='OLD')

C        The first record in the file must contain the title for the plot.
         READ(11,100)TITLE
C        The second record in the file must contain the title for the y axis.
         READ(11,200)(YAXISLABEL(I),I=15,1,-1)
C        The third record in the file must contain the title for the x axis.
         READ(11,100)XAXISLABEL

C        Input all the x and y data values until a -999 value is encountered.
C        The final data value for x must be -999.
C        Determine the minimum and maximum values for x and y as the values
C        are being input.  Count the number of records.
         READ(11,300) X(1), Y(1)
         XMIN = X(1)
         XMAX = X(1)
         YMIN = Y(1)
         YMAX = Y(1)
         KNT=0
         DO WHILE (X(KNT+1).NE.-999)
            KNT = KNT +1
            IF (X(KNT).LT.XMIN) XMIN = X(KNT)
            IF (X(KNT).GT.XMAX) XMAX = X(KNT)
            IF (Y(KNT).LT.YMIN) YMIN = Y(KNT)
            IF (Y(KNT).GT.YMAX) YMAX = Y(KNT)

            READ (11,300) X(KNT+1), Y(KNT+1)
         END DO
         CLOSE(11)
         RETURN
         END


C                                                   Program SCATPLOT.FOR
C
         SUBROUTINE SCALE AXES (XMIN,XMAX,XINC,YMIN,YMAX,YINC,XRANGE,
     -                 YRANGE,LENGTHXAXIS,LENGTHYAXIS,NUMXINC,NUMYINC)
C

C                    The subroutine prints the recorded minimum and
C                    maximum values input for your data.  Then it
C                    prompts you to enter the minimum, maximum and
C                    increment you choose for scaling.  (Note -
C                    The reason for allowing the user to enter the
C                    values is that the minimum might be 7 and the
C                    maximum might be 29.  Seven and 29 would be
C                    unusual beginning and ending points on a plot.
C                    You would probably choose 5 and 30.

         INTEGER XMIN,XMAX,YMIN,YMAX
         WRITE(6,*)'YOU WILL NEED TO SPECIFY THE SCALING FOR YOUR PLOT'
         WRITE(6,*)'THE FOLLOWING ARE RECORDED MAXIMUMS AND MINIMUMS'
         WRITE(6,*)'FOR THE X VALUES   MIN=',XMIN,'   MAX=',XMAX
         WRITE(6,*)'FOR THE Y VALUES   MIN=',YMIN,'   MAX=',YMAX
         WRITE(6,*)
```

```
            WRITE(6,*)'PLEASE SPECIFY SCALING FOR YOUR PLOT'
            WRITE(6,*)'ENTER MINIMUM, MAXIMUM & INCREMENT FOR THE X AXIS.'
            READ(5,*) XMIN,XMAX,XINC
            WRITE(6,*)'ENTER MINIMUM, MAXIMUM & INCREMENT FOR THE Y AXIS.'
            READ(5,*) YMIN,YMAX,YINC

            NUMXINC = INT( (XMAX-XMIN) / XINC) + 1
            NUMYINC = INT( (YMAX-YMIN) / YINC) + 1

            XRANGE = XMAX - XMIN
            YRANGE = YMAX - YMIN
            LENGTHXAXIS = (NUMXINC-1) * 5 + 1
            LENGTHYAXIS = (NUMYINC-1) * 3 + 1

            RETURN
            END

C                                             Program SCATPLOT.FOR
C
            _____
            SUBROUTINE MAKELABELS (LABEL,MIN,MAX,AINC,NUMINC,LENGTHAXIS,XY)
C
C           _____
C                         The subroutine stores the values to be used for
C                         tick mark labels at each tick mark.  The subroutine
C                         uses the minimum value entered by the user as the
C                         starting value and adds the increment value until
C                         the number of tick marks has reached the maximum
C                         number of tick marks.
            INTEGER LABEL(11)
100         FORMAT(' ','THERE CAN BE NO MORE THAN 10 INCREMENT STEPS',
         -  /,'PLEASE REENTER ',A,' INCREMENT FOR 10 OR FEWER STEPS')
            CHARACTER XY*1
            LABELNO = 1
            LABEL(1) = MIN
            DO WHILE (LABEL(LABELNO).LT.MAX)
               LABELNO = LABELNO + 1
               IF (LABELNO.GT.11) THEN
                  WRITE(6,100)
                  READ(5,*)AINC
                  NUMINC = INT ((MAX-MIN)/AINC + 1)
                  IF (XY.EQ.'X')LENGTHAXIS=(NUMINC-1)*5+1
                  IF (XY.EQ.'Y')LENGTHAXIS=(NUMINC-1)*3+1
                  LABELNO=2
                     END IF
               LABEL(LABELNO)=LABEL(LABELNO-1)+AINC
            END DO
            RETURN
            END
C
            _____
            SUBROUTINE SCALE_DATA (X,XMIN,XRANGE,LENGTHXAXIS,KNT,
         -           Y,YMIN,YRANGE,LENGTHYAXIS,PLOT)
C
C           _____
C                         The subroutine scales input data values to fit
C                         into the array of 30 lines and 50 columns to be
C                         printed.  First the array PLOT is filled with
C                         blank characters.  Then for each data value, the
C                         scaled location for the value is determined and an
C                         asterisk is stored in the array at that location.
```

```
CHARACTER PLOT(0:30,0:50)*1
INTEGER X(50),Y(50),XMIN,YMIN

DO LINE = 0,30
   DO ICOL = 0,50
      PLOT(LINE,ICOL) = ' '
   END DO
END DO
DO I = 1,KNT
   NUMCOLUMN = (X(I)-XMIN)/XRANGE * LENGTHXAXIS - 1
   NUMLINE = (Y(I)-YMIN)/YRANGE * LENGTHYAXIS + 3
   PLOT(NUMLINE,NUMCOLUMN)='*'
END DO
RETURN
END


C                                               Program SCATPLOT.FOR
C
      SUBROUTINE DRAWPLOT(LENGTHXAXIS,NUMXINC,XLABEL,XAXISLABEL,
     -           LENGTHYAXIS,NUMYINC,YLABEL,YAXISLABEL,
     -           KNT,TITLE,PLOT)
C
C                    The subroutine first prints the plot title.
C                    The linenumber which is the top of the plot
C                    in the array named PLOT is established.  Beginning
C                    at the top, the subroutine prints the character
C                    for the label for the y axis, the value to
C                    be printed for the tick mark and the line of
C                    data to be plotted.  Then for the two succeding
C                    lines, the tick marks are not printed. Only the
C                    character for the y axis label and the line
C                    of data are printed.  After all the lines of
C                    the plot are printed, the line is printed for the
C                    x axis, the tick marks for the x axis are printed,
C                    and the title to the x axis is printed.
      CHARACTER PLOT(0:30,0:50)*1,TITLE*40,YAXISLABEL(30)*1,
     -      XAXISLABEL*40,XTICKMARKS(11)*5,XAXISLINE(50)*1
      INTEGER XLABEL(11),YLABEL(11)
      DATA XTICKMARKS,XAXISLINE/11*'    1', 50*'-'/
100   FORMAT(' ',A,7X,I5,' - 1',60A)
200   FORMAT(' ',A,'            1',60A)
300   FORMAT(/,' ',20X,A)
400   FORMAT(' ',16X,50A)
500   FORMAT(' ',12X,11A)
600   FORMAT(' ',12X,10I5)

      WRITE(6,300)TITLE                !Print the plot title
      LINENUMBER = NUMYINC * 3 + 1     !Start at the top line.

C     The DO loop is used to count the number of tick marks that
C     are to be labeled,  starting at the top and coming down.
      DO LABELNUM = NUMYINC, 2, -1
         LINENUMBER = LINENUMBER  - 1
C        Print a line with a tick mark label.
         WRITE(6,100)YAXISLABEL(LINENUMBER),YLABEL(LABELNUM),
     -            (PLOT(LINENUMBER,N),N=0,LENGTHXAXIS)
```

```
C          Print two lines between the tick marks.
           DO IBETWEEN = 1,2
               LINENUMBER = LINENUMBER - 1
               WRITE(6,200)YAXISLABEL(LINENUMBER),
      -                (PLOT(LINENUMBER,N),N=0,LENGTHXAXIS)
           END DO
        END DO
C       Print the last line of the plot with the last y tick mark.
        WRITE(6,100)YAXISLABEL(1),YLABEL(1),(PLOT(0,N),N=0,LENGTHXAXIS)
        WRITE(6,400)(XAXISLINE(I),I=1,LENGTHXAXIS)  !Print line for x axis.
        WRITE(6,500)(XTICKMARKS(I),I=1,NUMXINC)     !Print tick marks for x axis.
        WRITE(6,600)(XLABEL(I),I=1,NUMXINC)         !Print x tick mark values.
        WRITE(6,300)XAXISLABEL                      !Print x axis title.
        RETURN
        END
```

```
$ FORTRAN SCATPLOT
$ LINK SCATPLOT
$ RUN SCATPLOT
```

Example 14.4
User Input and Output

```
YOU WILL NEED TO SPECIFY THE SCALING FOR YOUR PLOT
THE FOLLOWING ARE RECORDED MAXIMUMS AND MINIMUMS
FOR THE X VALUES    MIN=        60      MAX=        370
FOR THE Y VALUES    MIN=        50      MAX=        210

PLEASE SPECIFY SCALING FOR YOUR PLOT
ENTER MINIMUM, MAXIMUM & INCREMENT FOR THE X AXIS.
0,400,50                                                    user input

ENTER MINIMUM, MAXIMUM & INCREMENT FOR THE Y AXIS.
0,250,50                                                    user input
```

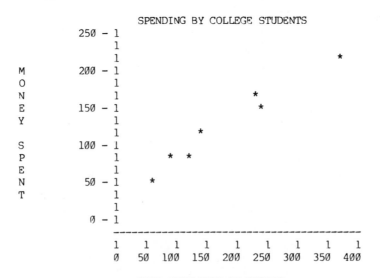

14.4
DATA CONSIDERATIONS
FOR APPLICATIONS

For most common applications, it is not necessary to understand the way that data is stored inside the computer; however it is beneficial to have a general understanding of the way that data is stored. In some cases, you may need to specify a particular way for data to be stored.

Data is stored inside the computer as a series of bits in which an electrical current is either flowing or the current is not flowing. We think of this as a series of 1's and 0's.

The smallest unit of data inside a computer is a bit, that is one position with a value of a one or a zero. The association between bits of data have different implications depending on whether a real number is stored, an integer number is stored, or alphanumeric data is stored.

Like many other computers, the number of bits in one word for the VAX computer is 32. A word is the number of bits addressed as a unit unless some other number of bits is specified. For instance, if the value 10 is stored in the memory location named NUM in a program, there are up to 31 bits that could be used to represent that number, because one of the 32 bits is used to represent the plus or minus sign. The value ten would actually be represented with the following configuration.

00000000000000000000000000001010
                                 ↑ ↑
                          Current Flowing

Each bit represents a power of 2.
2^{31} .... 2^6 2^5 2^4 2^3 2^2 2^1 2^0

The decimal value 10 then =	8	+	2
=	2^3	+	2^1
which is the binary value	1 0	1	0

For a REAL number, the significant digits in the number are stored as well as the plus or minus sign and the location of the decimal point in the number. Using the 32 bits in a word on the VAX to store one numeric value, the following are the ranges for the values that can be stored.

INTEGER range: -2147483648 to $+2147483648$

REAL range: $0.29*10^{-38}$ to $1.7*10^{+38}$

If this range of values will not store a number as large or as small as you need, you can use the double precision facility in the FORTRAN language to allow values to occupy two words, that is 64 bits. The 32 bits in a word are divided into 4 bytes. Each byte contains 8 bits. Most data is stored in the 4 byte, 32 bit word.

The double precision declaration can be used to declare that two words be used to represent a value. Since two words would be 8 bytes, a double precision value can be declared as a REAL*8 value. The following two sample programs indicate declarations and formats for double precision.

```
      REAL*8 BIGX, BIGY
      READ(5,10) BIGX, BIGY
      WRITE(6,20) BIGX, BIGY
10    FORMAT(D10.5, D9.1)
20    FORMAT(' ',D11.5, D10.2)
      END
```

                    or

```
      DOUBLE PRECISION BIGX, BIGY
      READ(5,10) BIGX, BIGY
      WRITE(6,20) BIGX, BIGY
10    FORMAT(D10.5, D9.1)
20    FORMAT(' ',D11.5, D10.2)
      END
```

An E format can be used to allow you to enter data and to print data in exponential format. The E format can be used with either single or double precision values.

```
      REAL*8, X, Y
      READ(5,10) X
      READ(5,10) Y
      WRITE(6,20) X, Y
10    FORMAT(E10.4)
20    FORMAT(' ',E11.4,2X,E11.4)
      END
```

The following example is included to demonstrate data declarations. A DATA DECLARATION sets a value or values in memory at the time that a program begins to execute. Notice that the two-dimensional array is stored column-wise in the data declaration. Observe the output to see how the data is stored. There is no input to the program.

```
$ EDIT DATDECLAR.FOR                                    Example 14.5
      REAL VALUE(8)
      INTEGER NUMBERS(5,2)
      DATA A,B,I,M/ 2.3, 11.78, 4,56/
```

```
         DATA VALUE/1.1, 6.8, 3.2, 5.5, 3.4, 6.6, 7.7, 9.8/
         DATA NUMBERS/90,80,70,60,0,100,89,79,69,59/
         WRITE(6,100)A,B,I,M
100      FORMAT(' A=',F5.2,' B=',F5.2,' I=',I3,' M=',I3)
         WRITE([6,200)VALUE
200      FORMAT(' VALUE ',8F5.1)
         DO I = 1,5
             WRITE(6,300)NUMBERS(I,1),NUMBERS(I,2)
         END DO
300      FORMAT(' NUMBERS ',2I5)
         STOP
         END
$ FORT DATDECLAR
$ LINK DATDECLAR
$ RUN DATDECLAR

A= 2.30 B=11.78 I=  4 M= 56
VALUE    1.1  6.8  3.2  5.5  3.4  6.6  7.7  9.8
NUMBERS      90  100
NUMBERS      80   89
NUMBERS      70   79
NUMBERS      60   69
NUMBERS       0   59
```

Example 14.5
Output

14.5
SUMMARY

It is useful to develop and test general subroutines for performing tasks that you may need repeatedly. Algorithms exist for many of the applications that are employed frequently in computing.

Sorting is a function performed well by a computer, and selecting the correct sorting algorithm can be very important. The *bubble sort,* the *shell sort* and the *quick sort* are frequently employed sort algorithms.

Often a set of data is stored on disk and then a program is written to allow a user at the terminal to interact with that data. Such a program then accepts input from both the disk and the terminal.

14.6
EXERCISES

14.1. A *binary search* is a more efficient way to look through an array to find a match for a value than a linear search. In a linear search, each element in the array is compared one after another until a match is found. To use a binary search, the elements in the array that is being searched must be sorted into either ascending or descending order. (See Figure 14.6.)

Divide the array in half and compare the search value with the middle element in the array. That will determine if comparisons

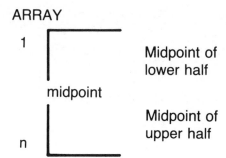

FIGURE 14.6

should be made in the upper half of the array or the lower half of the array. Then compare with the midpoint of the half in which the value is determined to be located. Continue to divide the list and compare with the midpoint until the element is found.

Write a binary search subroutine that is completely general and can be invoked whenever the need for such a routine occurs in a program.

14.2.   Write a program that includes a quick sort. The algorithm will be the same as that in this chapter, but develop your own code. Modify the algorithm slightly to do the following. When a list is divided into two sublists, always put the longer sublist on the stack first. Test the program with the following data: 34 −2.3 987.7 588 321 876 33 −0.23 1000 12

14.3.   Write a program to input two lists of data, sort each list, and then merge the sorted lists. The lists might not be the same length.

Input lists		Sorted lists		Merged list
7	14	2	3	2
9	3	7	4	3
2	4	9	9	4
	9		14	7
				9
				9
				14

14.4.   Write a program to produce a bar chart for a set of sales data. The program should input the plot title and axes labels as data. Axes should be labeled with tick mark values and the data should be scaled. Make the plot program general. Test the program with the following two sets of sample data. The plots should be more precise than the oversimplified plots shown.

Easy Printer Company
Ribbon Sales

Year	
1981	12000
1982	14500
1983	17800
1984	19520

Easy Printer Company

Ribbon Sales

```
        Easy Printer Company
Ribbon 20000 |                      *
Sales        |                 *    *
       15000 |            *    *    *
             |       *    *    *    *
       10000 |       *    *    *    *
             +-----------------------------
              1981  1982  1983  1984
                       Year
```

The Shoe Sole
Shoe Sales

Year	
1981	6200
1982	7450
1983	9780

The Shoe Sole

```
        The Shoe Sole
Shoe  10000 |
Sales       |                           *
            |                 *         *
            |       *         *         *
      5000  |       *         *         *
            +-----------------------------
             1981           1982      1983
                      Year
```

14.5.   The problem generally known as the Towers of Hanoi will aid in developing programming and logic skills. There are three posts on a board. On one post, there is a stack of rings, the top ring being the smallest ring and the bottom ring being the largest ring. The problem is to move all the rings to another post with the largest ring at the bottom and the smallest ring at the top. (See Figure 14.7.)

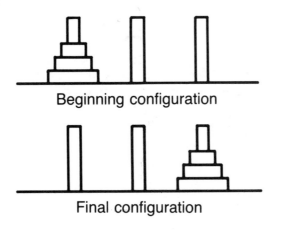

Beginning configuration

Final configuration

FIGURE 14.7

The rules for moving the rings are that only one ring can be moved at one time and that no ring can be placed on top of a smaller ring. Write a program to restack the rings on another post.

14.6. This project includes writing four FORTRAN programs. First, write a program to generate a set of 1000 data records and store the records in a data file. The data should be generated as three random values per record using the following criteria.

Value 1 in each record is sex and should be F for female or M for male. This could be generated as a 1 or a 0 and converted to F or M.

Value 2 in each record should be an age and should be generated as random numbers between 0 and 100.

Value 3 in each record should be the number of books read in 1 year and should be generated as random numbers between 0 and 20. (Example 10.2 in the text provides an example of creating data sets.)

A few of the records that might be created are the following:

Sex	Age	Books read
F	29	4
M	38	12
M	4	7
F	82	18
F	61	9
M	18	11
M	52	6
M	9	13
F	31	2

Then write three programs that include selection and sorting. Write the program using a bubble sort for the problem. Then modify the program to use a shell sort for the problem. And then modify the program to use a quick sort for the problem.

First sort the data by male or female. Then select the age group below 50 and sort the data by the number of books read. Then select the age group 50 and over and sort the data by number of books read.

FEMALE
    UNDER 50
            BOOKS READ
                2
                4
        50 AND OVER
            BOOKS READ
                9
                18

```
MALE
  UNDER 50
          BOOKS READ
             7
            11
            12
            13
50 AND OVER
          BOOKS READ
             6
```

The original records are:

```
F   31    2
F   29    4

F   61    9
F   82   18

M    4    7
M   18   11
M   38   12
M    9   13

M   52    6
```

15

Developing
Large Programs

This chapter summarizes some of the factors that should be considered in developing large programs. Methods for developing large computer programs that are well designed, useful, and correct are the topics for many entire books.

15.1
PROGRAM DESIGN

A detailed and systematic procedure for organizing a simple problem in such a way that it can be solved with a computer is demonstrated in Chapter 4. That procedure involves writing down everything that you know about a problem and then rearranging and clarifying the steps until there is a logical solution to the problem. Writing very large programs requires a level of consideration above the logic of accessing and manipulating individual data elements.

For large problems, it is best to begin by analyzing the overall problem, dividing the problem into manageable subtasks, and developing the relationships between the subtasks. Only after the subtasks are completely defined should you consider the details of writing programming code. This approach to developing a computer program is called *top down design.*

The first step in developing a program might be to make an overall statement about the problem.

GENERATE PROBLEM STATEMENT

The second step is to specify the major parts involved in solving the problem. (See Figure 15.1.)

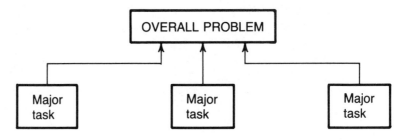

FIGURE 15.1

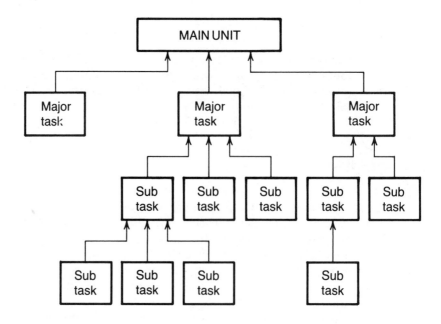

FIGURE 15.2

If a problem is large, you are probably still considering broad problems at this level, and you will need to continue to divide the problem into subtasks until each module specifies a task that can be easily understood. (See Figure 15.2.)

Once you have completely defined a problem by specifying each subtask involved in producing the desired result, you can begin to consider each module as a subroutine or a series of subroutines. In developing a module, you must first consider the relationship of data elements and structures between program units. Then you can begin to develop the code for processing individual data elements in a subroutine.

15.2
PROGRAM STRUCTURE

Solving the overall problem is performed as the modules for each task are defined. After the modules are clearly defined, the programming code to actually perform the necessary processes is considered.

The top level of design begins with the main program. Design continues as the modules are developed and the links are developed. When you actually write the code to process individual data elements for each subroutine, you need to select the appropriate FORTRAN structures to perform the necessary processing. If you have divided a problem into well-defined tasks, writing the code should not be overly difficult.

The few FORTRAN structures are used in various combinations to produce the results that you need. The important concept is that these structures provide one entry point and one exit point from a task. The primary routine is the MAIN program with one entry point and one exit, that is, the STOP END.

```
PROGRAM

STOP
END
```

In general, the main program should be a series of calls to subroutines. The entry point and exit point from a subroutine are well defined.

```
SUBROUTINE

RETURN
END
```

Inside each subroutine, the structures for repetition and selection are used, either separately or in various combinations. Each structure should be used with one entry point and one exit point. Always using one entry and one exit point makes a program readable and thus easy to debug and verify correctness.

■ Structures for Repetition and Selection

Repetition.

```
DO loop_control_value = begin_value, end_value, increment
    statements to be executed repeatedly
END  DO
```

Selection.

```
IF   (condition) THEN
    statements to execute if condition is true
END  IF
```

```
IF   (condition) THEN
    statements to execute if condition is true
    ELSE
    statements to execute if condition is false
END  IF
```

Repetition and Selection.

```
DO WHILE (condition)
    statements to execute repeatedly while the condition is true
END  DO
```

In most cases combinations of the basic structures are used for writing the code for a task.

Combinations of Control Structures.

```
DO loop_control_value = begin_value, end_value, increment
    IF (condition) THEN
        IF (condition) THEN
            block of statements
        ELSE
            block of statements
        END IF
    ELSE
        IF (condition) THEN
            block of statements
        ELSE
            block of statements
```

```
                END IF
          END IF
      END DO
```

15.3
PROGRAM CORRECTNESS

Because a realistic large program usually contains many combinations of program structures to process data elements, there are opportunities to introduce errors into a program. The time spent debugging a large program can be far greater than the time spent writing the program if the program is not well designed. These techniques are helpful in writing correct programs:

1. Make sure that the overall problem is completely understood.

2. Divide the problem into definable tasks. If any task seems long or complex, divide it into more manageable subtasks.

3. Carefully define the data structures to be used in the program and the methods for transferring data between the various parts of the program.

4. Select program structures to implement the logic of each task that obviously correspond to the problem to be solved. A program should ideally read like a story of the solution to the problem.

5. Select symbolic names that describe the data being stored.

15.4
GENERAL PROGRAMS

If you write a program to perform some operations exactly 10 times and then you need to perform those same operations 11 times, you will have to make major modifications in the program. You should always write programs with as much generality built into the program as possible.

Procedures that you can incorporate in programs to make them general include the following:

1. Use variables as counters for loops.

2. Use variable dimensions for arrays after the initial declaration.

3. Allow the user to enter the name or names of files to be accessed at run time.

4. Develop a library of general subroutines to perform the procedures that you might often need to perform. Then incorporate those tested subroutines in programs as needed.

15.5
PROGRAMMING STYLE

Program style can contribute significantly to the readability of a program. If a program is formatted on the printed page in a systematic way and all the elements are well defined, it is certainly easier to understand the program and to modify it at a later time.

Many organizations have a set of rules for indentation, spacing, and documentation for programs. If no such rules are provided for you, you may develop your own style of programming. The following methods used in programming enhance a program's readability.

1. An overall description of the program should be at the beginning of the main program.

2. A description of the procedures used in each module should be included at the beginning of each module in the program.

3. A listing and description of the variables for each unit in the program should be included at the beginning of the unit.

4. Each substructure in a program should be indented at least three spaces to visually identify the beginning and end of structures.

5. Blank lines should be inserted around groups of statements that are related.

6. Describe the input that should be provided for the program. Often an example set of data is useful for documentation.

7. Describe the output that would be produced by the program. Example output could be included in the documentation.

15.6
RUN TIME ERROR RECOVERY

A program should be written to be able to recover if an error in input data or processing occurs. The structures in the FORTRAN language provide adequate features for setting error flags and ending procedures systematically.

If a program is processing data including the ages of people, and an age of 646 years is encountered, there is obviously a problem. Statements can be included in a program to check for errors, set flags if errors occur, and record error information. The following is indicative of code that might be included in detecting and recording errors.

```
READ (11,100) AGE
DO WHILE (AGE.LT.100)
      :            :
   READ(11,100) AGE
END DO

IF (AGE.GT.100) THEN
   ERRORFLAG = 'YES'
   SEVERITY__CODE = 1
   WRITE(6,200)SUBROUTINE__NAME
   WRITE(6,300)RECORD__NUMBER
END IF

IF (SEVERITY__CODE.EQ.1) CALL RECORD__ERROR
IF (SEVERITY__CODE.EQ.2) CALL TERMINATE__PROGRAM
```

15.7
TESTING

Testing and debugging a program can consume large amounts of time. Writing well-designed, well-coded, and well-documented programs is the greatest tool in testing a program.

The approach to testing a program historically has been to run a program many times through the various procedures that are included in a program, using test data and verifying the results. The problem with relying entirely on this approach is that a particular combination of procedures that could break the program might never occur in test runs.

Another approach to testing a program is for a programmer or a team of programmers to systematically step through code and verify that the desired result would be produced by the code. This approach to testing can be used only with clearly written and well-documented programs. Work is currently underway to develop methods for proving the correctness of programs. For now, a combination of stepping through a program and executing test runs is generally the procedure used for testing.

15.8
APPLICATION

The one application in this chapter is a program for generating a class grade summary. The program produces individual student information, class summary information, and assigns letter grades for a class of students. The program is general enough to be used in most classrooms. The description of the program is included in the documentation for the program.

The primary tasks to be performed in solving the problem are the following. (See Figure 15.3.)

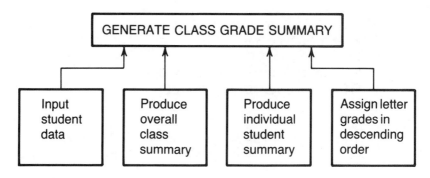

FIGURE 15.3

The program units in the program to input the data and produce the required results are the following. (See Figure 15.4.)

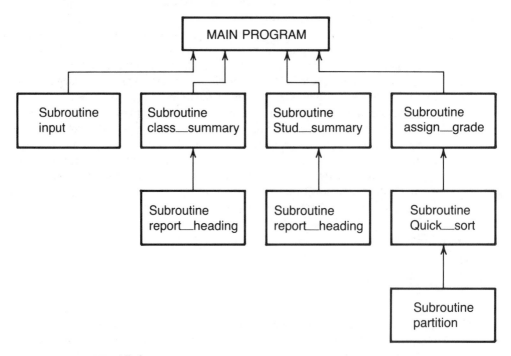

FIGURE 15.4

■ Example 15.1: General Grading Program

A GENERAL GRADING PROGRAM

The program produces a report of class summary statistics
and individual student scores and weighted averages.
The program generates a list of student names and letter
grades sorted in descending order by the average student
scores calculated with weighted exams. Observe the output
from the program following the program.

The program accepts data for a class of students as input from
a file. The program allows a teacher to use any number of exams
with any weight assigned to each exam, any number of students,
and any number of letter grades.
   The restrictions for the program are the following:
      Maximum number of students is 100.
      Maximum number of letter grades is 10.
      Maximum number of exams is 10 (An easy way to include
         homework is to add up all the homework scores
         for a student and count that total as an exam
         with some specified weight.

In order to provide data for the program, you need to create
a data file containing the data in the order specified. Observe
the example data file on the following page. Create the input
data file with the following format:

Record 1	Name of the class - Maximum 30 characters
Record 2	Teacher's name - Maximum 30 characters
Record 3	Date of class - Maximum 30 characters
Record 4	Number of exams - Integer, free format
Record 5	Weight for each exam - Weights can contain a decimal part. Separate values by a space. Homework scores might be assigned a weight of 0.1 or some partial exam weight.
Record 6	Letter grades for the class - Do NOT include spaces between letter grades.
Record 7	The upper bound for the highest grade category.
Record 8	The upper bound for the second highest grade.
:	As long as there are more grade categories corresponding to the letter grades that you
:	entered in record 6, enter the upper bound for for each category.
Final records	Enter all the student records one after another until there are no more records to enter. The student name should be entered in the first 15 character positions in each record followed by up to ten scores for each student. Each score should occupy three character positions on a line with blanks where there are not numbers.

(Continued)

```
After the data file is created and saved, invoke the program
with the command:
                RUN CLASSGRAD
```

The input to the program is provided in the data file. The data file is created with an editor. When the program runs, the user will be prompted to enter the name of the file containing the class data.

The description of the fields in the data is provided in the previous external documentation.

Example 15.1
Displayed at the terminal when the program runs.

```
Enter the name of the file with class data.
```

User input at the terminal.

```
cc585.dat
```

Example 15.1
Input from the file named CC585.DAT

```
COMPUTER CONCEPTS   CC585
Dr. Frank Shrub
Spring Quarter 1984
4                 NUMBER OF EXAMS
1 1 1 2           WEIGHT OF EXAMS
ABCDF             LETTER GRADES
100            A upper bound
89             B upper bound
79             C upper bound
64             D upper bound
49             F upper bound
Adams, Alice      88 79 83 99
Berry, Ben        83 73 86 67
Denver, Denice    71 78 73 70
Eastman, Jim      92 94 96 98
Harvey, Henry     50 54 58 62
Lariless, David   93 95 97 99
Rider, Arliss     97 98 99100
Sanders, Jane     73 61 82 75
Portman, Tom      69 72 65 63
```

Example 15.1

```
C$EDIT CLASSGRAD.FOR
C                   A GENERAL GRADING PROGRAM

C       The program inputs data for a class of students from a file.
C       The program prompts the user to enter the name of the file
C       where the data is stored.
C       The program allows a teacher to use any number of exams with
C       any weight assigned to each exam, any number of students, and
C       any number of letter grades, limited only by the dimensions
C       of the arrays in the program.
```

```
C     The program produces a report of class summary statistics
C     and individual student scores and weighted averages.
C     The program generates a list of student names and letter
C     grades sorted in descending order by the average student
C     scores calculated with weighted exams.


C     Symbolic names:
C     BOUND(10)          Upper boundary score for a letter grade.
C     GRADE(100,10)      Individual scores for each of ten
C                        possible exams for up to 100 students.
C     STUDAVE(100)       Weighted average for each student.
C     WEIGHTS(10)        Weight for each exam.  The final exam
C                        might be weighted twice a midterm exam.
C     CLASSTITLE(3)      A character array with 30 characters in
C                        each of 3 rows of title to describe the
C                        class: classname, teacher and date.
C     LETTERGRADE(10)    Up to ten letter grades to be assigned.
C                        Grades could be ABC or PF or 12345, etc.
C     NAME(100)          Student names up to 15 characters each.
C     NUMSTUD            The number of students in the class.
C     NUMEXAMS           The number of exams.


      REAL BOUND(10),GRADE(100,10),STUDAVE(100),WEIGHTS(10)
      CHARACTER CLASSTITLE(3)*30,LETTERGRADE(10)*1, NAME(100)*15
      INTEGER NUMSTUD, NUMEXAMS



      CALL INPUT (BOUND,CLASSTITLE,GRADE,LETTERGRADE,NAME,
     -            NUMEXAMS,NUMSTUD,WEIGHTS)

      CALL CLAS_SUMRY(CLASSTITLE,GRADE,NUMEXAMS,NUMSTUD,WEIGHTS)

      CALL STUD_SUMMARY(CLASSTITLE,GRADE,NAME,NUMEXAMS,NUMSTUD,
     -            STUDAVE,WEIGHTS)

      CALL ASSIGNGRADE(BOUND,CLASSTITLE,LETTERGRADE,NAME,NUMSTUD,
     -            STUDAVE)
      STOP
      END



!                                          Program CLASSGRAD.FOR
C-----------------------------------------------------------------
      SUBROUTINE INPUT (BOUND,CLASSTITLE,GRADE,LETTERGRADE,NAME,
     -            NUMEXAMS,NUMSTUD,WEIGHTS)
C-----------------------------------------------------------------
C     All data is input in this subroutine.
C-----------------------------------------------------------------
      REAL WEIGHTS(*),BOUND(*),GRADE(100,*)
      CHARACTER LETTERGRADE(10)*1, NAME(*)*15,CLASSTITLE(*)*30,
     -            FILENAME*30
100   FORMAT(A)
200   FORMAT(10A)
300   FORMAT(A,10F3.0)
```

```
C       Prompt user to enter the name of the file with class data.
        WRITE(6,*)'Enter the name of file containing the class data.'
C       Read the name of the file and open the file.
        READ(5,100)FILENAME
        OPEN(11,FILE=FILENAME,STATUS='OLD')

C       Read the name of the class
        READ (11,100)CLASSTITLE(1)
C       Read the name of the teacher
        READ (11,100)CLASSTITLE(2)
C       Read the quarter date.
        READ(11,100)CLASSTITLE(3)

C       Read the number of exams for the class and the weight for
C       each exam.  (i.e. The final exam might be wieghted twice
C       a midterm exam.)
        READ(11,*) NUMEXAMS
        READ(11,*) (WEIGHTS(I), I=1,NUMEXAMS)

C       Enter the letter grades for the class.  Enter each grade one
C       after another with no spaces in between up to 10 categories.
        READ(11,200) LETTERGRADE
C       Look for the blank at the end of the letter grades to
C       determine how many grade categories there are.
        NUMLETTERGRADES = 0
        DO WHILE (LETTERGRADE(NUMLETTERGRADES+1) .NE. ' ')
          NUMLETTERGRADES = NUMLETTERGRADES + 1
        END DO
C       Enter the upper boundary for each of the letter grades.
        DO I=1,NUMLETTERGRADES
          READ(11,*) BOUND(I)
        END DO

C       Enter all the grades for all the students and count the
C       number of students.
        READ(11,300,IOSTAT=IEND) NAME(1),(GRADE(1,N),N=1,NUMEXAMS)
        NUMSTUD = 0
        DO WHILE (IEND .EQ. 0)
          NUMSTUD = NUMSTUD+1
          READ(11,300,IOSTAT=IEND) NAME(NUMSTUD+1),
     -        (GRADE(NUMSTUD+1,N),N=1,NUMEXAMS)
        END DO

        CLOSE(11)
        RETURN
        END

!                                          Program CLASSGRAD.FOR
C------------------------------------------------------------------
        SUBROUTINE CLAS_SUMRY(CLASSTITLE,GRADE,NUMEXAMS,NUMSTUD,WEIGHTS)
C------------------------------------------------------------------
C       Calculate and print the summary statistics for the class
C       including the average and standard deviation for each exam
C       and the overall weighted class average and standard deviation
C------------------------------------------------------------------
        REAL GRADE(100,*), WEIGHTS(*)
        REAL EXAMAVERAGE(10),EXAMTOTAL(10),STANDARD_DEVIATION(10)
        CHARACTER HEADING*30, CLASSTITLE(*)*30
```

```
100       FORMAT(' ','AVERAGE',T17,11F9.2)
200       FORMAT(/,' ','STANDARD',/,' DEVIATION',T17,11F9.2)

          HEADING = 'CLASS SUMMARY'
          CALL REPORT_HEADING(CLASSTITLE,NUMEXAMS,WEIGHTS,HEADING)

C         Calculate class average for each exam.
          CLASSTOT = 0
          DO IEXAM=1,NUMEXAMS
             EXAMTOTAL(IEXAM) = 0
             DO ISTUD=1,NUMSTUD
                EXAMTOTAL(IEXAM) = EXAMTOTAL(IEXAM) + GRADE(ISTUD,IEXAM)
             END DO
             EXAMAVERAGE(IEXAM) = EXAMTOTAL(IEXAM) / NUMSTUD
          END DO

C         Calculate weighted class average over all exams.
          WEIGHTTOTAL = 0
          CLASSTOTAL = 0
          DO IEXAM=1,NUMEXAMS
             CLASSTOT = CLASSTOT + WEIGHTS(IEXAM)*EXAMTOTAL(IEXAM)
             WEIGHTTOTAL = WEIGHTTOTAL + WEIGHTS(IEXAM)
          END DO
          WEIGHTED_CLASS_AVERAGE = CLASSTOT / (WEIGHTTOTAL*NUMSTUD)
          WRITE(6,100) WEIGHTED_CLASS_AVERAGE,
     -                 (EXAMAVERAGE(IEXAM),IEXAM=1,NUMEXAMS)

C         Calculate standard deviation for each exam.
          WEIGHTSUMXSQUARE = 0
          NUMWEIGHT = 0
          DO IEXAM=1,NUMEXAMS
             SUMXSQUARE = 0
             DO ISTUD=1,NUMSTUD
                SUMXSQUARE = SUMXSQUARE +
     -                       GRADE(ISTUD,IEXAM)*GRADE(ISTUD,IEXAM)
             END DO
             STANDARD_DEVIATION(IEXAM) = SQRT( ( SUMXSQUARE -
     -       (EXAMTOTAL(IEXAM)*EXAMTOTAL(IEXAM))/NUMSTUD) / (NUMSTUD-1) )
             WEIGHTSUMXSQUARE =
     -             WEIGHTSUMXSQUARE + SUMXSQUARE*WEIGHTS(IEXAM)
             NUMWEIGHT = NUMWEIGHT + NUMSTUD*WEIGHTS(IEXAM)
          END DO
          WEIGHTEDSD = SQRT( ( WEIGHTSUMXSQUARE -
     -    CLASSTOT*CLASSTOT/NUMWEIGHT) / (NUMWEIGHT-1) )
          WRITE(6,200) WEIGHTEDSD,(STANDARD_DEVIATION(IEXAM),
     -                                    IEXAM=1,NUMEXAMS)

          RETURN
          END


      !                                        Program CLASSGRAD.FOR
      C----------------------------------------------------------------
          SUBROUTINE REPORT_HEADING(CLASSTITLE,NUMEXAMS,WEIGHTS,HEADING)
      C----------------------------------------------------------------
      C     Print the heading and titles for the class summary statistics
      C     and the individual student output.
      C----------------------------------------------------------------
```

```
              REAL WEIGHTS(*)
              CHARACTER WEIGHTPRINT(10)*9,EXAMPRINT(10)*9,HEADING*30,
         -            CLASSTITLE(*)*30
              INTEGER EXAMNUMBERS(10)

100      FORMAT('1',3(//,' ',T30,A) )
200      FORMAT(' ',/,' ',14('_'),//,' ',A,//,' ',14('_') )
300      FORMAT(//,' ',T19,'OVERALL',T29,10A)
400      FORMAT(' ',T29,10(3X,I2,4X),/)
500      FORMAT(/,' ',T19,'WEIGHTED',T28,10A)
600      FORMAT(' ',T29,10(2X,F4.1,3X),//)
700      FORMAT(' ',A,F9.2,10F9.0)
1000     FORMAT(' ')


C        Values are stored in arrays so that a variable number of
C        elements up to the NUMEXAMS can be printed across a line
C        in the WRITE statements below.

         DO I=1,NUMEXAMS
           EXAMNUMBERS(I) = I
           WEIGHTPRINT(I) =' WEIGHTED '
           EXAMPRINT(I)   =' EXAM #   '
         END DO

         WRITE(6,100) (CLASSTITLE(LINE),LINE=1,3)
         WRITE(6,200) HEADING
         WRITE(6,300) (EXAMPRINT(NSCORE),NSCORE=1,NUMEXAMS)
         WRITE(6,400) (EXAMNUMBERS(NSCORE),NSCORE=1,NUMEXAMS)
         WRITE(6,500) (WEIGHTPRINT(NSCORE),NSCORE=1,NUMEXAMS)
         WRITE(6,600) (WEIGHTS(NSCORE),NSCORE=1,NUMEXAMS)
         WRITE(6,1000)                 !Print blank line


         RETURN
         END


!                                             Program CLASSGRAD.FOR
C-----------------------------------------------------------------------
         SUBROUTINE STUD_SUMMARY(CLASSTITLE,GRADE,NAME,NUMEXAMS,NUMSTUD,
         -            STUDAVE,WEIGHTS)
C-----------------------------------------------------------------------
C        Calculates weighted averages for individual students and
C        prints a summary of individual scores and weighted averages.
C-----------------------------------------------------------------------

         REAL WEIGHTS(*), STUDAVE(*), GRADE(100,*)
         CHARACTER NAME(*)*15, HEADING*30, CLASSTITLE(*)*30
         INTEGER EXAMNUMBERS(10)

         HEADING = 'STUDENT SUMMARY'
         CALL REPORT_HEADING(CLASSTITLE,NUMEXAMS,WEIGHTS,HEADING)


100      FORMAT(' ',A,F9.2,10F9.0)
1000     FORMAT(' ')
```

```
          WEIGHTTOTAL = 0
          DO IEXAM = 1, NUMEXAMS
             WEIGHTTOTAL = WEIGHTTOTAL + WEIGHTS(IEXAM)
          END DO


C         Calculates the weighted student averages.
          DO ISTUD=1,NUMSTUD
             STUDTOTAL = 0
             DO IEXAM=1,NUMEXAMS
               STUDTOTAL = STUDTOTAL + WEIGHTS(IEXAM) * GRADE(ISTUD,IEXAM)
             END DO
             STUDAVE(ISTUD) = STUDTOTAL/WEIGHTTOTAL
          END DO
          WRITE(6,1000)              !Print blank line
          DO ISTUD = 1, NUMSTUD
             WRITE(6,100)NAME(ISTUD),STUDAVE(ISTUD),
        -       (GRADE(ISTUD,IEXAM),IEXAM=1,NUMEXAMS)
          END DO
          RETURN
          END
!                                                   Program CLASSGRAD.FOR
C--------------------------------------------------------------------------
          SUBROUTINE ASSIGNGRADE(BOUND,CLASSTITLE,LETTERGRADE,NAME,
        -                    NUMSTUD,STUDAVE)
C--------------------------------------------------------------------------
C         Prints a list of names and grades sorted by grades in
C         descending order.
C--------------------------------------------------------------------------

          CHARACTER NAME(*)*15, LETTERGRADE(10)*1, CLASSTITLE(*)*30
          REAL STUDAVE(*),BOUND(*)
100       FORMAT('1',3(//,' ',T30,A) )
200       FORMAT(' ',////,' ',26('_'),//,' ',
        - 'LETTER GRADES FOR STUDENTS',/,
        - ' ','RANKED IN DESCENDING ORDER',//,' ',26('_'),///,
        - ' ',T23,'GRADE',T35,'WEIGHTED AVERAGE',/)
300       FORMAT (' ',A,T25,A,T40,F8.2)

          WRITE(6,100) (CLASSTITLE(LINE),LINE=1,3)
          WRITE (6,200)

C         Invoke the sort routine to sort the average grades for students
C         into descending order and to keep the names with the grades.
          CALL QUICK_SORT (NAME,NUMSTUD,STUDAVE)

C         Go through the list of students sorted by average and print
C         the grade for the category in which the student falls.
          DO I=1,NUMSTUD
            NCATEGORY=0
            DO WHILE (STUDAVE(I) .LE. BOUND(NCATEGORY+1))
              NCATEGORY = NCATEGORY + 1
            END DO
            WRITE (6,300) NAME(I),LETTERGRADE(NCATEGORY),STUDAVE(I)
          END DO
          RETURN
          END
```

```
!                                                    Program CLASSGRAD.FOR
C------------------------------------------------------------------------
          SUBROUTINE QUICK_SORT (NAME,NUMSTUD,STUDAVE)
C------------------------------------------------------------------------
C         Sort names and grades into descending order.
C------------------------------------------------------------------------


          CHARACTER NAME(*)*15
          REAL STUDAVE(*)
          INTEGER TOPSTACK(100),BOTTOMSTACK(100),TOP,BOTTOM,B
C

C         Initialize stack to point to top of the list of data and the
C         bottom of the list of data to be sorted.
          POINTER = 1
          TOPSTACK(POINTER) = 1
          BOTTOMSTACK(POINTER) = NUMSTUD
C
C         As long as the pointer to the stacks is > 0, there are sets
C         of data to be sorted.


          DO WHILE (POINTER .GT. 0)

            IF (TOPSTACK(POINTER) .GE. BOTTOMSTACK(POINTER)) THEN

               POINTER = POINTER-1

            ELSE



C           Set the pointer to top and bottom of sublist to be processed.
            TOP = TOPSTACK(POINTER)
            BOTTOM = BOTTOMSTACK(POINTER)

C           Invoke the subroutine to divide the sublist to be processed
C           into two succeeding sublists with one element in place between
C           the sublists developed.
            CALL PARTITION_LIST (NAME,STUDAVE,TOP, BOTTOM, B)

C              Put the two new sublists on the stack
               TOPSTACK(POINTER) = TOP
               BOTTOMSTACK(POINTER) = B - 1
               POINTER = POINTER+1
               TOPSTACK(POINTER) = B + 1
               BOTTOMSTACK(POINTER) = BOTTOM



            END IF
          END DO

          RETURN
          END
```

```
!                                          Program CLASSGRAD.FOR
C-------------------------------------------------------------------
       SUBROUTINE PARTITION_LIST (NAMELIST,STUDAVE,TOP,BOTTOM,B)
C-------------------------------------------------------------------
C      Partitions the list of scores into a top sublist and a bottom sublist.
C      Every element in the top sublist is greater than every element in
C      the bottom sublist. The names are kept with the associated scores.
C-------------------------------------------------------------------

       CHARACTER NAMELIST(*)*15, NHOLD*15, NTEMP*15
       REAL STUDAVE(*)
       INTEGER TOP,BOTTOM,T,B

C      Establish value for comparison. The value from the top of the stack
C      is assumed to be the VALUE_IN_PLACE for comparison.
       VALUE_IN_PLACE = STUDAVE(TOP)
       NHOLD = NAMELIST(TOP)
C      Set pointers to the top and bottom of this sublist to be sorted.
       T = TOP
       B = BOTTOM+1

C      Go through the sublist comparing each element with the VALUE_IN_PLACE.
C      The bottom pointer will move from the bottom and the top pointer will
C      move from the top finding the one value that can be put in place.
C      Move through array until top (T) pointer reaches bottom (B) pointer.
       DO WHILE (T .LT. B)
          B = B-1
C      As long as the values in the sublist are < the comparison value, the
C      program continues to move up from the bottom of the list and compare.
       DO WHILE (STUDAVE(B) .LT. VALUE_IN_PLACE)
          B = B-1
       END DO
C      When a value is found to be out of place coming from the bottom,
C      the program starts to make comparisons coming from the top.
       T = T+1

C      As long as the values in the sublist are > the comparison value, and
C      the top pointer is still above the bottom pointer in the list, the
C      program continues to move down from the top of the list and compare.
       DO WHILE((STUDAVE(T).GT.VALUE_IN_PLACE).AND.(T.LT.B))
          T = T+1
       END DO

C      If top pointer is still above the  bottom pointer, exchange top and
C      bottom entries.  Exchange both names and scores.
       IF (T .LT. B) THEN
          NTEMP = NAMELIST(T)
          NAMELIST(T) = NAMELIST(B)
          NAMELIST(B) = NTEMP
          STEMP = STUDAVE(T)
          STUDAVE(T) = STUDAVE(B)
          STUDAVE(B) = STEMP
       END IF
       END DO
```

(Continued)

```
C       Put the new VALUE_IN_PLACE keeping the associated name.
        STUDAVE(TOP) = STUDAVE(B)
        STUDAVE(B) = VALUE_IN_PLACE
        NAMELIST(TOP) = NAMELIST(B)
        NAMELIST(B) = NHOLD
        RETURN
        END
```

COMPUTER CONCEPTS   CC585   Example 15.1
                                 Output
Dr. Frank Shrub

Spring Quarter 1984

CLASS SUMMARY

	OVERALL	EXAM # 1	EXAM # 2	EXAM # 3	EXAM # 4
	WEIGHTED	WEIGHTED 1.0	WEIGHTED 1.0	WEIGHTED 1.0	WEIGHTED 2.0
AVERAGE	80.56	79.56	78.22	82.11	81.44
STANDARD DEVIATION	15.17	15.10	15.30	14.46	17.08

COMPUTER CONCEPTS   CC585   Example 15.1
                                 Output
Dr. Frank Shrub

Spring Quarter 1984

STUDENT SUMMARY

	OVERALL	EXAM # 1	EXAM # 2	EXAM # 3	EXAM # 4
	WEIGHTED	WEIGHTED 1.0	WEIGHTED 1.0	WEIGHTED 1.0	WEIGHTED 2.0
Adams, Alice	89.60	88.	79.	83.	99.
Berry, Ben	75.20	83.	73.	86.	67.
Denver, Denice	72.40	71.	78.	73.	70.
Eastman, Jim	95.60	92.	94.	96.	98.
Harvey, Henry	57.20	50.	54.	58.	62.
Lariless, David	96.60	93.	95.	97.	99.
Rider, Arliss	98.80	97.	98.	99.	100.
Sanders, Jane	73.20	73.	61.	82.	75.
Portman, Tom	66.40	69.	72.	65.	63.

Example 15.1
Output

```
COMPUTER CONCEPTS   CC585

Dr. Frank Shrub

Spring Quarter 1984
```

```
LETTER GRADES FOR STUDENTS
RANKED IN DESCENDING ORDER
```

	GRADE	WEIGHTED AVERAGE
Rider, Arliss	A	98.80
Lariless, David	A	96.60
Eastman, Jim	A	95.60
Adams, Alice	A	89.60
Berry, Ben	C	75.20
Sanders, Jane	C	73.20
Denver, Denice	C	72.40
Portman, Tom	C	66.40
Harvey, Henry	D	57.20

15.9
SUMMARY

Developing a large program requires that the overall problem be analyzed and broken down into definable tasks. Generally each of the tasks is written as a *subroutine*. The *main program* then serves only to control the flow of the program into subroutines.

Program correctness and style are closely related. Writing programs that are easy to read and understand also makes it easy to write correct programs.

General programs should be written to run under various conditions as much as possible rather than for a specific set of data.

A program should be able to either recover and continue processing if an error occurs or terminate in a predefined way and record the error. Testing a program in the final analysis requires running the program under various conditions and verifying that the results are the expected results.

15.10
EXERCISES

15.1. Develop the following program. The number of employees that a company has is unknown from week to week, but it is never more than 50. A file contains the following information for each employee. A few example records are listed below the heading for the data.

SOCIAL SECURITY NUMBER	NAME	DEPARTMENT CODE NUMBER	JOB CODE NUMBER	RATE OF PAY PER HOUR	HOURS WORKED
459668286	Jan Sellers	9	101	35.00	47
321876982	John Flower	7	123	4.75	40
289873654	Tom Howard	5	328	5.50	41
398229837	Carol Dyson	7	119	8.20	40
345432898	Paul Tiers	9	123	22.75	40
253664398	Linda Smith	5	119	9.90	42
349872266	Gordon Johns	3	123	18.59	43

Generate tables reporting total costs per department and total costs per job code for the week of data shown. Individal employee information should be sorted by social security number for each report.

The names of each department and job code should be read in as variables that can be associated with the numerical codes in the employee data when the program runs.

Department 3	Analysis	Job code 101	Adams Project
Department 5	Design	Job code 119	Mabrey Project
Department 7	Development	Job code 123	Goolsby Project
Department 9	Production	Job code 328	Rose Project

Output should be produced for each department with the data sorted by social security number. Sample output for Department 9 would be the following.

```
                    DEPARTMENT  9

                    PRODUCTION

     345432898   Paul Tiers     9    123    22.75      40
     459668286   Jan Sellers    9    101    35.00      47
                                             _____

     Total expenditures for
     Department 9                                $2555.00
```

Output should be produced for each job code with the data sorted by social security number. Sample output for job code 123 would be the following.

JOB CODE 123

GOOLSBY PROJECT

321876982	John Flower	7	123	4.75	40
345432898	Paul Tiers	9	123	22.75	40
349872266	Gordon Johns	3	123	18.59	43

| Total cost of project | | | | $1899.37 | |

You should provide additional data for the problem.

15.2. Samples are collected weekly from each of 13 bodies of water in the state of Tennessee. There are various numbers of collection points at each body of water. Some sites may have one collection point and some may have ten. Various parameters are recorded. The parameters that might be recorded are water temperature, dissolved oxygen, pH, and nitrogen. Not all parameters are measured at each site. Dates are recorded for each sample.

Data would include the following.

SAMPLING SITE	COLLECTION POINT	DATE	PARAMETER	MEASUREMENT	WEATHER
1	1	01 02 84	pH	6.8	Sun
1	1	01 02 84	DO	5.05	Rain
1	1	01 02 84	TEMP	2.9	Rain
1	1	01 02 84	NH4N	0.5	Rain
1	2	01 02 84	DO	4.79	Sun
1	2	01 02 84	TEMP	2.7	Sun
2	1	01 07 84	NH4N	0.3	Sun

Develop a program to analyze the data. Data were collected over a 12-month period. Averages should be generated for the following sets of data.

Average for all collection points at all sampling sites for each parameter.

Average by sampling site over all collection points for each parameter.

Average by month over all sites and collection points for each parameter.

Perform statistical analyses to study the impact of rainy and sunny weather.

15.3.   Develop a bookkeeping system and inventory control program for an automobile dealership. Develop your own criteria for variables.

15.4.   Develop an on-line registration system for a college. Develop your own criteria for variables, including adding and dropping classes, class size, cost for classes, and the like.

Appendices

APPENDIX A
An Introduction to
Using the VAX System:
A Tutorial

A.1
AN OVERVIEW FOR LEARNING
TO USE THE SYSTEM

The VAX/VMS operating system is covered in this guide. The Digital Command Language (DCL) is used in this guide to direct the VAX to perform operations. A dollar sign symbol, ($), on the terminal screen will prompt you to enter a command to the system.

In order to use the VAX computer to create and run FORTRAN programs, you need to know how to perform the tasks listed below. A step by step tutorial is provided for each concept that you need for getting started.

YOU NEED TO KNOW HOW TO:	YOU CAN LEARN HOW IN:
Login to the system	Appendix A.2 (page 395).
Use a terminal	Appendix A.2 (page 396).
Logout from the system	Appendix A.2 (page 400).
Use files on the VAX	Appendix A.2 (page 401).
Create and modify files with an editor	Appendices A.3 (page 403) and A.4 (page 416). A.3 covers line-editing using a terminal with no special features. All users can use the EDT line-editor. A.4 covers full-screen editing for terminals with the features available on a DEC VT100 terminal.
Delete and print files	Appendix A.5 (page 471).
Enter a FORTRAN program file	Appendix B (page 473).
Enter commands to execute FORTRAN program	Appendix B (page 473).
Direct input and output for FORTRAN	Appendix B and Chapter 3 in text.
Develop FORTRAN programs to solve problems	Throughout the text.

The tutorials in Appendix A and B show everything that you should enter at a terminal and all the responses the computer displays. The best way to learn with the tutorial is to type in the examples exactly as shown and observe what is happening. The method for logging in the first time might be unique for your computer and the command, EDT, might be EDIT/EDT for your computer, but everything else should be just as shown. It should take from one to three hours to enter and run the examples in Appendices A and B, and then you should have a background for using the VAX and can proceed with using the computer productively for entering and running FORTRAN programs!

A.2

LOGGING IN AND USING THE VAX SYSTEM

IN THE TUTORIALS, EVERYTHING THAT YOU SHOULD TYPE AND THE KEYS THAT YOU SHOULD PRESS AND THE OUTPUT DISPLAYED AT THE TERMINAL ARE PRINTED ON THE LEFT OF EACH PAGE.

IN THE TUTORIALS, THE EXPLANATIONS OF WHAT YOU SHOULD DO AND WHAT IS HAPPENING ARE PRINTED ON THE RIGHT OF EACH PAGE.

LOGGING INTO THE VAX

You need to press the [RETURN] key on a terminal connected to the VAX. You will not be prompted to press the [RETURN] key.

[RETURN]

You will be prompted to enter your username.

The flashing light on the screen is called a cursor. The cursor is a pointer to where the next transaction on the screen can occur.

USERNAME :

Type your username. Then press the [RETURN] key.

USERNAME: yourusername   [RETURN]

You are prompted to enter your password. Your password is the key to your account. Only you should know the password. Select a password that you can remember, because you must use the password each time you log in. When you type in your password, it will not appear on the screen. Type the letters in your password firmly and press the [RETURN] key.

PASSWORD: yourpassword [RETURN]

You are now logged into the VAX

The dollar sign on the screen means that the VAX is waiting for you to enter a command to begin a task. The command language used in this guide to direct the VAX to perform operations is called the Digital Command Language, DCL.

USING THE TERMINAL

Before beginning to create and modify files, you need to learn some features of using the terminal with the VAX.

One of the Digital Command Language commands is SHOW. You can request various kinds of information with the SHOW command. Try using the SHOW TIME command. Type the characters SHOW TIME and press the [RETURN] key. If you make a mistake typing, continue reading to find out ways to correct your mistakes.

```
$ SHOW TIME  [RETURN]

    11-JULY-1983 08:55:31
```

DELETING CHARACTERS AS YOU TYPE

If you make a typing mistake as you are typing, the [DELETE] key or the [RUBOUT] key can be used for backing up so that you can retype the characters which were incorrectly typed. Each time you press the [DELETE] key or the [RUBOUT] key, the character to the left of the cursor is deleted.

For practice deleting one character at a time, type in some characters in the SHOW TIME command in the wrong order. Do not press the return key. Type the characters SHOW TIEM.

```
$ SHOW TIEM
```

Use the [DELETE] key or the [RUBOUT] key to back up one character at the time.

```
        [DELETE] or [RUBOUT]
```

Now press the [DELETE] or [RUBOUT] key again.

```
$ SHOW TIE
        [DELETE] or [RUBOUT]
```

The E is removed from the screen.

```
  $ SHOW TI
```

Now you can enter the M and the E to spell TIME correctly and press the [RETURN] key.

```
$ SHOW TIME [RETURN]

    11-JULY-1983 08:58:28
```

UNRECOGNIZED COMMANDS

If you enter a command which is not recognized by the VAX, a message is displayed that the command is not recognized. If you misspell SHOW and press [RETURN] you will get a message like this.

$ SHOE TIME [RETURN]

The computer searches for the command SHOE and can not find the command, so a message is displayed indicating that the command is not recognized.

%DCL, unrecognized command
    \SHOE\TIME

You should have a dollar sign on the screen now. You can retype the command correctly.

DELETING A LINE AS IT IS BEING TYPED

If you make several mistakes as you are typing a line you may want to abandon the line and begin the line again. You could use the [DELETE] key or the [RUBOUT] key to back all the way to the beginning of a line; however, if the line is long, you may want to use the [CONTROL/U] to abandon the entire line. A [CTRL/U] represents the action of pressing and holding the [CTRL] key down while you type the character [U] key.

Practice using [CTRL/U]. First, type a line of characters. Then press the [CTRL] key, and while the [CTRL] key is depressed, type the character [U] key. The cursor moves to the next line and the line which you were entering is ignored. You can begin the line again.

$ SHOW ERRRORRRS   [CTRL/U]

A caret symbol and U is displayed on the screen when you use a [CONTROL/U] to ignore a line.

^U

THE HELP COMMAND

Now you have a dollar sign on the screen again, and you can enter a valid command. You can enter the Digital Command Language command to request HELP. After you have typed the word HELP, press the [RETURN] key in order to see the Digital Command Language, DCL, commands for which HELP can be displayed at the terminal.

$ HELP   [RETURN]

Output similar to the following appears on the terminal screen. Since every VAX system is different, the HELP information that you see varies.

THE HELP INFORMATION YOU SEE WILL VARY

Information available:

ALLOCATE	ANALYZE	APPEND	ASSIGN	BACKUP	BASIC	BLISS
CANCEL	CLOSE	COBOL	CONTINUE	COPY	CORAL	CREATE
DEALLOCATE	DEASSIGN	DEBUG	DECK	DEFINE	DELETE	DEPOSIT
DIFFERENCES		DIRECTORY	DISMOUNT	DUMP	EDIT	EOD
EOJ	ERRORS	EXAMINE	EXIT	FORTRAN	GOTO	HELP
IF	INITIALIZE	INQUIRE	JOB	LEXICAL	LIBRARY	LINK
LOGIN	LOGOUT	MACRO	MAIL	MCR	MERGE	MESSAGE
MOUNT	ON	OPEN	PASCAL	PASSWORD	PATCH	PLI
PRINT	PROCEDURE	PURGE	READ	RENAME	REPLY	REQUEST
RMS	RUN	SET	SHOW	SORT	SPECIFY	START
STOP	SUBMIT	SYMBOLS	SYNCHRONIZE		SYSTEM	TECO
TYPE	UNLOCK	VTEDIT	WAIT	WRITE		

topic?

[Press the [RETURN] key to exit HELP]

The purpose for using the HELP command at this point is to demonstrate using the terminal.

In order to get out of HELP mode, press the [RETURN] key until there is a $ on the screen.

You should go on through this tutorial before returning to the HELP facility for HELP on particular topics.

STOPPING PROCESSING

Before you begin to use a computer, you need to know how to interrupt processing if your procedure is not executing as it should be. Perhaps a procedure which you start seems to be running too long or you know for sure that you want to stop processing, you can stop processing with a [CONTROL/Y]. A [CTRL/Y] represents the action of pressing and holding the [CTRL] key down while you type the character [Y].

Use the HELP command to practice stopping a process. Since you have a dollar sign on the screen, you can enter a command. Enter the HELP command and press the [return] key. Then stop the process by using a [CTRL/Y]. You might do this two or three times, so that you will remember that a [CTRL/Y] terminates processing and waits for you to enter another command.

$ HELP   [RETURN]

After the HELP output begins to display, press the [CTRL] key. While the [CTRL] key is depressed, type the character [Y] key.

Information available:

ALLOCATE	ANALYZE	APPEND	ASSIGN	BACKUP	BASIC	BLISS
CANCEL	CLOSE	COBOL	CONTINUE	COPY	CORAL	CREATE
DEALLOCATE	DEASSIGN	DEBUG	DECK	DEFINE	DELETE	DEPOSIT

[CTRL/Y]

A ^Y displayed on the screen indicates that processing has stopped.

^Y

The dollar sign displayed at the terminal by the system indicates that you may enter another command.

$

INTERRUPTING AND RESUMING TERMINAL DISPLAY

If more than about 20 lines is being displayed at the terminal, the display scrolls. The display of output on the screen can be suspended to allow you time to read the lines and then the display can be resumed by using control keys.

If there is a [NO SCROLL] key on your terminal, you can suspend display by depressing that key and subsequently resume display by depressing the [NO SCROLL] key again.

A [CTRL/S] key can be used to suspend display at any terminal. Press and hold the [CTRL] key and while the [CTRL] key is depressed, press the [S] key to suspend display at the terminal. The [CTRL/Q] is subsequently used to resume display at a terminal. To resume

display after it has been suspended with the
[CTRL/S], press and hold the [CTRL] key and
while the [CTRL] key is depressed, press the
[Q] key.

Enter the HELP command to practice suspending
display at the terminal.

$ HELP   [RETURN]

Now use a [CTRL/S] or depress the [NO SCROLL]
key to suspend display.

[CTRL/S] or [NO SCROLL]

Use a [CTRL/Q] to resume display if you used
a [CTRL/S] to suspend display or depress the
[NO SCROLL] key to resume display if you used
the [NO SCROLL] key to suspend display.
Display will resume exactly where it stopped.

[CTRL/Q] or [NO SCROLL]

screen output is not shown

LOGGING OUT

In order to terminate communication with the   computer,   you
type the characters LO and press the [RETURN] key.   Try
logging out now.   You can login again   immediately,   if   you
choose.

$ lo   [RETURN]
     USER logged out at 11-JULY-1983 10:59:30.65

A SUMMARY OF USING A TERMINAL WITH THE VAX

Begin communications by pressing the [RETURN] key.

Enter your USERNAME. Then press the [RETURN] key.

Enter the password which you selected.
The password will not display on the screen.
Then press the [RETURN] key.

When a dollar sign appears at the terminal,
the VAX is waiting for a command from you.

Logout by typing the characters LO and pressing the
[RETURN] key.

TERMINAL CONTROL KEYS

[DELETE]
[RUBOUT] -- Delete a character as you are typing a line
            and move the cursor one space to the left.
[CTRL/U] -- Disregard the entire line which you are typing.
[CTRL/Y] -- Terminate the current process, display a
            dollar sign on the screen and wait for
            for you to enter another command.
[CTRL/S] -- Suspend display at the terminal.
[CTRL/Q] -- Resume display at the terminal.
[NO SCROLL] Suspend and resume display at the terminal.
[SHIFT]   Use upper case characters like a typewriter.
[CAPS/LOCK] Lock and unlock upper case letters.

VAX FILE NAMES

    To use a computer effectively, you need to enter information into
the computer and store it for later use. A set of information stored on
a computer is called a FILE. The set of information is stored in a group
of logically related records which are arranged in a specific order. The
set of records in a file must be assigned a name and treated as a unit.
A RECORD is an individual set of data items entered as a unit. A RECORD
can usually be thought of as a line of type.

    If there is a class of students, all the information about all the
students could be stored in a file. For each student, there might be
recorded three grades and a name. A RECORD then would include all four
of the items about each student. There would be one RECORD for each
student. The following records for a small class are used in this
tutorial.

            86 74 80 ADAMS
            75 80 95 BOX
            93 87 90 CARR
            95 85 90 DAVIS
            82 83 84 EDWARDS

    You must give the VAX a name to use for storing your file. You must
use a FILENAME from one to nine characters and then a period and then an
extension of one to three characters. Possible characters for names and
extensions include letters of the alphabet and numerical digits 0 through
9. An appropriate filename for the set of class grades used for the
tutorial is GRADES.DAT.

Examples: PAYROLL.FOR   GRADES.DAT   DIVISION3.DAT

    Usually the extension you select indicates the type of file you are
creating. You usually use FOR for FORTRAN and DAT for data.

In addition to the filename and extension, a file has a version number. In most cases, you do not need to specify the version number, but the VAX will always be referencing a particular version number. A version number is 1 the first time a file is created, and then the version number is incremented by one each time the file is modified and saved. The version number follows the extension after a semicolon.

Examples: PAYROLL.FOR;1   GRADES.DAT;5   DIVISION3.DAT;9

CREATING FILES WITH THE EDT EDITOR

An editor is a set of commands the computer can recognize to allow you to interact with the computer in order to store, modify or retrieve information. You can use an editor to do the following:

    Enter data into a file
    Change the data in a file
    Add to the data in a file
    Save a file

After you have logged into the computer, you are ready to create a file and save it. If you are not logged into the VAX, follow the instructions at the beginning of this tutorial.

The VAX editor used in this guide is the EDT editor. Two approaches to using the EDT editor are covered.

        The EDT line-editor can be used with any terminal that works with the VAX. The line editor requires no special terminal features. The Digital Equipment Corporation's VT100 terminals provide special features for the EDT full-screen editor. If you are using a terminal that is not compatible with VT100 terminals, then you should use the EDT line editor covered in Appendix A.3.

        If you are using a VT100 terminal or a terminal with the special features of a VT100 terminal, then you should use the EDT full-screen editor covered in Appendix A.4.

Remember that you can use the [DELETE] key or the [RUBOUT] key to back-up as you are typing a line, and you can use a [CTRL/U] to disregard the complete line on which you are typing.

You can use either upper or lower case letters or a combination of upper and lower case. Pressing the key marked [SHIFT] or [CAPS/LOCK] on the left of the keyboard changes to or from all capital letters.

When there is a dollar sign on the screen, you can begin an edit session. It will be easier for you to follow the examples if you use the filenames and data in the examples as they are shown. Then you can experiment with your own data after you complete the tutorial.

Begin now in Appendix A.3 if you do not have a VT100 compatible terminal. Begin now in Appendix A.4 on page 416 if you have a VT100 compatible terminal. After completing Appendix A.3 or A.4, look at Appendix A.5 on page 471 and then go through the tutorial in Appendix B.

A.3
USING THE EDT LINE EDITOR

CREATING AND SAVING A SIMPLE FILE
DIRECTORY
TYPING FILES AT THE TERMINAL
PRINTING FILES ON A PRINTER
USING THE EDT EDITOR

Enter the EDT command and the filename and extension GRADES.DAT and press the [RETURN] key to begin an edit session.

$ EDT GRADES.DAT   [RETURN]

The message that the editor displays means that it looked for a file called GRADES.DAT and did not find one. Since that file does not exist, it is giving you some space to create a new file. The [EOB] means the end of the buffer area – that is the end of the space for you to work.

Input file does not exist
[EOB]
*

The [EOB] marker which represents the end of your workspace is displayed on the screen. The asterisk is a prompt for you to enter a command. Whenever there is an asterisk on the screen, you can enter a command for the EDT editor.

In order to enter records into your file, you need to use the INSERT command. Press the [RETURN] key after typing the word INSERT.

*insert [RETURN]

The cursor will be positioned 16 spaces from the left margin. Now you can enter one record after another. Press the [RETURN] key after each record is entered. Type in the data as shown now. If you make mistakes, just keep going. There are lots of fix-up examples in the guide.

Enter three scores and a name and press the [RETURN] key.

86 74 80 ADAMS   [RETURN]

You can enter another record and press the [RETURN] key.

75 80 95 BOX   [RETURN]

Now you can enter more records, pressing the [RETURN] key after each record is entered.

93 87 90 CARR   [RETURN]
95 85 90 DAVIS   [RETURN]

Assume that there are only five students in this class. Enter the last record and press [RETURN]. Enter the grades and name for EDWARDS.

82 83 84 EDWARDS   [RETURN]

Now specify to the EDT editor that you have finished entering records with a [CONTROL/Z]. Press the [CTRL] key and while the [CTRL] key is depressed press the character [Z] key.

[CTRL/Z]

An asterisk will appear at the bottom of the screen. The asterisk, *, is a prompt for the EDT editor, indicating that you should enter an EDT command.

Now you need to enter the EXIT command and press the [RETURN] key, and your file will be saved in the file named GRADES.DAT. You specified the filename when you entered the EDT command at the beginning of this edit session. If you made a lot of typing mistakes and you want to eliminate this file and start over, you can use the QUIT command instead of the EXIT command.

* EXIT   [RETURN]

The following message indicates that your file is saved.

[USER]GRADES.DAT;1 5 LINES

The message [USER]GRADES.DAT;1 5 LINES means that your file is saved on the disk drive under your username that the filename is GRADES.DAT version 1. There are five records in the file.

You now have a dollar sign on the screen again. Once again, the system is waiting for a DCL command from you to begin another task.

You can type the DIRECTORY command to list the names of the files in your directory. Since you have saved a file named GRADES.DAT, that file name is listed when you enter the DIRECTORY COMMAND.

$ DIRECTORY

   Directory _USER

   GRADES.DAT;1

   Total of 1 file

You again have a $ prompt on the screen to indicate that the system is waiting for a command from you.

When there is a dollar sign on the screen, there are two commands which you can use to look at the contents of a file. You need to specify the name of the file which you want to see or to print. The TYPE command is used to display a file at the terminal. The PRINT command is used to print a copy of a file on a printer.

Enter the TYPE command, the name of a file, and the extension and press the [RETURN] key.

$ TYPE GRADES.DAT   [RETURN]

The file which you specify will be displayed at the terminal where you are working. If this were a long file, you could stop and resume scrolling by using a [CTRL/S] and a [CTRL/Q].

86 74 80 ADAMS
75 80 95 BOX
93 87 90 CARR
95 85 90 DAVIS
82 83 84 EDWARDS

You can send a copy of your file to a hard copy printer with the PRINT command. The output usually goes to a printer associated with the terminals where you are working.

$ PRINT GRADES.DAT   [RETURN]

A message is displayed to tell you that output is scheduled to print.

Job 118 entered on queue

DISPLAYING RECORDS AT THE TERMINAL USING THE EDT LINE EDITOR

Consider again the GRADES.DAT file which you entered. If you typed in the example, you now have a data file stored which contains records for five students. Now follow the next editing sessions to learn some ways to look at and modify your data.

Log into the computer if you are not

logged-in. Look at Appendix A.2 for logging-in instructions.

Begin another edit session. Enter the EDT command and the name of the file to edit. Press the [RETURN] key after each line you type.

```
$ edt grades.dat
```

The latest version of your file is brought into memory for editing. The first line of your GRADES file is displayed.

```
1        86 74 80 ADAMS
```

The * prompt on the screen indicates that you may now enter an EDT command. Some EDT commands which could be used are Type, Delete, Replace, and Substitute.

This example simply uses the Type command to demonstrate different ways for looking at a file.

Enter the Type Whole command to display all the records.

```
* t w
```

All the records are typed on the screen.

```
1        86 74 80 ADAMS
2        75 80 95 BOX
3        93 87 90 CARR
4        95 85 90 DAVIS
5        82 83 84 EDWARDS
```

Type a particular line by specifying the line number.

```
* t 3
3        93 87 90 CARR
```

Entering the T command with no line number indicates that the current line should be Typed. Line number 3 is still the current line from the previous access to a line.

```
* t
3        93 87 90 CARR
```

The word BEGIN can be used to access the first record in the file.

```
* t begin

1        86 74 80 ADAMS
```

The word END can be used to access the end of the file. The Whole file can be displayed with the Type Whole or Type BEGIN:END command.

```
* t begin:end

1        86 74 80 ADAMS
2        75 80 95 BOX
3        93 87 90 CARR
4        95 85 90 DAVIS
5        82 83 84 EDWARDS
```

You can Type from the beginning to a particular line number.

```
* t begin:4
```

```
1       86 74 80 ADAMS
2       75 80 95 BOX
3       93 87 90 CARR
4       95 85 90 DAVIS
```

You can type lines which contain a specified string of characters. The string of characters could be several characters or words.

```
* t begin:end all 'A'
```

```
1       86 74 80 ADAMS
3       93 87 90 CARR
4       95 85 90 DAVIS
5       82 83 84 EDWARDS
```

Type line 2.

```
* t 2
```

```
2       75 80 95 BOX
```

By pressing the [RETURN] key in edit mode, the succeeding line is displayed automatically. Press the [RETURN] key.

```
* [RETURN]
3       93 87 90 CARR
```

Press the [RETURN] key again to display the succeeding line in the file.

```
* [RETURN]
4       95 85 90 DAVIS
```

By entering a minus sign before pressing the [RETURN] key, you can display the preceding record in the file.

```
* - [RETURN]
3       93 87 90 CARR
```

Entering the Type command with an increment number and a plus or minus sign displays the relative line specified. Using the T command to indicate the current line, the line displayed is relative to the current line.

```
* t +2
5       82 83 84 EDWARDS
```

You have made no changes in your file. You have only used the Type command to display records in the file. You can use the QUIT command to end the edit session. If you had made any changes in the file which you wanted to save, you would need to use the EXIT command.

```
* QUIT
```

Now you have ended the edit session. There is again a dollar sign on the screen indicating that the computer is waiting for a DCL command from you.

You have just used the Type command in the editor to display individual records in your file. Now that you are out of the editor, you can use the TYPE command to display your entire file on the terminal

screen or the PRINT command to print your
entire file on the printer.

```
$ type grades.dat
 86 74 80 ADAMS
 75 80 95 BOX
 93 87 90 CARR
 95 85 90 DAVIS
 82 83 84 EDWARDS

$ print grades.dat
  job entered on queue
```

ADDING RECORDS TO A FILE USING THE EDT LINE EDITOR

Consider again the GRADES.DAT file which you
entered. New records are added to the file
at specified locations in this example.

Begin an edit session with the file
GRADES.DAT which should be in your directory.

```
$ edt grades.dat
```

The first line of your GRADES file is
displayed.

```
1        86 74 80 ADAMS
```

You could Type the Whole file to look at all
the records.

```
* t w
 1       86 74 80 ADAMS
 2       75 80 95 BOX
 3       93 87 90 CARR
 4       95 85 90 DAVIS
 5       82 83 84 EDWARDS
```

You can use the Insert command to add records
to the file. If you do not specify where in
the file that records should be inserted, the
added records will be inserted prior to the
record that is the current record. When you
begin an edit session, the current record is
the first record, and records added with the
simple Insert command will be added to the
beginning of the file. You could specify
that records be added at the beginning of the
file with the I BEGIN command.

```
* i
```

Now you can enter any number of records. For
the example, add two new records. Press the
[RETURN] key after each record that is
entered.

```
        81 88 94 AARON
        77 79 81 ABRAHMS
```

End the Insert mode with a [CTRL/Z].

```
[CTRL/Z]
```

The line which is the current line is
displayed at the terminal

```
1       86 74 80 ADAMS
```

You will have an asterisk on the screen again
and you can enter any EDT command.

Use the Type Whole command to look at the contents of the entire file. Decimal line numbers preceding line one have been added.

```
* t w
0.1      81 88 94 AARON
0.2      77 79 81 ABRAHMS
1        86 74 80 ADAMS
2        75 80 95 BOX
3        93 87 90 CARR
4        95 85 90 DAVIS
5        82 83 84 EDWARDS
[EOB]
```

You can specify a particular location where added lines should be inserted. You can insert lines at the end of the file.

```
* i end
```

Enter any number of records and terminate the Insert mode with a [CTRL/Z].

```
         65 66 67 ZIMMER
         [CTRL/Z]
[EOB]
```

Now Type the file.

```
* t w
0.1      81 88 94 AARON
0.2      77 79 81 ABRAHMS
1        86 74 80 ADAMS
2        75 80 95 BOX
3        93 87 90 CARR
4        95 85 90 DAVIS
5        82 83 84 EDWARDS
6        65 66 67 ZIMMER
```

You can specify that lines be added at any point in the file by using a particular line number. The records which you enter will be added to the file preceding the line number indicated.

```
* i 4
```

Enter some number of records.

```
         56 68 72 COMER
         68 69 77 CULLINS
         [CTRL/Z]
```

The line which is the current line is displayed at the terminal.

```
4        95 85 90 DAVIS
```

Use the Type Whole command to observe the result.

```
* t w
0.1      81 88 94 AARON
0.2      77 79 81 ABRAHMS
1        86 74 80 ADAMS
2        75 80 95 BOX
3        93 87 90 CARR
3.1      56 68 72 COMER
3.2      68 69 77 CULLINS
4        95 85 90 DAVIS
5        82 83 84 EDWARDS
6        65 66 67 ZIMMER
```

```
    [EOB]
                              You can also enter text following  an  insert
                              command and a semicolon.
    * i 7;65 43 58 NOORDER
    [EOB]
                              Look one more time at the file.
    * t w
    0.1        81 88 94 AARON
    0.2        77 79 81 ABRAHMS
    1          86 74 80 ADAMS
    2          75 80 95 BOX
    3          93 87 90 CARR
    3.1        56 68 72 COMER
    3.2        68 69 77 CULLINS
    4          95 85 90 DAVIS
    5          82 83 84 EDWARDS
    6          65 66 67 ZIMMER
    7          65 43 58 NOORDER
                              You could RESequence the file to renumber the
                              lines in increments of one.
    * RES
      11 lines resequenced
                              Look at the records again.
    * t w
    1          81 88 94 AARON
    2          77 79 81 ABRAHMS
    3          86 74 80 ADAMS
    4          75 80 95 BOX
    5          93 87 90 CARR
    6          56 68 72 COMER
    7          68 69 77 CULLINS
    8          95 85 90 DAVIS
    9          82 83 84 EDWARDS
    10         65 66 67 ZIMMER
    11         65 43 58 NOORDER
                              You could enter the EXIT command to save this
                              file  or  you could enter the QUIT command to
                              terminate the edit session without saving the
                              changes  made in the file.  For this example,
                              enter the QUIT command.
    * QUIT




    DELETING RECORDS IN A FILE USING THE EDT LINE EDITOR

                              Begin  an  edit  session  with  your  file
                              GRADES.DAT.
    $ edt grades.dat
                              The first line is displayed.
    1          86 74 80 ADAMS
                              Look at all the records.
    * t w
    1          86 74 80 ADAMS
    2          75 80 95 BOX
    3          93 87 90 CARR
    4          95 85 90 DAVIS
    5          82 83 84 EDWARDS
```

Delete a particular record in the file by specifying the line number to delete.

* d 2

A message displays that one line was deleted and the current line is displayed at the terminal.

```
1 line deleted
3          93 87 90 CARR
```

Observe that the line is gone.

```
* t w
1          86 74 80 ADAMS
3          93 87 90 CARR
4          95 85 90 DAVIS
5          82 83 84 EDWARDS
```

Delete a range of lines by specifying the first line number and the final line number separated by a colon.

```
* d 4:5
2 lines deleted
[EOB]
```

Look to see that the records are gone.

```
* t w
1          86 74 80 ADAMS
3          93 87 90 CARR
```

Delete all the records in a file by specifying the BEGINing to the END.

```
* d begin:end
2 lines deleted
[EOB]
```

Now there are no more records in your file.

```
* t w
[EOB]
```

The [EOB] marker is displayed because you are at the end of the buffer space for your file.

Since you need the GRADES.DAT file to work with again, use the QUIT command to end the edit session.

```
* quit
```

REPLACING RECORDS IN A FILE USING THE EDT LINE EDITOR

The REPLACE command in the EDT line mode causes a line or lines to be deleted and allows you to enter INSERT mode. You can then enter one or more records followed by pressing the [RETURN] key. The INSERT mode then is terminated when you use a [CTRL/Z].

Consider again the GRADES.DAT file which you entered.

Begin an edit session with the file GRADES.DAT which should be in your directory.

```
$ edt grades.dat
```

The first line of your GRADES file is displayed.

```
1          86 74 80 ADAMS
```

You could Type the Whole file to look at all the records.

```
* t w
1            86 74 80 ADAMS
2            75 80 95 BOX
3            93 87 90 CARR
4            95 85 90 DAVIS
5            82 83 84 EDWARDS
[EOB]
```
Replace the second record in the file.
```
* r 2
  1 line deleted
```
Line 2 is deleted and you are in the INSERT mode. You can enter as many records as you choose. After you have entered all the records which you need to enter, use the [CTRL/Z] to terminate INSERT mode. Enter two records for the example.
```
             55 65 75 BEX
             72 83 74 BURLEY
             [CTRL/Z]
```
The current line is displayed.
```
3            93 87 90 CARR
```
Now observe the file.
```
* t w
1            86 74 80 ADAMS
1.1          55 65 75 BEX
1.2          72 83 74 BURLEY
3            93 87 90 CARR
4            95 85 90 DAVIS
5            82 83 84 EDWARDS
```
Use the Replace command to delete lines 4 and 5 and begin the INSERT mode for entering new lines.
```
* r 4:5
  2 lines deleted
```
Enter some more lines now. Press the [RETURN] key following each line entered.
```
             55 56 57 COMELATE
             88 78 68 WESTON
             68 76 85 THOMAS
             89 87 85 PARROT
```
Terminate the INSERT mode with a [CTRL/Z].
```
             [CTRL/Z]
[EOB]
```
Now look at the file.
```
* t w
1            86 74 80 ADAMS
1.1          55 65 75 BEX
1.2          72 83 74 BURLEY
3            93 87 90 CARR
4            55 56 57 COMELATE
5            88 78 68 WESTON
6            68 76 85 THOMAS
7            89 87 85 PARROT
[EOB]
```
You could save the file with the EXIT command. For now use the QUIT command to keep the GRADES.DAT file in its original form.
```
* quit
```

FINDING RECORDS AND STRINGS IN A FILE USING THE EDT LINE EDITOR
SUBSTITUTING STRINGS OF CHARACTERS IN A FILE

Begin an edit session with your file
GRADES.DAT.

$ edt grades.dat

The first line of the file is displayed.

1   86 74 80 ADAMS

Look at all the records.

* t w
1   86 74 80 ADAMS
2   75 80 95 BOX
3   93 87 90 CARR
4   95 85 90 DAVIS
5   82 83 84 EDWARDS
[EOB]

Look at the HELP for the EDT editor.
Whenever an asterisk is displayed on the
screen, you can enter the HELP command to get
general information about EDT. You can enter
a particular command for which you want HELP.

* help

The output is not printed here. Observe the
display at the terminal.

* help type

The output is not printed here. Observe the
display at the terminal.

You can move the line pointer in the file to
a particular record with the Find command.
You can specify that you want line 3 to be
the current line by using the Find command
followed by the line number.

* f 3

Line 3 is now the current line. Use the Type
current line command which is the T command
with no range specified. Observe the current
line.

* t
3   93 87 90 CARR

Using the Find command, you can locate a
string of characters. The string of
characters follows the Find command enclosed
in single quotation marks.

* f 'WAR'

The editor locates the characters WAR in the
name EDWARDS and the line that contains the
string becomes the current line. Type
current line.

* t
5   82 83 84 EDWARDS

You may need to find a line or a string of
characters just to observe some records, to
insert new records at that point, to delete a
line or for any other editing purpose. If
there are 500 records in a file, the Find
command becomes very important.

Now try the Substitute command to substitute
a character or a string of characters for

some specified string of characters. There are many forms of the Substitute command. The following is the form of the command used here.

        S/oldtext/newtext/linenumber
        S/oldtext/newtext/range-of-linenumbers

The S means to substitute the characters between the second set of slashes for the text which is between the first set of slashes in the record or records specified.

Substitute the name CERR for the name CARR in line number 3.

```
* s/CARR/CERR/3
```

The line is displayed.

```
3        93 87 90 CERR
1 substitution
```

Observe what happens when you substitute the letter Z for every occurrence in the file of the character A.

```
* s/A/Z/begin:end
1        86 74 80 ZDZMS
4        95 85 90 DZVIS
5        82 83 84 EDWZRDS
4 substitions
```

Type the file to observe.

```
* t w
1        86 74 80 ZDZMS
2        75 80 95 BOX
3        93 87 90 CERR
4        95 85 90 DZVIS
5        82 83 84 EDWZRDS
[EOB]
```

You could change the Z's back to A's with the Substitute command. You could make other changes. For now, use the QUIT command to terminate this edit session.

```
* quit
```

MOVING RECORDS FROM ONE LOCATION TO ANOTHER USING THE EDT LINE EDITOR

Begin an edit session with the file GRADES.DAT which should be in your directory.

```
$ edt grades.dat
```

The first line of your GRADES file is displayed.

```
1        86 74 80 ADAMS
```

Type the Whole file to see all the records.

```
* t w
1        86 74 80 ADAMS
2        75 80 95 BOX
3        93 87 90 CARR
4        95 85 90 DAVIS
5        82 83 84 EDWARDS
[EOB]
```

Use the Move command to transfer the record which is now line 2 to line 4 in the file. Since line 4 exists, the record will be moved to a line immediately preceding line 4.

```
* m 2 to 4
1 line moved
```

Type the file to observe the location of the moved record.

```
* t w
1        86 74 80 ADAMS
3        93 87 90 CARR
3.1      75 80 95 BOX
4        95 85 90 DAVIS
5        82 83 84 EDWARDS
[EOB]
```

You can Move a range of records to some other location in the file. Move lines 4 through 5 to the location immediately preceding line 1 in the file.

```
* m 4:5 to 1
2 lines moved
```

Type the file to observe the result.

```
* t w
0.1      95 85 90 DAVIS
0.2      82 83 84 EDWARDS
1        86 74 80 ADAMS
3        93 87 90 CARR
3.1      75 80 95 BOX
[EOB]
```

Use the QUIT command to terminate the edit session without saving the changes made in the file. You could use the EXIT command if you wanted to save the changes.

```
* quit
```

COPYING RECORDS FROM ONE LOCATION TO ANOTHER USING THE EDT LINE EDITOR

Begin an edit session with the file GRADES.DAT which should be in your directory.

```
$ edt grades.dat
```

The first line of the file is displayed.

```
1        86 74 80 ADAMS
```

Type the Whole file to look at all records.

```
* t w
1        86 74 80 ADAMS
2        75 80 95 BOX
3        93 87 90 CARR
4        95 85 90 DAVIS
5        82 83 84 EDWARDS
[EOB]
```

You can use the editor to make a copy of a record or a group of records at some other location in the file.

Make a copy of line 2 immediately preceding line 4.

```
* co  2 to 4
1 line copied
```

Notice that the copy of line 2 is inserted at line 3.1. Line 1 remains in the file at its original position.

```
* t w
1        86 74 80 ADAMS
2        75 80 95 BOX
3        93 87 90 CARR
3.1      75 80 95 BOX
4        95 85 90 DAVIS
5        82 83 84 EDWARDS
[EOB]
```

Copy a range of lines to another location in a file.

```
* co 1:3 to end
3 lines copied
```

Observe added lines at the end of the file.

```
* t w
1        86 74 80 ADAMS
2        75 80 95 BOX
3        93 87 90 CARR
3.1      75 80 95 BOX
4        95 85 90 DAVIS
5        82 83 84 EDWARDS
6        86 74 80 ADAMS
7        75 80 95 BOX
8        93 87 90 CARR
```

Terminate the edit session with the QUIT command. You could enter the EXIT command if you wished to save the changes.

```
* quit
```

A.4
USING THE EDT
FULL-SCREEN EDITOR

CREATING AND SAVING A SIMPLE FILE
DIRECTORY
TYPING FILES AT THE TERMINAL
PRINTING FILES ON A PRINTER
USING THE EDT EDITOR

```
$ EDT GRADES.DAT
      [RETURN]
```

The message that the editor prints means that it looked for a file called GRADES.DAT and did not find one. Since that file does not exist, it is giving you some space to create a new file. The [EOB] means the end of the buffer area - that is the end of the space for you to work.

```
$ EDT GRADES.DAT
      Input file does not exist
      [EOB]
```

There is an asterisk on the screen now. Before you start to enter data, you need to indicate to the editor that you will be using the VT100 terminal with the keypad mode. (The keypad will be described in another example.) Type the CHANGE command and press [RETURN] to enter the correct editing mode.

```
$ EDT GRADES.DAT
     Input file does not exist
     [EOB]
*  CHANGE
                  [RETURN]
```

Now the [EOB] marker which represents the end of your workspace is at the top of the screen.

```
  [EOB]
```

As you type in data, the [EOB] marker will move down to give you more space. Type in the data as shown now. If you make mistakes, just keep going. There are lots of fix-up examples in the guide. Enter three scores and a name and press the [RETURN] key. Notice that the [EOB] marker moves down below the line which you enter.

```
  86 74 80 ADAMS
  [EOB]
                  [RETURN]
```

You can enter another record and press the [RETURN] key.

```
  86 74 80 ADAMS
  75 80 95 BOX
  [EOB]
                  [RETURN]
```

Now you can enter more records, pressing the [RETURN] key after each record is entered.

```
  86 74 80 ADAMS
  75 80 95 BOX
  93 87 90 CARR
  [EOB]
                  [RETURN]
```

```
  86 74 80 ADAMS
  75 80 95 BOX
  93 87 90 CARR
  95 85 90 DAVIS
  [EOB]
                  [RETURN]
```

Assume that there were only five students in this class. Enter the last record. Do not press [RETURN] after the record is entered. Enter the grades and name for EDWARDS and then specify to the EDT editor that you have finished entering records with a [CONTROL/Z]. Press the [CTRL] key and while the [CTRL] key is depressed press the character Z key.

```
86 74 80 ADAMS
75 80 95 BOX
93 87 90 CARR
95 85 90 DAVIS
82 83 84 EDWARDS
[EOB]
                    [CTRL/Z]
```

An asterisk will appear at the bottom of the screen.

Now you need to enter the EXIT command and press the [RETURN] key and your file will be saved in the file named GRADES.DAT. You specified the filename when you entered the EDT command at the beginning of this edit session. If you made a lot of typing mistakes and you want to eliminate this file and start over, you can use the QUIT command instead of the EXIT command.

```
[EOB]


* EXIT
                [RETURN]
```

The VAX will print a message telling you that your file is saved.

```
[EOB]


* EXIT

_DRA1:[HAPPY]GRADES.DAT;1 5 LINES
```

The message _DRA1:[HAPPY]GRADES.DAT;1 5 LINES means that your file is saved on the disk drive named DRA1 under the username of HAPPY and that the filename is GRADES.DAT version 1. There are five records in the file. (If you pressed the [RETURN] key after entering the record for Edwards, you have an extra blank record and the message says that you have 6 lines. It will create no problems for now.)

You now have a dollar sign on the screen again. Once again, the system is waiting for a DCL command from you to begin another task.

You can type the DIRECTORY command to list the names of the files in your directory. Since you have saved a file named GRADES.DAT, that file name is listed when you enter the DIRECTORY COMMAND.

```
$ DIRECTORY

    Directory _DRA1:[HAPPY]

    GRADES.DAT;1

    Total of 1 file
```

You again have a $ prompt on the screen to indicate that the system is waiting for a command from you.

When there is a dollar sign on the screen, there are two commands which you can use to look at the contents of a file. You need to specify the name of the file which you want to see or to print. The TYPE command is used to print a file at the terminal. The PRINT command is used to send a copy of a file to a printer.

Enter the TYPE command and the name of a file and press the [RETURN] key.

```
$ TYPE GRADES.DAT
                    [RETURN]
```

The file which you specify will be printed at the terminal where you are working. If this were a long file, you could stop and resume scrolling with the [NO SCROLL] key.

```
$ TYPE GRADES.DAT

   86 74 80 ADAMS
   75 80 95 BOX
   93 87 90 CARR
   95 85 90 DAVIS
   82 83 84 EDWARDS
```

You can send a copy of your file to a hard copy printer with the PRINT command. The output will go to a printer associated with the terminals where you are working.

```
$ PRINT GRADES.DAT
                    [RETURN]
```

A message prints to tell you that output is scheduled to print on the system printer.

```
$ PRINT GRADES.DAT

   Job 118 entered on queue SYS$PRINT
```

You can get your printout from the printer associated with the terminals you are using as soon as the output completes printing.

ENDING AN EDIT SESSION WITHOUT SAVING
INPUT AND CHANGES MADE IN SESSION
USING THE EDT EDITOR

Enter the edit mode again. Use the file GRADES.DAT which you created in the previous example. In this example, you can delete a name from one of the existing records. Then instead of saving the file with the change, you use the QUIT command which terminates the session without saving the change.

Enter the EDT command and the filename to enter the edit mode. Then press the [RETURN] key.

```
$ EDT GRADES.DAT

             [RETURN]
```

The first record in your file will be printed.

```
$ EDT GRADES.DAT
1   86 74 80 ADAMS
*
```

You can enter the change command to enter Keypad Edit mode.

```
$ EDT GRADES.DAT
1   86 74 80 ADAMS
*change
             [RETURN]
```

The records in your file are printed at the terminal. If there are more records than will fit on the screen, only the first 22 records will print initially.

The flashing cursor is represented by the underline character in this example. The cursor is located at the position of the first character in the first record.

The up, down, left and right arrows are at the top of your keyboard. Press the right arrow to move the cursor to the end of the name ADAMS.

```
_86 74 80 ADAMS
 75 80 95 BOX
 93 87 90 CARR
 95 85 90 DAVIS
 82 83 84 EDWARDS
[EOB]
             [Press right arrow repeatedly]
```

Now press the [DELETE] key repeatedly to delete the characters in the name ADAMS.

```
 86 74 80 ADAMS_
 75 80 95 BOX
 93 87 90 CARR
 95 85 90 DAVIS
 82 83 84 EDWARDS
[EOB]
             [Press [DELETE] key repeatedly]
```

Often you make several inputs and changes and then you may realize that you have made a mess of things and you just want to start over. The following procedure will allow you to abandon a file.

The first record has been changed in this edit session. If you now want to end this edit session without saving the change you made, you do the following. End the Keypad Edit mode with a [CONTROL/Z] and end the edit session with the QUIT command.

Press and hold the [CTRL] key. While the [CTRL] key is depressed type the character Z.

```
86 74 80 _
75 80 95 BOX
93 87 90 CARR
95 85 90 DAVIS
82 83 84 EDWARDS
[EOB]
                [CTRL/Z]
```

Now you have an asterisk on the screen. You can enter the QUIT command and the file created during the edit session will not be saved.

```
[EOB]


* QUIT
        [RETURN]
```

You can use the TYPE command to look at your file and see that the saved version of your file was not altered.

```
$ TYPE GRADES.DAT

                [RETURN]
```

```
$ TYPE GRADES.DAT

86 74 80 ADAMS
75 80 95 BOX
93 87 90 CARR
95 85 90 DAVIS
82 83 84 EDWARDS
```

If you ever need to terminate an edit session without saving the input or the changes made in the session, the QUIT command allows you to do that.

If you chose to save the changes you made, you would use the EXIT command instead of the QUIT command.

USING THE EDT EDITOR
DELETING CHARACTERS AND LINES AS YOU TYPE
SAVING AN EDIT FILE

Another small data file can be entered to practice using the EDT editor in KEYPAD MODE. The following student records are used for this example.

```
69 82 84 Asford
75 70 79 Bentley
99 99 99 Camaro
80 80 80 Dendy
91 94 89 Foxley
88 82 93 Garr
70 69 74 Haroldson
92 89 96 Israelson
76 72 79 Kilmichael
80 87 91 Martinez
```

You can invoke the EDT editor by typing the EDT command and a filename followed by a [RETURN]. Once you are in the editor, you can enter the CHANGE command to specify that you are using KEYPAD EDITING.

```
$ EDT NEWCLASS.DAT

            [RETURN]
```

The VAX looks for the file named NEWCLASS.DAT. When the file is not found, it creates some work space for you. Enter the keypad mode with the CHANGE command. Press the [RETURN] key after you type the word "change."

```
$ EDT NEWCLASS.DAT
      Input file does not exist

  * CHANGE
            [RETURN]
```

You will have the End of Buffer [EOB] marker on the screen.

```
  [EOB]
```

Enter the first record containing student scores. As before, leave a space to the left of the first score and one space between each score, because the maximum score might be 100 and would require three positions.

If the name should be Asford, the b is a typing mistake. You can use the [DELETE] key on the main keyboard to delete the mistyped character.

```
  69 82 84 Asb_
  [EOB]
            [DELETE]
```

Now you can continue typing the line correctly and press the [RETURN] key.

```
  69 82 84 Asford_
  [EOB]
            [RETURN]
```

You can enter another line and press the [RETURN] key.

```
69 82 84 Asford
75 70 79 Bentley_
[EOB]
                [RETURN]
```

If you make several mistakes as you are entering a line, you can use the [DELETE] key repeatedly to back up. If you enter the characters, Wow, when you should have entered Camaro, you can press the [DELETE] key 3 times to back up and then retype the name correctly.

```
69 82 84 Asford
75 70 79 Bentley
99 99 99 Wow_
[EOB]
        [Press the [DELETE] key three times]
```

The cursor is at the location where you should enter the name Camaro.

```
69 82 84 Asford
75 70 79 Bentley
99 99 99 _
[EOB]
```

Now enter the correct name, Camaro, and press the [RETURN] key.

```
69 82 84 Asford
75 70 79 Bentley
99 99 99 Camaro_
[EOB]
          [RETURN]
```

If you make several mistakes as you are entering a line you can use a [CONTROL/U] to erase the entire line. The [CTRL/U] is executed by pressing and holding the key marked [CTRL] and while the [CTRL] key is depressed type the letter U.

```
69 82 84 Asford
75 70 79 Bentley
99 99 99 Camaro
30 30 30 Dindy_
[EOB]
              [CTRL/U]
```

Now you can enter the Dendy record correctly.

```
69 82 84 Asford
75 70 79 Bentley
99 99 99 Camaro
80 80 80 Dendy_
[EOB]
            [RETURN]
```

Enter another five records and press the [RETURN] key after each record.

```
    69 82 84 Asford
    75 70 79 Bentley
    99 99 99 Camaro
    80 80 80 Dendy
    91 94 89 Foxley
    88 82 93 Garr
    70 69 74 Haroldson
    92 89 96 Israelson
    76 72 79 Kilmichael

[EOB]
                    [Press the [RETURN] key after]
                    [each record is entered      ]
```

Enter one more record. Do not press the [RETURN] key. Terminate the KEYPAD EDITING with a [CTRL/Z].

```
    69 82 84 Asford
    75 70 79 Bentley
    99 99 99 Camaro
    80 80 80 Dendy
    91 94 89 Foxley
    88 82 93 Garr
    70 69 74 Haroldson
    92 89 96 Israelson
    76 72 79 Kilmichael
    80 87 91 Martinez_
[EOB]
                    [CTRL/Z]
```

```
    [EOB]

 * EXIT
                [RETURN]
```

Now you have a dollar sign on the screen. The VAX is waiting for a Digital Command Language command from you. Use the DIRECTORY command to observe that you now have two files in your directory.

```
$ DIR
     Directory _DRA1:[HAPPY]
     GRADES.DAT;1          NEWCLASS.DAT;1

     Total of 2 files
```

USING THE EDT EDITOR
USING THE KEYBOARD ARROWS TO MOVE THE CURSOR

After you enter the EDT Keypad Editing mode, a full-screen of data is printed on the screen. If your file contains fewer than 22 records, those records will all be printed on the screen. You can use the arrows at the upper right of your keyboard to move the cursor around the screen in the EDT Keypad Editing. If your file contains more than 22 records, pressing the up and down keyboard arrows at the top or bottom of the screen causes succeeding lines to be printed on the screen.

You can not use the arrow keys for giving commands when there is a dollar sign on the screen.

Practice using the arrows with the following example. Enter the EDT command and press the [RETURN] key to enter editing mode. Use the example file named NEWCLASS.DAT which you created in the previous example.

```
$ EDT NEWCLASS.DAT

           [RETURN]
```

The VAX looks for the file named NEWCLASS.DAT. The first record of your file is printed. Enter the Keypad Mode with the CHANGE command. Press the [RETURN] key after you type the word change.

```
$ EDT NEWCLASS.DAT
 1  69 82 84 Asford

* CHANGE
               [RETURN]
```

The contents of your file will be printed on the screen. Now you can use the arrows to move the cursor. The cursor is at the first character of the first record now. Press the 'down' arrow several times until the cursor is at the beginning of the record for Haroldson.

```
_69 82 84 Asford
 75 70 79 Bentley
 99 99 99 Camaro
 80 80 80 Dendy
 91 94 89 Foxley
 88 82 93 Garr
 70 69 74 Haroldson
 92 89 96 Israelson
 76 72 79 Kilmichael
 80 87 91 Martinez
[EOB]
          [Press the 'down' arrow until the cursor]
          [is at the beginning of the record for Haroldson]
```

Now you can use the 'right' arrow.

```
 69 82 84 Asford
 75 70 79 Bentley
 99 99 99 Camaro
 80 80 80 Dendy
 91 94 89 Foxley
 88 82 93 Garr
_70 69 74 Haroldson
 92 89 96 Israelson
 76 72 79 Kilmichael
 80 87 91 Martinez
[EOB]
        [Press the 'right' arrow until the cursor]
        [is at the end of the name Haroldson]
```

```
 69 82 84 Asford
 75 70 79 Bentley
 99 99 99 Camaro
 80 80 80 Dendy
 91 94 89 Foxley
 88 82 93 Garr
 70 69 74 Haroldson_
 92 89 96 Israelson
 76 72 79 Kilmichael
 80 87 91 Martinez
[EOB]
                [Press the [DELETE] key repeatly]
                [to delete the name Haroldson]
```

Use the 'up' arrow.

```
 69 82 84 Asford
 75 70 79 Bentley
 99 99 99 Camaro
 80 80 80 Dendy
 91 94 89 Foxley
 88 82 93 Garr
 70 69 74 _
 92 89 96 Israelson
 76 72 79 Kilmichael
 80 87 91 Martinez
[EOB]
                [Press the 'up' arrow until the cursor]
                [is at the beginning of the name Bentley]
```

Use the 'right' arrow to move to the end of the the name Bentley.

```
 69 82 84 Asford
 75 70 79 Bentley
 99 99 99 Camaro
 80 80 80 Dendy
 91 94 89 Foxley
 88 82 93 Garr
 70 69 74
 92 89 96 Israelson
 76 72 79 Kilmichael
 80 87 91 Martinez
[EOB]
                [Press the 'right' arrow until the cursor]
                [is at the end of the name Bentley]
```

Now delete the name Bentley.

```
   69 82 84 Asford
   75 70 79 Bentley_
   99 99 99 Camaro
   80 80 80 Dendy
   91 94 89 Foxley
   88 82 93 Garr
   70 69 74
   92 89 96 Israelson
   76 72 79 Kilmichael
   80 87 91 Martinez
   [EOB]
                [Press the [DELETE] key repeatly]
                [to delete the name Bentley]
```

Continue using the arrows and the [DELETE] key to delete all the names from the records. Do not be concerned about deleting names or records, because you can end this edit session with the QUIT command.

Notice that the [DELETE] key always deletes the character to the left of the cursor.

```
   69 82 84 Asford
   75 70 79 _
   99 99 99 Camaro
   80 80 80 Dendy
   91 94 89 Foxley
   88 82 93 Garr
   70 69 74
   92 89 96 Israelson
   76 72 79 Kilmichael
   80 87 91 Martinez
   [EOB]
                [Use the arrows and the [DELETE] key]
                [to delete the names from all the records]
```

After you have practiced using the arrows, use the [CTRL/Z] to end the Keypad Edit mode.

```
   69 82 84
   75 70 79
   99 99 99
   80 80 80
   91 94 89
   88 82 93
   70 69 74
   92 89 96
   76 72 79
   80 87 91_
   [EOB]
                [CTRL/Z]
```

End the edit session with the QUIT command, so that the changes which you made in this session will not be saved.

```
[EOB]

* QUIT
            [RETURN]
```

When you are in the Keypad Edit mode, you can use the arrows to move the cursor. Now that you have a dollar sign on the screen, you need to enter a Digital Command Language command. You enter DCL commands a line at the time. You can not use the arrows to move around the screen until you return to the EDT Keypad Edit mode.

Since you ended the edit session with the QUIT command, changes which you made in this session were not saved. You can use the TYPE command to observe that your file, NEWCLASS.DAT is unaltered.

```
$ TYPE NEWCLASS.DAT

            [RETURN]
```

The file which was saved with the EXIT command is printed.

```
69 82 84 Asford
75 70 79 Bentley
99 99 99 Camaro
80 80 80 Dendy
91 94 89 Foxley
88 82 93 Garr
70 69 74 Haroldson
92 89 96 Israelson
76 72 79 Kilmichael
80 87 91 Martinez
```

You have a dollar sign on the screen again. You can enter a command to begin a new task.

USING THE EDT EDITOR
THE VT100 KEYPAD

The VT100 terminal has a main keyboard with all the letters of the alphabet, the numbers, the arrows and other special characters.

In addition to the main keyboard, there is a separate KEYPAD located to the right of the keyboard. The keypad keys on the VT100 have special functions when used in an EDT edit session. Look at the keypad. The characters PF1 are printed on the key at the upper left of the keypad. The numbers 0 through 9 and some other characters are printed on other keys. When you enter the command EDT and then enter the CHANGE command, these keys assume special functions. It is helpful if your terminal has a plastic overlay with the keypad functions specified.

```
-------------------------------------------------------------
-----------------------------
:     :     :     :     :
: PF1 : PF2 : PF3 : PF4 :
:     :     :     :     :
-----------------------------
:     :     :     :     :
: 7   : 8   : 9   : -   :
:     :     :     :     :
-----------------------------
:     :     :     :     :
: 4   : 5   : 6   : ,   :
:     :     :     :     :
-----------------------------
:     :     :     :     :
: 1   : 2   : 3   :     :
:     :     :     :enter:
-----------------------:     :
:     :     :     :
: 0         : .   :     :
:     :     :     :
-----------------------------
-------------------------------------------------------------
```

The key marked PF1 at the upper left of the keypad is named the
[GOLD] key for keypad editing. The [GOLD] key is used like a shift
key for a typewritter.

The second key on the top row, which is marked PF2, is called the
[HELP] key for keypad editing. The [HELP] key can be used in
keypad editing to request that definitions of key functions be printed
at the terminal.

Now you should get into the EDT editor and use the HELP key.
You should have a $ on the screen. Enter the EDT command and
specify a filename. For this example, use the file named
NEWCLASS.DAT which you created. Then press the [RETURN] key.

```
$ EDT NEWCLASS.DAT

        [RETURN]
```

Now you should type the CHANGE command and press [RETURN]
to specify that you will be using KEYPAD EDITING.

```
$ EDT NEWCLASS.DAT

1   69 82 84 Asford

* CHANGE
            [RETURN]
```

The records in your file are printed on the screen. Press the
[HELP] key now. If your keypad does not have a plastic overlay
marking the [HELP] key, press the key marked PF2. It is the second
key on the top row of the keypad.

```
 ┌──────────────────────────────────────────────────────┐
 │  _69 82 84 Asford                                      │
 │   75 70 79 Bentley                                     │
 │   99 99 99 Camaro                                      │
 │   80 80 80 Dendy                                       │
 │   91 94 89 Foxley                                      │
 │   88 82 93 Garr                                        │
 │   70 69 74 Haroldson                                   │
 │   92 89 96 Israelson                                   │
 │   76 72 79 Kilmichael                                  │
 │   80 87 91 Martinez                                    │
 │  [EOB]                                                 │
 │                    [HELP]                              │
 └──────────────────────────────────────────────────────┘
```

The keypad keys are displayed on the screen.

```
------------------------------------------------------------
         ---------------------------------------------------
         :          :         :             :            :
         :  GOLD    :  HELP   :  FNDNXT     :  DEL L     :
         :          :         :    FIND     :  UND L     :
         :          :         :             :            :
         ---------------------------------------------------
         :          :         :             :            :
         :  PAGE    :  SECT   :  APPEND     :  DEL W     :
Type a key :COMMAND  :  FILL   :  REPLACE    :  UND W     :
for help on :        :         :             :            :
that key. ---------------------------------------------------
         :          :         :             :            :
         :  ADVANCE :  BACKUP :     CUT     :  DEL C     :
         :  BOTTOM  :  TOP    :   PASTE     :  UND C     :
         :          :         :             :            :
         ---------------------------------------------------
To exit, type :       :         :             :            :
a space.  :  WORD    :  EOL    :    CHAR     :            :
         : CHNGCASE : DEL EOL :  SPECINS    :            :
         :          :         :             :  ENTER     :
         -----------------------------------;            :
         :          :         :             :  SUBS      :
         :      LINE          :  SELECT     :            :
         :    OPEN LINE       :  RESET      :            :
         :          :         :             :            :
         ---------------------------------------------------
```

         [Press the [SPACE BAR] to end KEYPAD help]

Press a key to see a description of a function of a key. Press the
third key down on the right. If you have a plastic overlay for the
keypad, the key is marked with function [DEL C/UND C]. If you do
not have a plastic overlay, the key is marked with a comma. The
function of the key is to delete the character at the position where the
cursor is located. The 'SHIFT' function, [UND C] restores the most
recently deleted character. The 'SHIFT' function of UNDeleting a
Character is invoked by first pressing the [GOLD] key AND THEN
pressing the [DEL C/UND C] key. Each function is covered in an
example. Try pressing other keys to become familiar with some of the
functions of the keys.

An example is the best way to demonstrate what happens as you use the function keys in keypad editing. End this edit session and look at the following examples of the functions of the keys.

For now use a [CONTROL/Z] to get out of keypad editing.

```
_69 82 84 Asford
 75 70 79 Bentley
 99 99 99 Camaro
 80 80 80 Dendy
 91 94 89 Foxley
 88 82 93 Garr
 70 69 74 Haroldson
 92 89 96 Israelson
 76 72 79 Kilmichael
 80 87 91 Martinez
[EOB]
            [CTRL/Z]
```

Then type the characters QUIT and press return to end the edit session. The QUIT command causes the edit session to terminate without saving anything. Nothing was entered in this example to save.

```
[EOB]

* QUIT
        [RETURN]
```

At any time during an EDT Keypad Edit session, you can press the [HELP] key on the keypad to get the definition of the function of a key. Your file will not be affected by pressing the [HELP] key.

USING THE EDT EDITOR
USING THE KEYPAD FUNCTIONS
[ADVANCE] [BACKUP] [LINE] [EOL]

Another data file can be entered to demonstrate some of the functions of the keys on the keypad. The following student records are used for creating the file:

```
69 82 84 Akasofu
75 70 79 Allen
82 76 81 Bedford
71 78 86 Benson
65 69 67 Cain
79 82 80 Cuccarese
58 89 93 Dixon
89 95 92 Drew
76 70 74 Fuller
```

Since the example numbers represent scores, you might assume that there could be maximum scores of 100. In order to follow the examples easily, it is best if you leave one space to the left of each score, so you will need to press the space bar once before typing the first score for each student.

You can invoke the EDT editor by typing the EDT command and a filename. After you are in the editor, you can enter the CHANGE command to specify that you are using KEYPAD EDITING. If you forget to enter the filename, you will be prompted to enter the filename. For this example, use the filename, SOMECLASS.DAT.

```
$ EDT [RETURN]
File: SOMECLASS.DAT
Input file does not exist
[EOB]
* CHANGE
```

You have the End of Buffer [EOB] marker on the screen. You can begin to enter records. If you need to know a function of a key on the keypad at any time, you can press the [HELP] key - that is the key marked [PF2]. For now, enter some of the student records into your file. You should enter only the records shown in the following example so that you can practice inserting records. Press [RETURN] after the first three records. Do not press [RETURN] after the record for Drew. If you press return after entering the Drew record, you will create a blank record.

```
69 82 84 Akasofu [RETURN]
75 70 79 Allen [RETURN]
65 69 67 Cain [RETURN]
89 95 92 Drew
[EOB]
```

NOTE If you get lost in following this or any example and want to start over, refer to the previous example for instructions on using the QUIT command.

If you need to enter a student record for a student named Bedford, you would probably want to make it the third record to keep the records in alphabetical order. In order to insert new data at a particular place in a file you first need to move the cursor to that place in the file. From a previous example, you know that you could use the up-arrow to move the cursor up in the file. That is probably the easiest way, but try using the [LINE] key function instead. The line key may be marked [BLINE]. The key is the wide key at at the bottom of the keypad. In order to get the line function to move backwards in the file, you need to first press the [BACKUP] key. Then press the [LINE] key. You will remain in BACKUP mode until you press the [ADVANCE] key.

```
69 82 84 Akasofu
75 70 79 Allen
65 69 67 Cain
89 95 92 Drew _
[EOB]
                [BACKUP]
```

```
69 82 84 Akasofu
75 70 79 Allen
65 69 67 Cain
89 95 92 Drew_
[EOB]
                [LINE]
```

The [LINE] command moves the cursor back to the beginning of the line for Drew. Press the [LINE] key again.

```
69 82 84 Akasofu
75 70 79 Allen
65 69 67 Cain
_89 95 92 Drew
[EOB]
                [LINE]
```

Now the cursor is at the beginning of Cain's record. Since you are moving backwards in the file, pressing the [EOL] key will cause the cursor to move to the end of the previous line.

```
69 82 84 Akasofu
75 70 79 Allen
_65 69 67 Cain
 89 95 92 Drew
[EOB]
                [EOL]
```

The cursor should be at the end of the word Allen. Now you can press [RETURN] to get a blank line for typing the new record.

```
69 82 84 Akasofu
75 70 79 Allen_
65 69 67 Cain
89 95 92 Drew
[EOB]
                [RETURN]
```

Notice that there is a blank line on the screen. The cursor is at the beginning of the blank line.

```
69 82 84 Akasofu
75 70 79 Allen

_
65 69 67 Cain
89 95 92 Drew
[EOB]
```

Enter a line for a student named Bedford. Press [RETURN] and you will get another line.

```
69 82 84 Akasofu
75 70 79 Allen
82 76 81 Bedford_
65 69 67 Cain
89 95 92 Drew
[EOB]
                [RETURN]
```

Now you have another blank line for entering a record.

```
 69 82 84 Akasofu
 75 70 79 Allen
 82 76 81 Bedford
_
 65 69 67 Cain
 89 95 92 Drew
[EOB]
```

Enter a line for a student named Benson. There are no more records to enter at this place in the file, so you should not press [RETURN].

```
 69 82 84 Akasofu
 75 70 79 Allen
 82 76 81 Bedford
 71 78 86 Benson_
 65 69 67 Cain
 89 95 92 Drew
```

(If you press [RETURN] you will get an extra line. You might just try it and then use the [DELETE] key to erase the last code which is the RETURN code. The extra line is removed.) After you become familiar with KEYPAD EDITING, you will find many ways for entering data.

```
 69 82 84 Akasofu
 75 70 79 Allen
 82 76 81 Bedford
 71 78 86 Benson _
 65 69 67 Cain
 89 95 92 Drew
[EOB]
                 [RETURN]
```

```
 69 82 84 Akasofu
 75 70 79 Allen
 82 76 81 Bedford
 71 78 86 Benson
_
 65 69 67 Cain
 89 95 92 Drew
[EOB]
                 [DELETE]
```

When you pressed the [BACKUP] key when you started to move backwards through your file, the editor was set in the BACKUP mode. Now press the [ADVANCE] key so that you can move forward in your file. Insert the names Cuccarese and Dixon in your file.

```
 69 82 84 Akasofu
 75 70 79 Allen
 82 76 81 Bedford
 71 78 86 Benson_
 65 69 67 Cain
 89 95 92 Drew
[EOB]
                 [ADVANCE]
```

```
69 82 84 Akasofu
75 70 79 Allen
82 76 81 Bedford
71 78 86 Benson_
65 69 67 Cain
89 95 92 Drew
[EOB]
                    [LINE]
```

Use the [EOL] command to move to the end of the line.   You can also use the arrows to move the cursor on the screen.

```
69 82 84 Akasofu
75 70 79 Allen
82 76 81 Bedford
71 78 86 Benson
_65 69 67 Cain
 89 95 92 Drew
[EOB]
                    [EOL]
```

When the cursor is at the end of the name Cain, press [RETURN] to give yourself another line to enter a record.

```
69 82 84 Akasofu
75 70 79 Allen
82 76 81 Bedford
71 78 86 Benson
65 69 67 Cain_
89 95 92 Drew
[EOB]
                    [RETURN]
```

Now you have a blank line for entering a new record.

```
69 82 84 Akasofu
75 70 79 Allen
82 76 81 Bedford
71 78 86 Benson
65 69 67 Cain

_
 89 95 92 Drew
[EOB]
```

Enter the record for Cuccarese and press [RETURN].

```
69 82 84 Akasofu
75 70 79 Allen
82 76 81 Bedford
71 78 86 Benson
65 69 67 Cain
79 82 80 Cuccarese_
89 95 92 Drew
[EOB]
                    [RETURN]
```

Now you have a blank line to enter another record.

```
69 82 84 Akasofu
75 70 79 Allen
82 76 81 Bedford
71 78 86 Benson
65 69 67 Cain
79 82 80 Cuccarese

89 95 92 Drew
[EOB]
```

There is one more record to enter in this example session, but before entering that, you should use the [HELP] key to look at the descriptions for the function keys which you have used. First press the [HELP] key and then press the key [BACKUP]. Then look at the descriptions for [ADVANCE] and [LINE]

Enter the record for Dixon, but do not press [RETURN], because there are no more records to enter at this point.

```
69 82 84 Akasofu
75 70 79 Allen
82 76 81 Bedford
71 78 86 Benson
65 69 67 Cain
79 82 80 Cuccarese
58 89 93 Dixon_
89 95 92 Drew
[EOB]
```

Now use the arrows to move to the end of the file which is marked with the [EOB] marker and enter another record.

```
69 82 84 Akasofu
75 70 79 Allen
82 76 81 Bedford
71 78 86 Benson
65 69 67 Cain
79 82 80 Cuccarese
58 89 93 Dixon_
89 95 92 Drew
[EOB]
        [Use arrows to move cursor to [EOB] on the screen]
```

```
69 82 84 Akasofu
75 70 79 Allen
82 76 81 Bedford
71 78 86 Benson
65 69 67 Cain
79 82 80 Cuccarese
58 89 93 Dixon
89 95 92 Drew
[EOB]
```

Now you can enter the final record for this example edit session. Use a [CTRL/Z] after the record to terminate the KEYPAD EDITING mode.

```
  69 82 84 Akasofu
  75 70 79 Allen
  82 76 81 Bedford
  71 78 86 Benson
  65 69 67 Cain
  79 82 80 Cuccarese
  58 89 93 Dixon
  89 95 92 Drew
  76 70 74 Fuller_
[EOB]
                    [CTRL/Z]
```

Now you need to save the file with the EXIT command. Remember that if you made a lot of mistakes and you would like to start over, you can use the QUIT command and your file will not be saved.

```
[EOB]


* EXIT
            [RETURN]
```

The VAX confirms that your file has been saved.

```
[EOB]


* EXIT
_DRA1:[HAPPY]SOMECLASS.DAT;1 9 LINES
```

Now you have a dollar sign on the screen. You can enter a DCL command now. Enter the DIRECTORY command to see that the files you have entered are listed.

```
$ DIRECTORY
  Directory _DRA1:[HAPPY]

  SOMECLASS.DAT;1    GRADES.DAT;1    NEWCLASS.DAT;1

  Total of 3 files
```

You could print any of the files at the terminal with the TYPE command or you could send a copy of a file to a printer with the PRINT command. The TYPE and PRINT commands are Digital Command Language, DCL, commands. You can use DCL commands when there is a dollar sign on the screen.

```
$ TYPE SOMECLASS.DAT [RETURN]
```

The contents of the file will be printed on the screen.

```
69 82 84 Akasofu
75 70 79 Allen
82 76 81 Bedford
71 78 86 Benson
65 69 67 Cain
79 82 80 Cuccarese
58 89 93 Dixon
89 95 92 Drew
76 70 74 Fuller
```

The PRINT command sends the output to a printer.

```
$ PRINT SOMECLASS.DAT

Job 250 entered on queue SYS$PRINT
```

USING THE EDT EDITOR KEYPAD FUNCTIONS
DELETING CHARACTERS, WORDS AND LINES
[HELP] [CHAR] [DEL CHAR] [WORD] [DEL WORD]
[LINE] [DEL LINE]

Pressing the function key marked [CHAR] will move the cursor one character in the current direction. The default direction is forward in the file unless you have used the [BACKUP] key to alter the direction. After the [BACKUP] key is used, the [CHAR] key will cause the cursor to move one character backwards in the file. The [ADVANCE] key is used to reset the direction forward in the file.

Pressing the [WORD] key causes the cursor to move over the current word to the next blank space. A word is considered to be all the characters before a space is encountered. The direction that the cursor moves is forward unless the [BACKUP] key has been used to set the direction. The [ADVANCE] key can be used to reset the direction to forward.

Begin an edit session with the file which is saved with the name NEWCLASS.DAT. Enter the EDT command and your filename and press [RETURN]. After the VAX prints the first line of your file, you should type the CHANGE command and press [RETURN].

```
$ EDT NEWCLASS.DAT [RETURN]
1 69 82 84 Asford
[EOB]
* CHANGE
```

The records from your file are printed on the screen.

```
_69 82 84 Asford
 75 70 79 Bentley
 99 99 99 Camaro
 80 80 80 Dendy
 91 94 89 Foxley
 88 82 93 Garr
 70 69 74 Haroldson
 92 89 96 Israelson
 76 72 79 Kilmichael
 80 87 91 Martinez
[EOB]
```

Press the [HELP] key (the PF2 key) on the keypad. You can press the [HELP] key at any time without regard to the location of the cursor.

```
_69 82 84 Asford
 75 70 79 Bentley
 99 99 99 Camaro
 80 80 80 Dendy
 91 94 89 Foxley
 88 82 93 Garr
 70 69 74 Haroldson
 92 89 96 Israelson
 76 72 79 Kilmichael
 80 87 91 Martinez
[EOB]
              [HELP]
```

Observe the positions of the [CHAR], [WORD], [DEL CHARACTER], [DEL WORD], and the [DEL LINE] keys. You have already used the [LINE] bar at the bottom of the keypad. You have used the [BACKUP] key and the [ADVANCE] key. Use these keys along with the arrows and the [DELETE] key in this example.

```
-----------------------------------------------------------
-----------------------------
:          :         :       :////////////:
:  GOLD    :   HELP  : FNDNXT :/  DEL L  /:
:          :         :  FIND  :/  UND L  /:
:          :         :       :////////////:
-----------------------------------------------------------
:          :         :       :////////////:
:  PAGE    :   SECT  : APPEND :/  DEL W  /:
:  COMMAND :   FILL  : REPLACE:/  UND W  /:
:          :         :       :////////////:
-----------------------------------------------------------
:          :         :       :////////////:
:  ADVANCE :  BACKUP :  CUT   :/  DEL C  /:
:  BOTTOM  :   TOP   :  PASTE :/  UND C  /:
:          :         :       :////////////:
-----------------------------------------------------------
:////////////:         :////////////:
:/  WORD  /:   EOL   :/  CHAR   /:
:/CHNGCASE/: DEL EOL :/ SPECINS /:
:////////////:         :////////////:      ENTER    :
---------------------------------------:             :
:                      :            :    SUBS    :
:          LINE        : SELECT  :             :
:       OPEN LINE      : RESET   :             :
:                      :         :             :
-----------------------------------------------------------

[Press the [SPACE BAR] to return to your file]
-----------------------------------------------------------
```

The flashing cursor on the screen is at the beginning of the first line of your file. The underline character is used to represent the cursor in this guide. Press the [CHAR] key to move one key to the right.

```
 _69 82 84 Asford
  75 70 79 Bentley
  99 99 99 Camaro
  80 80 80 Dendy
  91 94 89 Foxley
  88 82 93 Garr
  70 69 74 Haroldson
  92 89 96 Israelson
  76 72 79 Kilmichael
  80 87 91 Martinez
 [EOB]
                        [CHAR]
```

Now press the [CHAR] key repeatedly to move to the d in the word Asford.

```
  69 82 84 Asford
  75 70 79 Bentley
  99 99 99 Camaro
  80 80 80 Dendy
  91 94 89 Foxley
  88 82 93 Garr
  70 69 74 Haroldson
  92 89 96 Israelson
  76 72 79 Kilmichael
  80 87 91 Martinez
 [EOB]
    [Press the [CHAR] key repeatedly to move]
    [the cursor to the letter d in Asford]
```

Press the [CHAR] key a few more times and the cursor moves down to the next line.

```
  69 82 84 Asford
  75 70 79 Bentley
  99 99 99 Camaro
  80 80 80 Dendy
  91 94 89 Foxley
  88 82 93 Garr
  70 69 74 Haroldson
  92 89 96 Israelson
  76 72 79 Kilmichael
  80 87 91 Martinez
       [Press the [CHAR] key a few more times]
 [EOB]
```

Notice that the cursor moves to the next line. Now press the [BACKUP] key to change the direction from forward to backward in the file.

```
  69 82 84 Asford
  75 70 79 Bentley
  99 99 99 Camaro
  80 80 80 Dendy
  91 94 89 Foxley
  88 82 93 Garr
  70 69 74 Haroldson
  92 89 96 Israelson
  76 72 79 Kilmichael
  80 87 91 Martinez
 [EOB]
                        [BACKUP]
```

Press the [CHAR] key. The cursor moves back one character.

```
 69 82 84 Asford
 75 70 79 Bentley
 99 99 99 Camaro
 80 80 80 Dendy
 91 94 89 Foxley
 88 82 93 Garr
 70 69 74 Haroldson
 92 89 96 Israelson
 76 72 79 Kilmichael
 80 87 91 Martinez
[EOB]
            [CHAR]
```

Since you pressed the [BACKUP] key, you are still in BACKUP mode. Continue pressing the [CHAR] key until the cursor is on the 2 in the score 82 for Asford.

```
 69 82 84 Asford
 75 70 79 Bentley
 99 99 99 Camaro
 80 80 80 Dendy
 91 94 89 Foxley
 88 82 93 Garr
 70 69 74 Haroldson
 92 89 96 Israelson
 76 72 79 Kilmichael
 80 87 91 Martinez
[EOB]
        [Press the [CHAR]key until the cursor]
        [is on the 2 in the score 82 for Asford]
```

Press the [DEL CHAR] key.

```
 69 82 84 Asford
 75 70 79 Bentley
 99 99 99 Camaro
 80 80 80 Dendy
 91 94 89 Foxley
 88 82 93 Garr
 70 69 74 Haroldson
 92 89 96 Israelson
 76 72 79 Kilmichael
 80 87 91 Martinez
[EOB]
              [DEL CHAR]
```

The 2 is deleted.

```
 69 8_84 Asford
 75 70 79 Bentley
 99 99 99 Camaro
 80 80 80 Dendy
 91 94 89 Foxley
 88 82 93 Garr
 70 69 74 Haroldson
 92 89 96 Israelson
 76 72 79 Kilmichael
 80 87 91 Martinez
[EOB]
```

You could enter a 5 now if the score should actually have been 85.

```
69 85_84 Asford
75 70 79 Bentley
99 99 99 Camaro
80 80 80 Dendy
91 94 89 Foxley
88 82 93 Garr
70 69 74 Haroldson
92 89 96 Israelson
76 72 79 Kilmichael
80 87 91 Martinez
[EOB]
```

Now press the [ADVANCE] key to set the direction to forward again.

```
69 85_84 Asford
75 70 79 Bentley
99 99 99 Camaro
80 80 80 Dendy
91 94 89 Foxley
88 82 93 Garr
70 69 74 Haroldson
92 89 96 Israelson
76 72 79 Kilmichael
80 87 91 Martinez
[EOB]
              [ADVANCE]
```

The [WORD] key causes the cursor to move over a group of contiguous characters through the blank space following the characters.

Press the [WORD] key repeatedly to move over words and observe what happens. Stop the cursor at the beginning of the name, Dendy.

```
69 85_84 Asford
75 70 79 Bentley
99 99 99 Camaro
80 80 80 Dendy
91 94 89 Foxley
88 82 93 Garr
70 69 74 Haroldson
92 89 96 Israelson
76 72 79 Kilmichael
80 87 91 Martinez
[EOB]
    [Press the [WORD] key repeatedly]
```

Now press the [DEL WORD] key. The name Dendy is erased.

```
       69 85 84 Asford
       75 70 79 Bentley
       99 99 99 Camaro
       80 80 80 Dendy
       91 94 89 Foxley
       88 82 93 Garr
       70 69 74 Haroldson
       92 89 96 Israelson
       76 72 79 Kilmichael
       80 87 91 Martinez
       [EOB]
                        [DEL WORD]
```

You could enter a new name in that place or correct the spelling after the name is deleted.

```
       69 85 84 Asford
       75 70 79 Bentley
       99 99 99 Camaro
       80 80 80 _
       91 94 89 Foxley
       88 82 93 Garr
       70 69 74 Haroldson
       92 89 96 Israelson
       76 72 79 Kilmichael
       80 87 91 Martinez
       [EOB]
```

Enter the name Dixon in place of the deleted name.

```
       69 85 84 Asford
       75 70 79 Bentley
       99 99 99 Camaro
       80 80 80 Dixon_
       91 94 89 Foxley
       88 82 93 Garr
       70 69 74 Haroldson
       92 89 96 Israelson
       76 72 79 Kilmichael
       80 87 91 Martinez
       [EOB]
```

Move the cursor to the beginning of the line 88 82 93 Garr using [CHAR] and [WORD] keys.

```
       69 85 84 Asford
       75 70 79 Bentley
       99 99 99 Camaro
       80 80 80 Dixon
       91 94 89 Foxley
      _88 82 93 Garr
       70 69 74 Haroldson
       92 89 96 Israelson
       76 72 79 Kilmichael
       80 87 91 Martinez
       [EOB]
```

Use the [LINE] key to move down another line.

```
69 85 84 Asford
75 70 79 Bentley
99 99 99 Camaro
80 80 80 Dixon
91 94 89 Foxley
_88 82 93 Garr
 70 69 74 Haroldson
92 89 96 Israelson
76 72 79 Kilmichael
80 87 91 Martinez
[EOB]
                    [LINE]
```

The cursor is at the beginning of the line for Haroldson.   Use the [DELETE LINE] key to delete the line.

```
69 85 84 Asford
75 70 79 Bentley
99 99 99 Camaro
80 80 80 Dixon
91 94 89 Foxley
88 82 93 Garr
_70 69 74 Haroldson
 92 89 96 Israelson
76 72 79 Kilmichael
80 87 91 Martinez
[EOB]
                 [DEL LINE]
```

The Haroldson line is deleted.   Press the key marked [EOL] to move the cursor to the end of the line.

```
69 85 84 Asford
75 70 79 Bentley
99 99 99 Camaro
80 80 80 Dixon
91 94 89 Foxley
88 82 93 Garr
_92 89 96 Israelson
 76 72 79 Kilmichael
80 87 91 Martinez
[EOB]
                 [EOL]
```

Observe that the cursor moves to the end of the line.

```
69 85 84 Asford
75 70 79 Bentley
99 99 99 Camaro
80 80 80 Dixon
91 94 89 Foxley
88 82 93 Garr
92 89 96 Israelson_
76 72 79 Kilmichael
80 87 91 Martinez
[EOB]
```

Try moving around the screen now using the arrows, and the keys

[CHAR], [WORD], [LINE], [EOL], [BACKUP] and [ADVANCE].   Try
using the [DEL CHAR], [DEL WORD] and [DEL LINE] keys.   Try
adding data to the file and changing records in the file.   Practice as
long as you need to feel comfortable with these keys.   End the KEYPAD
edit session with a [CTRL/Z].

```
    69 85 84 Asford
    75 70 79 Bentley
    99 99 99 Camaro
    80 80 80 Dixon
    91 94 89 Foxley
    88 82 93 Garr
    92 89 96 Israelson_
    76 72 79 Kilmichael
    80 87 91 Martinez
   [EOB]
                        [CTRL/Z]
```

Use the QUIT command and observe that this version of your file is
not saved.   The previous version of the file is saved and unaltered
when you use the QUIT command.

```
   [EOB]

   * QUIT
```

Now you have a dollar sign on the screen.   You can enter a
command to begin another task.

USING THE EDT EDITOR KEYPAD FUNCTIONS
RESTORING DELETED CHARACTERS, WORDS AND LINES
[UNDL CHR] [UNDL WRD] [UNDL LIN]

The VAX Keypad editor has a special feature that allows you to
UNDELETE strings of characters which you have deleted.   If you have
ever remembered that you were making a mistake just as you deleted a
character or word or record, you will appreciate this feature!

Begin another edit session with the file which is saved with the
name NEWCLASS.DAT.   Enter the EDT command and your filename and
press [RETURN].   After the VAX prints the first line of your file, you
should type the CHANGE command and press [RETURN].

```
   $ EDT NEWCLASS.DAT
    1 69 82 84 Asford
    [EOB]
    * CHANGE
```

The records from your file are printed on the screen.

```
 _69 82 84 Asford
  75 70 79 Bentley
  99 99 99 Camaro
  80 80 80 Dendy
  91 94 89 Foxley
  88 82 93 Garr
  70 69 74 Haroldson
  92 89 96 Israelson
  76 72 79 Kilmichael
  80 87 91 Martinez
 [EOB]
```

This example demonstrates how to restore characters, words and lines which have been deleted. Press the [HELP] key (the PF2 key) on the keypad. You can press the [HELP] key at any time without regard to the location of the cursor.

```
 _69 82 84 Asford
  75 70 79 Bentley
  99 99 99 Camaro
  80 80 80 Dendy
  91 94 89 Foxley
  88 82 93 Garr
  70 69 74 Haroldson
  92 89 96 Israelson
  76 72 79 Kilmichael
  80 87 91 Martinez
 [EOB]
              [HELP]
```

Observe the positions of the 'undelete' keys. The 'undelete' keys are the shift keys for the [DEL CHARACTER], [DEL WORD], and the [DEL LINE] keys. Observe the position of the [GOLD] key which is used for a shift key in keyboard editing.

In order to use the shift of a key you need to first press the [GOLD] key AND AFTER THAT press the function key which you want to use. You press the function key AFTER pressing the GOLD key.

```
-----------------------------------------------------------
:         :         :         ://///////////:
:  GOLD   :  HELP   : FNDNXT   :/  DEL L  /:
:         :         : FIND     :/  UND L  /:
:         :         :         ://///////////:
-----------------------------------------------------------
:         :         :         ://///////////:
:  PAGE   :  SECT   : APPEND   :/  DEL W  /:
: COMMAND :  FILL   : REPLACE  :/  UND W  /:
:         :         :         ://///////////:
-----------------------------------------------------------
:         :         :         ://///////////:
: ADVANCE : BACKUP  : CUT      :/  DEL C  /:
: BOTTOM  :  TOP    : PASTE    :/  UND C  /:
:         :         :         ://///////////:
-----------------------------------------------------------
:         :         :         :            :
:  WORD   :  EOL    : CHAR     :            :
: CHNGCASE : DEL EOL : SPECINS :            :
:         :         :         :   ENTER    :
------------------------------------------;            :
:         :         :         :   SUBS     :
:     LINE          : SELECT   :            :
:   OPEN LINE       : RESET    :            :
:         :         :         :            :
-----------------------------------------------------------
```

[Press the [SPACE BAR] to return to your file]

Press the [CHAR] key to move one key to the right.

```
_69 82 84 Asford
 75 70 79 Bentley
 99 99 99 Camaro
 80 80 80 Dendy
 91 94 89 Foxley
 88 82 93 Garr
 70 69 74 Haroldson
 92 89 96 Israelson
 76 72 79 Kilmichael
 80 87 91 Martinez
[EOB]
                    [CHAR]
```

The cursor is now on the 6 in the score 69 for Asford.   Press the [DEL CHAR] key.

```
 69 82 84 Asford
 75 70 79 Bentley
 99 99 99 Camaro
 80 80 80 Dendy
 91 94 89 Foxley
 88 82 93 Garr
 70 69 74 Haroldson
 92 89 96 Israelson
 76 72 79 Kilmichael
 80 87 91 Martinez
[EOB]
            [DEL CHAR]
```

The character 6 is deleted from the screen.

```
 9 82 84 Asford
 75 70 79 Bentley
 99 99 99 Camaro
 80 80 80 Dendy
 91 94 89 Foxley
 88 82 93 Garr
 70 69 74 Haroldson
 92 89 96 Israelson
 76 72 79 Kilmichael
 80 87 91 Martinez
[EOB]
```

In fact the character, 6, is stored in a buffer. The most recently deleted character is always stored in a buffer. Now you can use the [GOLD] key to shift to the [UNDELETE CHARACTER] key to restore the character which you deleted. First press the [GOLD] key.

```
 9 82 84 Asford
 75 70 79 Bentley
 99 99 99 Camaro
 80 80 80 Dendy
 91 94 89 Foxley
 88 82 93 Garr
 70 69 74 Haroldson
 92 89 96 Israelson
 76 72 79 Kilmichael
 80 87 91 Martinez
[EOB]
                    [GOLD]
```

```
┌─────────────────────────────────────────────────────────┐
│    9 82 84 Asford                                         │
│   75 70 79 Bentley                                        │
│   99 99 99 Camaro                                         │
│   80 80 80 Dendy                                          │
│   91 94 89 Foxley                                         │
│   88 82 93 Garr                                           │
│   70 69 74 Haroldson                                      │
│   92 89 96 Israelson                                      │
│   76 72 79 Kilmichael                                     │
│   80 87 91 Martinez                                       │
│  [EOB]                                                    │
│                     [UNDEL CHAR]                          │
└─────────────────────────────────────────────────────────┘
```

The character, 6, which was stored in a buffer is now put back into your file.

Now use the [CHAR], [WORD] and [LINE] keys to move the cursor to the beginning of the name, Camaro.

```
┌─────────────────────────────────────────────────────────┐
│   69 82 84 Asford                                         │
│   75 70 79 Bentley                                        │
│   99 99 99 Camaro                                         │
│   80 80 80 Dendy                                          │
│   91 94 89 Foxley                                         │
│   88 82 93 Garr                                           │
│   70 69 74 Haroldson                                      │
│   92 89 96 Israelson                                      │
│   76 72 79 Kilmichael                                     │
│   80 87 91 Martinez                                       │
│  [EOB]                                                    │
│      [Use the [CHAR], [WORD] and [LINE] keys to move]     │
│      [the cursor to the beginning of the name, Camaro]    │
└─────────────────────────────────────────────────────────┘
```

Use the [DELETE WORD] key to delete the name.

```
┌─────────────────────────────────────────────────────────┐
│   69 82 84 Asford                                         │
│   75 70 79 Bentley                                        │
│   99 99 99 Camaro                                         │
│   80 80 80 Dendy                                          │
│   91 94 89 Foxley                                         │
│   88 82 93 Garr                                           │
│   70 69 74 Haroldson                                      │
│   92 89 96 Israelson                                      │
│   76 72 79 Kilmichael                                     │
│   80 87 91 Martinez                                       │
│  [EOB]                                                    │
│                   [DEL WORD]                              │
└─────────────────────────────────────────────────────────┘
```

The word, Camaro, is deleted from the screen.

The word, Camaro, is stored in a buffer so that it can be restored with the [UNDELETE WORD] function. Press the [GOLD] key and then the [UNDELETE WORD] key.

```
    69 82 84 Asford
    75 70 79 Bentley
    99 99 99_
    80 80 80 Dendy
    91 94 89 Foxley
    88 82 93 Garr
    70 69 74 Haroldson
    92 89 96 Israelson
    76 72 79 Kilmichael
    80 87 91 Martinez
[EOB]
                   [GOLD]
```

Now press the [UNDELETE WORD] key.

```
    69 85_84 Asford
    75 70 79 Bentley
    99 99 99 _
    80 80 80 Dendy
    91 94 89 Foxley
    88 82 93 Garr
    70 69 74 Haroldson
    92 89 96 Israelson
    76 72 79 Kilmichael
    80 87 91 Martinez
[EOB]
              [UNDELETE WORD]
```

Use the [CHAR], [WORD] and [LINE] keys to move to the beginning of the record for Haroldson.

```
    69 85 84 Asford
    75 70 79 Bentley
    99 99 99 Camaro_
    80 80 80 Dixon
    91 94 89 Foxley
    88 82 93 Garr
    70 69 74 Haroldson
    92 89 96 Israelson
    76 72 79 Kilmichael
    80 87 91 Martinez
[EOB]
    [Use the [CHAR], [WORD] and [LINE] keys to move]
    [to the beginning of the record for Haroldson]
```

Use the [DELETE LINE] key to delete the line.

```
    69 85 84 Asford
    75 70 79 Bentley
    99 99 99 Camaro
    80 80 80 Dixon
    91 94 89 Foxley
    88 82 93 Garr
  _70 69 74 Haroldson
    92 89 96 Israelson
    76 72 79 Kilmichael
    80 87 91 Martinez
[EOB]
                  [DEL LINE]
```

The Haroldson line is deleted.

The line for Haroldson which was deleted is stored in a buffer. The [UNDELETE LINE] function can be used to restore the line. First press the [GOLD] key.

```
69 85 84 Asford
75 70 79 Bentley
99 99 99 Camaro
80 80 80 Dixon
91 94 89 Foxley
88 82 93 Garr
_92 89 96 Israelson
76 72 79 Kilmichael
80 87 91 Martinez
[EOB]
              [GOLD]
```

After you press the [GOLD] key, then press the [UNDELETE LINE] key and observe that the line is indeed restored.

```
69 85 84 Asford
75 70 79 Bentley
99 99 99 Camaro
80 80 80 Dixon
91 94 89 Foxley
88 82 93 Garr
_92 89 96 Israelson
76 72 79 Kilmichael
80 87 91 Martinez
[EOB]
              [UNDELETE LINE]
```

End the KEYPAD edit session with a [CTRL/Z].

```
69 85 84 Asford
75 70 79 Bentley
99 99 99 Camaro
80 80 80 Dixon
91 94 89 Foxley
88 82 93 Garr
92 89 96 Israelson
_70 69 74 Haroldson
76 72 79 Kilmichael
80 87 91 Martinez
[EOB]
                [CTRL/Z]
```

Use the QUIT command and observe that this version of your file is not saved. The previous version of the file is saved and unaltered when you use the QUIT command.

```
[EOB]

* QUIT
```

In this example, you see that you can use the UNDELETE function keys to restore characters, words and lines which have been deleted.

Now you have a dollar sign on the screen. You can enter a command to begin another task.

USING THE EDT EDITOR KEYPAD FUNCTIONS
COPYING AND MOVING DELETED CHARACTERS, WORDS AND LINES
[UNDL CHR]   [UNDL WRD]   [UNDL LIN]

The [UNDELETE] functions of the VAX Keypad editor allow you to copy and move characters, words and lines which you have deleted.

Begin another edit session with the file which is saved with the name NEWCLASS.DAT. Enter the EDT command and your filename and press [RETURN]. After the VAX prints the first line of your file, you should type the CHANGE command and press [RETURN].

```
$ EDT NEWCLASS.DAT
1 69 82 84 Asford
[EOB]
* CHANGE
```

The records from your file are printed on the screen.

```
_69 82 84 Asford
 75 70 79 Bentley
 99 99 99 Camaro
 80 80 80 Dendy
 91 94 89 Foxley
 88 82 93 Garr
 70 69 74 Haroldson
 92 89 96 Israelson
 76 72 79 Kilmichael
 80 87 91 Martinez
[EOB]
```

This example deletes characters, words and lines, and then moves and copies the deleted characters, words and lines.

Again you will be using the [DELETE] keys and the [UNDELETE] keys. The [UNDELETE] keys are the shift keys for the [DEL CHARACTER], [DEL WORD], and the [DEL LINE] keys. The [GOLD] key is used for a shift key in keypad editing.

Press the [CHAR] key to move one key to the right.

```
_69 82 84 Asford
 75 70 79 Bentley
 99 99 99 Camaro
 80 80 80 Dendy
 91 94 89 Foxley
 88 82 93 Garr
 70 69 74 Haroldson
 92 89 96 Israelson
 76 72 79 Kilmichael
 80 87 91 Martinez
[EOB]
                [CHAR]
```

The cursor is now on the 6 in the score 69 for Asford. Press the [DEL CHAR] key.

```
    69 82 84 Asford
    75 70 79 Bentley
    99 99 99 Camaro
    80 80 80 Dendy
    91 94 89 Foxley
    88 82 93 Garr
    70 69 74 Haroldson
    92 89 96 Israelson
    76 72 79 Kilmichael
    80 87 91 Martinez
    [EOB]
                    [DEL CHAR]
```

The character 6 is deleted from the screen.

```
    9 82 84 Asford
    75 70 79 Bentley
    99 99 99 Camaro
    80 80 80 Dendy
    91 94 89 Foxley
    88 82 93 Garr
    70 69 74 Haroldson
    92 89 96 Israelson
    76 72 79 Kilmichael
    80 87 91 Martinez
    [EOB]
```

In fact the character 6 is stored in a buffer. The most recently deleted character is always stored in a buffer. Now you can use the [GOLD] key to shift to the [UNDELETE CHARACTER] key to restore the character which you deleted. First press the [GOLD] key and then the [UNDELETE CHARACTER] key.

```
    9 82 84 Asford
    75 70 79 Bentley
    99 99 99 Camaro
    80 80 80 Dendy
    91 94 89 Foxley
    88 82 93 Garr
    70 69 74 Haroldson
    92 89 96 Israelson
    76 72 79 Kilmichael
    80 87 91 Martinez
    [EOB]
                    [GOLD]
                    [UNDEL CHAR]
```

The character 6 which was stored in a buffer is now put back into your file.

The character 6 which was stored in the buffer when you pressed the [DELETE CHAR] key is still stored in the buffer. The character 6 will remain in the buffer until you press the [DELETE CHAR] key again to put something else in the buffer.

Since the 6 is still stored in the buffer you can use the [UNDELETE CHAR] function to put the 6 at some other place in your file. Move the cursor with the [LINE] key to the beginning of the record for Foxley.

```
   69 82 84 Asford
   75 70 79 Bentley
   99 99 99 Camaro
   80 80 80 Dendy
   91 94 89 Foxley
   88 82 93 Garr
   70 69 74 Haroldson
   92 89 96 Israelson
   76 72 79 Kilmichael
   80 87 91 Martinez
 [EOB]
    [Use [LINE] key to move the cursor]
    [to the score 91 for Foxley]
```

Press the [UNDELETE CHAR] key and observe that a 6 is put in your file at the point where the cursor is located.

```
   69 82 84 Asford
   75 70 79 Bentley
   99 99 99 Camaro
   80 80 80 Dendy
 _91 94 89 Foxley
   88 82 93 Garr
   70 69 74 Haroldson
   92 89 96 Israelson
   76 72 79 Kilmichael
   80 87 91 Martinez
 [EOB]              [GOLD]
                 [UNDELETE CHAR]
```

The 6 is still stored in the buffer. Press the [EOL] key to move the cursor to the end of the record for Foxley.

```
   69 82 84 Asford
   75 70 79 Bentley
   99 99 99 Camaro
   80 80 80 Dendy
 6 91 94 89 Foxley
   88 82 93 Garr
   70 69 74 Haroldson
   92 89 96 Israelson
   76 72 79 Kilmichael
   80 87 91 Martinez
 [EOB]
              [EOL]
```

Press the [UNDELETE CHAR] key three times and observe that three 6's are put in your file at the point where the cursor is located.

```
┌─────────────────────────────────────────────────────────────┐
│   69 82 84 Asford                                            │
│   75 70 79 Bentley                                           │
│   99 99 99 Camaro                                            │
│   80 80 80 Dendy                                             │
│  6 91 94 89 Foxley_                                          │
│   88 82 93 Garr                                              │
│   70 69 74 Haroldson                                         │
│   92 89 96 Israelson                                         │
│   76 72 79 Kilmichael                                        │
│   80 87 91 Martinez                                          │
│  [EOB]                              [GOLD]                   │
│              [Press the [UNDELETE CHAR] key three times]     │
│                                                              │
└─────────────────────────────────────────────────────────────┘
```

The same concepts apply to deleting, restoring and moving words and lines as those shown for characters.

Move the cursor to the beginning of the name Camaro.

```
┌─────────────────────────────────────────────────────────────┐
│   69 82 84 Asford                                            │
│   75 70 79 Bentley                                           │
│   99 99 99 Camaro                                            │
│   80 80 80 Dendy                                             │
│  6 91 94 89 Foxley666_                                       │
│   88 82 93 Garr                                              │
│   70 69 74 Haroldson                                         │
│   92 89 96 Israelson                                         │
│   76 72 79 Kilmichael                                        │
│   80 87 91 Martinez                                          │
│  [EOB]                                                       │
│              [Move cursor the beginning of name Camaro]      │
│                                                              │
└─────────────────────────────────────────────────────────────┘
```

Use the [DELETE WORD] key to delete the name.

```
┌─────────────────────────────────────────────────────────────┐
│   69 82 84 Asford                                            │
│   75 70 79 Bentley                                           │
│   99 99 99 Camaro                                            │
│   80 80 80 Dendy                                             │
│   91 94 89 Foxley                                            │
│   88 82 93 Garr                                              │
│   70 69 74 Haroldson                                         │
│   92 89 96 Israelson                                         │
│   76 72 79 Kilmichael                                        │
│   80 87 91 Martinez                                          │
│  [EOB]                                                       │
│              [DEL WORD]                                      │
│                                                              │
└─────────────────────────────────────────────────────────────┘
```

The word, Camaro is deleted from the screen.

The word, Camaro, is stored in a buffer so that it can be restored with the [UNDELETE WORD] function. Instead of putting the name Camaro back where it came from, move the cursor to the end of the first record in the file.

```
69 82 84 Asford
75 70 79 Bentley
99 99 99_
80 80 80 Dendy
 6 91 94 89 Foxley666
88 82 93 Garr
70 69 74 Haroldson
92 89 96 Israelson
76 72 79 Kilmichael
80 87 91 Martinez
[EOB]
            [Move cursor to end of the Asford record]
```

Now press the [GOLD] and the [UNDELETE WORD] key.

```
69 85 84 Asford_
75 70 79 Bentley
99 99 99
80 80 80 Dendy
 6 91 94 89 Foxley666
88 82 93 Garr
70 69 74 Haroldson
92 89 96 Israelson
76 72 79 Kilmichael
80 87 91 Martinez
[EOB]
                [GOLD]
                [UNDELETE WORD]
```

Now, if you want to move the Asford name where the Camaro name was, you can use the [DELETE WORD] function again. Move the cursor to the beginning of the name, Asford. First, you need to be sure to insert a space between the name Asford and the name Camaro, otherwise the two names will be taken as one word when you use the [DELETE WORD] and [UNDELETE WORD] functions.

```
69 85 84 Asford Camaro_
75 70 79 Bentley
99 99 99
80 80 80 Dendy
 6 91 94 89 Foxley666
88 82 93 Garr
70 69 74 Haroldson
92 89 96 Israelson
76 72 79 Kilmichael
80 87 91 Martinez
[EOB]
    [Insert a space between the names Asford and Camaro]
    [Move the cursor to the beginning of the name Asford]
```

Now use the [DELETE WORD] key to delete the name Asford.

```
     69 85 84 Asford Camaro
     75 70 79 Bentley
     99 99 99
     80 80 80 Dendy
   6 91 94 89 Foxley666
     88 82 93 Garr
     70 69 74 Haroldson
     92 89 96 Israelson
     76 72 79 Kilmichael
     80 87 91 Martinez
   [EOB]
       [DELETE WORD]
```

Move the cursor to the location to which you want to insert the name, Asford, maybe in the place where the name Camaro was located.

```
     69 85 84 Camaro
     75 70 79 Bentley
     99 99 99
     80 80 80 Dixon
   6 91 94 89 Foxley666
     88 82 93 Garr
     70 69 74 Haroldson
     92 89 96 Israelson
     76 72 79 Kilmichael
     80 87 91 Martinez
   [EOB]
       [Move the cursor to the location where the name]
       [is missing in the third record.]
```

Use the [GOLD] key and the [UNDELETE WORD] key to move the name Asford to this location.

```
     69 85 84 Camaro
     75 70 79 Bentley
     99 99 99 _
     80 80 80 Dixon
   6 91 94 89 Foxley666
     88 82 93 Garr
     70 69 74 Haroldson
     92 89 96 Israelson
     76 72 79 Kilmichael
     80 87 91 Martinez
   [EOB]
         [GOLD]
       [UNDELETE WORD]
```

You can use the [DELETE LINE] key and the [UNDELETE LINE] key to delete and move and copy lines. Move the cursor to the beginning of the record for Haroldson.

```
     69 85 84 Camaro
     75 70 79 Bentley
     99 99 99 Asford_
     80 80 80 Dixon
   6 91 94 89 Foxley666
     88 82 93 Garr
     70 69 74 Haroldson
     92 89 96 Israelson
     76 72 79 Kilmichael
     80 87 91 Martinez
   [EOB]
       [Move cursor to beginning of Haroldson record]
```

Use the [DELETE LINE] key to delete the line.

```
    69 85 84 Asford
    75 70 79 Bentley
    99 99 99 Camaro
    80 80 80 Dixon
    91 94 89 Foxley
    88 82 93 Garr
   _70 69 74 Haroldson
    92 89 96 Israelson
    76 72 79 Kilmichael
    80 87 91 Martinez
   [EOB]
                       [DEL LINE]
```

The Haroldson line is deleted. The line for Haroldson which was deleted is stored in a buffer. The [UNDELETE LINE] function can be used to restore the line at the current position, or you can use the [UNDELETE LINE] function to move the line to another position in the file. For this example move the line to another position. First you need to move the cursor to the position where you want to insert the line.

```
    69 85 84 Camaro
    75 70 79 Bentley
    99 99 99 Asford
    80 80 80 Dixon
   6 91 94 89 Foxley666
    88 82 93 Garr
   _92 89 96 Israelson
    76 72 79 Kilmichael
    80 87 91 Martinez
   [EOB]
   [Move the cursor to the beginning of the Bentley record]
```

Now press the [GOLD] key and then the [UNDELETE LINE] key to move the Harolson record.

```
    69 85 84 Camaro
   _75 70 79 Bentley
    99 99 99 Asford
    80 80 80 Dixon
   6 91 94 89 Foxley666
    88 82 93 Garr
    92 89 96 Israelson
    76 72 79 Kilmichael
    80 87 91 Martinez
   [EOB]
               [GOLD]
               [UNDELETE LINE]
```

End the KEYPAD edit session with a [CTRL/Z].

```
 69 85 84 Camaro
 70 69 74 Haroldson_
 75 70 79 Bentley
 99 99 99 Asford
 80 80 80 Dixon
6 91 94 89 Foxley666
 88 82 93 Garr
 92 89 96 Israelson
 76 72 79 Kilmichael
 80 87 91 Martinez
[EOB]
                      [CTRL/Z]
```

Use the QUIT command and observe that this version of your file is not saved. The previous version of the file is saved and unaltered when you use the QUIT command.

```
[EOB]

* QUIT
```

In this example, you see that you can use the DELETE and UNDELETE function keys to restore, move and copy characters, words and lines.

Now you have a dollar sign on the screen. You can enter a command to begin another task.

USING THE EDT EDITOR KEYPAD FUNCTIONS
MOVING SEGMENTS OF TEXT
DELETING SEGMENTS OF TEXT
[SELECT] [CUT] [PASTE]

The [SELECT] and [CUT] functions of the keypad editor can be used to delete a section of text from a file. The [PASTE] function of the keypad editor allows you to restore deleted text and to move or copy the selected sections of text within a file.

Moving text means that you take a section of text from one place in a file and move it to another place in the file. Copying text means that you create a copy of a section of text at some place in a file while retaining the text at the original location in the file.

This example illustrates how to move a section of text from one location in the file to another location in the file.

Begin another edit session with the file which is saved with the name NEWCLASS.DAT. Enter the EDT command and your filename and press [RETURN]. After the VAX prints the first line of your file, you should type the CHANGE command and press [RETURN].

```
$ EDT NEWCLASS.DAT
  1 69 82 84 Asford
[EOB]
* CHANGE
```

The records from your file are printed on the screen.

```
_69 82 84 Asford
 75 70 79 Bentley
 99 99 99 Camaro
 80 80 80 Dendy
 91 94 89 Foxley
 88 82 93 Garr
 70 69 74 Haroldson
 92 89 96 Israelson
 76 72 79 Kilmichael
 80 87 91 Martinez
[EOB]
```

The concept of deleting, moving and copying text is the same as the concept of deleting, moving and copying characters, words and lines in the previous section.

Assume that you want to move the records for Camaro through Foxley to the end of your file.

```
69 82 84 Asford
75 70 79 Bentley
99 99 99 Camaro    ----------
80 80 80 Dendy                 |--->------|
91 94 89 Foxley   ----------            |
88 82 93 Garr                           |
70 69 74 Haroldson                      |
92 89 96 Israelson                      |
76 72 79 Kilmichael                     |
80 87 91 Martinez                       |
                  <-------------------|
```

Press the [LINE] key twice to move the cursor to the beginning of the record for Camaro.

```
_69 82 84 Asford
 75 70 79 Bentley
 99 99 99 Camaro
 80 80 80 Dendy
 91 94 89 Foxley
 88 82 93 Garr
 70 69 74 Haroldson
 92 89 96 Israelson
 76 72 79 Kilmichael
 80 87 91 Martinez
[EOB]
          Press the [LINE] key twice.
```

The cursor is at the beginning of the line for Camaro. In order to use the EDT editor to move the three records for Camaro, Dendy and Foxley, you need to SELECT a region which includes the three records. With the cursor at the top of the region of text which you want to move, you press the [SELECT] key. Then you will move the cursor to

the bottom of the section of text which you want to move and press the
[CUT] key. With the SELECT and CUT keys, you select a region of
text which you want to move.

For now, press the [SELECT] key.

```
      69 82 84 Asford
      75 70 79 Bentley
     _99 99 99 Camaro
      80 80 80 Dendy
      91 94 89 Foxley
      88 82 93 Garr
      70 69 74 Haroldson
      92 89 96 Israelson
      76 72 79 Kilmichael
      80 87 91 Martinez
     [EOB]
                     [SELECT]
```

The first character location in the record Camaro has been selected
as the first location in the SELECT field. Now press the [LINE] key
once to include the record for Camaro in the SELECT field.

```
      69 82 84 Asford
      75 70 79 Bentley
     _99 99 99 Camaro
      80 80 80 Dendy
      91 94 89 Foxley
      88 82 93 Garr
      70 69 74 Haroldson
      92 89 96 Israelson
      76 72 79 Kilmichael
      80 87 91 Martinez
     [EOB]
                     [LINE]
```

Notice that the line which you SELECTED is printed black on white
on the screen to indicate that this line is in the SELECT region. Now
press the [LINE] key twice to move the cursor down to the beginning
of the record for Garr. By moving the cursor to the beginning of the
record for Garr, you have moved the cursor past the RETURN code for
the record Foxley. If you do not include the RETURN code at the end
of the line, you will be left with a blank line.

```
      69 82 84 Asford
      75 70 79 Bentley
     /99/99/99/Camaro/
     _80 80 80 Dendy
      91 94 89 Foxley
      88 82 93 Garr
      70 69 74 Haroldson
      92 89 96 Israelson
      76 72 79 Kilmichael
      80 87 91 Martinez
     [EOB]
                     Press the [LINE] key twice
```

Now you have the block of records which you want to select in the
SELECT FIELD. Notice that all the lines which you SELECTED are

printed black on white on the screen to indicate that these lines are in the SELECT region. Now press the [CUT] key to enter the SELECTED lines in a buffer so that you can move the records.

```
    69 82 84 Asford
    75 70 79 Bentley
    /99/99/99/Camaro/
    /80/80/80/Dendy/
    /91/94/89/Foxley/
    /88 82 93 Garr
    70 69 74 Haroldson
    92 89 96 Israelson
    76 72 79 Kilmichael
    80 87 91 Martinez
    [EOB]
                  [CUT]
```

Now the records for Camaro, Dendy and Foxley are stored in a buffer where you can use them to move the records to a new location.

When you press the [SELECT] key and then select a region of text by moving the cursor to another point and then pressing the [CUT] key, the text included in the selected region is deleted from the screen.

```
    69 82 84 Asford
    75 70 79 Bentley
   _88 82 93 Garr
    70 69 74 Haroldson
    92 89 96 Israelson
    76 72 79 Kilmichael
    80 87 91 Martinez
    [EOB]
```

These three records will remain in the buffer until you select another range of records with the [SELECT] and [CUT] keys.

At this point, you have deleted the text. If you want only to delete text, you need do no more. The [PASTE] key could be used to restore the deleted text into the same location in your file from which the text came.

Since the three records which you want to move are stored in the text buffer, you can easily move those records to another location in your file. First, you need to move the cursor to the location in the file where you want to move the records, that is the end of this file marked by the End of Buffer, [EOB], marker. Move the cursor with the [LINE] key to the [EOB] marker.

```
    69 82 84 Asford
    75 70 79 Bentley
   _88 82 93 Garr
    70 69 74 Haroldson
    92 89 96 Israelson
    76 72 79 Kilmichael
    80 87 91 Martinez
    [EOB]
       [Use [LINE] key to move the cursor]
       [to the end of buffer, [EOB], marker ]
```

Now press the [GOLD] key and then the [PASTE] key. The selected text which you have stored in a buffer is put in your file at the point where the cursor is located.

```
69 82 84 Asford
75 70 79 Bentley
88 82 93 Garr
70 69 74 Haroldson
92 89 96 Israelson
76 72 79 Kilmichael
80 87 91 Martinez

[EOB]
                    [GOLD]
                    [PASTE]
```

Now the records which were in your text buffer are inserted at the end of your main buffer displayed on the screen.

You have used the [SELECT] and [CUT] keys to select the lines of text to be stored in a text buffer. Then you moved the cursor to the position where you wanted to move the selected text. Finally, you used the [GOLD] and [PASTE] keys to insert the text at the cursor position.

Terminate the keypad edit session with a [CTRL/Z].

```
69 82 84 Asford
75 70 79 Bentley
88 82 93 Garr
70 69 74 Haroldson
92 89 96 Israelson
76 72 79 Kilmichael
80 87 91 Martinez
99 99 99 Camaro
80 80 80 Dendy
91 94 89 Foxley _
                [CTRL/Z]
[EOB]
```

Use the QUIT command to end the edit session without saving the edit session.

```
[EOB]
* QUIT
```

USING THE EDT EDITOR KEYPAD FUNCTIONS
COPYING SEGMENTS OF TEXT
[SELECT] [CUT] [PASTE]

The [SELECT] and [CUT] functions of the keypad editor can be used to delete a section of text from a file. The [PASTE] function of the keypad editor allows you to restore deleted text and to move or copy the selected sections of text within a file.

This example illustrates how to copy a section of text into a new location in the text while retaining the text in the original location. The following procedure is used for copying with the EDT editor. Press the [SELECT] key to mark one border of the text to be copied and then press the [CUT] key to mark the second border. After you have SELECTED and CUT the text, that text is in a buffer making the text available either for moving or copying. You immediately press the [PASTE] key to put the text back into the location where it was originally. The text is still in the buffer after the paste, so you move the cursor to the location where you want to copy the text and paste again.

Begin another edit session with the file which is saved with the name NEWCLASS.DAT. Enter the EDT command and your filename and press the [RETURN] key. After the VAX prints the first line of your file, you should type the CHANGE command and press the [RETURN] key.

```
$ EDT NEWCLASS.DAT
1 69 82 84 Asford
[EOB]
* CHANGE
```

The records from your file are printed on the screen.

```
_69 82 84 Asford
 75 70 79 Bentley
 99 99 99 Camaro
 80 80 80 Dendy
 91 94 89 Foxley
 88 82 93 Garr
 70 69 74 Haroldson
 92 89 96 Israelson
 76 72 79 Kilmichael
 80 87 91 Martinez
[EOB]
```

Assume that you want to copy the records for Camaro through Foxley at the end of your file.

```
69 82 84 Asford
75 70 79 Bentley
99 99 99 Camaro    ----------
80 80 80 Dendy               |--->------|
91 94 89 Foxley    ----------           |
88 82 93 Garr                           |
70 69 74 Haroldson                      |
92 89 96 Israelson                      |
76 72 79 Kilmichael                     |
80 87 91 Martinez                       |
99 99 99 Camaro    ----------           |
80 80 80 Dendy               |---<------|
91 94 89 Foxley    ----------
```

Press the [LINE] key twice to move the cursor to the beginning of the record for Camaro.

```
 _69 82 84 Asford
  75 70 79 Bentley
  99 99 99 Camaro
  80 80 80 Dendy
  91 94 89 Foxley
  88 82 93 Garr
  70 69 74 Haroldson
  92 89 96 Israelson
  76 72 79 Kilmichael
  80 87 91 Martinez
 [EOB]
                Press the [LINE] key twice.
```

The cursor is at the beginning of the line for Camaro. In order to use the EDT editor to copy the three records for Camaro, Dendy and Foxley, you need to SELECT a region which includes the three records. With the cursor at the top of the region of text which you want to copy, you press the [SELECT] key. Then you will move the cursor to the bottom of the section of text which you want to copy and press the [CUT] key. With the SELECT and CUT keys, you select a region of text which you want to copy.

For now, press the [SELECT] key.

```
  69 82 84 Asford
  75 70 79 Bentley
 _99 99 99 Camaro
  80 80 80 Dendy
  91 94 89 Foxley
  88 82 93 Garr
  70 69 74 Haroldson
  92 89 96 Israelson
  76 72 79 Kilmichael
  80 87 91 Martinez
 [EOB]
                  [SELECT]
```

The first character location in the record Camaro has been selected as the first location in the SELECT field. Now press the [LINE] key once to include the record for Camaro in the SELECT field.

```
  69 82 84 Asford
  75 70 79 Bentley
 _99 99 99 Camaro
  80 80 80 Dendy
  91 94 89 Foxley
  88 82 93 Garr
  70 69 74 Haroldson
  92 89 96 Israelson
  76 72 79 Kilmichael
  80 87 91 Martinez
 [EOB]
                  [LINE]
```

Notice that the line which you SELECTED is printed black on white on the screen to indicate that this line is in the SELECT region. Now press the [LINE] key twice to move the cursor down to the beginning of the record for Garr. By moving the cursor to the beginning of the record for Garr, you have moved the cursor past the RETURN code for

the record Foxley. If you do not include the RETURN code at the end
of the line, you will be left with a blank line.

```
  69 82 84 Asford
  75 70 79 Bentley
/99/99/99/Camaro/
_80 80 80 Dendy
  91 94 89 Foxley
  88 82 93 Garr
  70 69 74 Haroldson
  92 89 96 Israelson
  73 72 79 Kilmichael
  80 87 91 Martinez
[EOB]
                Press the [LINE] key twice
```

Now you have the block of records which you want to select in the
SELECT FIELD. Notice that all the lines which you SELECTED are
printed black on white on the screen to indicate that these lines are in
the SELECT region. Now press the [CUT] key to enter the SELECTED
lines in a buffer so that you can move the records.

```
  69 82 84 Asford
  75 70 79 Bentley
/99/99/99/Camaro/
/80/80/80/Dendy/
/91/94/89/Foxley/
/88 82 93 Garr
  70 69 74 Haroldson
  92 89 96 Israelson
  76 72 79 Kilmichael
  80 87 91 Martinez
[EOB]
                [CUT]
```

Now the records for Camaro, Dendy and Foxley are stored in a
buffer where you can use them to copy the records to a new location.

When you press the [SELECT] key and then select a region of text
by moving the cursor to another point and then pressing the [CUT]
key, the text included in the selected region is deleted from the
screen.

```
  69 82 84 Asford
  75 70 79 Bentley
_88 82 93 Garr
  70 69 74 Haroldson
  92 89 96 Israelson
  76 72 79 Kilmichael
  80 87 91 Martinez
[EOB]
                [CUT]
```

These three records will remain in the text buffer until you select
another range of records with the [SELECT] and [CUT] keys.

At this point, you have deleted the text and stored the text in a text buffer. Press the [GOLD] key and then the [PASTE] key to insert the deleted text into the original location in your file.

```
69 82 84 Asford
75 70 79 Bentley
_88 82 93 Garr
70 69 74 Haroldson
92 89 96 Israelson
76 72 79 Kilmichael
80 87 91 Martinez
[EOB]
              [GOLD] [PASTE]
```

Pasting the records back into the same location in the text from which the text was cut is the first part of copying text. The file now looks as it did before the [CUT].

```
69 82 84 Asford
75 70 79 Bentley
99 99 99 Camaro
80 80 80 Dendy
91 94 89 Foxley
_88 82 93 Garr
70 69 74 Haroldson
92 89 96 Israelson
76 72 79 Kilmichael
80 87 91 Martinez
[EOB]
```

Since the three records which you want to copy are stored in the text buffer, now you can copy those records to another location in your file. First, you need to move the cursor to the location in the file where you want to move the records; that is the end of this file which is marked by the end of buffer [EOB] marker. Move the cursor with the [LINE] key to the [EOB] marker.

```
69 82 84 Asford
75 70 79 Bentley
99 99 99 Camaro
80 80 80 Dendy
91 94 89 Foxley
_88 82 93 Garr
70 69 74 Haroldson
92 89 96 Israelson
76 72 79 Kilmichael
80 87 91 Martinez
[EOB]
   [Press the [LINE] key to move the cursor]
   [to the end of buffer, [EOB], marker ]
```

Now press the [GOLD] key and then the [PASTE] key. The selected text which you have stored in a buffer is put into your file at the point where the cursor is located.

```
     69 82 84 Asford
     75 70 79 Bentley
     99 99 99 Camaro
     80 80 80 Dendy
     91 94 89 Foxley
     88 82 93 Garr
     70 69 74 Haroldson
     92 89 96 Israelson
     76 72 79 Kilmichael
     80 87 91 Martinez
    _[EOB]
                [GOLD]  [PASTE]
```

Now the records which are in your text buffer are inserted at the end of your main buffer displayed on the screen.

You have used the [SELECT] and [CUT] keys to select the lines of text to be stored in a text buffer. You have used the [GOLD] and [PASTE] keys to insert the text at the original location in the text. Then you moved the cursor to the position where you wanted to copy the selected text. Finally, you used the [GOLD] and [PASTE] keys to insert the text at the cursor position.

Terminate the keypad edit session with a [CTRL/Z].

```
     69 82 84 Asford
     75 70 79 Bentley
     99 99 99 Camaro
     80 80 80 Dendy
     91 94 89 Foxley
     88 82 93 Garr
     70 69 74 Haroldson
     92 89 96 Israelson
     76 72 79 Kilmichael
     80 87 91 Martinez
     99 99 99 Camaro
     80 80 80 Dendy
     91 94 89 Foxley _
    [EOB]
                [CTRL/Z]
```

Use the QUIT command to end the edit session without saving the edit session.

```
     [EOB]
    * QUIT
```

USING THE EDT EDITOR KEYPAD FUNCTIONS
FINDING TEXT
[FIND] [FINDNEXT]

The keypad FIND command can be used to locate a string of characters in a file.

```
$ EDT NEWCLASS.DAT
 1 69 82 84 Asford
 [EOB]
 * CHANGE
```

The records from your file are printed on the screen.

```
_69 82 84 Asford
 75 70 79 Bentley
 99 99 99 Camaro
 80 80 80 Dendy
 91 94 89 Foxley
 88 82 93 Garr
 70 69 74 Haroldson
 92 89 96 Israelson
 76 72 79 Kilmichael
 80 87 91 Martinez
 [EOB]
```

You might need to find the name, ISRAELSON. First press the [GOLD] key and then the [FIND] key.

```
_69 82 84 Asford
 75 70 79 Bentley
 99 99 99 Camaro
 80 80 80 Dendy
 91 94 89 Foxley
 88 82 93 Garr
 70 69 74 Haroldson
 92 89 96 Israelson
 76 72 79 Kilmichael
 80 87 91 Martinez
 [EOB]
            [GOLD] [FIND]
```

A message is printed on the screen asking for the text you want to find. You should enter the text to find and press the [ENTER] key if you wish to search in the same direction that the line pointer is moving through your file. You can specify the direction for the search by pressing either the [ADVANCE] or [BACKUP] key.

```
_69 82 84 Asford
 75 70 79 Bentley
 99 99 99 Camaro
 80 80 80 Dendy
 91 94 89 Foxley
 88 82 93 Garr
 70 69 74 Haroldson
 92 89 96 Israelson
 76 72 79 Kilmichael
 80 87 91 Martinez
 [EOB]
 Search for: Israelson
             [ADVANCE]
```

The cursor is moved to the first character in the name, Israelson.

You might want to find the occurrence of the grade 89 in the BACKUP direction. First press the [GOLD] key and then the [FIND] key.

```
       69 82 84 Asford
       75 70 79 Bentley
       99 99 99 Camaro
       80 80 80 Dendy
       91 94 89 Foxley
       88 82 93 Garr
       70 69 74 Haroldson
       92 89 96 Israelson
       76 72 79 Kilmichael
       80 87 91 Martinez
       [EOB]
                   [GOLD] [FIND]
```

A message is printed on the screen asking for the text you want to find. Specify the direction for the search by pressing the [BACKUP] key.

```
       69 82 84 Asford
       75 70 79 Bentley
       99 99 99 Camaro
       80 80 80 Dendy
       91 94 89 Foxley
       88 82 93 Garr
       70 69 74 Haroldson
       92 89 96 Israelson
       76 72 79 Kilmichael
       80 87 91 Martinez
       [EOB]
       Search for: 89
                   [BACKUP]
```

The cursor is moved to the 89 in the BACKUP direction.

```
       69 82 84 Asford
       75 70 79 Bentley
       99 99 99 Camaro
       80 80 80 Dendy
       91 94 89 Foxley
       88 82 93 Garr
       70 69 74 Haroldson
       92 89 96 Israelson
       76 72 79 Kilmichael
       80 87 91 Martinez
       [EOB]
```

You could use the [FINDNEXT] key following a find command to find the next occurrence of the characters specified in the previous find command.

```
┌─────────────────────────────────────────────────┐
│    69 82 84 Asford                               │
│    75 70 79 Bentley                              │
│    99 99 99 Camaro                               │
│    80 80 80 Dendy                                │
│    91 94 89 Foxley                               │
│    88 82 93 Garr                                 │
│    70 69 74 Haroldson                            │
│    92 89 96 Israelson                            │
│    76 72 79 Kilmichael                           │
│    80 87 91 Martinez                             │
│   [EOB]                                          │
│                    [FINDNEXT]                    │
└─────────────────────────────────────────────────┘
```

The cursor moves to the next set of the specified characters, 89, in the BACKUP direction since that was the direction specified.

```
┌─────────────────────────────────────────────────┐
│    69 82 84 Asford                               │
│    75 70 79 Bentley                              │
│    99 99 99 Camaro                               │
│    80 80 80 Dendy                                │
│    91 94 89 Foxley                               │
│    88 82 93 Garr                                 │
│    70 69 74 Haroldson                            │
│    92 89 96 Israelson                            │
│    76 72 79 Kilmichael                           │
│    80 87 91 Martinez                             │
│   [EOB]                                          │
│                    [FINDNEXT]                    │
└─────────────────────────────────────────────────┘
```

You could continue to use the [FINDNEXT] key to find all the occurrences of 89 in the file in the [BACKUP] direction.

If your file fills more than one screen of print, the search will continue through the file whether the search string is on the screen or not. You can quit the edit session for this example and terminate the keypad edit session with a [CTRL/Z].

```
┌─────────────────────────────────────────────────┐
│    69 82 84 Asford                               │
│    75 70 79 Bentley                              │
│    99 99 99 Camaro                               │
│    80 80 80 Dendy                                │
│    91 94 i Foxley                                │
│    88 82 93 Garr                                 │
│    70 69 74 Haroldson                            │
│    92 89 96 Israelson                            │
│    76 72 79 Kilmichael                           │
│    80 87 91 Martinez                             │
│                      [CTRL/Z]                    │
│   [EOB]                                          │
└─────────────────────────────────────────────────┘
```

Use the QUIT command to end the edit session without saving the edit session.

```
┌─────────────────────────────────────────────────┐
│    [EOB]                                         │
│    * QUIT                                        │
└─────────────────────────────────────────────────┘
```

A.5

DISPLAYING, PRINTING, AND DELETING FILES DIRECTORY

You can display a file at your terminal with the TYPE command.
$ type filename.ext
If the file GRADES.DAT is in your directory, you can display that file at the terminal.

`$ type grades.dat`

The output is displayed at the terminal.

You can print a file in your directory on the printer.
$ print filename.ext
You can print your file named GRADES.DAT.

`$ print grades.dat`

The file is printed on a printer.

There is a limited amount of space on the disk packs for the VAX. You should delete all files which you do not need.

The following directory is used for an example. The files with extensions .FOR would probably be FORTRAN program source code. The files with extensions .EXE are files which contain executable code.

```
$ directory
AMOUNTS.EXE;2    AMOUNTS.FOR;3    COSTDAT.DAT;2    PRICE.DAT;1
PRINTCOST.EXE;1  PRINTCOST.FOR;1  TREES.DAT;4
```

You can delete a particular file by specifying the filename, the extension and the version number. If there is only one version of the file, you can delete the file simply by using the delete command with the filename and extension followed by a period.

```
$ del price.dat;1    (or $ del price.dat.)
$ directory
AMOUNTS.EXE;2    AMOUNTS.FOR;3    COSTDAT.DAT;2    PRINTCOST.EXE;1
PRINTCOST.FOR;1  TREES.DAT;4
```

An asterisk in the position of the filename means that all filenames are referenced. The asterisk is called a wild card. An asterisk in the position of the extension means that all extensions are referenced. An asterisk in the position of the version number means that all versions are referenced. You can delete all the files with a particular extension by specifying the extension and putting asterisks for wild cards in the filename position and the version number position. The following command deletes all the executable files.

```
$ del *.exe;*
$ directory
  AMOUNTS.FOR;3   COSTDAT.DAT;2   PRINTCOST.FOR;1 TREES.DAT;4
```

You can delete all the files with the filename PRINTCOST with the following command. This command will select all versions with all extensions for files with the filename PRINTCOST. In this case, both the EXEcutable code and the FORtran code are deleted.

```
$ del printcost.*;*
$ directory
  AMOUNTS.FOR;3   COSTDAT.DAT;2   TREES.DAT;4
```

You can use an asterisk to specify all versions even if there is only one version of a particular filename in the directory.

```
$ del costdat.dat;*
$ directory
  AMOUNTS.FOR;3   TREES.DAT;4
```

The asterisks provide an easy way to access files on the VAX, but you must be careful with asterisks. You can delete all versions of all files with the following command.

```
$ del *.*;*
$ directory
  No files found
```

You can use the DIRECTORY/FULL command to look at the attributes of all your files. You can specify a filename to observe the attributes with DIRECTORY/FULL.

```
$ DIR/FULL
  output not shown
  output would include file attributes for all your files
$DIR/FULL filename.ext
  output not shown
  output would be the file attributes for the file specified
```

APPENDIX B
An Introduction to
Running FORTRAN Programs
on the VAX

CREATING, COMPILING, LINKING, AND RUNNING THE PROGRAM

To create and run a FORTRAN program on the VAX, you need to do the following:

```
first:   Enter and save program instructions
              EDIT filename.for
second:  Compile the program
              FORTRAN filename
third:   Link the program
              LINK filename
fourth:  Run the program
              RUN filename
```

Look at the following FORTRAN program. The program represents the calculation of some pay based on a rate and hours worked.

```
RATE = 4.00
HOURS = 3.0
PAY = RATE * HOURS
PRINT *, 'PAY IS',PAY
STOP
END
```

The names, RATE, HOURS, and PAY are called SYMBOLIC NAMES or VARIABLE NAMES. A SYMBOLIC NAME consists of 31 characters or fewer and can contain letters, numbers and the underline character.

When the statements in the program are executed, the program stores each of two numbers in a memory location, multiplies the two numbers together, stores the result, and finally displays the result at the terminal.

You start by entering the statements in the program using the editor. You should actually go through the tutorial in Appendix A at the terminal before beginning to enter a FORTRAN program.

473

Enter the EDIT command and your filename and press the [RETURN] key.

```
$ edit payone.for
  Input file does not exist
  [EOB]
*
```

Enter the INSERT command if you are using the EDT line editor. Enter the CHANGE command if you are using the EDT full-screen editor. Refer to Appendix A for details about using the EDT editor.

Enter each FORTRAN statement, pressing the [RETURN] key after each statement. All FORTRAN statements in this example must begin in column seven or beyond. (Statement numbers can be used with statements. If statement numbers are used, the statement numbers should begin in column one.) The [TAB] key on the keyboard moves the cursor over to column 9 to begin entering your FORTRAN statements. Press the [RETURN] key after entering each statement in the program.

SPECIAL NOTE ABOUT USING THE EDT LINE EDITOR

When you enter the INSERT mode in the EDT line editor, you will be in column 16 on the screen, but that is really column one for a FORTRAN program. Since FORTRAN statements must begin in column seven or beyond, use the [TAB] key to move to column nine to start entering FORTRAN statements.

```
      RATE = 4.00
      HOURS = 3.0
      PAY = RATE * HOURS
      PRINT *, 'PAY IS',PAY
      STOP
      END

[EOB]
```

[Use the TAB key to move the cursor over before each statement.]
[Press the [RETURN] key after typing each statement.   ]

[Use [CTRL/Z] to end the insert mode.   ]
[Save the file and end the edit session with the EXIT command.]

After the program is entered and saved with the editor, you need to enter:
the FORTRAN command to translate the program into machine code
the LINK command to link the code into executable code
the RUN command to execute the instructions in the program.

Enter the FORTRAN command to compile the program, that is to translate the instructions into machine code.

$ fortran payone

IF THERE ARE SYNTAX ERRORS IN THE PROGRAM, ERROR MESSAGES WILL BE DISPLAYED. If there are syntax errors, you will need to use the editor to modify your program.

BEGIN ANOTHER EDIT SESSION and use the commands in the editor to make changes in your file if there are errors in the program. With the editor, you can add records to the file, delete records from the file or modify records in the file. A tutorial for entering and modifying files is in Appendix A.

After the program is successfully compiled, enter the LINK command to link the instructions in the program into executable form.

$ link payone

When you enter the RUN command, the instructions in the program are executed.

$ run payone

The output is displayed at the terminal.

PAY IS 12.00
FORTRAN STOP

The following is a brief description of the statements in the program. The first three statements are ASSIGNMENT STATEMENTS. An ASSIGNMENT STATEMENT specifies that the value of the expression on the right of the equal sign be stored in the memory location specified on the left of the equal sign.

$$RATE = 4.00$$
$$HOURS = 3.0$$
$$PAY = RATE * HOURS$$

The PRINT statement directs output. The PRINT statement specifies that the 'PAY IS' characters between single quotation marks and the value in the location named PAY be displayed at the terminal.

PRINT *, 'PAY IS',PAY

Characters between single quotes in a PRINT statement are displayed just as they appear between the quotes. A symbolic name without quotation marks in a PRINT statement indicates that the value which is stored in that location should be displayed.

CREATING A LISTING OF A PROGRAM
LISTING ERROR MESSAGES

You can use the LIST option with the FORTRAN command to produce a file containing your program along with compile information and error messages attached to particular statements if there are syntax errors.

```
$ fortran/list payone
```

Display the list file at the terminal with the TYPE command or print the list file to observe the location of the syntax errors in your program.

```
$ type payone.lis
$ print payone.lis
```

If there are errors in the program, begin another edit session and use the commands in the editor to make changes in your file. With the editor, you can add records to the file, delete records from the file or modify records in the file. A tutorial for entering and modifying files is in Appendix A.

After the program compiles with no error messages, enter the LINK command to produce executable code and the RUN command to execute the instructions in your program.

```
$ link payone
$ run payone
```

The output is displayed.

```
PAY IS 12.00
FORTRAN STOP
```

ACCEPTING INPUT FROM THE TERMINAL
DISPLAYING OUTPUT AT THE TERMINAL

Create the FORTRAN program file with the editor. Unit 5 is by default assigned to input from the terminal. Unit 6 is by default assigned to output to the terminal.

```
$ edit termio.for

    WRITE(6,*)'Enter value one.'
    READ(5,*)VALUE1
    WRITE(6,*)'Enter value two.'
    READ(5,*)VALUE2
    AVERAGE = (VALUE1 + VALUE2) / 2.0
    WRITE(6,*)'The average value is',AVERAGE
    STOP
    END
```

Enter the FORTRAN command to compile the program, that is to translate the program into machine code.

```
$ fortran termio
```

Enter the LINK command to produce executable code.

```
$ link termio
```
Enter the RUN command to begin executing the instructions in the program one after another.

```
$ run termio
```
The first WRITE statement causes the message 'Enter Value One' to be displayed at the terminal.

```
Enter value one.
4.4
```
You should enter a value.

The prompt from the second WRITE statement is displayed at the terminal.

```
Enter value two.
2.2
```
You should enter the second value.

The calculated output is displayed when the third WRITE statement is executed.

```
The average value is      3.300000
```

PROVIDING INPUT FROM A DATA FILE
SENDING OUTPUT TO A DATA FILE
PRINTING THE OUTPUT

```
$ edit fortfile.dat
   4,9.7
   8,4.5
```
Create and save an input data file with two records using the editor. Refer to Appendix A for details about entering files.

Then create and save the FORTRAN program file with the editor. The file unit numbers of 11 and 12 are arbitrary.

```
$ edit fortfile.for

          OPEN (11,FILE='FORTFILE.DAT',STATUS='OLD')
          OPEN (12,FILE='FORTFILE.OUT',STATUS='NEW')
          READ (11,*) A,B
          AVERAGE = (A+B) / 2.0
          WRITE(12,*) AVERAGE
          READ (11,*) C,D
          DIFFERENCE = D - C
          WRITE(12,*) DIFFERENCE
          CLOSE(11)
          CLOSE(12)
          STOP
          END
$ fortran fortfile
$ link fortfile
$ run fortfile
```
Now compile link and run the program.

The first READ statement copies the two values 4 and 9.7 from the file named FORTFILE.DAT into the memory locations A and B. The next statement calculates the average of the two values. Then the first WRITE statement copies the value stored in memory location AVERAGE into the file named FORTFILE.OUT.

The second READ statement copies the two values from the second record into the memory locations named C and D in the program. The value in memory location named C is then subtracted from the memory location named D. The second WRITE statement copies the value stored in the memory location named DIFFERENCE to the output data file named FORTFILE.OUT.

After the program executes, the output from the two WRITE statements is stored in the file named FORTFILE.OUT. You can display that file at the terminal.

```
$ type fortfile.out
   6.850000
  -3.500000
```

You can PRINT the file on the printer.

```
$ print fortfile.out
```

ACCEPTING INPUT FROM THE TERMINAL AND A DISK FILE
DISPLAYING OUTPUT AT THE TERMINAL

First create and save the data file for input to the program.

```
$ edit values.dat
3
4
1
2
5
```

Create the FORTRAN program file with the editor. Unit 5 is by default assigned to input from the terminal. Unit 6 is by default assigned to output to the terminal. Unit 11 is an arbitrary number used for the disk file unit.

```
$edit varyname.for
C      This program prompts the user to enter the name of the
C      file where a set of data is stored.  Then the program
C      opens that file and reads the data from the file.

       CHARACTER FILENAME*20
       WRITE(6,*)'Enter name of file where data is stored.'
       READ(5,100)FILENAME
100    FORMAT(A)

       OPEN(11,FILE=FILENAME,STATUS='OLD')
       TOTAL = 0
       DO NUM = 1,5
          READ(11,*)VALUE
          TOTAL = TOTAL + VALUE
       END DO
       WRITE(6,*)'Total value is',TOTAL
       STOP
       END
```

```
$ fortran varyname
$ link varyname
$ run varyname
```

The program displays the prompt.

Enter name of file where data is stored.

You enter the filename in upper or lower case letters.

values.dat

The program reads the data from the file, calculates the total and displays the result at the terminal.

Total value is   15.0000

READING TO THE END OF FILE

First create and save the input data file using the editor.

```
$ edit convert.dat
   0
  32
  50
  70
 100
 212
```

Create the FORTRAN program file with the editor. The OPEN statements link the READ and WRITE statements to the external data files. The IOSTAT option in the READ statement is a flag which is zero as long as a READ statement executes successfully. When an end of file is reached and there are no more data records, the flag is set to a positive number. The program can check that flag to see if there are any more records in the file.

```
$ edit convert.for
        OPEN(1,FILE='CONVERT.DAT',STATUS='OLD')
        OPEN(2,FILE='CONVERT.OUT',STATUS='NEW')
  100   FORMAT(F3.0)
  200   FORMAT(F6.1)

        READ(1,100,IOSTAT=IEND)DEGREE
        DO WHILE (IEND.EQ.0)
           CELSIUS = 5.0 / 9.0 *  (DEGREE - 32.0)
           WRITE (2,200)CELSIUS
           READ(1,100,IOSTAT=IEND)DEGREE
        END DO

        CLOSE(1)
        CLOSE(2)
        STOP
        END
```

```
$ fortran convert          Compile link and run the program.
$ link convert
$ run convert              As the program executes, the output is stored
                           in a file named CONVERT.OUT.
$ type convert.out         You can display the output at the terminal
-17.8                      with the TYPE command.
  0.0
 10.0
 21.1
 37.8
100.0

$ print convert.out        You can print the output on a printer.
```

SUBMITTING A JOB FROM CARDS

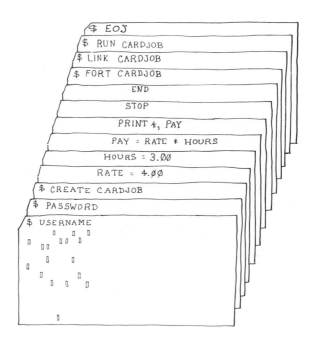

Figure B.1

APPENDIX C
FORTRAN Structures:
Quick Reference

DO LOOPS

```
$ edit doloop.for
      WRITE(6,*)'The standard DO LOOP'
      DO 10 I = 1,4
         WRITE(6,*)'I=',I
10    CONTINUE

      WRITE(6,*)'VAX DO LOOP with END DO'
      DO J = 1,3
         WRITE(6,*)'J=',J
      END DO

      WRITE(6,*)'The DO WHILE LOOP which executes for as long as',
     -          'the condition in the DO statement is true.'
      KOUNT = 0
      DO 20 WHILE (KOUNT.LT.5)
         KOUNT = KOUNT + 1
         WRITE(6,*)'KOUNT=',KOUNT
20    CONTINUE

      WRITE(6,*)'The DO WHILE LOOP without the statement number'
      NUMBER = 7
      DO WHILE (NUMBER.GT.4)
         NUMBER = NUMBER - 1
         WRITE(6,*)'NUMBER=',NUMBER
      END DO

      WRITE(6,*)'Nested DO LOOP - For each time through the outside',
     -          'DO LOOP, the inside loop is executed the number',
     -          'of times specified.'
      DO LOOPOUTSIDE = 1,2
         WRITE(6,*)'LOOP OUTSIDE = ',LOOPOUTSIDE
         DO LOOPINSIDE = 1,3
            WRITE(6,*)'    LOOP INSIDE =',LOOPINSIDE
         END DO
      END DO

      STOP
      END
$ fortran doloop
$ link doloop
$ run doloop

The standard DO LOOP                              Output
 I=            1
 I=            2
 I=            3
 I=            4
```

```
VAX DO LOOP with END DO
J=            1
J=            2
J=            3
The DO WHILE LOOP which executes for as long as
the condition in the DO statement is true.
KOUNT=            1
KOUNT=            2
KOUNT=            3
KOUNT=            4
KOUNT=            5
The DO WHILE LOOP without the statement number
NUMBER=            6
NUMBER=            5
NUMBER=            4
Nested DO LOOP - For each time through the outside
DO LOOP, the inside loop is executed the numberof times specified.
LOOP OUTSIDE =            1
     LOOP INSIDE =            1
     LOOP INSIDE =            2
     LOOP INSIDE =            3
LOOP OUTSIDE =            2
     LOOP INSIDE =            1
     LOOP INSIDE =            2
     LOOP INSIDE =            3
```

IF STATEMENTS

```
$ edit if1.for
C        The program shows some forms of IF statements.

         CHARACTER*17  SOMENAME, ANOTHERNAME
         VALUE = 19.8

         IF (VALUE .EQ. 19.8) WRITE(6,100)
100      FORMAT(' The Value is equal to 19.8')

         IF (VALUE .GT. 13.4 .AND. VALUE .LT. 25.6) WRITE(6,200)
200      FORMAT(' The Value is between 13.4 and 25.6')

         IF (VALUE .LT. 50.0 .OR. VALUE .GT. 100.00) WRITE(6,300)
300      FORMAT(' The Value is less than 50 or greater than 100.')

         N = 17
         IF (.NOT.N.EQ.12)WRITE(6,400)
400      FORMAT(' The Value is not equal to 12.')

         SOMENAME = 'Reba Bivens Hardy'
         ANOTHERNAME = 'Reba Bivens Hardy'
         IF (SOMENAME.EQ.ANOTHERNAME) Write(6,500)
500      FORMAT(' The names are the same.')

         STOP
         END
```

```
$ fortran if1
$ link if1
$ run if1
```

```
The Value is equal to 19.8
The Value is between 13.4 and 25.6
The Value is less than 50 or greater than 100.
The Value is not equal to 12.
The names are the same.
```

IF THEN ELSE STATEMENTS

```
$ edit if2.for
C       An Example of the block structured IF THEN ELSE

        NUMBER = 10

        IF (NUMBER.LT.5) THEN
           COST = 23.98 * NUMBER
           WRITE(6,*)' UNIT COST = 23.98, TOTAL COST = ',COST
        ELSE
           COST = 19.98 * NUMBER
           WRITE(6,*)' UNIT COST = 19.98, TOTAL COST = ',COST
        END IF

        STOP
        END
$ fortran if2
$ link if2
$ run if2
```

```
  UNIT COST = 19.98, TOTAL COST =    199.8000
```

```
$ edit if3.for
C       An example of IF statements with multiple ELSE statements.

        CHARACTER GRADE*1

        ISCORE = 72
        IF (ISCORE.GE.90) THEN
             GRADE = 'A'
           ELSE IF (ISCORE.GE.80 .AND. ISCORE.LT.90) THEN
             GRADE = 'B'
           ELSE IF (ISCORE.GE.65 .AND. ISCORE.LT.80) THEN
             GRADE = 'C'
           ELSE
             GRADE = 'D'
        END IF
```

```
                    WRITE(6,100)GRADE
         100        FORMAT(' GRADE : ',A)

                    STOP
                    END
         $ fortran if3
         $ link if3
         $ run if3
```
```
         GRADE : C
```


ONE DIMENSIONAL ARRAYS


```
$ edit arrays1d.for
        DIMENSION SCORE(4)

        Write (6,*)'Enter four scores, one score per record.'
        DO NUM = 1,4
           READ(5,*)SCORE(NUM)
        END DO

        Write (6,*)'SCOREs printed one value per record'
        DO NUM = 1,4
           WRITE(6,*)SCORE(NUM)
        END DO

        Write (6,*)'SCOREs printed across the line'
        WRITE(6,100)(SCORE(NUM),NUM=1,4)
100     FORMAT(' ',4F6.0)

        STOP
        END

$ fortran arrays1d
$ link arrays1d
$ run arrays1d
```

You are prompted to enter
four scores per student.

```
Enter four scores, one score per record.
```

Enter the four values.

```
96
72
67
49
```

The output is displayed.

```
  SCOREs printed one value per record
     96.00000
     72.00000
     67.00000
     49.00000
  SCOREs printed across the line
     96.   72.   67.   49.
```

TWO DIMENSIONAL ARRAYS

```
$ edit arrays2d.for
        DIMENSION SCORES(4,3)

        DO ISTUD = 1,4
           WRITE(6,*)'Enter three scores for one student'
           READ(5,*) (SCORES(ISTUD,NUM),NUM=1,3)
        END DO

        WRITE(6,*)'The scores and the average for each student'
        DO ISTUD = 1,4
           TOTAL = 0
           DO ISCORE = 1, 3
              TOTAL = TOTAL + SCORES(ISTUD,ISCORE)
           END DO
           AVERAGE = TOTAL/3.0
           WRITE(6,100)ISTUD,(SCORES(ISTUD,ISCORE),ISCORE=1,3),AVERAGE
        END DO
100     FORMAT(' ',I1,3F5.0,'  AVERAGE=',F6.1)

        STOP
        END

$ fortran arrays2d
$ link arrays2d
$ run arrays2d
```

> You are prompted to enter values and you enter scores for a student following each prompt.

```
Enter three scores for one student
94, 88, 81
Enter three scores for one student
69, 77, 79
Enter three scores for one student
88, 77, 70
Enter three scores for one student
75, 69, 59
```

> The output is displayed.

```
The scores and the average for each student
1  94.  88.  81.  AVERAGE=  87.7
2  69.  77.  79.  AVERAGE=  75.0
3  88.  77.  70.  AVERAGE=  78.3
4  75.  69.  59.  AVERAGE=  67.7
```

CHARACTER ARRAYS

```
$ edit charactr.for
        CHARACTER STUDENT(3)*15,STATE(3)*10

        WRITE(6,*)'Enter the name of each student and then the'
        WRITE(6,*)'students home state on the following line.'
```

```
        DO ISTUD = 1,3
           READ(5,100)STUDENT(ISTUD)
           READ(5,100)STATE(ISTUD)
        END DO
100     FORMAT(A)

        WRITE(6,*)'Students and their home states'
        DO ISTUD = 1,3
           WRITE(6,200)STUDENT(ISTUD),STATE(ISTUD)
        END DO
200     FORMAT(' ',2A)

        STOP
        END

$ fortran charactr
$ link charactr
$ run charactr
```

You are prompted to enter data.

Enter the name of each student and then the students home state on the following line.

You enter the names and states pressing the [RETURN] key after each entry.

```
Greg Mullican
Tennessee
Kathy Paige
Florida
Tim Barnett
Illinois
```

The following output is displayed.

```
Students and their home states
Greg Mullican  Tennessee
Kathy Paige    Florida
Tim Barnett    Illinois
```

FUNCTIONS

```
$ edit funct.for
        WRITE(6,*)'Enter three values on one line.'
        READ(5,*)VALUE1, VALUE2, VALUE3

C       Invoke a function to calculate the total of the values.
        SUMVALUES = TOTAL(VALUE1,VALUE2,VALUE3)

        WRITE(6,*)'The TOTAL calculated is', SUMVALUES

        STOP
        END
```

```
      FUNCTION TOTAL(VALUE1,VALUE2,VALUE3)
      TOTAL = VALUE1+VALUE2+VALUE3
      RETURN
      END
```

```
$ fortran funct
$ link funct
$ run funct
```

You are prompted to enter values.

Enter three values on one line.

Enter the three values.

  45.16, 31.72, 23.12

The following output is displayed.

The TOTAL calculated is   100.0000

                     SUBROUTINES

```
$ edit subr.for
      DIMENSION SCORES(20,4),AVERAGE(20)
      NUM = 3
      CALL INPUT (SCORES,NUM)
      CALL STUDAVERAGE (SCORES,NUM,AVERAGE)
      CALL OUTPUT (SCORES,NUM,AVERAGE)
      STOP
      END

      SUBROUTINE INPUT(SCORES,NUM)
      DIMENSION SCORES(20,4)
      Write(6,*)'Enter 4 scores for each student'
      DO ISTUD = 1,NUM
         READ(5,100)(SCORES(ISTUD,ISCORE),ISCORE=1,4)
      END DO
100   FORMAT(4F3.0)
      RETURN
      END

      SUBROUTINE STUDAVERAGE(SCORES,NUM,AVERAGE)
C     CALCULATE THE AVERAGE FOR EACH STUDENT
      DIMENSION SCORES(20,NUM),AVERAGE(NUM)
      DO ISTUD = 1,NUM
         TOTAL = 0
         DO ISCORE = 1,4
            TOTAL = TOTAL + SCORES(ISTUD,ISCORE)
         END DO
         AVERAGE(ISTUD) = TOTAL/4.0
      END DO
      RETURN
      END

      SUBROUTINE OUTPUT(SCORES,NUM,AVERAGE)
      DIMENSION SCORES(20,*),AVERAGE(*)
      WRITE(6,*)'Student scores and average'
      DO ISTUD = 1,NUM
         WRITE(6,100)ISTUD,(SCORES(ISTUD,N),N=1,4),AVERAGE(ISTUD)
      END DO
```

```
100     FORMAT(' ',I2,4F5.0,F6.1)
        RETURN
        END
$ fortran subr
$ link subr
$ run subr                                You are prompted to enter values.
 Enter 4 scores for each student
 87 65 79 81
 77 91 85 85
 61 75 69 72
 Student scores and average                The output is displayed.
   1  87.  65.  79.  81.  78.0
   2  77.  91.  85.  85.  84.5
   3  61.  75.  69.  72.  69.3
```

APPENDIX D
FORTRAN Formats:
Quick Reference

FREE FORMAT

```
$ edit freeformt.for
      PRINT *, 'Input two values free format'
      PRINT *, 'Values may be separated by a space or a comma.'
      READ *, X,Y
      PRINT *, X,Y

C     Using the READ and WRITE with unit numbers 5 and 6
C     allows more flexibility in programs.
      WRITE(6,*) 'Input two values free format'
      READ(5,*) X, Y
      WRITE(6,*) X, Y
      STOP
      END
$ fortran freeformt
$ link freeformt
$ run freeformt
```

                                              You are prompted to enter
                                              values.

```
Input two values free format
Values may be separated by a space or a comma.
3.4, 5.678
```

                                              The values are output free
                                              format.

```
   3.400000      5.678000
```

                                              You are prompted to enter
                                              two more values.

```
Input two values free format
88 0.98743
```

                                              The values are output free
                                              format.

```
   88.00000      0.9874300
```

INTEGER FORMAT

```
$ edit iformat.for
      WRITE(6,100)
100   FORMAT(' ','Input two integer values')
      READ(5,200)NUM1, NUM2
200   FORMAT(I3,2X,I7)
      WRITE(6,300)NUM1,NUM2
300   FORMAT(' ',2I10)
      STOP
      END
```

489

```
$ fortran iformat
$ link iformat
$ run iformat
```

Input two integer values   A prompt is displayed.

119 2345872   You enter the values.

    119   2345872   The output is displayed.

F FORMAT

```
$ edit fformat.for
                      WRITE(6,100)
100     FORMAT(' ','Enter two values with formats F5.1 and F7.2')
        READ(6,200) X, Y
200     FORMAT(F5.1,F7.2)
        WRITE(6,300)X,Y
300     FORMAT(' ','The formatted values are',2X,F5.1,2X,F7.2)
        STOP
        END

$ fortran fformat
$ link fformat
$ run fformat
```

                                  You are prompted to enter
                                  values.

Enter two values with formats F5.1 and F7.2

                                  Now enter the values.
34.5 56.78

                                  The output is displayed.

The formatted values are 34.5   56.78

ALPHANUMERIC FORMAT

```
$ edit aformat.for
        CHARACTER*25 NAME1,NAME2,NAME3
        WRITE(6,100)
100     FORMAT(' ','Enter name 25 characters or fewer.')
        READ(5,200)NAME1
200     FORMAT(A)
        WRITE(6,100)
        READ(5,200)NAME2
        WRITE(6,100)
        READ(5,200)NAME3
        WRITE(6,300)NAME1,NAME2,NAME3
300     FORMAT(' ',3A)
        STOP
        END
```

```
$ fortran aformat
$ link aformat
$ run aformat
```

You are prompted three times to enter names and you should enter a name following each prompt.

```
Enter name 25 characters or fewer.
Reba Bivens Hardy
Enter name 25 characters or fewer.
Odell Hardy
Enter name 25 characters or fewer.
Jewell Dixon Middlebrooks
```

The names are displayed on one line of output.

```
Reba Bivens Hardy          Odell Hardy              Jewel Dixon Middlebrooks
```

DOUBLE PRECISION FORMAT

```
$ edit dformat.for
        REAL*8 X, Y, Z
        READ(5,10) X, Y, Z
        WRITE(6,20) X, Y
        WRITE(6,30) Z
10      FORMAT(D7.1, D6.1, D6.4)
20      FORMAT(' ',D11.4, D10.3)
30      FORMAT(' ',D12.5)
        STOP
        END
$ fortran dformat
$ link dformat
$ run dformat
```

A line of numbers is entered. Using the input format the first seven numbers will be stored in the memory location named X, the next six numbers will be stored in the memory location named Y and the final 6 numbers will be stored in the memory location named Z.

```
1234567123456123456
```

The following output lines are displayed.

```
0.1235D+06    0.123D+05
0.12346D+02
```

E FORMAT

```
$ edit eformat.for
C       Reading and writing with an E format
```

```
        REAL*8 X, Y, Z
        READ(5,10) X
        READ(5,10) Y
        READ(5,10) Z
        WRITE(6,20) X, Y, Z
10      FORMAT(E8.4)
20      FORMAT(' ',E12.3,2X,E12.5,2X,E12.5)
        STOP
        END
$ fortran eformat
$ link eformat
$ run eformat
```

Input three values, one value per record.

```
23.5E+02
0.15E-02
1234.567
```

The following output line is displayed.

```
0.235E+04    0.15000E-02    0.12346E+04
```

APPENDIX E
Using the VAX:
Quick Reference

VAX LOGON   Press the [RETURN] key to begin.
  Username:
  Password:

VAX LOGOUT
$ LO

THE SYSTEM
VAX 11/780   The hardware made by Digital Equipment Corporation.
VMS   Virtual Memory System - the operating system.
DCL   Digital Command Language.
$ Prompt for a DCL command.
EDT   An editor for creating and modifying files.
*   Prompt for user to enter a command for the EDT editor.

THE TERMINAL
[RETURN] key   Transmits information from terminal to computer.
[DELETE] key   The [DELETE] or the [RUBOUT] key deletes the character
[RUBOUT] key   to the left of the cursor and moves the cursor one space
                    to the left. Never use the [BACKSPACE] key (causes problems).
[TAB]   Tabs to columns 9, 17, 25, etc.
[SHIFT]   Shifts to upper case letters like a typewritter.
[CAPS/LOCK]   Locks and unlocks upper case letters.
CONTROL keys   The CONTROL key marked [CTRL] at the left of the keyboard
                    is used with other characters on the keyboard to send commands
                    to the computer. When you use the CONTROL key, you press and
                    hold the [CTRL] key and while the [CTRL] key is depressed, you
                    type the letter key specified.
[CTRL/U]   Disregards the entire line which you are typing.
[CTRL/S]   Suspends display at the terminal.
[CTRL/Q]   Resumes display at the terminal.
                    (Note: The [NO-SCROLL] key may be used on VT-100 compatible
                    terminals to suspend and resume display.

FILENAMES AND COMPLETE FILE SPECIFICATIONS
name.extension
name   Nine Characters or fewer.
extension   Three characters or fewer (Represents the kind of file. -
                    FOR (FORtran), DAT (DATa)
name.extension;version
                    Usually the version number represents the number of
                    times the file has been saved. In most cases, it is not
                    necessary to specify a version number.

DIRECTORY
$ DIR   Display filenames.
$ DIR/FULL   Display filenames and file attributes.

DELETING FILES
$ DEL filename.ext.   Delete the current version of the specified file.
$ DEL filename.ext;version Delete the specified file.
$ DEL filename.*;*   Delete all files with specified filename.
$ Del *.ext;*   Delete all files with specified extension.
$ DEL filename.ext;*   Delete all versions of specified file.
$ DEL *.*;*   Delete all files.
$ PURGE   Retain only the last version of each file.
                           (PURGE is applicable only in multi-version environments.)

DISPLAYING A FILE AT THE TERMINAL
$ TYPE filename.ext   Display file from your directory.
  [CTRL/S]   Suspend display. (Gives you time to read.)
  [CTRL/Q]   Resume display.
                            CAUTION: NEVER TYPE A FILE WITH AN
                                      EXTENSION OF OBJ OR EXE.

PRINTING A FILE ON A PRINTER
$ PRINT filename.ext   Print file on system printer.
                            CAUTION: NEVER PRINT A FILE WITH AN
                                      EXTENSION OF OBJ OR EXE.

RUNNING A FORTRAN PROGRAM
                            The extension for the filename should be FOR.
$ FORT filename   Compile the program.
$ LINK filename   Link the object code.
$ RUN filename   Execute the instructions in the program.

                            The FORT/LIST option can be used to compile
                            the program and produce a program listing
                            with the errors marked.
$ FORT/LIST filename   When the program compiles or attempts to
                            compile, the LIST option creates a file
                            with the specified filename and extention
                            LIS. The LIS file will contain a listing
                            of the program with any syntax error
                            messages included at the line where the
                            error occurs. That file can then be observed.
$ PRINT filename.LIS   PRINT listing on the printer.
$ TYPE filename.LIS   Display listing at the terminal.
$ LINK filename   Link the object code.
$ RUN filename   Execute the instructions in the program.

INTERRUPTING AND RESUMING PROGRAM EXECUTION

[CTRL/Y]   Interrupts the current process, displays
                            a dollar sign on the screen and waits for
                            you to enter another command.

$ SHOW STATUS   Display execution status.

$ CONTINUE   Resume the execution that was interrupted
                            with the [CTRL/Y].

CHANGING A PASSWORD

$ SET PASSWORD   Command to reset a password.

$ Old Password: Enter your current password.

$ New Password: Enter new password.

$ Verification: Enter the new password again.

COPYING FROM ONE FILE TO ANOTHER

$ COPY   The COPY command like most DCL commands

_From: oldfilename.ext   will prompt you to enter appropriate

_To: newfilename.ext   parameters.

RENAMING A FILE

$ RENAME   The RENAME command like most DCL commands

$ _From: oldfilename.ext   will prompt you to enter appropriate

$ _To: newfilename.ext   parameters.

APPENDIX F
EDT Line Editor:
Quick Reference

`$ EDT filename.extension`	When an asterisk is on the screen, EDT editor commands can be entered. The Insert command allows records to be inserted in a file.
`* i`	Press the [RETURN] key after each line of type. After all the records are entered, use a [CTRL/Z] to exit the insert mode.
`[CTRL/Z]`	When an asterisk is again on the screen, any EDT command can be entered. Use the following commands to modify the records you entered.
`* co`	COPY to make a copy of some lines of text.
`* d`	DELETE a line or lines of text.
`* f`	FIND a specified line of text or string of text.
`* h`	HELP to display EDT information.
`* i`	INSERT to insert more records into a file.
`* m`	MOVE to move some line or lines of text.
`* r`	REPLACE to delete a line or lines of text and to begin insert mode for adding lines.
`* res`	RESEQUENCE to renumber the lines of text.
`* s`	SUBSTITUTE to substitute a string of characters by another string of characters.
`* t`	TYPE to type a line or lines of text.

After you have entered records in the INSERT mode, and possibly made changes in the records with the editor commands such as Delete, Substitute, etc., you should save the file or end the edit session without saving the input and changes made in the session.

EXIT (EX) ends an edit session and saves the file created or modified in the edit session.

`* ex`

QUIT ends an edit session without saving the input or changes made in the edit session. If a file is saved from a previous session, that file remains saved and unaltered.

NOTE: Options for the EDT commands listed above are on the following pages.

NOTE: If an EDT edit session is abnormally terminated, (if you accidentally break out of the EDT editor) you can usually recover most of your edit session by using the EDT/RECOVER option. A file with your filename and extension of JOU is created by an abnormal exit from the editor. To recover the work in the journal file, enter the EDT/RECOVER command followed by the filename and no extension.

`$ EDT/RECOVER filename`

496

```
COPY        CO   Copy a record or a group of records at some other
                 location in the file. The original records are unaltered.
                 COPY[range-1]TO[range-2][/QUERY][/DUPLICATE:n]
* co ln1 to ln2     Make a copy of line number 1 at location line number 2.
* co ln1:ln2 to ln3 Make a copy of the group of line numbers including line
                    number 1 and line number 2 at the location beginning
                    immediately preceding line number 3.
* co ln1 to end     Copy a record to the end of the file.
```

```
DELETE      D    Deletes a line or lines of text.
                 DELETE [range][/QUERY]
* d                 Delete current line.
* d ln              Delete specified line number.
* d ln1:ln2         Delete range including linenumber 1 through linenumber 2.
* d begin:end       Delete all records.
* d before          Delete all records preceding current record.
                    The QUERY option allows you to decide whether or not to
                    delete a line. A line is printed followed by a question
                    mark. You respond Y—Yes, N—No, or Q—Quit.
* d ln/query        Prints line to delete followed by a question mark.
* d ln1:ln2/query Prints each line of text followed by a question mark.
```

```
EXIT        EX   Exit the edit session and save the file.
* ex
```

```
FIND        F    The Type command contains a more complete set of options
                 for finding and displaying a range or string of text.
                 The Find command locates a specified line of text or
                 locates a string of text. (Searches from the current line
                 toward the end of the file.) The located line is not typed.
* f ln              Locate a specific line number.
* f 'string'        Locate a specific string of text.
```

```
HELP        H    Displays EDT information.
* h                 Displays the topics for which EDT help is available.
* h topic           Displays information about the topic specified.
```

```
INSERT      I    Allows you to enter records into a file.
                 INSERT [range][;text to be inserted]
* i                 Records will be inserted before current record.
* i ln              Records will be inserted before linenumber specified.
* i end             Records will be inserted following the last record.
  [CTRL/Z]          Terminates insert mode.

* i ln;text         Inserts the specified text immediately preceding the
                    specified linenumber.
```

MOVE   M   Move a record from one location in a file to another
location in the file.
                MOVE[range-1]TO[range-2][/QUERRY]
* m ln1 to ln2   Move the record in line number 1 to line number 2.
* m ln1:ln2 to ln3   Move the range of lines including line number 1 and
line number 2 to the location beginning immediately
preceding line number 3.

QUIT   Ends the current editing session without saving
the input or changes made in the editing session.
* quit

REPLACE   R   Delete a line or lines of text and enter insert
mode to allow a line or lines to be entered. After
lines are inserted, use a [CTRL/Z] to end insert mode.
                REPLACE [range] [;text to be inserted]
* r ln   Delete specified line and begin insert mode.
* r ln1:ln2   Delete specified range and begin insert mode.
[CTRL/Z]

* r ln;text   Replace the text in the specified line number
with the text following the semicolon.

RESEQUENCE RES Renumber the lines of text.
                RESEQUENCE [range][/SEQUENCE[:initial[:increment]]
* res   Resequence entire file.
* res lin1:lin2 Resequence specified range.
* res lin1:lin2/seq:initial
* res lin1:lin2/seq:initial:increment
                     Resequence specified range beginning
with the initial value specified for
the new sequence numbers and adding
the specified increments for line numbers.

SUBSTITUTE S   Substitute a string of characters for another
string of characters in one occurrence or in
multiple occurrences of the characters.
            SUBSTITUTE/oldtxt/newtxt/[range][/BRIEF[:n]]/QUERY][/NOTYPE]
* s/oldtext/newtext/ln   Substitute the newtext specified for the oldtext
specified in the linenumber specified.
* s/oldtext/newtext/ln1:ln2 Substitute text in the range of lines specified.

SUBSTITUTE NEXT

                  SUBSTITUTE NEXT /oldtext/newtext/
* s n /oldtext/newtext/   Substitute the new text for the next occurence
of the oldtext specified.
* s n   Make the same substitution in the NEXT occurrence
of the oldtext as was made in the previous
substitute command.

TYPE   T   Display a line or lines of text in the file.
                         TYPE [range][/BRIEF[:n]][/STAY]
* t   Type the current line.
* t ln   Type specified line number.
* t w   Type Whole file.
* t ln1:ln2   Type range of lines.
* t begin:end   Type whole file.
* t begin:ln   Type from beginning through specified line.
* t ln:end   Type from the specified line through the end.

* t ln1:ln2 all 'string' Type all the lines in the specified range
                          that contain the 'string' of characters.
* t +num   Type the line number relative to the current line.
* t -num
*   [RETURN]   Pressing the [RETURN] key displays the succeeding record.
*   - [RETURN]   Pressing the minus sign and then the [RETURN] key
                         displays the preceeding record.

INCLUDE   COPY AN EXTERNAL FILE INTO BUFFER FOR THE EDT EDITOR.

* include filename.ext   Copy the specified file into the buffer at the
                                location immediately preceding the current line.

* include filename.ext linenumber   Copy the specified file into the buffer
                                     at the line immediately preceding the
                                     linenumber specified.

Additional information about using the VAX system, the EDT editor and FORTRAN on the VAX can be obtained from the following manuals published by the Digital Equipment Corporation.

VAX/VMS Command Language User's Guide
EDT Editor Manual
VAX-11 FORTRAN User's Guide
VAX-11 FORTRAN Reference Manual

Index

INDEX FOR EXAMPLES

A format, 121, 190, 490
Airplane seat assignment, 169
Animal population analysis, 193
APPLICATIONS, ADVANCED:
  Business report with bar chart, 254
  Correlation coefficient, 260
  Frequency distribution, 335
  General grading program, 379
  On-line employee information sort, 353
  Regression analysis, 260
  Sales analysis, 295
  Scatter plot of data, 260
  Scatter plot program, 357
APPLICATIONS, INTERMEDIATE:
  Airplane seat assignment, 169
  Animal population analysis, 193
  Boat tax assessment, 190
  Compound Interest table, 189
  Factorial, 108
  Inflation problem, 107
  Logical relationship, 110
  Mailing labels, 136
  Parkfund contributions logic problem, 191
  Pay calculation, IF THEN ELSE, 159
  Plant research project, 137
  Problem solving, 113
  Rainfall with DO loop, 106
  Selecting records, 159
  Simple interest, 109
APPLICATIONS, SIMPLE (*See* PRO-
  GRAMS, SIMPLE)
Area of polygon, 315
Arithmetic precedence, 29, 31
Arithmetic GO TO, 156
ARRAY, ONE-DIMENSIONAL:
  Accessing array with DO loop, 208
  Assigning values to array, 204
  Counting input elements, 220
  General approach to arrays, 220
  Implied DO loops, 222
  Input and output, 222
  INTEGER, REAL, CHARACTER ar-
    rays, 217
  Manipulating data in array, 219
  Ordering data input to array, 214
  Plotting with array, 224, 225
  Program needs array, 202
  Quick reference, 484
  Simple input for array, 206
ARRAY, TWO-DIMENSIONAL:
  Accessing 2D array with DO loops, 280
  General approach, 295

Implied DO loops, 293
Input for 2D array, 277
Input row by row for 2D array, 279
Output for 2D array, 284
Program needing 2D array, 273
Quick reference, 485
Realistic program, 286
Simple assignment for 2D array, 274
Assignment statement, 25
Bar chart, 254
Boat tax assessment, 190
Bubble sort, 247
Business report with bar chart, 254
Case structure, 157
Category distribution, 335
Character comparisons, 148
Common declaration, 333, 334
Compiling program, 13, 473
Compound Interest table, 189
Compound interest, 185, 186
Computed GO TO, 158
Correlation coefficient, 260
COS library function, 42
Counting concept, 90
Counting number of input records, 220
Cumulative total, 96
D format, 364, 491
Debugging, 73
Destructive READ, 63
DO LOOP:
  Compound interest, 185, 186
  Controlling number of loops, 180
  Counting concept, 90
  DO loops, 481
  Iterative processing, 181
  Nested DO loop, 176, 178, 481
  Prime numbers, 187
  Processing in a DO loop, 98, 100, 106,
    107, 109, 110
  Simple DO loop, 94, 98
  Variable counter, 102
  Variable nested DO loops, 179
DO WHILE LOOP:
  DO WHILE loops, 481
  DO WHILE structure, 182
  Flag for End of File, 183
  Iterative processing, 182
  Prime numbers, 187
  Read to End of File, IOSTAT, 184
Documentation, 76
E format, 364, 491
END= option in READ statement, 105
End of File, IOSTAT, 184
F format, 126, 490

Factorial, 108
FILES:
  Counting number of input records, 220
  Creating subset files, 239
  Destructive READ, 63
  END=option in READ statement, 105
  Files, 56
  Flag for End of File, 183
  IOSTAT option in READ statement, 184,
    190, 220
  Merging files, 64
  Reading input from disk file, 60, 61
  Reading to End of File, 105, 183, 184,
    190, 220, 239, 479
  Storing and using input data, 63
  Writing output to disk file, 58
Flag for End of File, 183
FORMATS:
  A format, 121, 190, 490
  D format, 364, 491
  E format, 364, 491
  F format, 126, 490
  Formatted input, 129, 131
  Formatted output, 123
  Formatted report heading, 135
  Generating a formatted table, 135
  I format, 126, 489
  Input formats for data with no spaces,
    133
  Mailing labels, 136
  Storing and printing characters, 121
  T format, 135
  Unformatted output, 122, 489
Formatted report heading, 135
Frequency distribution, 335
FUNCTION—USER WRITTEN:
  Area of polygon, 315
  Function with array, 312
  Parameters, 309
  Simple Function, 307, 486
General approach to arrays, 220
General grading program, 379
GO TO, 103, 104, 105, 156, 157, 158
I format, 126, 489
IF STATEMENTS:
  Block structured IF, 150, 151
  Character comparisons, 148
  Complex IF THEN ELSE, 153
  Compound conditions, 147
  Location of max value in set of records,
    163
  Maximum value in set of records, 162
  Minimum value in a record, 163, 165
  Minimum value in set of records, 165

  Multiple ELSE statements, 156
  Nested IF THEN ELSE, 154
  Relational operators, 147
  Selection, 149
  Simple IF statements, 144, 145, 482
  Tax calculation, 153
  The IF THEN ELSE structure, 152, 483
Implied DO Loops, 221, 222, 225, 292, 293,
  298
Inflation problem, 107
INPUT:
  from disk file, 60, 61, 66, 477
  from terminal and file, 478
  from terminal, 51, 66, 476
  Implied DO Loops, 221, 222, 225, 292,
    293, 298
  Quick reference, 476–479
  Reading to End of File, 184, 189, 195,
    220, 479
INTEGER:
  Arithmetic, 32, 33, 37
  Declaration, 34
  Library function, 36
  INTEGER, REAL, CHARACTER ar-
    rays, 217
IOSTAT option in READ statement, 184,
  190, 220
Iterative processing, 181, 182
Labeling output, 27, 37
Linking program, 14, 473
Location of max value in set of records, 163
LOG—natural log library function, 36
LOG10 library function, 36
Logic of a program, 74
Logical relationship, 110
Loop with END=option, 105
Loop with GO TO, 104
Mailbox concept, 4, 5
Mailing labels, 136
Maximum library function, 36
Maximum value in set of records, 162
Merging files, 64
MIN library function, 36
Minimum value in a record, 163, 165
Minimum value in set of records, 165
Mixed mode arithmetic, 33
Modular programming, 328, 336, 346, 351,
  353, 358, 381
Multiple ELSE statements, 156
Nearest integer (NINT) library function, 36
Nested DO loop, 176, 178, 481
Nested IF THEN ELSE, 154
On-line employee information sort, 353
OUTPUT:

Implied DO Loops, 221, 222, 225, 292, 293, 298
Printing output, 477
Running the first program, 473
to disk file, 58, 61, 66, 477
to terminal, 51, 61, 66, 476, 478
Parameters, 34, 306, 309, 324
Parkfund contributions logic problem, 191
Pay calculation, IF THEN ELSE, 159
Payroll with overtime, 84
Percentage calculation, 37
Plant research project, 137
PLOTTING:
 Bar chart, 254
 General scatter plot, 357
 Plot of regression line, 260
 Plotting rainfall, 225
 Plotting with array, 224, 225
 Scatter plot, 260
Prime numbers, 187
Print statement, 27
Printing output at terminal, 49
Printing output, 477
Problem solving, 81, 113
Processing in a DO loop, 98, 100, 106, 107, 109, 110
Processing multiple records, 39, 40
Program entry, 11, 473
PROGRAMS, SIMPLE:
 Arithmetic precedence, 29, 31
 Assignment statement, 25
 Compiling program, 13
 Cosine library function, 42
 Counting concept, 90
 Cumulative total, 96
 Debugging, 73
 Documentation, 76
 Integer arithmetic, 32, 33, 37
 Integer declaration, 34
 Integer library function, 36
 Labeling output, 27, 37
 Linking program, 14
 Log—natural log library function, 36
 Log10 library function, 36
 Logic of a program, 74
 Mailbox concept, 4, 5
 Maximum library function, 36
 Minimum library function, 36
 Mixed mode arithmetic, 33
 Nearest integer library function, 36
 Payroll with overtime, 84
 Percentage calculation, 37
 Print statement, 27
 Printing output at terminal, 49

Problem solving, 81
Processing multiple records, 39, 40
Program entry, 11, 473
READ statement, 51
Reading input from a terminal, 51
Real arithmetic, 32, 33
Real declaration, 34
Running program, 14
Running the first program, 473
Sine library function, 42
Square root library function, 35
Syntax error, 72
Trigonometry application, 41, 42
Unreadable code, 81
Using memory locations repeatedly, 40
WRITE statement, 49
Writing multiple lines of output, 50
Writing multiple values on a line, 49
Writing output to terminal, 49
Quick reference, 476–479
Quick sort, 344, 380
Rainfall with DO loop, 106
READ statement, 51
Read to End of File, IOSTAT, 184
Reading to End of File, 184, 189, 195, 220, 479
Real arithmetic, 32, 33
REAL declaration, 34
Regression analysis, 260
Relational operators, 147
Running program, 14, 473
Running the first program, 473
Sales analysis, 295
Scatter plot of data, 260, 357
Scatter plot, 260, 357
SELECTION:
 Selection, 149
 Selecting and arranging subsets, 235
 Selecting random subset, 239
 Selecting records, 159
 Selection and analysis, 242
Shell sort, 350, 353
Simple interest, 109
Sine library function, 42
SORTING:
 Bubble sort, 247
 Interactive sort, 353
 Quick sort, 344, 380
 Shell sort, 350, 353
 Sorting Alphanumeric data, 252
 Sorting associated values, 250
 Sorting by category, 335
Square root library function, 35
Subprograms, 329

SUBROUTINES:
  COMMON declaration, 333, 334
  General approach, 335
  Modular programming, 328, 336, 346,
    351, 353, 358, 381
  Parameters, 326
  Quick reference, 487
  Simple subroutine, 322
  Subprograms, 329
Subset files, 239
Syntax error, 72

T format, 135
Tax calculation, 153
Trigonometry application, 41, 42
Unconditional transfer, 103
Unformatted output, 122, 489
Unreadable code, 81
WRITE statement, 49
Writing multiple lines of output, 50
Writing multiple values on a line,
  49
Writing output to terminal, 49

INDEX FOR APPENDICES

A first program to run, 473
Adding records to file:
    EDT line editor, 403, 408, 497
    EDT full-screen editor, 417, 433
Alphanumeric format, 490
Array:
    One-dimensional, 484
    Two-dimensional, 485
    Character, 485
Asterisk in DELETE command, 472
Beginning an edit session:
    EDT full-screen, 416
    EDT line editor, 403, 496
CHANGE - EDT full-screen, 417
Character array, 485
Character deletion, 396
Character format, 490
Compile program, 473, 475, 477
CONTINUE process command (DCL), 495
Control keys:
    CTRL/Q 400, 401
    CTRL/S, 400, 401
    CTRL/U, 397, 401
    CTRL/Y, 399, 401
COPY file, 495
Copying characters, words in file, EDT full-
    screen editor, 451
Copying lines in file:
    EDT full-screen editor, 451
    EDT line editor, 415, 497
Copying segments of text:
    EDT full-screen editor, 462
    EDT line editor, 416, 497
Creating a simple file:
    EDT full-screen editor, 416, 421
    EDT line editor, 403
DELETE file, 471, 472, 494
Deleting:
    Characters as you type, 438
    Files, 471, 472, 494
    Lines:
        EDT full-screen editor, 438
        EDT line editor, 410, 497
    Segments of text:
        EDT full-screen editor, 458
        EDT line editor, 411, 497
Digital Command Language (DCL):
    CONTINUE process command, 495
    COPY file, 495
    DELETE file, 471, 472, 494
    DIRECTORY command, 405, 418, 471,
        472, 494

EDIT command, 394, 403, 416
FORTRAN compile, 473, 494
FORTRAN/LIST compile, 476, 494
HELP, 398
Interrupt process, 398, 495
LINK command, 473, 494
Logout, 400
PASSWORD SET, 495
PRINT file, 405, 419, 471, 494
RENAME file, 495
RUN program, 473, 494
SCROLL screen control, 400
SHOW command, 396
TYPE file (display file), 405, 419, 471, 494
DIRECTORY command (DCL), 405, 418,
    471, 472, 494
DIRECTORY/FULL, 472
Display:
    File at terminal, 471
    Records at terminal:
        EDT full-screen editor, 420, 432, 433
        EDT line editor, 405, 499
DO loop, 481
DO WHILE loop, 481
Double precision format, 491
E format, 491
EDIT command (DCL), 394, 403, 416
    EDT full-screen editor (*see* Editor, EDT
        full-screen)
    EDT line editor (*see* Editor, EDT line)
Editor—Creating files, 402
Editor, EDT full-screen:
    Adding records to file, 417, 433
    Beginning edit session, 416
    Change to full-screen, 417
    Copying characters, words, lines, 451
    Copying segments of text, 462
    Creating a simple file, 416, 421
    Deleting characters, 438
    Deleting lines, 438
    Deleting segments of text, 458
    Deleting words, 438
    Ending keypad mode, 418
    Exiting a file, 418, 424
    Finding strings of characters, 468, 469,
        470
    Inserting records in file, 417, 433
    Keyboard arrows, 425
    Keypad, 428, 430, 431
    Moving characters, words, lines, 451
    Moving segments of text, 458
    Quiting an edit session, 419, 421
    Restoring deleted characters, 445
    Saving a file, 418, 424

Tutorial, 416
Editor, EDT line:
  Adding records to file, 408, 497
  Beginning an edit session, 403, 496
  COPYing records in a file, 415, 497
  Creating a simple file, 403
  DELETing records in a file, 410, 497
  Displaying records, 405, 499
  Ending insert mode, 404
  EXITing a file, 404, 497
  FINDing strings in a file, 413, 497
  HELP, 413, 497
  INCLUDE external file, 499
  INSERTing records in file, 403, 408, 409,
    496, 497
  MOVing records in a file, 414, 498
  Quick reference, 496
  QUITing an edit session, 407, 498
  REPLACing records in file, 411, 498
  RESequence line numbers, 410, 498
  Saving a file, 404, 497
  Substituting strings in file, 413, 498
  Tutorial, 403
  TYPing records, 406, 499
End of File—Reading to EOF, 479
Ending:
  Edit session—EDT line editor, 404, 407,
    497, 498
  Edit session—EDT full-screen editor, 418,
    419, 421, 424,
  Insert mode—EDT line editor, 404
  Keypad mode—EDT full-screen editor,
    418
Exiting a file:
  EDT full-screen editor, 418, 424
  EDT line editor, 404, 497
Extension for filename, 401
Filename, 401
Files on the VAX, 401
Finding strings in a file:
  EDT full-screen editor, 468, 469, 470
  EDT line editor, 413, 497
  Files DIRECTORY, 405, 418, 471, 472,
    494
Finishing:
  Edit session—EDT line editor, 404, 407,
    497, 498
  Edit session—EDT full-screen editor, 418,
    419, 421, 424,
  Insert mode—EDT line editor, 404
  Keypad mode—EDT full-screen editor,
    418
Floating point format, 490

FORTRAN compile, 473, 475, 477, 494
FORTRAN/LIST compile, 476, 494
FORTRAN structures quick reference, 481
FORMAT quick reference:
  A format, 490
  D format, 491
  E format, 491
  F format, 490
  Free format, 489
  I format, 489
FORTRAN—Quick reference examples:
  Alphanumeric format, 490
  Character array, 485
  DO Loops, 481
  DO WHILE Loops, 481
  Double precision, 491
  E format, 491
  F format, 490
  Free format, 489
  Function, 486
  IF THEN ELSE statements, 483
  IF statements, 482
  Input from file, 477, 479
  Input from terminal, 476
  Input from terminal and disk, 478
  Integer format, 489
  Nested DO loops, 481
  One-dimensional array, 484
  Output to disk, 477, 479
  Output to terminal, 476, 478
  Printing output, 477
  Reading to End of file, 479
  Running the first program, 473
  Submitting with cards, 480
  Subroutine, 487
  Two-dimensional array, 485
Function, 486
HELP:
  with EDT full-screen editor, 430
  with EDT line editor, 413, 497
  VAX HELP commands, 398
IF, 482
IF THEN ELSE, 483
Include external file with EDT editor, 499
Input:
  Formats (*see* FORMAT Quick reference)
  from file, 477, 479
  from terminal, 476
  from terminal and disk, 478
Inserting records in file:
  EDT full-screen editor, 417, 433
  EDT line editor, 403, 408, 409, 496, 497
Integer format, 489

Interrupting:
    Process (DCL), 398, 495
    Terminal display, 399, 400
    Scrolling, 399, 400
Keyboard arrows—EDT full-screen, 425
Keypad, EDT full-screen, 428, 430, 431
Keys—terminal:
    CTRL/Q, 400, 401
    CTRL/S, 400, 401
    CTRL/U, 397, 401
    CTRL/Y, 399, 401
    [DELETE] [RUBOUT], 396, 401
    [NO SCROLL], 400, 401
    [SHIFT], 401
Keypad keys for EDT full-screen editor:
    [ADVANCE], 434
    [BACKUP], 432, 469
    [CHARACTER], 440
    [CUT], 461, 465
    [DEL LINE], 444
    [DEL WORD], 443
    [DELETE CHAR], 441
    [DELETE], 434
    [EOL], 433
    [FIND], 468
    [FINDNEXT], 470
    [GOLD], 446
    [HELP], 430, 439
    [LINE], 433
    [PASTE], 462, 466
    [SELECT], 460, 464
    [UNDELETE CHAR], 448
    [UNDELETE LINE], 450
    [UNDELETE WORD], 449
    [WORD], 442
LINK program, 473, 475, 477, 494,
Logging out from the VAX, 400
Logging in to the VAX, 395
Moving:
    Characters, words, lines—EDT full-screen, 451
    Lines in a file—EDT line editor, 414, 498
    Segments of text—EDT full-screen, 458
Nested DO loop, 481
One-dimensional array, 484
Overview for using the VAX, 394
PASSWORD SET, 495
Password for the VAX, 395
PRINT file on printer, 405, 419, 471, 494
    Display file at terminal (*see* Display)
Process interrupt, 398, 399, 495
PROGRAM RUNNING:
    Alphanumeric format, 490

Character array, 485
DO Loops, 481
DO WHILE Loops, 481
Double precision, 491
E format, 491
F format, 490
Free format, 489
Function, 486
IF THEN ELSE statements, 483
IF statements, 482
Input from file, 477, 479
Input from terminal, 476
Input from terminal and disk, 478
Integer format, 489
Nested DO loops, 481
One-dimensional array, 484
Output to disk, 477, 479
Output to terminal, 476, 478
Printing output, 477
Reading to End of file, 479
Running the first program, 473
Submitting with cards, 480
Subroutine, 487
Two-dimensional array, 485
Quick reference:
    EDT line editor, 496
    FORTRAN structures, 481 (*see also* PRO-
    GRAM RUNNING.)
    Formats, 489 (*see also* FORMAT quick
    reference.)
Quiting an edit session:
    EDT full-screen, 419, 421
    EDT line editor, 407, 498
Real format, 490
RENAME file, 495
Replacing records in a file:
    EDT full-screen editor, 450
    EDT line editor, 411, 498
Resequence line numbers, EDT line editor,
    410, 498
Restoring deleted characters, words, lines,
    EDT full-screen editor, 445
Running FORTRAN program (*see* PRO-
    GRAM RUNNING)
Saving a file:
    EDT full-screen, 418, 424
    EDT line editor, 404, 497
Scientific notation format, 491
SCROLL display control, 399, 400
SHOW command (DCL), 396
Stopping:
    Edit session—EDT line editor, 404, 407,
    497, 498

Edit session—EDT full-screen editor, 418, 419, 421, 424,
Insert mode—EDT line editor, 404
Keypad mode—EDT full-screen editor, 418
Process, 398, 399
Structures of FORTRAN:
  Alphanumeric format, 490
  Character array, 485
  DO Loops, 481
  DO WHILE Loops, 481
  Double precision, 491
  E format, 491
  F format, 490
  Free format, 489
  Function, 486
  IF THEN ELSE statements, 483
  IF statements, 482
  Input from file, 477, 479
  Input from terminal, 476
  Input from terminal and disk, 478
  Integer format, 489
  Nested DO loops, 481
  One-dimensional array, 484
  Output to disk, 477, 479
  Output to terminal, 476, 478
  Printing output, 477
  Reading to End of file, 479
  Running the first program, 473
  Submitting with cards, 480
  Subroutine, 487
  Two-dimensional array, 485
Subroutines, 487
Substituting strings in file:

EDT full-screen editor, 443
EDT line editor, 413, 498
System commands [see Digital Command Language (DCL)]
TYPE file (display file), 405, 419, 471, 494
Terminal - Using with the VAX, 396–401
Tutorial:
  EDT full-screen editor, 416
  EDT line editor, 403
  for using the VAX, 394
Two-dimensional array, 485
Unformatted input, 489
Unrecognized command, 397
Username for the VAX, 395
Using the VAX, 394
VAX system commands (see Digital Command Language)
VAX terminal keys, 401
VAX use:
  Deleting files, 471
  Displaying and printing files, 471
  Learning, 394
  Logging in, 395
  Logging out, 400
  Password, 395
  Running FORTRAN programs, 473
  Username, 395
  Using EDT full-screen editor, 416
  Using EDT line editor, 403
  Using files on the VAX, 401
  Using the terminal, 396
VAX/VMS, 394
WHILE, DO WHILE loop, 481

GENERAL INDEX

A first program to run, 473
A FORMAT, 121, 126, 128
ABSolute (ABS) library function, 35
ACCumulator (ACC) object code, 12, 13
Accuracy, 114, 363, 364
ACOS library function, 35
Addition, 29
Addressable locations, 18
Algorithm, 77, 79, 83
Alphanumeric data, 118, 119, 120, 121
Alphanumeric format, quick reference example, 490
Analysis of a problem, 77, 78, 82, 85, 371, 389
Analysis of data, 257, 258, 261
ANSI, 3
Appendices, tutorial (*see* INDEX FOR APPENDICES)
Argument:
　for library function, 35
　for subroutine, 324, 326
　for user-written function, 306, 311
Arithmetic example, 33
Arithmetic expression, 29, 43
Arithmetic GO TO, 155, 156
Arithmetic Logic Unit, 9, 10, 16, 17, 18
Arithmetic operator, 29, 43
Arithmetic precedence, 29, 31
Array:
　Access with DO loop, 207, 208
　CHARACTER, 217
　　Quick reference example, 485
　General approach, 219
　INTEGER, 217
　One-dimensional, 200, 201, 203, 204, 205, 206, 213, 225, 232
　　Quick reference example, 484
　Ordering data in array, 214
　Plotting, 223, 224
　REAL, 217
　Subset, 233, 235
　Two-dimensional array, 270, 271, 272, 274, 275, 276, 277, 279
　　Description, 271, 272
　　DIMENSION, 275
　　Input introduction, 277, 279
　　Introduction, 274, 276
　　Quick reference example, 485
ASIN library function, 35
Assignment statement, 23, 43
ATAN library function, 35
Auxiliary storage, 8, 10

Average calculation, 106
Bar chart, 253, 254, 255
Binary search, 365
Bit unit of storage, 363
Block structured IF, 149, 150, 483
Bubble sort, 244, 247
Bug in program, 74
Business report, 253, 254, 255
Calculations example, 38, 39
CALL statement, invoking subroutine, 321, 323, 324, 326, 337
Carriage control, in format statement, 123, 124, 125, 126, 138
Case structure, 155, 157, 158
Central Processing Unit, 9, 10, 18
Character:
　array declaration, 217
　array quick reference example, 485
　comparisons, 148
　data, 118, 119, 121
　declaration, 121, 138
　deletion at terminal, 396
　format, 121, 122, 490
　strings, 120
Circuit boards, 9
Class grade report, 388
Class score summary, with weighted scores, 382
CLOSE statement, 58, 61, 64, 65
Code stored electronically, 6
Codes, 21
Columns for program entry, 23, 42
Comment statement, 75
Comments for program, 75, 76
COMMON BLOCK, 332
COMMON declaration, for subprograms, 331, 332, 333, 334
Compile program, 12, 55, 72, 475
　with LIST, 72
Compiler, 12
Compound interest, 157, 185, 186, 188
Computed GO TO, 157, 158
Computer, 9
　Configuration, 9
　Language, 22
　Program, 22
Condition in IF statement, 143, 144, 146, 147, 151, 152, 153, 170
Conditional statement, 142, 143, 145, 170
Consequent statement, in IF statement, 143, 146
Constant, 28, 43
Continuation of FORTRAN statement, 24, 43, 114

Contributions problem, 191
Control structures, 373
Control unit, 18, 9, 10, 11, 14, 15
Correcting a program, 73
Correlation coefficient, 257, 258, 259, 261
COS library function, 35, 42
Counter, 91, 92, 93, 114
    for DO loop, 92, 93, 94, 101, 176
Counting number of elements, 220
CPU—Central processing unit, 9, 10
Cumulative total, 96, 98, 99, 105, 113, 114
Current, 6
D format, 364, 491
DATA declaration, 235, 237, 262
    for two-dimensional array, 364
Data:
    Alphanumeric, 118, 119, 120
    Base, 352
    Character, 118, 119, 120
    Considerations, 363
    Files, 46, 57
    Numeric, 118, 119
Debugging, 73, 74, 75, 377
Decimal format, 129
Declaration:
    INTEGER, REAL, CHARACTER, 298
    INTEGER and REAL, 34
Default, 50, 65
Definable task 328, 321
Deleting characters, at the terminal, 396
Deleting files, 57, 471, 472, 494
Descriptive labels for output, 27
Designing a program, 371
Destructive READ, 62, 63
Developing:
    a program, 71
    Large programs, 370
Device number, 49
Digital Command Language (DCL):
    CONTINUE process command, 495
    COPY file, 495
    DELETE file, 471, 472, 494
    DIRECTORY command, 405, 418, 471,
        472, 494
    EDIT command, 394, 416, 403
    FORTRAN compile, 473, 494
    FORTRAN/LIST program, 476, 494
    HELP command, 398
    Interrupting processing, 398, 495
    LINK command, 473, 494
    Logging out, 400
    PASSWORD SET command, 495
    PRINT file, 405, 419, 471, 494
    RENAME file, 495
    RUN program, 473, 494
    Scroll control, 400
    SHOW command, 396
    TYPE (display) file, 405, 419, 471, 494
    Terminal display control, 400
DIMENSION:
    INTEGER, REAL, CHARACTER, 217
    in function, 311
    in subroutine, 325, 326
    One-dimensional array, 205, 206
    Two-dimensional array, 298
Directory, 55, 56, 59, 405, 418, 471, 472, 494
Display value, 17
Displaying VAX files, at the terminal, 471
Division, 29
DO WHILE loop, 175, 181, 182, 195
    Reading to End of File, 184, 189
    Quick reference example, 481
DO loop, 88, 91, 93, 94, 95, 97, 100, 101,
    106, 107, 108, 109, 110, 113, 114, 176,
    185
    CONTINUE, 93
    Counter, 98, 99
    Cumulative total, 98, 99
    DO WHILE, 187, 195, 175
        Reading to End of File, 184, 189
    END DO, 92
    Implied, 225, 292, 293, 298
    Nested, 175, 176, 177, 178, 179, 180, 181,
        195
    Quick reference example, 481
    Standard, 101
    Structure, 175
    Variable increments, 100, 101, 102, 176
    with array, 207, 208
    with counter, 92, 94, 95
    with one-dimensional array, 225
    with two-dimensional array, 280, 281, 283
Documentation, 75, 76, 376, 379
Dollar sign, 6
Double precision:
    Declaration, 364
    D Format, 364
    Quick reference example, 491
E format, 364
    Quick reference example, 491
Edit, 11, 18, 23, 24, 25, 42, 48
Editor:
    Creating files, 402
    EDT full-screen editor:
        Tutorial, 416
        Commands (see Editor, EDT full-
            screen)
    EDT line editor:

Tutorial, 403
Commands (*see* Editor, EDT line)
Editor, EDT full-screen, 416
  Beginning an edit session, 416
  Copying characters, words, lines, 451
  Copying segments of text, 462
  Creating a simple file, 416, 421
  Deleting characters, 438
  Deleting lines, 438
  Deleting segments of text, 458
  Deleting words, 438
  Keyboard arrows, 425
  Keypad, 428, 430
  Keypad cursor control, 431
  Moving characters, words, lines, 451
  Moving segments of text, 458
  Quiting an edit session, 419, 421
  Restoring deleted characters, 445
  Restoring deleted lines, 445
  Restoring deleted words, 445
  Saving a file, 418, 424
  Tutorial, 416
Editor, EDT line, 403
  Adding records to file, 408, 497
  Beginning an edit session, 403, 496
  Copying records in a file, 415, 497
  Creating a simple file, 403
  Deleting records in a file, 410, 497
  Displaying records at terminal, 405, 499
  Finding strings in a file, 413, 497
  Help, 413, 497
  Include external file, 499
  Moving records in a file, 414, 498
  Quick reference, 496
  Quiting an edit session, 407, 498
  Replacing records in a file, 411, 498
  Resequence line numbers, 498, 410
  Saving a file, 404, 497
  Substituting strings in file, 413, 498
  Tutorial, 403
EDT full-screen editor (*see* Editor, EDT full-screen)
EDT line editor (*see* Editor, EDT line)
Electronic code, 6
ELSE, with IF statement, 151, 171
ELSE IF, with nested IF THEN ELSE, 154
END DO, 92, 114, 176,
END IF, 149, 171
End of File, reading to, 105, 106, 183, 184, 189, 479
END statement, 23
END=clause, reading to End of File, 105, 106
EOF—End of File, 105

Entering a program, 23, 24, 42
Equal sign, 23
Error in syntax, 71, 72, 74
Error messages, 72, 73
Error recovery, 376
EXAMPLES (*see* INDEX OF EXAMPLES)
Executable code, 12, 13, 14, 18, 56
Execution of program, 9, 12, 14, 25, 26, 43
EXP library function, 35
Exponential format, 364
Exponentiation, 29
Expression—arithmetic, 29
Extension for filename, 13
F FORMAT, 123, 124, 125, 126, 128
Factorial program, 108
Field, 23
  on output line, 125
File output from program, 58
File STATUS, 58
FILE specification, in OPEN statement, 65, 66
Filename, 11
Filename extension, 13
Files, 46, 47, 53, 55, 56, 57, 58, 59, 60, 64, 66
  Data, 56, 57, 61, 64
  Deleting, 57, 471, 472, 494
  Executable code, 56, 57
  FORTRAN code, 57, 55, 56
  Object code, 55
  Input for program, 61
  Merging, 64
  Object code, 56, 57
  Output from program, 61, 62
  Output to disk, 62
  Source code, 55, 56, 57
  Writing to disk, 62
  on the VAX, 401
Flag, 183
Floating point format, 128
  Quick reference example, 490
Flow chart, 79, 80, 113
Format quick reference:
  Alphanumeric format, 490
  Character format, 490
  Double precision format, 491
  E format, 491
  Floating point format, 490
  Free format, 489
  Integer format, 489
  Real format, 490
  Scientific notation format, 491
  Unformatted input, 489
Formats, 118
Formatted table, 134

FORMAT statement, 119, 121, 123, 124, 125, 127
  A format, 121, 190, 490
  Carriage control, 123, 124, 125, 126
  D format, 364, 491
  Decimal specification, 123, 124, 125, 126, 128
  Description, 138
  E format, 126, 490
  Field, 125, 128
  Field descriptions, 138
  Floating point field, 123, 124, 125, 126, 128
  Generating a table, 134
  I format, 126, 489
  Integer field, 123, 124, 125, 126, 128, 129
  Real field, 129
  Skipped field, 123, 124
  Slashes—skipped line, 126
  T format, 135
FORTRAN 3, 22, 77
FORTRAN LIST option, 72
FORTRAN compile command, 12, 18, 24, 25, 43, 48, 55
FORTRAN program, running
  Input from file, 61, 477
  Input from terminal, 51, 476
  Input from terminal and disk, 478
  Output to disk, 58, 61, 477
  Output to terminal, 49, 51, 476, 478
  Printing output, 477
  Reading to End of File, 105, 184, 189, 479
  Submitting program with cards, 480
  Running the first program, 473
FORTRAN structures:
  Quick reference examples, 481
  Summary, 374
Fractions, 32
Free format, 49
Free format output, 49
Free format input, 51, 52
  Quick reference example, 489
Frequency distribution, 335
  Subroutine, 336
Function, 304, 305, 307
  Arguments, 316
  Arrays for arguments, 311
  DIMENSION statement, 311
  for area of polygon, 314
  Intrinsic library, 34, 305, 316
  Introduction, 306, 308
  Library, 34, 305
  Parameters, 308, 309, 316
  Quick reference example, 486

  Returning a value, 308
  Subprogram, 305
  Summary, 316
General approach:
  Grading program, 379
  Program design, 371
  Programs, 379
  Programming with arrays, 219
  Two-dimensional array program, 286, 294
GO TO:
  Case structure, 157
  Computed, 157
  Problems with, 104, 156
  Statement, 102, 105, 155
Grading program:
  General program, 379
  Grade assignment, 378
  Grade report, 388
Graphics:
  Introduction, 223, 224
  Bar chart, 253, 254, 255
  Scaling axes, 359
  Scatter plot, 256, 263, 358, 362
  with line printer, 357
Hard copy, 7
HELP:
  for EDT line editor, 413, 497
  for EDT full-screen editor, 429, 430, 439
  for VAX, 6, 398
I FORMAT, 123–128
IF THEN ELSE:
  Block IF structure, 171
  Complex, 153
  Flow chart, 168
  Nested, 154
  Problem solving, 166
  Quick reference example, 483
  Structure, 151, 152, 156, 159, 171
IF statement, 142, 144, 145, 146, 147, 170
  Block IF structure, 149, 150
  Quick reference example, 483
Implied DO loop:
  One-dimensional array, 221, 222, 225
  Two-dimensional array, 292, 293, 298
Index:
  Subscript for one-dimensional array, 205
  Subscript for two-dimensional array, 274
Inflation program, 107
Input, 46, 47, 52, 118
  Device, 10
  Format statements, 130, 131, 132
  Free format, 51, 489
  from disk file, 60, 61, 66, 477
  from terminal, 51, 66, 476

from terminal and disk file, 478
General considerations, 130
How to direct, 47
Implied DO loop:
    One-dimensional array, 221, 222, 225
    Two-dimensional array, 292, 293, 298
One-dimensional array, 206, 213, 214
Quick reference, 476, 477, 478, 479
to End of File, 105, 184, 189, 479
Two-dimensional array, 277, 279
Unformatted, 51, 489
Instructions, 20
INT library function, 35, 36
    in WRITE statement, 100
INTEGER:
    Arithmetic, 31, 32, 33, 38, 43
    Array declaration, 217
    Declaration, 34
    Format, 123–128
        Quick reference example, 489
    Symbolic names, 31
Intercept for regression line, 257, 258, 261
Interest:
    Compounded, 185, 186, 188
    Table, 108, 109
Intrinsic library function, 34, 35, 40, 305, 316
    Invoking, 35
Invoking:
    function, 306, 307, 308
    intrinsic library function, 35, 306
    subroutine, 321, 323, 337
IOSTAT option, reading to End of File, 184, 189, 195, 220
Iterative processing, 180, 182
Keyboard for terminal, 6
Keys for terminal, 401, 425
Keypad editing, 428, 430
Labeling output, 27
Language—computer, 22
Least squares method, 257, 258
Library function, 34, 35, 40, 305, 316
Line of FORTRAN, 23
Link, 13, 14
    Code, 12
    Command, 18, 24, 25, 43, 48, 56
List:
    Directed output, 50
    Option for compile, 72
    PRINT on printer, 405, 419, 471, 494
    Syntax error messages, 72
    TYPE—display at terminal, 59, 405, 419, 471, 494
Location—addressable, 5

LOG—library function, 35, 36
LOG10—library function, 35, 36
Logging-out from the VAX, 400
Logging-in to the VAX, 395
Logic, 70, 71, 85
    Error, 74
    of a program, 74, 77, 78, 82, 109, 110
    Problem, 191
Logical order, 112
Logical unit number, 58
Loops:
    Counter, 98, 99
    DO loop, 88, 91, 100
    DO WHILE loop, 187, 195, 175
    Nested, 175, 176, 195
    Repetitive processing, 88, 89, 90, 99, 103, 174
Machine code, 12
Magnetic disk memory, 7, 11, 47
Mailbox, 5, 9, 20
Mailing labels, 134
Main memory, 7, 11
Main program, 326, 329, 372
Manipulating data, in an array, 213
MAX—library function, 35, 36
Maximum value:
    Algorithm, 160
    in a set of records, 161
    location of max value, 162
Memory, 5, 7, 9, 10, 11, 14, 15, 18, 25, 28, 40
Memory location:
    Integer, 34, 217
    Real, 32, 217, 364
    Symbolic name, 25
Merging files, 64
MIN—library function, 35, 37
Minimum value:
    in a set of records, 164
    in one record, 163, 164
Mixed mode arithmetic, 33
MOD—library function, 35, 40
Modular design, 378
Modular programming, 381
Modules for program, 305, 321, 329, 373, 378
MOV—object code, 12
MUL—object code, 13
Multiplication, 16, 29
Natural Resources problem, 191
Nested DO loop:
    Introduction, 176–181
    Quick reference example, 481
    Summary, 195
Nested IF THEN ELSE, 154

NEW STATUS, 65
NINT—library function, 35, 36
   Application, 239, 240, 241
   in WRITE statement, 100
Numeric data, 118, 119
Object code, 12, 13, 55
Odometer in automobile, incrementing with
   DO loop, 174
OLD STATUS, 60, 65
One-dimensional array:
   Introduction, 200–232
   Quick reference example, 484
OPEN statement, 58, 60, 61, 64–67
Operator—numeric, 22
Ordering input data:
   One-dimensional array, 213
   Two-dimensional array, 283, 285
Output:
   Device, 10
   Directing, 47
   for program, 18
   Formatted, 122, 124
   Free format, 122
   General introduction, 46–50, 118
   Implied DO loop:
      One-dimensional array, 221, 222, 225
      Two-dimensional array, 292, 293, 298
   Numeric, 122
   One-dimensional array, 204, 208, 214
   Printing output, 59, 477
   to disk file, 58, 61, 66, 477
   to a terminal, 51, 61, 66, 476, 478
   Two-dimensional array, 275, 278, 281
   Unformatted, 122, 124
Overview for using the VAX, 394
Parameter:
   for library function, 35
   for function, 306, 311
   for subroutine, 324, 326
Parentheses, in arithmetic expressions, 30,
   31
Password for the VAX, 395
Plotting:
   Bar chart, 253, 254, 255
   Introduction, 223, 224
   Scaling axes, 359
   Scatter plot, 256, 263, 358, 362
   with line printer, 357
Precedence—arithmetic, 29, 30, 31
Predefined words, 21, 22, 42
Prime numbers, 186
PRINT:
   Characters on line, 27
   DCL command, 59

Display at terminal, 59, 405, 419, 471,
   494
on printer, 59, 405, 419, 471, 494
Quotation marks, 27
Simple report, 37
Statement, 18, 23, 26, 27, 48, 35
VAX files, 59, 405, 419, 471, 494
Printer, 7
Problem analysis, 77, 78, 82, 85, 371, 389
Problem solving, 70, 71, 77, 111, 113, 115,
   165, 166, 185, 191, 328, 371
Program:
   Correctness, 375
   Design, 371–378
   Development, 71
   Entry, 10, 23, 24, 42
   Execution, 10, 12, 43
   Introduction, 4, 18, 22, 42, 70
   Logic, 74, 77, 78, 82, 109, 110
   Modules, 305, 321, 329, 373, 378
   Output, 18
   Readability, 376
   Running:
      Input from file, 61, 477
      Input from terminal, 51, 476
      Input from terminal and disk, 478
      Output to disk, 58, 61, 477
      Output to terminal, 49, 51, 476
      Printing output, 58, 59, 477
      Reading to End of File, 105, 184, 189,
         479
      Running the first program, 473
      Submitting with cards, 480
   Structure, 373
   Style, 76, 328, 376
   Top down design, 372–378
Quick sort:
   Algorithm, 344, 345
   Implementation, 346, 386
   Trace of sort, 349
Quotation Marks, PRINT statement, 27
RANdom library function, 238, 239, 263
Random selection, 237
Rapid Access, 8
READ statement:
   General introduction, 51, 52, 60–67
   with FORMAT statement, 127
   with IOSTAT option, 184, 189
Reading:
   with format statements, 130, 131, 132
   with free format, 51, 489
   from disk file, 60, 61, 66
   from terminal, 51, 66
   Implied DO loop:

One-dimensional array, 221, 222, 225
Two-dimensional array, 292, 293, 298
One-dimensional array, 206, 213, 214
Quick reference, 476, 477, 478, 479
to End of File, 105, 184, 189
Two-dimensional array, 277, 279
Unformatted, 51, 489
Variable number of records, 104, 105
REAL:
    Array declaration, 217
    Arithmetic, 31, 32, 33, 38, 43
    Declaration, 34
    Format quick reference example, 490
    Library function, 35
    REAL*8 declaration, 364
    Symbolic names, 32
Recognized symbols, 21
Record, 23, 54
Regression analysis, 257–263
Relational Operator, 146, 147, 170
Relationship, 110
Remainder function, 40
Repetition:
    and selection, 373
    Control, 175
    Structures, 373
Research applications, 256
Retrieving information, 20
RETURN key, 6
RETURN statement:
    for function, 306, 316
    for subroutine, 322, 323, 337
RUN command, 25, 43, 48
RUN program, 14, 18
Running FORTRAN program:
    Input from file, 60, 61, 66, 477
    Input from terminal, 51, 66, 476
    Input from terminal and disk, 478
    Output to disk, 58, 61, 66, 477
    Output to terminal, 49, 51, 476, 478
    Printing output, 59, 477
    Reading to End of File, 105, 184, 189, 479
    Running the first program, 473
    Submitting with cards, 480
Save program, 8, 12, 404, 418, 424, 497
Scientific notation, 33, 114
    Quick reference example, 491
Selection, 148, 158, 159, 263
    and analysis, 242
    in array, 241
    Random subset of data, 237, 239
    Subset of data, 234, 235
    Structures, 373
Shell sort:

Algorithm, 350
    Implementation, 351, 353
Significant digits, 32, 114
Simple regression, 257, 258, 261
SIN library function, 35, 42
Slashes in FORMAT,
    skipping lines, 126
Solving a problem, 77, 111–115, 328, 371,
    165, 166, 185
Sorting, 247
    Algorithms, 343
    Alphanumeric data, 251
    Attribute, 354
    Bubble sort, 244, 250, 263, 344
    By category, 335, 336
    Frequency distribution, 335, 336
    Interactive sorting, 353
    Quick sort, 344
        Implementation, 346, 386
        Trace, 349
    Shell sort, 350
        Implementation, 351, 355
Source code, 12, 13, 81, 83
Special symbols, 21, 42
SQRT library function, 35
Stack structure, 344
Statement, 22, 23, 25, 42
    Number, 23
Statistical data analysis, 257, 258, 261
STATUS:
    of file in OPEN statement, 58, 60, 61
    option, OPEN statement, 64, 65, 66
STOP statement, 23
Storage range on VAX, 363
Storage unit, bit, word, 363
Store value, 15, 16, 17
Storing information, 20
Storing program, 8
String of characters, 27
Structured programs, 143, 149, 151, 166,
    328, 373, 374, 376
Structures of FORTRAN:
    Quick reference, 481
    Summary, 374
Student average score, with weighted scores,
    378
Style of programming, 76, 328, 376
Subprogram:
    COMMON declaration, 331, 332
    Function, 304
    Subroutine, 321
Subroutine, 320, 323, 325
    Argument list, 322, 324, 326
    Common algorithms, 343

589944

DIMENSION statement, 326
in program development, 343
in structured program, 337
Parameters, 322, 324
Quick reference example, 487
RETURN statement, 337
Structured programming, 328
Subprograms, 328
Top down design, 373
Subscript:
for one-dimensional array, 205, 206
for two-dimensional array, 276, 279
Subscripted variables, 205
Subset of data, 233, 235
Subtraction, 29
Sum—cumulative total, 96, 98, 99
Symbolic name, 21, 22, 27, 28, 31, 33, 34, 38, 42, 43, 94, 101, 120
Symbols, 21, 42
Syntax, 70, 71, 85
Syntax error, 71, 72, 73, 74
System commands (*see* Digital Command Language)
T FORMAT, tab to position, 126, 128
TAN—library function, 35
Terminal, 6, 18
Using with the VAX, 396
Testing, 377
Top down design, 328, 372
Total—cumulative total, 96, 98, 99, 105, 113, 114
Translate program, 12, 18
Trigonometry, 41, 42
Tutorial:
for using EDT full-screen editor, 416
for using EDT line editor, 403
for using the VAX, 394
(*See also* INDEX FOR APPENDICES)
Two-dimensional array:
Access with DO loop, 280, 281, 283
Description, 271
Introduction, 270, 274
Quick reference example, 485
Summary, 298

TYPE command (DCL), 59, 405, 419, 471, 494
Unformatted input, 51, 52, 119
Quick reference example, 489
Unformatted output, 119
Quick reference example, 489
Unit number for file, 50, 52, 58, 64, 65
Unit number in OPEN statement, 66
Username for VAX, 395
Using the VAX tutorials:
for using EDT full-screen editor, 416
for using EDT line editor, 403
for using the VAX, 394
(*See also* INDEX FOR APPENDICES)
VAX terminal keys, 401
VAX use:
Deleting files, 471
Displaying and printing files, 471
Learning, 394
Logging in, 395
Logging out, 400
Password, 395
Running FORTRAN programs, 473
Username, 395
Using EDT full-screen editor, 416
Using EDT line editor, 403
Using files on the VAX, 401
Using the terminal, 396
VAX/VMS, 394
Variable, 28
WHILE:
DO WHILE loop, 175
DO WHILE structure, 181
Quick reference example, 481
Word, unit of storage, 363
WRITE statement, 48, 50, 54, 58, 61, 65, 66, 67
with FORMAT, 123, 124, 125, 126
Writing:
Output to disk file, 58, 61, 66, 477
Output to terminal, 48, 49, 50, 51, 61, 66, 476, 478
X FORMAT, skipping fields, 123, 124, 126, 128